HISTORY OF THE NEGRO RACE IN AMERICA FROM 1619 TO 1880. VOL 1: NEGROES AS SLAVES, AS SOLDIERS, AND AS CITIZENS
BY
George Washington Williams

HISTORY OF THE NEGRO RACE IN AMERICA FROM 1619 TO 1880. VOL 1: NEGROES AS SLAVES, AS SOLDIERS, AND AS CITIZENS

Published by Firework Press

New York City, NY

First published circa 1891

Copyright © Firework Press, 2015

All rights reserved

Except in the United States of America, this book is sold subject to the condition that it shall not, by way of trade or otherwise, be lent, re-sold, hired out, or otherwise circulated without the publisher's prior consent in any form of binding or cover other than that in which it is published and without a similar condition including this condition being imposed on the subsequent purchaser.

ABOUT FIREWORK PRESS

Firework Press prints and publishes the greatest books about American history ever written, including seminal works written by our nation's most influential figures.

PREFACE.

I was requested to deliver an oration on the Fourth of July, 1876, at Avondale, O. It being the one-hundredth birthday of the American Republic, I determined to prepare an oration on the American Negro. I at once began an investigation of the records of the nation to secure material for the oration. I was surprised and delighted to find that the historical memorials of the Negro were so abundant, and so creditable to him. I pronounced my oration on the Fourth of July, 1876; and the warm and generous manner in which it was received, both by those who listened to it and by others who subsequently read it in pamphlet form, encouraged me to devote what leisure time I might have to a further study of the subject.

I found that the library of the Historical and Philosophical Society of Ohio, and the great Americana of Mr. Robert Clarke containing about eight thousand titles, both in Cincinnati, offered peculiar advantages to a student of American history. For two years I spent what time I could spare from professional cares in studying the whole problem of the African slave-trade; the founding of the British colonies in North America; the slave problem in the colonies; the rupture between the colonies and the British Government; the war of the Revolution; the political structure of the Continental government and Confederation; the slavery question in local and national legislation; and then traced the slavery and anti-slavery question down to the Rebellion. I became convinced that a history of the Colored people in America was required, because of the ample historically trustworthy material at hand; because the Colored people themselves had been the most vexatious problem in North America, from the time of its discovery down to the present day; because that in every attempt upon the life of the nation, whether by foes from without or within, the Colored people had always displayed a matchless patriotism and an incomparable heroism in the cause of Americans; and because such a history would give the world more correct ideas of the Colored people, and incite the latter to greater effort in the struggle of citizenship and manhood. The single reason that there was no history of the Negro race would have been a sufficient reason for writing one.

The labor incident upon the several public positions held by me precluded an earlier completion of this task; and, finding it absolutely impossible to write while discharging public duties or practising law, I retired from the public service several years ago, and since that time have devoted all my energies to this work. It is now nearly seven years since I began this wonderful task.

I have been possessed of a painful sense of the vastness of my work from first to last. I regret that for the sake of pressing the work into a single volume, favorable to a speedy sale,—at the sacrifice of the record of a most remarkable people,—I found my heart unwilling, and my best judgment protesting.

In the preparation of this work I have consulted over twelve thousand volumes,—about one thousand of which are referred to in the footnotes,—and thousands of pamphlets.

After wide and careful reading, extending through three years, I conceived the present plan of this history. I divided it into nine parts. Two thoughts led me to prepare the chapters under the head of PRELIMINARY CONSIDERATIONS. First, The defenders of slavery and the traducers of the Negro built their pro-slavery arguments upon biblical ethnology and the curse of Canaan. I am alive to the fact, that, while I am a believer in the Holy Bible, it is not the best authority on ethnology. As far as it goes, it is agreeable to my head and heart. Whatever science has added I have gladly appropriated. I make no claim, however, to be a specialist. While the curse of Canaan is no longer a question of debate, yet nevertheless the folly of the obsolete theory should be thoroughly understood by the young men of the Negro race who, though voting now, were not born when Sumter was fired upon. Second, A growing desire among the enlightened Negroes in America to learn all that is possible from research concerning the antiquity of the race,—Africa, its inhabitants, and the development of the Negro governments of Sierra Leone and Liberia, led me to furnish something to meet a felt need. If the Negro slave desired his native land before the Rebellion, will not the free, intelligent, and reflective American Negro turn to Africa with its problems of geography and missions, now that he can contribute something towards the improvement of the condition of humanity? Editors and writers everywhere throughout the world should spell the word Negro with a capital N; and when referring to the race as Colored people employ a capital C. I trust this will be observed.

In PART II., SLAVERY IN THE COLONIES, I have striven to give a succinct account of the establishment and growth of slavery under the English Crown. It involved almost infinite labor to go to the records of "the original thirteen colonies." It is proper to observe that this part is one of great value and interest.

In PART III., THE NEGRO DURING THE REVOLUTION, I found much of an almost romantic character. Many traditions have been put down, and many obscure truths elucidated. Some persons may think it irreverent to tell the truth in the plain, homely manner that characterizes my narrative; but, while I have nothing to regret in this particular, I can assure them that I have been actuated by none other spirit than that of candor. Where I have used documents it was with a desire to escape the charge of superficiality. If, however, I may be charged with seeking to escape the labor incident to thorough digestion, I answer, that, while men with the reputation of Bancroft and Hildreth could pass unchallenged when disregarding largely the use of documents and the citation of authorities, I would find myself challenged by a large number of critics. Moreover I have felt it would be almost cruel to mutilate some of the very rare old documents that shed such peerless light upon the subject in hand.

I have brought the first volume down to the close of the eighteenth century, detailing the great struggle through which the slavery problem passed. I have given as fair an idea of the debate on this question, in the convention that framed the Constitution, as possible. It was then and there that the hydra of slavery struck its fangs into the Constitution; and, once inoculated with the poison of the monster, the government was only able to purify itself in the flames of a great civil war.

The second volume opens with the present century, and closes with the year 1880. Unable to destroy slavery by constitutional law, the best thought and effort of this period were directed against the extension of the evil into the territory beyond the Ohio, Mississippi, and Missouri rivers. But having placed three-fifths of the slave population under the Constitution, having pledged the Constitution to the protection of slave property, it required an almost superhuman effort to confine the evil to one section of the country. Like a loathsome disease it spread itself over the body politic until our nation became the eyesore of the age, and a byword among the nations of the world. The time came when our beloved country had to submit to heroic treatment, and the cancer of slavery was removed by the sword.

In giving an account of the Anti-Slavery Agitation Movement, I have found myself able to deal briefly with methods and results only. I have striven to honor all the multifarious measures adopted to save the Negro and the Nation. I have not attempted to write a history of the Anti-Slavery Movement. Many noble men and women have not even been mentioned. It should not be forgotten that this is a history of the Negro race; and as such I have not run into the topic discussed by the late Henry Wilson in his "Rise and Fall of the Slave Power."

In discussing the problem of the rendition of fugitive slaves by the Union army, I have given the facts with temperate and honest criticism. And, in recounting the sufferings Negro troops endured as prisoners of war in the hands of the Rebels, I have avoided any spirit of bitterness. A great deal of the material on the war I purchased from the MS. library of Mr. Thomas S. Townsend of New-York City. The questions of vital, prison, labor, educational, and financial statistics cannot fail to interest intelligent people of all races and parties. These statistics are full of comfort and assurance to the Negro as well as to his friends.

Every cabinet minister of the President wrote me full information upon all the questions I asked, and promptly too. The refusal of the general and adjutant-general of the army did not destroy my hope of getting some information concerning the Negro regiments in the regular army. I visited the Indian Territory, Kansas, Texas, and New Mexico, where I have seen the Ninth and Tenth Regiments of cavalry, and the Twenty-fourth Regiment of infantry. The Twenty-fifth Regiment of infantry is at Fort Randall, Dakota. These are among the most effective troops in the regular army. The annual desertions in white regiments of cavalry vary from ninety-eight to a hundred and eighteen; while in Negro regiments of cavalry the desertions only average from six to nine per annum. The Negro regiments are composed of young men, intelligent, faithful, brave. I heard but one complaint from the lips of a score of white officers I met, and that was that the Negroes sometimes struck their horses over the head. Every distinction in law has disappeared, except in the regular army. Here Negroes are excluded from the artillery service and engineer's department. It is wrong, and Congress should place these brave black soldiers upon the same footing as the white troops.

I have to thank Drs. George H. Moore and S. Austin Allibone, of the Lenox Library, for the many kind favors shown me while pursuing my studies in New-York City. And I am under very great obligations to Dr. Moore for his admirable "History of Early Slavery in Massachusetts," without which I should have been put to great inconvenience. To Mr. John Austin Stevens, late editor of "The Magazine of American History," who, during several months residence in New-York City, placed his private library and office at my service, and did every thing in his power to aid my investigations, I return my sincerest thanks. To the Librarians of the New-York

Historical, Astor, and New-York Society Libraries, I return thanks for favors shown, and privileges granted. I am especially grateful to the Hon. Ainsworth R. Spofford, Librarian of Congress, for the manner in which he facilitated my researches during my sojourn in Washington. I had the use of many newspapers of the last century, and of other material to be found only in the Congressional Library.

To Sir T. Risely Griffith, Colonial Secretary and Treasurer of Sierra Leone, I am indebted for valuable statistics concerning that colony.

To the Assistant Librarian of the State Library of Ohio, the accomplished and efficient Miss Mary C. Harbough, I owe more than to any other person. Through her unwavering and untiring kindness and friendship, I have been enabled to use five hundred and seventy-six volumes from that library, besides newspaper files and Congressional Records. To Gov. Charles Foster, Chairman of the Board of Library Commissioners, I offer my profoundest thanks for the intelligent, active, and practical interest he has taken in the completion of this work. And to Major Charles Townsend, Secretary of State, I offer thanks for favors shown me in securing documents. To the Rev. J.L. Grover and his competent assistant, Mr. Charles H. Bell, of the Public Library of Columbus, I am indebted for the use of many works. They cheerfully rendered whatever aid they could, and for their kindness I return many thanks.

I am obliged to the Rev. Benjamin W. Arnett, Financial Secretary of the A.M.E. Church of the United States, for the statistics of his denomination. And to all persons who have sent me newspapers and pamphlets I desire to return thanks. I am grateful to C.A. Fleetwood, an efficient clerk in the War Department, for statistics on the Freedmen's Bank. And, above all and more than all, I return my profoundest thanks to my heavenly Father for the inspiration, health, and money by which I have been enabled to complete this great task.

I have mentioned such Colored men as I thought necessary. To give a biographical sketch of all the worthy Colored men in the United States, would require more space than has been occupied in this work.

Not as the blind panegyrist of my race, nor as the partisan apologist, but from a love for "the truth of history," I have striven to record the truth, the whole truth, and nothing but the truth. I have not striven to revive sectional animosities or race prejudices. I have avoided comment so far as it was consistent with a clear exposition of the truth. My whole aim has been to write a thoroughly trustworthy history; and what I have written, if it have no other merit, is reliable.

I commit this work to the public, white and black, to the friends and foes of the Negro, in the hope that the obsolete antagonisms which grew out of the relation of master and slave may speedily sink as storms beneath the horizon; and that the day will hasten when there shall be no North, no South, no Black, no White,—but all be American citizens, with equal duties and equal rights.

GEORGE W. WILLIAMS.
New York, November, 1882.

CHAPTER I.: THE UNITY OF MANKIND.

The Biblical Argument.—One Race and One Language.— One Blood.—The Curse of Canaan.

DURING the last half-century, many writers on ethnology, anthropology, and slavery have strenuously striven to place the Negro outside of the human family; and the disciples of these teachers have endeavored to justify their views by the most dehumanizing treatment of the Negro. But, fortunately for the Negro and for humanity at large, we live now in an epoch when race malice and sectional hate are disappearing beneath the horizon of a brighter and better future. The Negro in America is free. He is now an acknowledged factor in the affairs of the continent; and no community, state, or government, in this period of the world's history, can afford to be indifferent to his moral, social, intellectual, or political well-being.

It is proposed, in the first place, to call the attention to the absurd charge that the Negro does not belong to the human family. Happily, there are few left upon the face of the earth who still maintain this belief.

In the first chapter of the Book of Genesis it is clearly stated that "God created man," "male and female created he them;" that "the Lord God formed man of the dust of the ground, and breathed into his nostrils the breath of life; and man became a living soul;" and that "the Lord God took the man, and put him into the Garden of Eden to dress it and to keep it." It is noticeable that the sacred historian, in every reference to Adam, speaks of him as "man;" and that the divine injunction to them was,—Adam and Eve,—"Be fruitful, and multiply, and replenish the earth, and subdue it; and have dominion over the fish of the sea, and over the fowl of the air, and over every living thing that moveth upon the earth." As among the animals, so here in the higher order, there were two,—a pair,—"male and female," of the human species. We may begin with man, and run down the scale, and we are sure to find two of a kind, "male and female." This was the divine order. But they were to "be fruitful," were to "replenish the earth." That they did "multiply," we have the trustworthy testimony of God; and it was true that man and beast, fowl and fish, increased. We read that after their expulsion from the Garden of Eden, Eve bore Adam a family. Cain and Abel; and that they "peopled the earth."

After a number of years we find that wickedness increased in the earth; so much so that the Lord was provoked to destroy the earth with a flood, with the exception of Noah, his wife, his three sons and their wives,—eight souls in all. Of the animals, two of each kind were saved.

But the most interesting portion of Bible history comes after the Flood. We then have the history of the confusion of tongues, and the subsequent and consequent dispersion of mankind. In the eleventh chapter and first verse of Genesis it is recorded: "And the whole earth was of one language, and of one speech." "The whole earth" here means all the inhabitants of the earth,—all mankind. The medium of communication was common. Everybody used one language. In the sixth verse occurs this remarkable language: "And the Lord said, Behold, the people is one, and they have all one language." Attention is called to this verse, because we have here the testimony of the Lord that "the people is one," and that the language of the people is one. This verse establishes two very important facts; i.e., there was but one nationality, and hence but one language. The fact that they had but one language furnishes reasonable proof that they were of one blood; and the historian has covered the whole question very carefully by recording the great truth that they were one people, and had but one language. The seventh, eighth, and ninth verses of the eleventh chapter are not irrelevant: "Go to, let us go down, and there confound their language, that they may not understand one another's speech. So the Lord scattered them abroad from thence upon the face of all the earth; and they left off to build the city. Therefore is the name of it called Babel; because the Lord did there confound the language of all the earth; and from thence did the Lord scatter them abroad upon the face of all the earth."

It was the wickedness of the people that caused the Lord to disperse them, to confound their speech, and bring to nought their haughty work. Evidently this was the beginning of different families of men,—different nationalities, and hence different languages. In the ninth verse it reads, that "from thence did the Lord scatter them abroad upon the face of all the earth." There is no ambiguity about this language. He did not only "confound their language," but "scattered them from thence," from Babel, "upon the face of all the earth." Here, then, are two very important facts: their language was confused, and they were "scattered." They were not only "scattered," they were "scattered abroad upon the face of all the earth." That is, they were dispersed very widely, sent into the various and remote parts of the earth; and their nationality received its being from the latitudes to which the divinely appointed wave of dispersion bore them; and their subsequent racial character was to borrow its tone and color from climateric influences. Three great families, the Shemitic, Hamitic, and Japhetic, were suddenly built up. Many other families, or tribes, sprang from these; but these were the three great heads of all subsequent races of men.

In the seventeenth chapter of the Acts of the Apostles, twenty-sixth verse, we find the following language: "And hath made of one blood all nations of men for to dwell on all the face of the earth, and hath determined the times before appointed, and the bounds of their habitation." The Apostle Paul was a missionary. He was, at this time, on a mission to the far-famed city of Athens,—"the eye of Greece, and the fountain of learning and philosophy." He told the "men of Athens," that, as he travelled through their beautiful city, he had not been unmindful of its attractions; that he had not been indifferent to the claims of its citizens to scholarship and culture, and that among other things he noticed an altar erected to an unknown God. He went on to remark, that, great as their city and nation were, God, whose offspring they were, had created other nations, who lived beyond their verdant hills and swelling rivers. And, moreover, that God had created "all nations of men for to dwell on all the face of the earth" out "of one blood." He called their attention to the fact that God had fenced all the nations in by geographical boundaries,—had fixed the limits of their habitation.

We find two leading thoughts in the twenty-sixth verse; viz., that this passage establishes clearly and unmistakably the unity of mankind, in that God created them of one blood; second, he hath determined "the bounds of their habitation,"—hath located them geographically. The language quoted is very explicit. "He hath determined the bounds of their habitation," that is, "all the nations of men. We have, then, the fact, that there are different "nations of men," and that they are all "of one blood," and, therefore, have a common parent. This declaration was made by the Apostle Paul, an inspired writer, a teacher of great erudition, and a scholar in both the Hebrew and the Greek languages.

It should not be forgotten either, that in Paul's masterly discussion of the doctrine of sin,—the fall of man,—he always refers to Adam as the "one man" by whom sin came into the world. His Epistle to the Romans abounds in passages which prove very plainly the unity of mankind. The Acts of the Apostles, as well as the Gospels, prove the unity we seek to establish.

But there are a few who would admit the unity of mankind, and still insist that the Negro does not belong to the human family. It is so preposterous, that one has a keen sense of humiliation in the assured consciousness that he goes rather low to meet the enemies of God's poor; but it can certainly do no harm to meet them with the everlasting truth.

In the Gospel of Luke we read this remarkable historical statement: "And as they led him away, they laid hold upon one Simon, a Cyrenian, coming out of the country, and on him they laid the cross, that he might bear it after Jesus." By referring to the map, the reader will observe that Cyrene is in Libya, on the north coast of Africa. All the commentators we have been able to consult, on the passage quoted below, agree that this man Simon was a Negro,—a black man. John Melville produced a very remarkable sermon from this passage. And many of the most celebrated pictures of "The Crucifixion," in Europe, represent this Cyrenian as black, and give him a very prominent place in the most tragic scene ever witnessed on this earth. In the Acts of the Apostles we have a very full and interesting account of the conversion and immersion of the Ethiopian eunuch, "a man of Ethiopia, an eunuch of great authority under Candace, Queen of the Ethiopians, who had the charge of all her treasure, and had come to Jerusalem for to worship." Here, again, we find that all the commentators agree as to the nationality of the eunuch: he was a Negro; and, by implication, the passage quoted leads us to the belief that the Ethiopians were a numerous and wealthy people. Candace was the queen that made war against Augustus Cæsar twenty years before Christ, and, though not victorious, secured an honorable peace. She reigned in Upper Egypt,—up the Nile,—and lived at Meroe, that ancient city, the very cradle of Egyptian civilization.

But a few writers have asserted, and striven to prove, that the Egyptians and Ethiopians are quite a different people from the Negro. Jeremiah seems to have understood that these people about whom we have been writing were Negroes,—we mean black. "Can the Ethiopian," asks the prophet, "change his skin, or the leopard his spots?" The prophet was as thoroughly aware that the Ethiopian was black, as that the leopard had spots; and Luther's German has for the word "Ethiopia," "Negro-land,"—the country of the blacks. The word "Ethiop" in the Greek literally means "sunburn."

That these Ethiopians were black, we have, in addition to the valuable testimony of Jeremiah, the scholarly evidence of Herodotus, Homer, Josephus, Eusebius, Strabo, and others.

It will be necessary for us to use the term "Cush" farther along in this discussion: so we call attention at this time to the fact, that the Cushites, so frequently referred to in the Scriptures, are the same as the Ethiopians.

Driven from unscriptural and untenable ground on the unity of the races of mankind, the enemies of the Negro, falling back in confusion, intrench themselves in the curse of Canaan. "And Noah awoke from his wine, and knew what his younger son had done unto him. And he said, Cursed be Canaan; a servant of servants shall he be unto his brethren." This passage was the leading theme of the defenders of slavery in the pulpit for many years. Bishop Hopkins says,—

Now, the first thing to be done by those who adopt this view is, to prove, beyond a reasonable doubt, that Noah was inspired to pronounce this prophecy. Noah had been, as a rule, a righteous man. For more than a hundred years he had lifted up his voice against the growing wickedness of the world. His fidelity to the cause of God was unquestioned; and for his faith and correct living, he and his entire household were saved from the Deluge. But after his miraculous deliverance from the destruction that overcame the old world, his entire character is changed. There is not a single passage to show us that he continued his avocation as a preacher. He became a husbandman; he kept a vineyard; and, more than all, he drank of the wine and got drunk! Awaking from a state of inebriation, he knew that Ham had beheld his nakedness and "told his two brethren." But "Shem and Japheth took a garment, and laid it upon both their shoulders, and went backward, and covered the nakedness of their father; and their faces were backward, and they saw not their father's nakedness." It is quite natural to suppose, that, humiliated and chagrined at his sinful conduct, and angered at the behavior of his son and grandson, Ham and Canaan, Noah expressed his disapprobation of Canaan. It was his desire, on the impulse of the moment, that Canaan should suffer a humiliation somewhat commensurate with his offence; and, on the other hand, it was appropriate that he should commend the conduct of his other sons, who sought to hide their father's shame. And all this was done without any inspiration. He simply expressed himself as a fallible man.

Bishop Hopkins, however, is pleased to call this a "prophecy." In order to prophesy, in the scriptural meaning of the word, a man must have the divine unction, and must be moved by the Holy Ghost; and, in addition to this, it should be said, that a true prophecy always comes to pass,—is sure of fulfilment. Noah was not inspired when he pronounced his curse against Canaan, for the sufficient reason that it was not fulfilled. He was not speaking in the spirit of prophecy when he blessed Shem and Japheth, for the good reason that their descendants have often been in bondage. Now, if these words of Noah were prophetic, were inspired of God, we would naturally expect to find all of Canaan's descendants in bondage, and all of Shem's out of bondage,—free! If this prophecy—granting this point to the learned bishop for argument's sake—has not been fulfilled, then we conclude one of two things; namely, these are not the words of God, or they have not been fulfilled. But they were not the words of prophecy, and consequently never had any divine authority. It was Canaan upon whom Noah pronounced the curse: and Canaan was the son of Ham; and Ham, it is said, is the progenitor of the Negro race. The Canaanites were not bondmen, but freemen,—powerful tribes when the Hebrews invaded their country; and from the Canaanites descended the bold and intelligent Carthaginians, as is admitted by the majority of writers on this subject. From Ham proceeded the Egyptians, Libyans, the Phutim, and the Cushim or Ethiopians, who, colonizing the African side of the Red Sea, subsequently extended themselves indefinitely to the west and south of that great continent. Egypt was called Chemia, or the country of Ham; and it has been thought that the Egyptian's deity, Hammon or Ammon, was a deification of Ham. The Carthaginians were successful in numerous wars against the sturdy Romans. So in this, as in many other instances, the prophecy of Noah failed.

Following the chapter containing the prophecy of Noah, the historian records the genealogy of the descendants of Ham and Canaan. We will quote the entire account that we may be assisted to the truth.

Here is a very minute account of the family of Ham, who it is said was to share the fate of his son Canaan, and a clear account of the children of Canaan. "Nimrod," says the record, "began to be a mighty one in the earth. He was a mighty hunter before the Lord.... And the beginning of his kingdom," etc. We find that Cush was the oldest son of Ham, and the father of Nimrod the "mighty one in the earth," whose "kingdom" was so extensive. He founded the Babylonian empire, and was the father of the founder of the city of Nineveh, one of the grandest cities of the ancient world. These wonderful achievements were of the children of Cush, the ancestor of the Negroes. It is fair to suppose that this line of Ham's posterity was not lacking in powers necessary to found cities and kingdoms, and maintain government.

Thus far we have been enabled to see, according to the Bible record, that the posterity of Canaan did not go into bondage; that it was a powerful people, both in point of numbers and wealth; and, from the number and character of the cities it built, we infer that it was an intellectual posterity. We conclude that thus far there is no evidence, from a biblical standpoint, that Noah's prophecy was fulfilled. But, notwithstanding the absence of scriptural proof as to the bondage of the children of Canaan, the venerable Dr. Mede says, "There never has been a son of Ham who has shaken a sceptre over the head of Japheth. Shem has subdued Japheth, and Japheth has subdued Shem; but Ham has never subdued either." The doctor is either falsifying the facts of history, or is ignorant of history. The Hebrews were in bondage in Egypt for centuries. Egypt was peopled by Misraim, the second son of Ham. Who were the Shemites? They were Hebrews! The Shemites were in slavery to the Hamites. Melchizedek, whose name was expressive of his character,—king of righteousness (or a righteous king), was a worthy priest of the most high God; and Abimelech, whose name imports parental king, pleaded the integrity of his heart and the righteousness of his nation before God, and his plea was admitted. Yet both these personages appear to have been Canaanites." Melchizedek and Abimelech were Canaanites, and the most sacred and honorable characters in Old-Testament history. It was Abraham, a Shemite, who, meeting Melchizedek, a Canaanite, gave him a tenth of all his spoils. It was Nimrod, a Cushite, who "went to Asher, and built Nineveh," after subduing the Shemites, So it seems very plain that Noah's prophecy did not come true in every respect, and that it was not the word of God. "And God blessed Noah and his sons." God pronounces his blessing upon this entire family, and enjoins upon them to "be fruitful and multiply, and replenish the earth." Afterwards Noah seeks to abrogate the blessing of God by his "cursed be Canaan." But this was only the bitter expression of a drunken and humiliated parent lacking divine authority. No doubt he and his other two sons conformed their conduct to the spirit of the curse pronounced, and treated the Hamites accordingly. The scholarly Dr. William Jones says that Ham was the youngest son of Noah; that he had four sons, Cush, Misraim, Phut, and Canaan; and that they peopled Africa and part of Asia. The Hamites were the offspring of Noah, and one of the three great families that have peopled the earth.

FOOTNOTES:

Gen. i. 27.
Gen. ii. 7.
Gen. ii. 15.
Gen. i. 28.
Gen. vi. 5sq.
Encycl. of Geo., p. 255.
If the Apostle Paul had asserted that all men resembled each other in the color of their skin and the texture of their hair, or even in their physiological make-up, he would have been at war with observation and critical investigation. But, having announced a wonderful truth in reference to the unity of the human race as based upon one blood, science comes to his support, and through the microscope reveals the corpuscles of the blood, and shows that the globule is the same in all human blood.
Deut. xxxii. 8, 9: "When the Most High divided to the nations their inheritance, when he separated the sons of Adam, he set the bounds of the people according to the number of the children of Israel. For the Lord's portion is his people; Jacob is the lot of his inheritance."
Rom. v. 12, 14-21.
Luke xxiii, 26: Acts vi. 9, also second chapter, tenth verse. Matthew records the same fact in the twenty-seventh chapter, thirty-second verse. "And at they came out, they found a man of Cyrene, Simon by name: him they compelled to bear his cross."
See Melville's Sermons.
Acts viii. 27.
Pliny says the Ethiopian government subsisted for several generations in the hands of queens whose name was Candace.
See Liddell and Scott's Greek Lexicon.
Jones's Biblical Cyclopædia, p. 311.
The term Ethiope was anciently given to all those whose color was darkened by the sun.—Smyth's Unity of the Human Races, chap. i. p. 34.
Gen. ix. 24, 25. See also the twenty-sixth and twenty-seventh verses.
Bible Views of Slavery, p. 7.
Gen. ix. 23.
Plutarch, De Iside et Osiride. See also Dr. Morton, and Ethnological Journal, 4th No p. 172.
Gen. x. 6-20.
Dr. Bush.
Gen. ix. I.
Jones's Biblical Cyclopædia, p. 393. Ps. lxxviii. 51.
Ps. cv. 23.
If Noah's utterance were to be regarded as a prophecy, it applied only to the Canaanites, the descendants of Canaan, Noah's grandson. Nothing is said in reference to any person but Canaan

in the supposed prophecy.

CHAPTER II.: THE NEGRO IN THE LIGHT OF PHILOLOGY, ETHNOLOGY, AND EGYPTOLOGY.

Cushim and Ethiopia.—Ethiopians, White and Black.—Negro Characteristics.—The Dark Continent.—The Antiquity of the Negro.—Indisputable Evidence.—The Military and Social Condition of Negroes.—Cause of Color.—The Term Ethiopian.

THERE seems to be a great deal of ignorance and confusion in the use of the word "Negro;" and about as much trouble attends the proper classification of the inhabitants of Africa. In the preceding chapter we endeavored to prove, not that Ham and Canaan were the progenitors of the Negro races,—for that is admitted by the most consistent enemies of the blacks,—but that the human race is one, and that Noah's curse was not a divine prophecy.

The term "Negro" seems to be applied chiefly to the dark and woolly-haired people who inhabit Western Africa. But the Negro is to be found also in Eastern Africa. Zonaras says, "Chus is the person from whom the Cuseans are derived. They are the same people as the Ethiopians." This view is corroborated by Josephus. Apuleius, and Eusebius. The Hebrew term "Cush" is translated Ethiopia by the Septuagint, Vulgate, and by almost all other versions, ancient and modern, as well as by the English version. "It is not, therefore, to be doubted that the term 'Cushim' has by the interpretation of all ages been translated by 'Ethiopians,' because they were also known by their black color, and their transmigrations, which were easy and frequent." But while it is a fact, supported by both sacred and profane history, that the terms "Cush" and "Ethiopian" were used interchangeably, there seems to be no lack of proof that the same terms were applied frequently to a people who were not Negroes. It should be remembered, moreover, that there were nations who were black, and yet were not Negroes. And the only distinction amongst all these people, who are branches of the Hamitic family, is the texture of the hair. "But it is equally certain, as we have seen, that the term 'Cushite' is applied in Scripture to other branches of the same family; as, for instance, to the Midianites, from whom Moses selected his wife, and who could not have been Negroes. The term 'Cushite,' therefore, is used in Scripture as denoting nations who were not black, or in any respect Negroes, and also countries south of Egypt, whose inhabitants were Negroes; and yet both races are declared to be the descendants of Cush, the son of Ham. Even in Ezekiel's day the interior African nations were not of one race; for he represents Cush, Phut, Lud, and Chub, as either themselves constituting, or as being amalgamated with, 'a mingled people' (Ezek. xxx. 5); 'that is to say,' says Faber, 'it was a nation of Negroes who are represented as very numerous,—all the mingled people.'"

The term "Ethiopia" was anciently given to all those whose color was darkened by the sun. Herodotus, therefore, distinguishes the Eastern Ethiopians who had straight hair, from the Western Ethiopians who had curly or woolly hair.. They are a twofold people, lying extended in a long tract from the rising to the setting sun."

The conclusion is patent. The words "Ethiopia" and "Cush" were used always to describe a black people, or the country where such a people lived. The term "Negro," from the Latin "niger" and the French "noir," means black; and consequently is a modern term, with all the original meaning of Cush and Ethiopia, with a single exception. We called attention above to the fact that all Ethiopians were not of the pure Negro type, but were nevertheless a branch of the original Hamitic family from whence sprang all the dark races. The term "Negro" is now used to designate the people, who, in addition to their dark complexion, have curly or woolly hair. It is in this connection that we shall use the term in this work.

Africa, the home of the indigenous dark races, in a geographic and ethnographic sense, is the most wonderful country in the world It is thoroughly tropical. It has an area in English square miles of 11,556,600, with a population of 192,520,000 souls. It lies between the latitudes of 38° north and 35° south; and is, strictly speaking, an enormous peninsula, attached to Asia by the Isthmus of Suez. The most northern point is the cape, situated a little to the west of Cabo Blanco, and opposite Sicily, which lies in latitude 37° 20' 40" north, longitude 9° 41' east. Its southernmost point is Cabo d'Agulhas, in 34° 49' 15" south; the distance between these two points being 4,330 geographical, or about 5,000 English miles. The westernmost point is Cabo Verde, in longitude 17° 33' west; its easternmost, Cape Jerdaffun, in longitude 51° 21' east, latitude 10° 25' north, the distance between the two points being about the same as its length. The western coasts are washed by the Atlantic, the northern by the Mediterranean, and the eastern by the Indian Ocean. The shape of this "dark continent" is likened to a triangle or to an Oval. It is rich in oils, ivory, gold, and precious timber. It has beautiful lakes and mighty rivers, that are the insoluble problems of the present times.

Of the antiquity of the Negro there can be no doubt. He is known as thoroughly to history as any of the other families of men. He appears at the first dawn of history, and has continued down to the present time. The scholarly Gliddon says, that "the hieroglyphical designation of 'KeSH,' exclusively applied to African races as distinct from the Egyptian, has been found by Lepsius as far back as the monuments of the sixth dynasty, 3000 B.C. But the great influx of Negro and Mulatto races into Egypt as captives dated from the twelfth dynasty; when, about the twenty-second century, B.C., Pharaoh SESOUR-TASEN extended his conquests up the Nile far into Nigritia. After the eighteenth dynasty the monuments come down to the third century, A.D., without one single instance in the Pharaonic or Ptolemaic periods that Negro labor was ever directed to any agricultural or utilitarian objects." The Negro was found in great numbers with the Sukim, Thut, Lubin, and other African nations, who formed the strength of the army of the king of Egypt, Shishak, when he came against Rehoboam in the year 971 B.C.; and in his tomb, opened in 1849, there were found among his depicted army the exact representation of the genuine Negro race, both in color, hair, and physiognomy. Negroes are also represented in Egyptian paintings as connected with the military campaigns of the eighteenth dynasty. They formed a part of the army of Ibrahim Pacha, and were prized as gallant soldiers at Moncha and in South Arabia. And Herodotus assures us that Negroes were found in the armies of Sesostris and Xerxes; and, at the present time, they are no inconsiderable part of the standing army of Egypt. Herodotus states that eighteen of the Egyptian kings were Ethiopians.

It is quite remarkable to hear a writer like John P. Jeffries, who evidently is not very friendly in his criticisms of the Negro, make such a positive declaration as the following:—

It is difficult to find a writer on ethnology, ethnography, or Egyptology, who doubts the antiquity of the Negroes as a distinct people. Dr. John C. Nott of Mobile, Ala., a Southern man in the widest meaning, in his "Types of Mankind," while he tries to make his book acceptable to Southern slaveholders, strongly maintains the antiquity of the Negro.

In 1829 there was a remarkable Theban tomb opened by Mr. Wilkinson, and in 1840 it was carefully examined by Harris and Gliddon. There is a most wonderful collection of Negro scenes in it. Of one of these scenes even Dr. Nott says,—

It is rather strange that the feelings of Dr. Nott toward the Negro were so far mollified as to allow him to make a statement that destroys his heretofore specious reasoning about the political and social status of the Negro. He admits the antiquity of the Negro; but makes a special effort to place him in a servile state at all times, and to present him as a vanquished vassal before Ramses III. and other Egyptian kings. He sees no change in the Negro's condition, except that in slavery he is better fed and clothed than in his native home. But, nevertheless, the Negress of whom he makes mention, and the entire picture in the Theban tomb, put down the learned doctor's argument. Here is a Negro princess with Egyptian driver and groom, with a large army of attendants, going on a long journey to the tomb of her royal husband!

There is little room here to question the political and social conditions of the Negroes. They either had enjoyed a long and peaceful rule, or by their valor in offensive warfare had won honorable place by conquest. And the fact that black slaves are mentioned does not in any sense invalidate the historical trustworthiness of the pictures found in this Theban tomb; for Wilkinson says, in reference to the condition of society at this period,—

So we find that slavery was not, at this time, confined to any particular race of people. This Negro princess was as liable to purchase white as black slaves; and doubtless some were taken in successful wars with other nations, while others were purchased as servants.

But we have further evidence to offer in favor of the antiquity of the Negro. In Japan, and in many other parts of the East, there are to be found stupendous and magnificent temples, that are hoary with age. It is almost impossible to determine the antiquity of some of them, in which the idols are exact representations of woolly-haired Negroes, although the inhabitants of those countries to-day have straight hair. Among the Japanese, black is considered a color of good omen. In the temples of Siam we find the idols fashioned like unto Negroes. Osiris, one of the principal deities of the Egyptians, is frequently represented as black. Bubastis, also, the Diana of Greece, and a member of the great Egyptian Triad, is now on exhibition in the British Museum, sculptured in black basalt silting figure. Among the Hindus, Kali, the consort of Siva, one of their great Triad; Crishna, the eighth incarnation of Vishnu; and Vishnu also himself, the second of the Trimerti or Hindu Triad, are represented of a black color. Dr. Morton says,—

And the learned and indefatigable Hamilton Smith says,—

Now, these substantial and indisputable traces of the march of the Negro races through Japan and Asia lead us to conclude that the Negro race antedates all profane history. And while the great body of the Negro races have been located geographically in Africa, they have been, in no small sense, a cosmopolitan people. Their wanderings may be traced from the rising to the setting sun.

There is little room for speculation here to the candid searcher after truth. The evidence accumulates as we pursue our investigations. Monuments and temples, sepulchred stones and pyramids, rise up to declare the antiquity of the Negro races. Hamilton Smith, after careful and critical investigation, reaches the conclusion, that the Negro type of man was the most ancient, and the indigenous race of Asia, as far north as the lower range of the Himalaya Mountains, and presents at length many curious facts which cannot, he believes, be otherwise explained.

Taking the whole southern portion of Asia westward to Arabia, this conjecture—which likewise was a conclusion drawn, after patient research, by the late Sir T. Stanford Raffles— accounts, more satisfactorily than any other, for the Oriental habits, ideas, traditions, and words which can be traced among several of the present African tribes and in the South-Sea Islands. Traces of this black race are still found along the Himalaya range from the Indus to Indo-China, and the Malay peninsula, and in a mixed form all through the southern states to Ceylon.

But it is unnecessary to multiply evidence in proof of the antiquity of the Negro. His presence in this world was coetaneous with the other families of mankind: here he has toiled with a varied fortune; and here under God—his God—he will, in the process of time, work out all the sublime problems connected with his future as a man and a brother.

There are various opinions rife as to the cause of color and texture of hair in the Negro. The generally accepted theory years ago was, that the curse of Cain rested upon this race; while others saw in the dark skin of the Negro the curse of Noah pronounced against Canaan. These two explanations were comforting to that class who claimed that they had a right to buy and sell the Negro; and of whom the Saviour said, "For they bind heavy burdens and grievous to be borne, and lay them on men's shoulders; but they themselves will not move them with one of their fingers." But science has, of later years, attempted a solution of this problem. Peter Barrère, in his treatise on the subject, takes the ground that the bile in the human system has much to do with the color of the skin. This theory, however, has drawn the fire of a number of European scholars, who have combated it with more zeal than skill. It is said that the spinal and brain matter are of a dark, ashy color; and by careful examination it is proven that the blood of Ethiopians is black. These facts would seem to clothe this theory with at least a shadow of plausibility. But the opinion of Aristotle, Strabo, Alexander, and Blumenbach is, that the climate, temperature, and mode of life, have more to do with giving color than any thing else. This is certainly true among animals and plants. There are many instances on record where dogs and wolves, etc., have turned white in winter, and then assumed a different color in the spring. If you start at the north and move south, you will find, at first, that the flowers are very white and delicate; but, as you move toward the tropics, they begin to take on deeper and richer hues until they run into almost endless varieties. Guyot argues on the other side of the question to account for the intellectual diversity of the races of mankind.

The learned professor seeks to carry out his famous geographical argument, and, with great skill and labor, weaves his theory of the influence of climate upon the brain and character of man. But while no scholar would presume to combat the theory that plants take on the most gorgeous hues as one nears the equator, and that the races of mankind take on a darker color in their march toward the equator, certainly no student of Oriental history will assent to the unsupported doctrine, that the intensity of the climate of tropical countries affects the intellectual status of races. If any one be so prejudiced as to doubt this, let him turn to "Asiatic Researches," and learn that the dark races have made some of the most invaluable contributions to science, literature, civil-engineering, art, and architecture that the world has yet known. Here we find the cradle of civilization, ancient and remote.

Even changes and differences in color are to be noted in almost every community.

The artisan and farm-laborer may become exceedingly dark from exposure, and the sailor is frequently so affected by the weather that it is next to impossible to tell his nationality.

The same writer calls attention to the fact, that the people on the Cordilleras, who live under the mountains towards the west, and are, therefore, exposed to the Pacific Ocean, are quite, or nearly, as fair in complexion as the Europeans; whereas, on the contrary, the inhabitants of the opposite side, exposed to the burning sun and scorching winds, are copper-colored. Of this theory of climateric influence we shall say more farther on.

It is held by some eminent physicians in Europe and America, that the color of the skin depends upon substances external to the cutis vera. Outside of the cutis are certain layers of a substance various in consistence, and scarcely perceptible: here is the home and seat of color; and these may be regarded as secretions from the vessels of the cutis. The dark color of the Negro principally depends on the substance interposed between the true skin and the scarf-skin. This substance presents different appearances: and it is described sometimes as a sort of organized network or reticular tissue; at others, as a mere mucous or slimy layer; and it is odd that these somewhat incompatible ideas are both conveyed by the term reticulum mucosum given to the intermediate portion of the skin by its orignal discoverer, Malpighi. There is, no doubt, something plausible in all the theories advanced as to the color and hair of the Negro; but it is verily all speculation. One theory is about as valuable as another.

Nine hundred years before Christ the poet Homer, speaking of the death of Memnon, killed at the siege of Troy, says, "He was received by his Ethiopians." This is the first use of the word Ethiopia in the Greek; and it is derived from the roots αιθω, "to burn," and ωψ, "face." It is safe to assume, that, when God dispersed the sons of Noah, he fixed the "bounds of their habitation," and, that, from the earth and sky the various races have secured their civilization. He sent the different nations into separate parts of the earth. He gave to each its racial peculiarities, and adaptability for the climate into which it went. He gave color, language, and civilization; and, when by wisdom we fail to interpret his inscrutable ways, it is pleasant to know that "he worketh all things after the counsel of his own mind."

FOOTNOTES:

Edward W. Blyden, LL.D., of Liberia, says, "Supposing that this term was originally used as a phrase of contempt, is it not with us to elevate it? How often has it not happened that names originally given in reproach have been afterwards adopted as a title of honor by those against whom it was used?—Methodists, Quakers, etc. But as a proof that no unfavorable signification attached to the word when first employed, I may mention, that, long before the slave-trade began, travellers found the blacks on the coast of Africa preferring to be called Negroes" (see Purchas' Pilgrimage ...). And in all the pre-slavetrade literature the word was spelled with a capital N. It was the slavery of the blacks which afterwards degraded the term. To say that the name was invented to degrade the race, some of whose members were reduced to slavery, is to be guilty of what in grammar is called a hysteron proteron. The disgrace became attached to the name in consequence of slavery; and what we propose to do is, now that slavery is abolished, to restore it to its original place and legitimate use, and therefore to restore the capital N."

Prichard, vol. ii. p. 44.
Josephus, Antiq., lib. 2, chap. 6.
Poole.
Smyth's Unity Human Races, chap. II, p. 41.
Herodotus, vii., 69, 70. Ancient Univ. Hist., vol. xviii. pp. 254, 255.
Strabo, vol. I. p. 60.

It is not wise, to say the least, for intelligent Negroes in America to seek to drop the word "Negro." It is a good, strong, and healthy word, and ought to live. It should be covered with glory: let Negroes do it.

Journal of Ethnology, No. 7, p. 310.
Pickering's Races of Men, pp. 185-89.
Burckhardt's Travels, p. 341.
Euterpe, lib. 6.
Jeffries's Nat. Hist. of Human Race, p. 315.
Types of Mankind, p. 259.
Types of Mankind, p. 262.

Even in Africa it is found that Negroes possess great culture. Speaking of Sego, the capital of Bambara, Mr. Park says: "The view of this extensive city, the numerous, canoes upon the river, the crowded population, and the cultivated state of the surrounding country, formed altogether a prospect of civilization and magnificence which I little expected to find in the bosom of Africa." See Park's Travels, chap. ii. Mr. Park also adds, that the population of this city, Sego, is about thirty thousand. It had mosques, and even ferries were busy conveying men and horses over the Niger.

See Ambassades Mémorables de la Companie des Indes orientales des Provinces Unies vers les Empereurs du Japan, Amst., 1680; and Kaempfer.
Wilkinson's Egypt, vol. iii. p. 340.

Coleman's Mythology of the Hindus, p. 91. Dr. William Jones, vol. iii., p. 377.
Asiatic Researches, vol. vi. pp. 436-448.
Heber's Narrative, vol. i. p. 254.
Nat. Hist. of the Human Species, pp. 209, 214, 217.
Asiatic Researches, vol. i. p 427. Also Sir William Jones, vol. iii. 3d disc.
Nat. Hist. Human Species, p. 126.
Prichard, pp. 188-219.
Matt. xxiii. 4.
Discours sur la cause physicale de la couleur des nègres.
Earth and Man. Lecture x. pp. 254, 255.
Blumenbach, p. 107.

CHAPTER III.: PRIMITIVE NEGRO CIVILIZATION.

The Ancient and High Degree of Negro Civilization.—Egypt, Greece, and Rome borrow from the Negro the Civilization that made them Great.—Cause of the Decline and Fall of Negro Civilization.—Confounding the Terms "Negro" and "African."

IT is fair to presume that God gave all the races of mankind civilization to start with. We infer this from the known character of the Creator. Before Romulus founded Rome, before Homer sang, when Greece was in its infancy, and the world quite young, "hoary Meroe" was the chief city of the Negroes along the Nile. Its private and public buildings, its markets and public squares, its colossal walls and stupendous gates, its gorgeous chariots and alert footmen, its inventive genius and ripe scholarship, made it the cradle of civilization, and the mother of art. It was the queenly city of Ethiopia,—for it was founded by colonies of Negroes. Through its open gates long and ceaseless caravans, laden with gold, silver, ivory, frankincense, and palm-oil, poured the riches of Africa into the capacious lap of the city. The learning of this people, embalmed in the immortal hieroglyphic, flowed adown the Nile, and, like spray, spread over the delta of that time-honored stream, on by the beautiful and venerable city of Thebes,—the city of a hundred gates, another monument to Negro genius and civilization, and more ancient than the cities of the Delta,—until Greece and Rome stood transfixed before the ancient glory of Ethiopia! Homeric mythology borrowed its very essence from Negro hieroglyphics; Egypt borrowed her light from the venerable Negroes up the Nile. Greece went to school to the Egyptians, and Rome turned to Greece for law and the science of warfare. England dug down into Rome twenty centuries to learn to build and plant, to establish a government, and maintain it. Thus the flow of civilization has been from the East—the place of light—to the West; from the Oriental to the Occidental. (God fixed the mountains east and west in Europe.)

Is it asked what caused the decline of all this glory of the primitive Negro? why this people lost their position in the world's history? Idolatry! Sin!

Centuries have flown apace, tribes have perished, cities have risen and fallen, and even empires, whose boast was their duration, have crumbled, while Thebes and Meroe stood. And it is a remarkable fact, that the people who built those cities are less mortal than their handiwork. Notwithstanding their degradation, their woes and wrongs, the perils of the forest and dangers of the desert, this remarkable people have not been blotted out. They still live, and are multiplying in the earth. Certainly they have been preserved for some wise purpose, in the future to be unfolded.

But, again, what was the cause of the Negro's fall from his high state of civilization? It was forgetfulness of God, idolatry! "Righteousness exalteth a nation; but sin is a reproach to any people."

The Negro tribes of Africa are as widely separated by mental, moral, physical, and social qualities as the Irish, Huns, Copts, and Druids are. Their location on the Dark Continent, their surroundings, and the amount of light that has come to them from the outside world, are the thermometer of their civilization. It is as manifestly improper to call all Africans Negroes as to call, Americans Indians.

But in our examination of African tribes we shall not confine ourselves to that class of people known as Negroes, but call attention to other tribes as well. And while, in this country, all persons with a visible admixture of Negro blood in them are considered Negroes, it is technically incorrect. For the real Negro was not the sole subject sold into slavery: very many of the noblest types of mankind in Africa have, through the uncertainties of war, found their way to the horrors of the middle passage, and finally to the rice and cotton fields of the Carolinas and Virginias. So, in speaking of the race in this country, in subsequent chapters, I shall refer to them as colored people or Negroes.

FOOTNOTES:

Earth and Man, pp. 300-302.

It is a remarkable fact, that the absence of salt in the food of the Eastern nations, especially the dark nations or races, has been very deleterious. An African child will eat salt by the handful, and, once tasting it, will cry for it. The ocean is the womb of nature; and the Creator has wisely designed salt as the savor of life, the preservative element in human food.

Physical History of Mankind, vol. ii. pp. 45, 46.

CHAPTER IV.: NEGRO KINGDOMS OF AFRICA.

BENIN: Its Location.—Its Discovery by the Portuguese.—Introduction of the Catholic Religion.—The King as a Missionary,—His Fidelity to the Church Purchased by White Wife.—Decline of Religion.—Introduction of Slavery.—Suppression of the Trade by the English Government.—Restoration and Peace.

DAHOMEY: Its Location.—Origin of the Kingdom.—Meaning of the Name.—War.—Capture of the English Governor, and his Death.—The Military Establishment.—Women as Soldiers.—Wars and their Objects.—Human Sacrifices.—The King a Despot.—His Powers.—His Wives.—Polygamy.—Kingly Succession.—Coronation.—Civil and Criminal Law.—Revenue System.—Its Future.

YORUBA: Its Location.—Slavery and its Abolition.—Growth of the People of Abeokuta.—Missionaries and Teachers from Sierra Leone.—Prosperity and Peace attend the People.—Capacity of the People for Civilization.—Bishop Crowther.—His Influence.

BENIN.

THE vast territory stretching from the Volta River on the west to the Niger in the Gulf of Benin on the east, the Atlantic Ocean on the south, and the Kong Mountains on the north, embraces the three powerful Negro kingdoms of Benin, Dahomey, and Yoruba. From this country, more than from any other part of Africa, were the people sold into American slavery. Two or three hundred years ago there were several very powerful Negro empires in Western Africa. They had social and political government, and were certainly a very orderly people. But in 1485 Alfonso de Aviro, a Portuguese, discovered Benin, the most easterly province; and as an almost immediate result the slave-trade was begun. It is rather strange, too, in the face of the fact, that, when De Aviro returned to the court of Portugal, an ambassador from the Negro king of Benin accompanied him for the purpose of requesting the presence of Christian missionaries among this people. Portugal became interested, and despatched Fernando Po to the Gulf of Benin; who, after discovering the island that bears his name, ascended the Benin River to Gaton, where he located a Portuguese colony. The Romish Church lifted her standard here. The brothers of the Society of Jesus, if they did not convert the king, certainly had him in a humor to bring all of his regal powers to bear upon his subjects to turn them into the Catholic Church. He actually took the contract to turn his subjects over to this Church! But this shrewd savage did not agree to undertake this herculean task for nothing. He wanted a white wife. He told the missionaries that he would deliver his subjects to Christianity for a white wife, and they agreed to furnish her. Some priests were sent to the Island of St. Thomas to hunt the wife. This island had, even at that early day, a considerable white population. A strong appeal was made to the sisters there to consider this matter as a duty to the holy Church. It was set forth as a missionary enterprise. After some contemplation, one of the sisters agreed to accept the hand of the Negro king. It was a noble act, and one for which she should have been canonized, but we believe never was.

The Portuguese continued to come. Gaton grew. The missionary worked with a will. Attention was given to agriculture and commerce. But the climate was wretched. Sickness and death swept the Portuguese as the fiery breath of tropical lightning. They lost their influence over the people. They established the slave-trade, but the Church and slave-pen would not agree. The inhuman treatment they bestowed upon the people gave rise to the gravest suspicions as to the sincerity of the missionaries. History gives us the sum total of a religious effort that was not of God. There isn't a trace of Roman Catholicism in that country, and the last state of that people is worse than the former.

The slave-trade turned the heads of the natives. Their cruel and hardened hearts assented to the crime of man-stealing. They turned aside from agricultural pursuits. They left their fish-nets on the seashore, their cattle uncared for, their villages neglected, and went forth to battle against their weaker neighbors. They sold their prisoners of war to slave-dealers on the coast, who gave them rum and tobacco as an exceeding great reward. When war failed to give from its bloody and remorseless jaws the victims for whom a ready market awaited, they turned to duplicity, treachery, and cruelty. "And men's worst enemies were those of their own household." The person suspicioned of witchcraft was speedily found guilty, and adjudged to slavery. The guilty and the innocent often shared the same fate. The thief, the adulterer, and the aged were seized by the rapacity that pervaded the people, and were hurled into the hell of slavery.

Now, as a result of this condition of affairs, the population was depleted, the people grew indolent and vicious, and finally the empire was rent with political feuds. Two provinces was the result. One still bore the name of Benin, the other was called Waree. The capital of the former contains about 38,000 inhabitants, and the chief town and island of Waree only contain about 16,000 of a population.

Finally England was moved to a suppression of the slave-trade at this point. The ocean is very calm along this coast, which enabled her fleets to run down slave-vessels and make prizes of them. This had a salutary influence upon the natives. Peace and quietness came as angels. A spirit of thrift possessed the people. They turned to the cultivation of the fields and to commercial pursuits. On the river Bonny, and along other streams, large and flourishing palm-oil marts sprang up; and a score or more of vessels are needed to export the single article of palm-oil. The morals of the people are not what they ought to be; but they have, on the whole, made wonderful improvement during the last fifty years.

DAHOMEY.

This nation is flanked by Ashantee on the west, and Yoruba on the east; running from the seacoast on the south to the Kong mountains on the north. It is one hundred and eighty miles in width, by two hundred in breadth. Whydah is the principal town on the seacoast. The story runs, that, about two hundred and seventy-five years ago, Tacudons, chief of the Foys, carried a siege against the city of Abomey. He made a solemn vow to the gods, that, if they aided him in pushing the city to capitulate, he would build a palace in honor of the victory. He succeeded. He laid the foundations of his palace, and then upon them ripped open the bowels of Da. He called the building Da-Omi, which meant Da's belly. He took the title of King of Dahomey, which has remained until the present time. The neighboring tribes, proud and ambitious, overran the country, and swept Whydah and adjacent places with the torch and spear. Many whites fell into their hands as prisoners; all of whom were treated with great consideration, save the English governor of the above-named town. They put him to death, because, as they charged, he had incited and excited the people of Dahomey to resist their king.

    This is a remarkable people. They are as cruel as they are cunning. The entire population is converted into an army: even women are soldiers. Whole regiments of women are to be found in the army of the king of Dahomey, and they are the best foot-regiments in the kingdom. They are drilled at stated periods, are officered, and well disciplined. The army is so large, and is so constantly employed in predatory raids upon neighboring tribes, that the consuming element is greater than the producing. The object of these raids was threefold: to get slaves for human sacrifices, to pour the blood of the victims on the graves of their ancestors yearly, and to secure human skulls to pave the court of the king and to ornament the walls about the palace! After a successful war, the captives are brought to the capital of the kingdom. A large platform is erected in the great market space, encircled by a parapet about three feet high. The platform blazes with rich clothes, elaborate umbrellas, and all the evidences of kingly wealth and splendor, as well as the spoils taken in battle. The king occupies a seat in the centre of the platform, attended by his imperturbable wives. The captives, rum, tobacco, and cowries are now ready to be thrown to the surging mob below. They have fought gallantly, and now clamor for their reward. "Feed us, king!" they cry, "feed us, king! for we are hungry!" and as the poor captives are tossed to the mob they are despatched without ceremony!

    But let us turn from this bloody and barbarous scene. The king is the most absolute despot in the world. He is heir-at-law to all his subjects. He is regarded as a demigod. It is unlawful to indicate that the king eats, sleeps, or drinks. No one is allowed to approach him, except his nobles, who at a court levee disrobe themselves of all their elegant garments, and, prostrate upon the ground, they crawl into his royal presence. The whole people are the cringing lickspittles of the nobles in turn. Every private in the army is ambitious to please the king by valor. The king is literally monarch of all he surveys. He is proprietor of the land, and has at his disposal every thing animate or inanimate in his kingdom. He has about three thousand wives. Every man who would marry must buy his spouse from the king; and, while the system of polygamy obtains everywhere throughout the kingdom, the subject must have care not to secure so many wives that it would appear that he is attempting to rival the king. The robust women are consigned to the military service. But the real condition of woman in this kingdom is slavery of the vilest type. She owns nothing. She is always in the market, and lives in a state of constant dread of being sold. When the king dies, a large number of his wives are sacrificed upon his grave. This fact inspires them to take good care of him! In case of death, the king's brother, then his nephew, and so on, take the throne. An inauguration generally lasts six days, during which time hundreds of human lives are sacrificed in honor of the new monarch.

    The code of Dahomey is very severe. Witchcraft is punished with death; and in this regard stalwart old Massachusetts borrowed from the barbarian. Adultery is punished by slavery or sudden death. Thieves are also sold into slavery. Treason and cowardice and murder are punished by death. The civil code is as complicated as the criminal is severe. Over every village, is a Caboceer, equivalent to our mayor. He can convene a court by prostrating himself and kissing the ground. The court convenes, tries and condemns the criminal. If it be a death sentence, he is delivered to a man called the Milgan, or equivalent to our sheriff, who is the ranking officer in the state. If the criminal is sentenced to slavery, he is delivered to the Mayo, who is second in rank to the Milgan, or about like our turnkey or jailer. All sentences must be referred to the king for his approval; and all executions take place at the capital, where notice is given of the same by a public crier in the market-places.

The revenue system of this kingdom is oppressive. The majority of slaves taken in war are the property of the king. A tax is levied on each person or slave exported from the kingdom. In relation to domestic commerce, a tax is levied on every article of food and clothing. A custom-service is organized, and the tax-collectors are shrewd and exacting.

The religion of the people is idolatry and fetich, or superstition. They have large houses where they worship snakes; and so great is their reverence for the reptile, that, if any one kills one that has escaped, he is punished with death. But, above their wild and superstitious notions, there is an ever-present consciousness of a Supreme Being. They seldom mention the name of God, and then with fear and trembling.

But this people are not in a hopeless condition of degradation.

And we say Amen!

YORUBA.

This kingdom extends from the seacoast to the river Niger, by which it is separated from the kingdom of Nufi. It contains more territory than either Benin or Dahomey. Its principal seaport is Lagos. For many years it was a great slave-mart, and only gave up the traffic under the deadly presence of English guns. Its facilities for the trade were great. Portuguese and Spanish slave-traders took up their abode here, and, teaching the natives the use of fire-arms, made a stubborn stand for their lucrative enterprise; but in 1852 the slave-trade was stopped, and the slavers driven from the seacoast. The place came under the English flag; and, as a result, social order and business enterprise have been restored and quickened. The slave-trade wrought great havoc among this people. It is now about fifty-five years since a few weak and fainting tribes, decimated by the slave-trade, fled to Ogun, a stream seventy-five miles from the coast, where they took refuge in a cavern. In the course of time they were joined by other tribes that fled before the scourge of slave-hunters. Their common danger gave them a commonality of interests. They were, at first, reduced to very great want. They lived for a long time on berries, herbs, roots, and such articles of food as nature furnished without money and without price; but, leagued together to defend their common rights, they grew bold, and began to spread out around their hiding-place, and engage in agriculture. Homes and villages began to rise, and the desert to blossom as the rose. They finally chose a leader,—a wise and judicious man by the name of Shodeke; and one hundred and thirty towns were united under one government. In 1853, less than a generation, a feeble people had grown to be nearly one hundred thousand (100,000); and Abeokuta, named for their cave, contains at present nearly three hundred thousand souls.

In 1839 some colored men from Sierra Leone, desirous of engaging in trade, purchased a small vessel, and called at Lagos and Badagry. They had been slaves in this country, and had been taken to Sierra Leone, where they had received a Christian education. Their visit, therefore, was attended with no ordinary interest. They recognized many of their friends and kindred, and were agreeably surprised at the wonderful change that had taken place in so short a time. They returned to Sierra Leone, only to inspire their neighbors with a zeal for commercial and missionary enterprise. Within three years, five hundred of the best colored people of Sierra Leone set out for Lagos and Badagry on the seacoast, and then moved overland to Abeokuta, where they intended to make their home. In this company of noble men were merchants, mechanics, physicians, school-teachers, and clergymen. Their people had fought for deliverance from physical bondage: these brave missionaries had come to deliver them from intellectual and spiritual bondage. The people of Abeokuta gave the missionaries a hearty welcome. The colony received new blood and energy. School-buildings and churches rose on every hand. Commerce was revived, and even agriculture received more skilful attention. Peace and and plenty began to abound. Every thing wore a sunny smile, and many tribes were bound together by the golden cords of civilization, and sang their Te Deum together. Far-away England caught their songs of peace, and sent them agricultural implements, machinery, and Christian ministers and teachers. So, that, nowhere on the continent of Africa is there to be found so many renewed households, so many reclaimed tribes, such substantial results of a vigorous, Christian civilization.

 The forces that quickened the inhabitants of Abeokuta were not all objective, exoteric: there were subjective and inherent forces at work in the hearts of the people. They were capable of civilization,—longed for it; and the first blaze of light from without aroused their slumbering forces, and showed them the broad and ascending road that led to the heights of freedom and usefulness. That they sought this road with surprising alacrity, we have the most abundant evidence. Nor did all the leaders come from abroad. Adgai, in the Yoruba language, but Crowther, in English, was a native of this country. In 1822 he was sold into slavery at the port of Badagry. The vessel that was to bear him away to the "land of chains and stocks" was captured by a British man-of-war, and taken to Sierra Leone. Here he came under the influence of Christian teachers. He proved to be one of the best pupils in his school. He received a classical education, fitted for the ministry, and then hastened back to his native country to carry the gospel of peace. It is rather remarkable, but he found his mother and several sisters still "in the gall of bitterness and in the bonds of iniquity." The son and brother became their spiritual teacher, and, ere long, had the great satisfaction of seeing them "clothed, in their right mind, and sitting at the feet of Jesus." His influence has been almost boundless. A man of magnificent physical proportions,—tall, a straight body mounted by a ponderous head, shapely, with a kind eye, benevolent face, a rich cadence in his voice,—the "black Bishop" Crowther is a princely looking man, who would attract the attention of cultivated people anywhere. He is a man of eminent piety, broad scholarship, and good works. He has translated the Bible into the Yoruba language, founded schools, and directed the energies of his people with a matchless zeal. His beautiful and beneficent life is an argument in favor of the possibilities of Negro manhood so long injured by the dehumanizing influences of slavery. Others have caught the inspiration that has made Bishop

Crowther's life "as terrible as an army with banners" to the enemies of Christ and humanity, and are working to dissipate the darkness of that land of night.

FOOTNOTES:

The king of Dahomey is limited to 3,333 wives! It is hardly fair to suppose that his majesty feels cramped under the ungenerous act that limits the number of his wives.
Savage Africa, p. 51.
Western Africa, p. 207.

CHAPTER V.: THE ASHANTEE EMPIRE.

Its Location and Extent.—Its Famous Kings.—The Origin of the Ashantees Obscure.—The War with Denkera.—The Ashantees against the Field conquer Two Kingdoms and annex them.—Death of Osai Tutu.—The Envy of the King of Dahomey.—Invasion of the Ashantee Country by the King of Dahomey.—His Defeat shared by his Allies.—Akwasi pursues the Army of Dahomey into its own Country.—Gets a Mortal Wound and suffers a Humiliating Defeat.—The King of Dahomey sends the Royal Kudjoh His Congratulations.—Kwamina deposed for attempting to introduce Mohammedanism into the Kingdom.—The Ashantees conquer the Mohammedans.—Numerous Wars.—Invasion of the Fanti Country.—Death of Sir Charles McCarthy.—Treaty.—Peace.

THE kingdom of Ashantee lies between the Kong Mountains and the vast country of the Fantis. The country occupied by the Ashantees was, at the first, very small; but by a series of brilliant conquests they finally secured a territory of three hundred square miles. One of their most renowned kings, Osai Tutu, during the last century, added to Ashantee by conquest the kingdoms of Sarem, Buntuku, Warsaw, Denkera, and Axim. Very little is known as to the origin of the Ashantees. They were discovered in the early part of the eighteenth century in the great valley between the Kong Mountains and the river Niger, from whence they were driven by the Moors and Mohammedan Negroes. They exchanged the bow for fire-arms, and soon became a warlike people. Osai Tutu led in a desperate engagement against the king of Denkera, in which the latter was slain, his army was put to rout, and large quantities of booty fell into the hands of the victorious Ashantees. The king of Axim unwittingly united his forces to those of the discomforted Denkera, and, drawing the Ashantees into battle again, sustained heavy losses, and was put to flight. He was compelled to accept the most exacting conditions of peace, to pay the king of the Ashantees four thousand ounces of gold to defray the expenses of the war, and have his territory made tributary to the conqueror. In a subsequent battle Osai Tutu was surprised and killed. His courtiers and wives were made prisoners, with much goods. This enraged the Ashantees, and they reeked vengeance on the heads of the inhabitants of Kromanti, who laid the disastrous ambuscade. They failed, however, to recover the body of their slain king; but many of his attendants were retaken, and numerous enemies, whom they sacrificed to the manes of their dead king at Kumasi.

After the death of the noble Osai Tutu, dissensions arose among his followers. The tribes and kingdoms he had bound to his victorious chariot-wheels began to assert their independence. His life-work began to crumble. Disorder ran riot; and, after a few ambitious leaders were convinced that the throne of Ashantee demanded brains and courage, they cheerfully made way for the coronation of Osai Opoko, brother to the late king. He was equal to the existing state of affairs. He proved himself a statesman, a soldier, and a wise ruler. He organized his army, and took the field in person against the revolting tribes. He reconquered all the lost provinces. He defeated his most valorous foe, the king of Gaman, after driving him into the Kong Mountains. When his jealous underlings sought his overthrow by conspiracy, he conquered them by an appeal to arms.

His rule was attended by the most lasting and beneficent results. He died in 1742, and was succeeded by his brother, Osai Akwasi.

The fame and military prowess of the kings of the Ashantees were borne on every passing breeze, and told by every fleeing fugitive. The whole country was astounded by the marvellous achievements of this people, and not a little envy was felt among adjoining nations. The king of Dahomey especially felt like humiliating this people in battle. This spirit finally manifested itself in feuds, charges, complaints, and, laterally, by actual hostilities. The king of Dahomey felt that he had but one rival, the king of Ashantee. He felt quite sure of victory on account of the size, spirit, and discipline of his army. It was idle at this time, and was ordered to the Ashantee border. The first engagement took place near the Volta. The king of Dahomey had succeeded in securing an alliance with the armies of Kawaku and Bourony, but the valor and skill of the Ashantees were too much for the invading armies. If King Akwasi had simply maintained his defensive position, his victory would have been lasting; but, overjoyed at his success, he unwittingly pursued the enemy beyond the Volta, and carried war into the kingdom of Dahomey. Troops fight with great desperation in their own country. The Ashantee army was struck on its exposed flanks, its splendid companies of Caboceers went down before the intrepid Amazons. Back to the Volta, the boundary line between the two empires, fled the routed Ashantees. Akwasi received a mortal wound, from which he died in 1752, when his nephew, Osai Kudjoh, succeeded to the throne.

Three brothers had held the sceptre over this empire, but now it passed to another generation. The new king was worthy of his illustrious family. After the days of mourning for his royal uncle were ended, before he ascended the throne, several provinces revolted. He at once took the field, subdued his recalcitrant subjects, and made them pay a heavy tribute. He won other provinces by conquest, and awed the neighboring tribes until an unobstructed way was open to his invincible army across the country to Cape Palmas. His fame grew with each military manoeuvre, and each passing year witnessed new triumphs. Fawning followed envy in the heart of the king of Dahomey; and a large embassy was despatched to the powerful Kudjoh, congratulating him upon his military achievements, and seeking a friendly alliance between the two governments. Peace was now restored; and the armies of Ashantee very largely melted into agricultural communities, and great prosperity came. But King Kudjoh was growing old in the service of his people; and, as he could no longer give his personal attention to public affairs, dissensions arose in some of the remote provinces. With impaired vision and feeble health he, nevertheless, put an army into the field to punish the insubordinate tribes; but before operations began he died. His grandson, Osai Kwamina, was designated as legal successor to the throne in 1781. He took a solemn vow that he would not enter the palace until he secured the heads of Akombroh and Afosee, whom he knew had excited and incited the people to rebellion against his grandfather. His vengeance was swift and complete. The heads of the rebel leaders were long kept at Juntas as highly prized relics of the reign of King Kwamina. His reign was brief, however. He was deposed for attempting to introduce the Mohammedan religion into the kingdom. Osai Apoko was crowned as his successor in 1797. The Gaman and Kongo armies attached themselves to the declining fortunes of the deposed king, and gave battle for his lost crown. It was a lost cause. The new king could wield his sword as well as wear a crown. He died of a painful sickness, and was succeeded by his son, Osai Tutu Kwamina, in 1800.

The new king was quite youthful,—only seventeen; but he inherited splendid qualities from a race of excellent rulers. He re-organized his armies, and early won a reputation for courage, sagacity, and excellent ability, extraordinary in one so young. He inherited a bitter feeling against the Mohammedans, and made up his mind to chastise two of their chiefs, Ghofan and Ghobago, and make the territory of Banna tributary to Ashantee. He invaded their country, and burned their capital. In an engagement fought at Kaha, the entire Moslem army was defeated and captured. The king of Ghofan was wounded and made prisoner, and died in the camp of the Ashantee army. Two more provinces were bound to the throne of Kwamina; and we submit that this is an historical anomaly, in that a pagan people subdued an army that emblazoned its banner with the faith of the one God!

The Ashantee empire had reached the zenith of its glory. Its flag waved in triumph from the Volta to Bossumpea, and the Kong Mountains had echoed the exploits of the veterans that formed the strength of its army. The repose that even this uncivilized people longed for was denied them by a most unfortunate incident.

Asim was a province tributary to the Ashantee empire. Two of the chiefs of Asim became insubordinate, gave offence to the king, and then fled into the country of the Fantis, one of the most numerous and powerful tribes on the Gold Coast. The Fantis promised the fugitives armed protection. There was no extradition treaty in those days. The king despatched friendly messengers, who were instructed to set forth the faults of the offending subjects, and to request their return. The request was contemptuously denied, and the messengers subjected to a painful death. The king of Ashantee invaded the country of the enemy, and defeated the united forces of Fanti and Asim. He again made them an offer of peace, and was led to believe it would be accepted. But the routed army was gathering strength for another battle, although Chibbu and Apontee had indicated to the king that the conditions of peace were agreeable. The king sent an embassy to learn when a formal submission would take place; and they, also, were put to death. King Osai Tutu Kwamina took "the great oath," and vowed that he would never return from the seat of war or enter his capital without the heads of the rebellious chiefs. The Ashantee army shared the desperate feelings of their leader; and a war was begun, which for cruelty and carnage has no equal in the annals of the world's history. Pastoral communities, hamlets, villages, and towns were swept by the red waves of remorseless warfare. There was no mercy in battle: there were no prisoners taken by day, save to be spared for a painful death at nightfall. Their groans, mingling with the shouts of the victors, made the darkness doubly hideous; and the blood of the vanquished army, but a short distance removed, ran cold at the thoughts of the probable fate that waited them on the morrow. Old men and old women, young men and young women, the rollicking children whose light hearts knew no touch of sorrow, as well as the innocent babes clinging to the agitated bosoms of their mothers,—unable to distinguish between friend or foe,— felt the cruel stroke of war. All were driven to an inhospitable grave in the place where the fateful hand of war made them its victims, or perished in the sullen waters of the Volta. For nearly a hundred miles "the smoke of their torment" mounted the skies. Nothing was left in the rear of the Ashantee army, not even cattle or buildings. Pursued by a fleet-footed and impartial disaster, the fainting Fantis and their terrified allies turned their faces toward the seacoast. And why? Perhaps this fleeing army had a sort of superstitious belief that the sea might help them. Then, again, they knew that there were many English on the Gold Coast; that they had forts and troops. They trusted, also, that the young king of the Ashantees would not follow his enemy under the British flag and guns. They were mistaken. The two revolting chiefs took refuge in the fort at Anamabo. On came the intrepid king, thundering at the very gates of the English fort. The village was swept with the hot breath of battle. Thousands perished before this invincible army. The English soldiers poured hot shot and musketry into the columns of the advancing army; but on they marched to victory with an impurturbable air, worthy of "the old guard" under Ney at Waterloo. Preparations were completed for blowing up the walls of the fort; and it would have been but a few hours until the king of Ashantee would have taken the governor's chair, had not the English capitulated. During the negotiations one of the offending chiefs made good his escape to a little village called Cape Coast; but the other was delivered up, and, having been taken back to Kumasi, was tortured to death. Twelve thousand persons fell in the engagement at Anamabo, and thousands of lives were lost in other engagements. This took place in 1807.

In 1811 the king of Ashantee sent an array to Elmina to protect his subjects against predatory bands of Fantis. Three or four battles were fought, and were invariably won by the Ashantee troops.

Barbarians have about as long memories as civilized races. They are a kind-hearted people, but very dangerous and ugly when they are led to feel that they have been injured. "The great oath" means a great deal; and the king was not happy in the thought that one of the insolent chiefs had found refuge in the town of Cape Coast, which was in the Fanti country. So in 1817 he invaded this country, and called at Cape Coast, and reduced the place to the condition of a siege. The English authorities saw the Fantis dying under their eyes, and paid the fine imposed by the King of Ashantee, rather than bury the dead inhabitants of the beleaguered town. The Ashantees retired.

England began to notice the Ashantees. They had proven themselves to be a most heroic, intelligent, and aggressive people. The Fantis lay stretched between them and the seacoast. The frequent invasion of this country, for corrective purposes as the Ashantees believed, very seriously interrupted the trade of the coast; and England began to feel it. The English had been defeated once in an attempt to assist the Fantis, and now thought it wise to turn attention to a pacific policy, looking toward the establishment of amicable relations between the Ashantees and themselves. There had never been any unpleasant relations between the two governments, except in the instance named. The Ashantees rather felt very kindly toward England, and for prudential and commercial reasons desired to treat the authorities at the coast with great consideration. They knew that the English gave them a market for their gold, and an opportunity to purchase manufactured articles that they needed. But the Fantis, right under the English flag, receiving a rent for the ground on which the English had their fort and government buildings, grew so intolerably abusive towards their neighbors, the Ashantees, that the British saw nothing before them but interminable war. It was their desire to avoid it if possible. Accordingly, they sent an embassy to the king of the Ashantees, consisting of Gov. James, of the fort at Akra, a Mr. Bowdich, nephew to the governor-in-chief at Cape Coast, a Mr. Hutchinson, and the surgeon of the English settlement, Dr. Teddlie. Mr. Bowdich headed the embassy to the royal court, where they were kindly received. A treaty was made. The rent that the Fantis had been receiving for ground occupied by the English—four ounces of gold per month—was to be paid to the king of Ashantee, as his by right of conquest. Diplomatic relations were to be established between the two governments, and Mr. Hutchinson was to remain at Kumasi as the British resident minister. He was charged with the carrying out of so much of the treaty as related to his government. The treaty was at once forwarded to the home government, and Mr. Dupuis was appointed consul of his Majesty's government to the court of Ashantee. A policy was outlined that meant the opening up of commerce with the distant provinces of the Ashantee empire along the Kong Mountains. In those days it took a long time to sail from England to the Gold Coast in Western Africa; and before Consul Dupuis reached the coast, the king of Ashantee was engaged in a war with the king of Gaman. The Ashantee army was routed. The news of the disaster was hailed by the Fantis on the coast with the most boisterous and public demonstrations. This gave the king of Ashantee offence. The British authorities were quite passive about the conduct of the Fantis, although by solemn treaty they had become responsible for their deportment. The Fantis grew very insulting and offensive towards the Ashantees. The king of the latter called the attention of the authorities at the Cape to the conduct of the Fantis, but no official action was taken. In the mean while Mr. Dupuis was not allowed to proceed on his mission to the capital of the Ashantees. Affairs began to assume a very threatening attitude; and only after the most earnest request was he permitted to proceed to the palace of the king of Ashantee. He received a hearty welcome at the court, and was entertained with the most lavish kindness. After long and painstaking consideration, a treaty was decided upon that was mutually agreeable; but the self-conceited and swaggering insolence of the British authorities on the coast put it into the waste-basket. The commander of the British squadron put himself in harmony with the local authorities, and refused to give Consul Dupuis transportation to England for the commissioners of the Ashantee government, whom he had brought to the coast with the intention of taking to London with him.

 A war-cloud was gathering. Dupuis saw it. He sent word to the king of Ashantee to remember his oath, and refrain from hostilities until he could communicate with the British government. The treaty stipulated for the recognition, by the British authorities, of the authority of the Ashantee king over the Fantis. Only those immediately around the fort were subject to English law, and then not to an extent to exempt them from tax imposed by the Ashantee authorities.

 In the midst of these complications, Parliament, by a special act, abolished the charter of the African Company. This put all its forts, arsenals, and stations under the direct control of the crown. Sir Charles McCarthy was made governor-general of the British possessions on the Gold

Coast, and took up his head-quarters at Cape Coast in March, 1822. Two months had passed now since Dupuis had sailed for England; and not a syllable had reached the king's messenger, who, all this time, had waited to hear from England. The country was in an unsettled state. Gov, McCarthy was not equal to the situation. He fell an easy prey to the fawning and lying Fantis. They received him as the champion of their declining fortunes, and did every thing in their power to give him an unfriendly opinion of the Ashantees. The king of the Ashantees began to lose faith in the British. His faithful messenger returned from the coast bearing no friendly tidings. The king withdrew his troops from the seacoast, and began to put his army upon a good war-footing. When all was in readiness a Negro sergeant in the British service was seized, and put to a torturous death. This was a signal for the grand opening. Of course the British were bound to demand redress. Sir Charles McCarthy was informed by some Fantis scouts that the king of Ashantee, at the head of his army, was marching for Cape Coast. Sir Charles rallied his forces, and went forth to give him battle. His object was to fight the king at a distance from the cape, and thus prevent him from devastating the entire country as in former wars. Sir Charles McCarthy was a brave man, and worthy of old England; but in this instance his courage was foolhardy. He crossed the Prah River to meet a wily and desperate foe. His troops were the worthless natives, hastily gathered, and were intoxicated with the hope of deliverance from Ashantee rule. He should have waited for the trained troops of Major Chisholm. This was his fatal mistake. His pickets felt the enemy early in the morning of the 21st of January, 1824. A lively skirmish followed. In a short time the clamorous war-horns of the advancing Ashantees were heard, and a general engagement came on. The first fighting began along a shallow stream. The Ashantees came up with the courage and measured tread of a well-disciplined army. They made a well-directed charge to gain the opposite bank of the stream, but were repulsed by an admirable bayonet charge from Sir Charles's troops. The Ashantees then crossed the stream above and below the British army, and fell with such desperation upon its exposed and naked flanks, that it was bent into the shape of a letter A, and hurled back toward Cape Coast in dismay. Wounded and exhausted, toward evening Sir Charles fled from his exposed position to the troops of his allies under the command of the king of Denkera. He concentrated his artillery upon the heaviest columns of the enemy; but still they came undaunted, bearing down upon the centre like an avalanche. Sir Charles made an attempt to retreat with his staff, but met instant death at the hands of the Ashantees. His head was removed from the body and sent to Kumasi. His heart was eaten by the chiefs of the army that they might imbibe his courage, while his flesh was dried and issued in small rations among the line-officers for the same purpose. His bones were kept at the capital of the Ashantee kingdom as national fetiches.

 Major Chisholm and Capt. Laing, learning of the disaster that had well-nigh swallowed up Sir Charles's army, retreated to Cape Coast. There were about thirty thousand troops remaining, but they were so terrified at the disaster of the day that they could not be induced to make a stand against the gallant Ashantees. The king of Ashantee, instead of following the routed army to the gates of Cape Coast, where he could have dealt it a death-blow, offered the English conditions of peace. Capt. Ricketts met the Ashantee messengers at Elmina, and heard from them the friendly messages of the king. The Ashantees only wanted the British to surrender Kudjoh Chibbu of the province of Denkera; but this fugitive from the Ashantee king, while negotiations were pending, resolved to rally the allied armies and make a bold stroke. He crossed the Prah at the head of a considerable force, and fell upon the Ashantee army in its camp. The English were charmed by this bold stroke, and sent a reserve force; but the whole army was again defeated by the Ashantees, and came back to Cape Coast in complete confusion.

The Ashantee army were at the gates of the town. Col. Southerland arrived with re-enforcements, but was beaten into the fort by the unyielding courage of the attacking force. A new king, Osai Ockote, arrived with fresh troops, and won the confidence of the army by marching right under the British guns, and hissing defiance into the face of the foe. The conflict that followed was severe, and destructive to both life and property. All the native and British forces were compelled to retire to the fort; while the Ashantee troops, inspired by the dashing bearing of their new king, closed in around them like tongues of steel. The invading army was not daunted by the belching cannon that cut away battalion after battalion. On they pressed for revenge and victory. The screams of fainting women and terrified children, the groans of the dying, and the bitter imprecations of desperate combatants,—a mingling medley,—swelled the great diapason of noisy battle. The eyes of the beleaguered were turned toward the setting sun, whose enormous disk was leaning against the far-away mountains, and casting his red and vermilion over the dusky faces of dead Ashantees and Fantis; and, imparting a momentary beauty to the features of the dead white men who fell so far away from home and friends, he sank to rest. There was a sad, far-off look in the eye of the impatient sailor who kept his lonely watch on the vessel that lay at rest on the sea. Night was wished for, prayed for, yearned for. It came at last, and threw its broad sable pinions over the dead, the dying, and the living. Hostilities were to be renewed in the morning; but the small-pox broke out among the soldiers, and the king of Ashantee retired.

Sir Neill Campbell was appointed governor-general at Cape Coast. One of his first acts was to call for all the chiefs of the Fantis, and give them to understand that hostilities between themselves and the king of Ashantee must stop. He then required Osai Ockoto to deposit four thousand ounces of gold ($72,000), as a bond to keep the peace. In case he provoked hostilities, the seventy-two thousand dollars were to be used to purchase ammunition with which to chastise him. In 1831 the king was obliged to send two of his royal family, Kwanta Missah, his own son, and Ansah, the son of the late king, to be held as hostages. These boys were sent to England, where they were educated, but are now residents of Ashantee.

Warsaw and Denkera, interior provinces, were lost to the Ashantee empire; but, nevertheless, it still remains one of the most powerful Negro empires of Western Africa.

The king of Ashantee has a fair government. His power is well-nigh absolute. He has a House of Lords, who have a check-power. Coomassi is the famous city of gold, situated in the centre of the empire. The communication through to the seacoast is unobstructed; and it is rather remarkable that the Ashantees are the only nation in Africa, who, living in the interior, have direct communication with the Caucasian. They have felt the somewhat elevating influence of

Mohammedanism, and are not unconscious of the benefits derived by the literature and contact of the outside world. They are a remarkable people: brave, generous, industrious, and mentally capable. The day is not distant when the Ashantee kingdom will be won to the Saviour, and its inhabitants brought under the beneficent influences of Christian civilization.

FOOTNOTES:

"Massacre Of Maidens. London, Nov. 10, 1881.—Advices from Cape Coast Castle report that the king of Ashantee killed two hundred young girls for the purpose of using their blood for mixing mortar for repair of one of the state buildings. The report of the massacre was received from a refugee chosen for one of the victims. Such wholesale massacres are known to be a custom with the king."—Cinn. Commercial.

CHAPTER VI.: THE NEGRO TYPE.

Climate the Cause.—His Geographical Theatre.—He is susceptible to Christianity and Civilization.

IF the reader will turn to a map of Africa, the Mountains of the Moon will be found to run right through the centre of that continent. They divide Africa into two almost equal parts. In a dialectic sense, also, Africa is divided. The Mountains of the Moon, running east and west, seem to be nature's dividing line between two distinct peoples. North of these wonderful mountains the languages are numerous and quite distinct, and lacking affinity. For centuries these tribes have lived in the same latitude, under the same climatic influences, and yet, without a written standard, have preserved the idiomatic coloring of their tribal language without corruption. Thus they have eluded the fate that has overtaken all other races who without a written language, living together by the laws of affinity, sooner or later have found one medium of speech as inevitable as necessary.

But coming south of the Mountains of the Moon, until we reach the Cape of Good Hope, there is to be found one great family. Nor is the difference between the northern and southern tribes only linguistic. The physiological difference between these people is great. They range in color from the dead black up to pure white, and from the dwarfs on the banks of the Casemanche to the tall and giant-like Vei tribe of Cape Mount.

That climate has much to do with physical and mental character, we will not have to prove to any great extent. It is a fact as well established as any principle in pathology. Dr. Joseph Brown says,—

In his "Ashango Land," Paul B. du Chaillu devotes a large part of his fifteenth chapter to the Obongos, or Dwarfs. Nearly all African explorers and travellers have been much amazed at the diversity of color and stature among the tribes they met. This diversity in physical and mental character owes its existence to the diversity and perversity of African climate.

The Negro, who is but a fraction of the countless indigenous races of Africa, has been carried down to his low estate by the invincible forces of nature. Along the ancient volcanic tracts are to be found the Libyan race, with a tawny complexion, features quite Caucasian, and long black hair. On the sandstones are to be found an intermediate type, darker somewhat than their progenitors, lips thick, and nostrils wide at the base. Then comes the Negro down in the alluvia, with dark skin, woolly hair, and prognathous development.

The true Negro inhabits Northern Africa. When his country, of which we know absolutely nothing, has been crowded, the nomadic portion of the population has poured itself over the mountain terraces, and, descending into the swamps, has become degraded in body and mind.

Technically speaking, we do not believe the Negro is a distinct species.

The Negro is found in the low, marshy, and malarious districts. We think the Negro is produced in a descending scale. The African who moves from the mountain regions down into the miasmatic districts may be observed to lose his stature, his complexion, his hair, and his intellectual vigor: he finally becomes the Negro. Pathologically considered, he is weak, sickly, and short-lived. His legs are slender and almost calf-less: the head is developed in the direction of the passions, while the whole form is destitute of symmetry.

But the Negro is not beyond the influences of civilization and Christianization. Hundreds of thousands have perished in the cruel swamps of Africa; hundreds of thousands have been devoured by wild beasts of the forests; hundreds of thousands have perished before the steady and murderous columns of stronger tribes; hundreds of thousands have perished from fever, small-pox, and cutaneous diseases; hundreds of thousands have been sold into slavery; hundreds of thousands have perished in the "middle-passage;" hundreds of thousands have been landed in this New World in the West: and yet hundreds of thousands are still swarming in the low and marshy lands of Western Africa. Poor as this material is, out of it we have made, here in the United States, six million citizens; and out of this cast-away material of Africa, God has raised up many children.

To the candid student of ethnography, it must be conclusive that the Negro is but the most degraded and disfigured type of the primeval African. And still, with all his interminable woes and wrongs, the Negro on the west coast of Africa, in Liberia and Sierra Leone, as well as in the southern part of the United States, shows that centuries of savagehood and slavery have not drained him of all the elements of his manhood. History furnishes us with abundant and specific evidence of his capacity to civilize and Christianize. We shall speak of this at length in a subsequent chapter.

FOOTNOTES:

See Keith Johnson's Map of Africa, 1863.
Savage Africa, pp. 403, 404.
Savage Africa, p. 400.
Savage Africa, p. 412.
Savage Africa, p. 430.

CHAPTER VII.: AFRICAN IDIOSYNCRASIES.

Patriarchal Government.—Construction of Villages.—Negro Architecture.—Election of Kings.— Coronation Ceremony.—Succession.—African Queens.—Law, Civil and Criminal.—Priests.—Their Functions.—Marriage.—Warfare.—Agriculture.— Mechanic Arts.—Blacksmiths.

ALL the tribes on the continent of Africa are under, to a greater or less degree, the patriarchal form of government. It is usual for writers on Africa to speak of "kingdoms" and "empires;" but these kingdoms are called so more by compliment than with any desire to convey the real meaning that we get when the empire of Germany or kingdom of Spain is spoken of. The patriarchal government is the most ancient in Africa. It is true that great kingdoms have risen in Africa; but they were the result of devastating wars rather than the creation of political genius or governmental wisdom.

The above is a fair description of the internecine wars that have been carried on between the tribes in Africa, back "to a time whereof the memory of man runneth not to the contrary." In a preceding chapter we gave quite an extended account of four Negro empires. We call attention here to the villages of these people, and shall allow writers who have paid much attention to this subject to give their impressions. Speaking of a village of the Aviia tribe called Mandji, Du Chaillu says,—

But all the villages of these poor children of the desert are not so untidy as the one described above. There is a wide difference in the sanitary laws governing these villages.

The construction of houses in villages in Africa is almost uniform, as far as our studies have led us. Or, rather, we ought to modify this statement by saying there are but two plans of construction. One is where the houses are erected on the rectilinear, the other is where they are built on the circular plan. In the more warlike tribes the latter plan prevails. The hillsides and elevated places near the timber are sought as desirable locations for villages. The plan of architecture is simple. The diameter is first considered, and generally varies from ten to fifteen feet. A circle is drawn in the ground, and then long flexible sticks are driven into the earth. The builder, standing inside of the circle, binds the sticks together at the top; where they are secured together by the use of the "monkey-rope," a thick vine that stretches itself in great profusion from tree to tree in that country. Now, the reader can imagine a large umbrella with the handle broken off even with the ribs when closed up, and without any cloth,—nothing but the ribs left. Now open it, and place it on the ground before you, and you have a fair idea of the hut up to the present time. A reed thatching is laid over the frame, and secured firmly by parallel lashings about fifteen inches apart. The door is made last by cutting a hole in the side of the hut facing toward the centre of the contemplated circle of huts. The door is about eighteen inches in height, and just wide enough to admit the body of the owner. The sharp points, after the cutting, are guarded by plaited twigs. The door is made of quite a number of stout sticks driven into the ground at equal distances apart, through which, in and out, are woven pliant sticks. When this is accomplished, the maker cuts off the irregular ends to make it fit the door, and removes it to its place. Screens are often used inside to keep out the wind: they are made so as to be placed in whatever position the wind is blowing. Some of these houses are built with great care, and those with domed roofs are elaborately decorated inside with beads of various sizes and colors.

The furniture consists of a few mats, several baskets, a milk-pail, a number of earthen pots, a bundle of assagais, and a few other weapons of war. Next, to guard against the perils of the rainy season, a ditch about two feet in width and of equal depth is made about the new dwelling. Now multiply this hut by five hundred, preserving the circle, and you have the village. The palaver-house, or place for public debates, is situated in the centre of the circle of huts. Among the northern and southern tribes, a fence is built around their villages, when they are called "kraals." The space immediately outside of the fence is cleared, so as to put an enemy at a disadvantage in an attack upon the village. Among the agricultural tribes, as, for example, the Kaffirs, they drive their cattle into the kraal, and for the young build pens.

The other method of building villages is to have one long street, with a row of houses on each side, rectangular in shape. They are about twenty-five or thirty feet in length, and about twelve to fifteen feet in width. Six or eight posts are used to join the material of the sides to. The roofs are flat. Three rooms are allowed to each house. The two end rooms are larger than the centre one, where the door opens out into the street. Sometimes these rooms are plastered, but it is seldom; and then it is in the case of the well-to-do class.

We said, at the beginning of this chapter, that the government in Africa was largely patriarchal; and yet we have called attention to four great kingdoms. There is no contradiction here, although there may seem to be; for even kings are chosen by ballot, and a sort of a house of lords has a veto power over royal edicts.

Here are democracy and aristocracy blended somewhat. The king's power seems to be in deciding everyday affairs, while the weighty matters which affect the whole tribe are decided by the elders and the people. Mr. Reade says of such government,—

When a new king is elected, he has first to repair to the pontiff's house, who—apropos of priests—is more important than the king himself. The king prostrates himself, and, with loud cries, entreats the favor of this high priest. At first the old man inside, with a gruff voice, orders him away, says he cannot be annoyed; but the king enumerates the presents he has brought him, and finally the door opens, and the priest appears, clad in white, a looking-glass on his breast, and long white feathers in his head. The king is sprinkled, covered with dust, walked over, and then, finally, the priest lies upon him. He has to swear that he will obey, etc.; and then he is allowed to go to the coronation. Then follow days and nights of feasting, and, among some tribes, human sacrifices.

The right of succession is generally kept on the male side of the family. The crown passes from brother to brother, from uncle to nephew, from cousin to cousin. Where there are no brothers, the son takes the sceptre. In all our studies on Africa, we have found only two women reigning. A woman by the name of Shinga ascended the throne of the Congo empire in 1640. She rebelled against the ceremonies, sought to be introduced by Portuguese Catholic priests, who incited her nephew to treason. Defeated in several pitched battles, she fled into the Jaga country, where she was crowned with much success. In 1646 she won her throne again, and concluded an honorable peace with the Portuguese. The other queen was the bloodthirsty Tembandumba of the Jagas. She was of Arab blood, and a cannibal by practice. She fought many battles, achieved great victories, flirted with beautiful young savages, and finally was poisoned.

The African is not altogether without law.

We have found considerable civil and criminal law among the different tribes. We gave an account of the civil and criminal code of Dahomey in the chapter on that empire. In the Congo country all civil suits are brought before a judge. He sits on a mat under a large tree, and patiently hears the arguments pro and con. His decisions are final. There is no higher court, and hence no appeal. The criminal cases are brought before the Chitomé, or priest. He keeps a sacred fire burning in his house that is never suffered to go out. He is supported by the lavish and delicate gifts of the people, and is held to be sacred. No one is allowed to approach his house except on the most urgent business. He never dies, so say the people. When he is seriously sick his legal successor steals quietly into his house, and beats his brains out, or strangles him to death. It is his duty to hear all criminal cases, and to this end he makes a periodical circuit among the tribe. Murder, treason, adultery, killing the escaped snakes from the fetich-house,—and often stealing,—are punished by death, or by being sold into slavery. A girl who loses her standing, disgraces her family by an immoral act, is banished from the tribe. And in case of seduction the man is tied up and flogged. In case of adultery a large sum of money must be paid. If the guilty one is unable to pay the fine, then death or slavery is the penalty.

The laws of marriage among many tribes are very wholesome and elevating. When the age of puberty arrives, it is the custom in many tribes for the elderly women, who style themselves Negemba, to go into the forest, and prepare for the initiation of the igonji, or novice. They clear a large space, build a fire, which is kept burning for three days. They take the young woman into the fetich-house,—a new one for this ceremony,—where they go through some ordeal, that, thus far, has never been understood by men. When a young man wants a wife, there are two things necessary; viz., he must secure her consent, and then buy her. The apparent necessary element in African courtship is not a thing to be deprecated by the contracting parties. On the other hand, it is the sine qua non of matrimony. It is proof positive when a suitor gives cattle for his sweetheart, first, that he is wealthy; and, second, that he greatly values the lady he fain would make his bride. He first seeks the favor of the girl's parents. If she have none, then her next of kin, as in Israel in the days of Boaz. For it is a law among many tribes, that a young girl shall never be without a guardian. When the relatives are favorably impressed with the suitor, they are at great pains to sound his praise in the presence of the girl; who, after a while, consents to see him. The news is conveyed to him by a friend or relative of the girl. The suitor takes a bath, rubs his body with palm-oil, dons his best armor, and with beating heart and proud stride hastens to the presence of the fastidious charmer. She does not speak. He sits down, rises, turns around, runs, and goes through many exercises to show her that he is sound and healthy. The girl retires, and the anxious suitor receives the warm congratulations of the spectators on his noble bearing. The fair lady conveys her assent to the waiting lover, and the village rings with shouts of gladness. Next come the preliminary matters before the wedding. Marriage among most African tribes is a coetaneous contract. The bride is delivered when the price is paid by the bridegroom. No goods, no wife. Then follow the wedding and feasting, firing of guns, blowing of horns, music, and dancing.

Polygamy is almost universal in Africa, and poor woman is the greater sufferer from the accursed system. It is not enough that she is drained of her beauty and strength by the savage passions of man: she is the merest abject slave everywhere. The young women are beautiful, but it is only for a brief season: it soon passes like the fragile rose into the ashes of premature old age. In Dahomey she is a soldier; in Kaffir-land she tends the herds, and builds houses; and in Congo without her industry man would starve. Everywhere man's cruel hand is against her. Everywhere she is the slave of his unholy passions.

It is a mistaken notion that has obtained for many years, that the Negro in Africa is physically the most loathsome of all mankind. True, the Negro has been deformed by degradation and abuse; but this is not his normal condition. We have seen native Africans who were jet black, woolly-haired, and yet possessing fine teeth, beautiful features, tall, graceful, and athletic.

Dr. David Livingstone is certainly entitled to our utmost confidence in all matters that he writes about. Mr. Archibald Forbes says he has seen Africans dead upon the field of battle that would measure nine feet, and it was only a few months ago that we had the privilege of seeing a Zulu who was eight feet and eleven inches in height. As to the beauty of the Negro, nearly all African travellers agree.

We have quoted thus extensively from Mr. Reade because he has given a fair account of the peoples he met. He is a good writer, but sometimes gets real funny!

It is a fact that all uncivilized races are warlike. The tribes of Africa are a vast standing army. Fighting seems to be their employment. We went into this matter of armies so thoroughly in the fourth chapter that we shall not have much to say here. The bow and arrow, the spear and assagai were the primitive weapons of African warriors; but they have learned the use of fire-arms within the last quarter of a century. The shield and assagai are not, however, done away with. The young Prince Napoleon, whose dreadful death the reader may recall, was slain by an assagai. These armies are officered, disciplined, and drilled to great perfection, as the French and English troops have abundant reason to know.

And there are some legends told about African wars that would put the "Arabian Nights" to the blush.

In Africa, as in districts of Germany and Holland, woman is burdened with agricultural duties. The soil of Africa is very rich, and consequently Nature furnishes her untutored children with much spontaneous vegetation. It is a rather remarkable fact, that the average African warrior thinks it a degradation for him to engage in agriculture. He will fell trees, and help move a village, but will not go into the field to work. The women—generally the married ones—do the gardening. They carry the seed on their heads in a large basket, a hoe on their shoulder, and a baby slung on the back. They scatter the seed over the ground, and then break up the earth to the depth of three or four inches.

The cattle are cared for by the men, and women are not allowed to engage in the hunt for wild animals. The cattle among the mountain and sandstone tribes are of a fine stock, but those of the tribes in the alluvia, like their owners, are small and sickly.

The African pays more attention to his weapons of offensive warfare than he does to his wives; but in many instances he is quite skilful in the handicrafts.

Nearly all his mechanical genius seems to be exhausted in the perfection of his implements of war, and Dr. Livingstone is of the opinion, that when a certain perfection in the arts is reached, the natives pause. This, we think, is owing to their far remove from other nations. Livingstone says,—

Mr. Wood says,—

The blacksmith, then, is a person of some consequence in his village. He gives shape and point to the weapons by which game is to be secured and battles won. All seek his favor.

Verily, the day will come when these warlike tribes shall beat their spears into pruning-hooks, and their assagais into ploughshares, and shall learn war no more! The skill and cunning of their artificers shall be consecrated to the higher and nobler ends of civilization, and the noise of battle shall die amid the music of a varied industry!

FOOTNOTES:

Livingstone's Expedition to the Zambesi, pp. 216, 217.
Ashango Land, pp. 288, 289, 291, 292.
Western Africa, p. 257 sq.
Through the Dark Continent, vol. i. p. 489.
Uncivilized Races of Men, vol. i. chap, vii.
Equatorial Africa, pp. 377, 378.
Savage Africa, p. 216.
Expedition to Zambesi, pp. 626, 627.
Livingstone's Expedition to the Zambesi, pp. 307, 308.
Savage Africa, p. 219.
See Savage Africa, p. 207. Livingstone's Life-Work, pp. 47, 48. Uncivilized Races of Men, vol. 1. pp. 71-86; also Du Chaillu and Denham and Clappterton.
Savage Africa, pp. 424, 425.
Livingstone's Expedition to the Zambesi, pp 625, 626.
Savage Africa, pp 426, 427.
Uncivilized Races of Men, vol. i. p. 94.
Through the Dark Continent, vol. i. p. 344 sq.; also vol. ii. pp. 87, 88.
Livingstone's Zambesi, pp. 613-617.
Uncivilized Races of Men, vol. i. p. 146.
Ashango Land, pp 290, 291.
Uncivilized Races of Men, vol. i. pp. 97, 98.

CHAPTER VIII.: LANGUAGES, LITERATURE, AND RELIGION.

Structure of African Languages.—The Mpongwe, Mandingo, and Grebo.—Poetry: Epic, Idyllic, and Miscellaneous.—Religions and Superstitions.

PHILOLOGICALLY the inhabitants of Africa are divided into two distinct families. The dividing line that Nature drew across the continent is about two degrees north of the equator. Thus far science has not pushed her investigations into Northern Africa; and, therefore, little is known of the dialects of that section. But from what travellers have learned of portions of different tribes that have crossed the line, and made their way as far as the Cape of Good Hope, we infer, that, while there are many dialects in that region, they all belong to one common family. During the Saracen movement, in the second century of the Christian era, the Arab turned his face toward Central Africa. Everywhere traces of his language and religion are to be found. He transformed whole tribes of savages. He built cities, and planted fields; he tended flocks, and became trader. He poured new blood into crumbling principalities, and taught the fingers of the untutored savage to war. His religion, in many places, put out the ineffectual fires of the fetich-house, and lifted the grovelling thoughts of idolaters heavenward. His language, like the new juice of the vine, made its way to the very roots of Negro dialects, and gave them method and tone. In the song and narrative, in the prayer and precept, of the heathen, the Arabic comes careering across each sentence, giving cadence and beauty to all.

On the heels of the Mohammedan followed the Portuguese, the tried and true servants of Rome, bearing the double swords and keys. Not so extensive as the Arab, the influence of the Portuguese, nevertheless, has been quite considerable.

Transcriber's Note: A breve diacritical mark, a u-shaped symbol above a letter used to indicate special pronunciation, is found on several words in the original text. These letters are indicated here by the coding []x for a breve above any letter x. For example, the word "tonda" with a breve above the letter "o" will appear as "t[)o]nda" in the following text.

All along the coast of Northern Guinea, a distance of nearly fifteen hundred miles,—from Cape Mesurado to the mouth of the Niger,—the Kree, Grebo, and Basa form one general family, and speak the Mandu language. On the Ivory Coast another language is spoken between Frisco and Dick's Cove. It is designated as the Av[)e]kw[)o]m language, and in its verbal and inflective character is not closely related to the Mandu. The dialects of Popo, Dahomey, Ashantee, and Akra are resolvable into a family or language called the Fantyipin. All these dialects, to a greater or less extent, have incorporated many foreign words,—Dutch, French, Spanish, English, Portuguese, and even many words from Madagascar. The language of the Gold and Ivory Coasts we find much fuller than those on the Grain Coast. Wherever commerce or mechanical enterprise imparts a quickening touch, we find the vocabulary of the African amplified. Susceptible, apt, and cunning, the coast tribes, on account of their intercourse with the outside world, have been greatly changed. We are sorry that the change has not always been for the better. Uncivilized sailors, and brainless and heartless speculators, have sown the rankest seeds of an effete Caucasian civilization in the hearts of the unsuspecting Africans. These poor people have learned to cheat, lie, steal; are capable of remarkable diplomacy and treachery; have learned well the art of flattery and extreme cruelty. Mr. Wilson says,—

The Italics are our own. The above was written just a quarter of a century ago.

Mr. Stanley wrote the above in Africa in March, 1877. It was but a repetition of the experiences of Drs. Livingstone and Kirk, that, while the dialects west and south-west of the Mountains of the Moon are numerous, and apparently distinct, they are referable to one common parent. The Swahere language has held its place from the beginning. Closely allied to the Mpongwe, it is certainly one of great strength and beauty.

The dialects of Northern Africa are rough, irregular in structure, and unpleasant to the ear. The Mpongwe we are inclined to regard as the best of all the dialects we have examined. It is spoken, with but slight variations, among the Mpongwe, Ayomba, Oroungou, Rembo, Camma, Ogobay, Anenga, and Ngaloi tribes. A careful examination of several other dialects leads us to suspect that they, too, sustain a distant relationship to the Mpongwe.

Next to this remarkable language comes the Bakalai, with its numerous dialectic offspring, scattered amongst the following tribes: the Balengue, Mebenga, Bapoukow, Kombe, Mbiki, Mbousha, Mbondemo, Mbisho, Shekiani, Apingi, Evili, with other tribes of the interior.

The two families of languages we have just mentioned—the Mpongwe and the Bakalai—are distinguished for their system and grammatical structure. It is surprising that these unwritten languages should hold their place among roving, barbarous tribes through so many years. In the Mpongwe language and its dialects, the liquid and semi-vowel r is rolled with a fulness and richness harmonious to the ear. The Bakalai and its branches have no r; and it is no less true that all tribes that exclude this letter from their dialects are warlike, nomadic, and much inferior to the tribes that use it freely.

The Mpongwe language is spoken on each side of the Gabun, at Cape Lopez, and at Cape St. Catharin in Southern Guinea; the Mandingo, between Senegal and the Gambia; and the Grebo language, in and about Cape Palmas. It is about twelve hundred miles from Gabun to Cape Palmas, about two thousand miles from Gabun to Senegambia, and about six hundred miles from Cape Palmas to Gambia. It is fair to presume that these tribes are sufficiently distant from each other to be called strangers. An examination of their languages may not fail to interest.

It has been remarked somewhere, that a people's homes are the surest indications of the degree of civilization they have attained. It is certainly true, that deportment has much to do with the polish of language. The disposition, temperament, and morals of a people who have no written language go far toward giving their language its leading characteristics. The Grebo people are a well-made, quick, and commanding-looking people. In their intercourse with one another, however, they are unpolished, of sudden temper, and revengeful disposition. Their language is consequently monosyllabic. A great proportion of Grebo words are of the character indicated. A few verbs will illustrate. Kba, carry; la, kill; ya, bring; mu, go; wa, walk; ni, do; and so on. This is true of objects, or nouns. Ge, farm; bro, earth; w[)e]nh, sun; tu, tree; gi, leopard; na, fire; yi, eye; bo, leg; lu, head; nu, rain; kai, house. The Grebo people seem to have no idea of syllabication. They do not punctuate; but, speaking with the rapidity with which they move, run their words together until a whole sentence might be taken for one word. If any thing has angered a Grebo he will say, "E ya mu kra wudi;" being interpreted, "It has raised a great bone in my throat." But he says it so quickly that he pronounces it in this manner, yamukroure. There are phrases in this language that are beyond the ability of a foreigner to pronounce. It has no contractions, and often changes the first and second person of the personal pronoun, and the first and second person plural, by lowering or pitching the voice. The orthography remains the same, though the significations of those words are radically different.

The Mpongwe language is largely polysyllabic. It is burdened with personal pronouns, and its adjectives have numerous changes in addition to their degrees of comparison. We find no inflections to suggest case or gender. The adjective mpolo, which means "large," carries seven or eight forms. While it is impossible to tell whether a noun is masculine, feminine, or neuter, they use one adjective for all four declensions, changing its form to suit each.

The following form of declensions will serve to impart a clearer idea of the arbitrary changes in the use of the adjective:

We presume it would be a difficult task for a Mpongwe to explain the arbitrary law by which such changes are made. And yet he is as uniform and strict in his obedience to this law as if it were written out in an Mpongwe grammar, and taught in every village.

His verb has four moods; viz., indicative, imperative, conditional, and subjunctive. The auxiliary particle gives the indicative mood its grammatical being. The imperative is formed from the present of the indicative by changing its initial consonant into its reciprocal consonant as follows:—

    tonda, to love. ronda, love thou. denda, to do. lenda, do thou.

The conditional mood has a form of its own; but the conjunctive particles are used as auxiliaries at the same time, and different conjunctive particles are used with different tenses. The subjunctive, having but one form, in a sentence where there are two verbs is used as the second verb. So by the use of the auxiliary particles the verb can form the infinitive and potential mood. The Mpongwe verb carries four tenses,—present, past or historical, perfect past, and future. Upon the principle of alliteration the perfect past tense, representing an action as completed, is formed from the present tense by prefixing a, and by changing a-final into i: for example, t[)o]nda, "to love;" at[)o]ndi, "did love." The past or historical tense is derived from the imperative by prefixing a, and by changing a-final into i. Thus r[)o]nda, "love;" ar[)o]ndi, "have loved." The future tense is constructed by the aid of the auxiliary particle be, as follows: mi be t[)o]nda," I am going to love."

We have not been able to find a Mandingo grammar, except Mr. MacBrair's, which is, as far as we know, the only one in existence. We have had but little opportunity to study the structure of that language. But what scanty material we have at hand leads us to the conclusion that it is quite loosely put together. The saving element in its verb is the minuteness with which it defines the time of an action. The causative form is made by the use of a suffix. It does not use the verb "to go" or "come" in order to express a future tense. Numerous particles are used in the substantive verb sense. The Mandingo language is rather smooth. The letters v and z are not in it. About one-fifth of the verbs and nouns commence with vowels, and the noun always terminates in the letter o.

Here is a wide and interesting field for philologists: it should be cultivated.

The African's nature is as sunny as the climate he lives in. He is not brutal, as many advocates of slavery have asserted. It is the unanimous testimony of all explorers of, and travellers through, the Dark Continent, that the element of gentleness predominates among the more considerable tribes; that they have a keen sense of the beautiful, and are susceptible of whatever culture is brought within their reach. The Negro nature is not sluggish, but joyous and vivacious. In his songs he celebrates victories, and laughs at death with the complacency of the Greek Stoics.

"Rich man and poor fellow, all men must die: Bodies are only shadows. Why should I be sad?"

He can be deeply wrought upon by acts of kindness; and bears a friendship to those who show him favor, worthy of a better state of society. When Henry M. Stanley (God bless him! noble, brave soul!) was about emerging from the Dark Continent, he made a halt at Kabinda before he ended his miraculous journey at Zanzibar on the Pacific Ocean. He had been accompanied in his perilous journey by stout-hearted, brave, and faithful natives. Their mission almost completed, they began to sink into that listlessness which is often the precursor of death. They had been true to their master, and were now ready to die as bravely as they had lived. Read Mr. Stanley's account without emotion if you can:—

How many times we have read this marvellous narrative of Stanley's march through the Dark Continent, we do not know; but we do know that every time we have read it with tears and emotion, have blessed the noble Stanley, and thanked God for the grand character of his black followers! There is no romance equal to these two volumes. The trip was one awful tragedy from beginning to end, and the immortal deeds of his untutored guards are worthy of the famous Light Brigade.

On the fourth day of August, 1877, Henry M. Stanley arrived at the village of Nsanda on his way to the ocean. He had in his command one hundred and fifteen souls. Foot-sore, travel-soiled, and hungry, his people sank down exhausted. He tried to buy food from the natives; but they, with an indifference that was painful, told them to wait until market-day. A foraging party scoured the district for food, but found none. Starvation was imminent. The feeble travellers lay upon the ground in the camp, with death pictured on their dusky features. Stanley called his boat-captains to his tent, and explained the situation. He knew that he was within a few days march of Embomma, and that here were located one Englishman, one Frenchman, one Spaniard, and one Portuguese. He told the captains that he had addressed a letter to these persons for aid; and that resolute, swift, and courageous volunteers were needed to go for the relief,—without which the whole camp would be transformed into a common graveyard. We will now quote from Mr. Stanley again in proof of the noble nature of the Negro:—

What wonderful devotion! What sublime self-forgetfulness! The world has wept over such stories as Bianca and Héloise, and has built monuments that will stand,—

"While Fame her record keeps, Or Homer paints the hallowed spot Where Valor proudly sleeps,"—

and yet these black heroes are unremembered. "I will follow the track like a leopard," gives but a faint idea of the strong will of Uledi; and Kachéché's brave words are endowed with all the attributes of that heroic abandon with which a devoted general hurls the last fragment of wasting strength against a stubborn enemy. And besides, there is something so tender in these words that they seem to melt the heart. "We will walk and walk, and when we cannot walk we will crawl!" We have never read but one story that approaches this narrative of Mr. Stanley, and that was the tender devotion of Ruth to her mother-in-law. We read it in the Hebrew to Dr. O.S. Stearns of Newton, Mass.; and confess that, though it has been many years since, the blessed impression still remains, and our confidence in humanity is strengthened thereby.

Here are a few white men in the wilds of Africa, surrounded by the uncivilized children of the desert. They have money and valuable instruments, a large variety of gewgaws that possessed the power of charming the fancy of the average savage; and therefore the whites would have been a tempting prey to the blacks. But not a hair of their head was harmed. The white men had geographical fame to encourage them in the struggle,— friends and loved ones far away beyond the beautiful blue sea. These poor savages had nothing to steady their purposes save a paltry sum of money as day-wages,—no home, no friends; and yet they were as loyal as if a throne were awaiting them. No, no! nothing waited on their heroic devotion to a magnificent cause but a lonely death when they had brought the "master" to the sea. When their stomachs, pinched by hunger; when their limbs, stiff from travel; when their eyes, dim with the mists of death; when every vital force was slain by an heroic ambition to serve the great Stanley; when the fires of endeavor were burnt to feeble embers,—then, and only then, would these faithful Negroes fail in the fulfilment of their mission, so full of peril, and yet so grateful to them, because it was in the line of duty.

Cicero urged virtue as necessary to effective oratory. The great majority of Negroes in Africa are both orators and logicians. A people who have such noble qualities as this race seems to possess has, as a logical necessity, the poetic element in a large degree.

In speaking of Negro poetry, we shall do so under three different heads; viz., the Epic, Idyllic, Religious, or miscellaneous.

The epic poetry of Africa, so far as known, is certainly worthy of careful study. The child must babble before it can talk, and all barbarians have a sense of the sublime in speech. Mr. Taine, in his "History of English Literature," speaking of early Saxon poetry, says,—

This glowing description of the poetry of the primitive and hardy Saxon gives the reader an excellent idea of the vigorous, earnest, and gorgeous effusions of the African. Panda was king of the Kaffirs. He was considered quite a great warrior. It took a great many isi-bongas to describe his virtues. His chief isi-bongas was "O-Elephant." This was chosen to describe his strength and greatness. Mr. Wood gives an account of the song in honor of Panda:—

There is a daring insolence, morbid vanity, and huge description in this song of Panda, that make one feel like admitting that the sable bard did his work of flattery quite cleverly. It should not be forgotten by the reader, that, in the translation of these songs, much is lost of their original beauty and perspicuity. The following song was composed to celebrate the war triumphs of

Dinga, and is, withal, exciting, and possessed of good movement. It is, in some instances, much like the one quoted above:—

"Thou needy offspring of Umpikazi, Eyer of the cattle of men; Bird of Maube, fleet as a bullet, Sleek, erect, of beautiful parts; Thy cattle like the comb of the bees; O head too large, too huddled to move; Devourer of Moselekatze, son of Machobana; Devourer of 'Swazi, son of Sobuza; Breaker of the gates of Machobana; Devourer of Gundave of Machobana; A monster in size, of mighty power; Devourer of Ungwati of ancient race; Devourer of the kingly Uomape; Like heaven above, raining and shining."

The poet has seen fit to refer to the early life of his hero, to call attention to his boundless riches, and, finally, to celebrate his war achievements. It is highly descriptive, and in the Kaffir language is quite beautiful.

Tchaka sings a song himself, the ambitious sentiments of which would have been worthy of Alexander the Great or Napoleon Bonaparte. He had carried victory on his spear throughout all Kaffir-land. Everywhere the tribes had bowed their submissive necks to his yoke; everywhere he was hailed as king. But out of employment he was not happy. He sighed for more tribes to conquer, and thus delivered himself:—

"Thou hast finished, finished the nations! Where will you go out to battle now? Hey! where will you go out to battle now? Thou hast conquered kings! Where are you going to battle now? Thou hast finished, finished the nations! Where are you going to battle now? Hurrah, hurrah, hurrah! Where are you going to battle now?"

There is really something modern in this deep lament of the noble savage!

The following war song of the Wollof, though it lacks the sonorous and metrical elements of real poetry, contains true military aggressiveness, mixed with the theology of the fatalist.

A WAR SONG.

Mr. Reade says of the musicians he met up the Senegal,—

The idyllic poetry of Africa is very beautiful in its gorgeous native dress. It requires some knowledge of their mythology in order to thoroughly understand all their figures of speech. The following song is descriptive of the white man, and is the production of a Bushman.

"In the blue palace of the deep sea Dwells a strange creature: His skin as white as salt; His hair long and tangled as the sea-weed. He is more great than the princes of the earth; He is clothed with the skins of fishes,— Fishes more beautiful than birds. His house is built of brass rods; His garden is a forest of tobacco. On his soil white beads are scattered Like sand-grains on the seashore."

The following idyl, extemporized by one of Stanley's black soldiers, on the occasion of reaching Lake Nyanza, possesses more energy of movement, perspicuity of style, and warm, glowing imagery, than any song of its character we have yet met with from the lips of unlettered Negroes. It is certainly a noble song of triumph. It swells as it rises in its mission of praise. It breathes the same victorious air of the song of Miriam: "Sing ye to the Lord, for he hath triumphed gloriously; the horse and the rider hath he thrown into the sea." And in the last verse the child-nature of the singer riots like "The May Queen" of Tennyson.

THE SONG OF TRIUMPH.
"Sing, O friends, sing; the journey is ended: Sing aloud, O friends; sing to the great Nyanza. Sing all, sing loud, O friends, sing to the great sea; Give your last look to the lands behind, and then turn to the sea.
Long time ago you left your lands, Your wives and children, your brothers and your friends; Tell me, have you seen a sea like this Since you left the great salt sea?
CHORUS.
Then sing, O friends! sing; the journey is ended: Sing aloud, O friend! sing to this great sea.
This sea is fresh, is good and sweet; Your sea is salt, and bad, unfit to drink. This sea is like wine to drink for thirsty men; The salt sea—bah! it makes men sick.
Lift up your heads, O men, and gaze around; Try if you can see its end. See, it stretches moons away, This great, sweet, fresh-water sea.
We come from Usukuma land, The land of pastures, cattle, sheep and goats, The land of braves, warriors, and strong men, And, lo! this is the far-known Usukuma sea.
Ye friends, ye scorned at us in other days. Ah, ha! Wangwana. What say ye now? Ye have seen the land, its pastures and its herds, Ye now see the far-known Usukuma sea. Kaduma's land is just below; He is rich in cattle, sheep, and goats. The Msungu is rich in cloth and beads; His hand is open, and his heart is free.
To-morrow the Msungu must make us strong With meat and beer, wine and grain. We shall dance and play the livelong day, And eat and drink, and sing and play."
The religious and miscellaneous poetry is not of the highest order. One of the most remarkable men of the Kaffir tribe was Sicana, a powerful chief and a Christian. He was a poet, and composed hymns, which he repeated to his people till they could retain them upon their memories. The following is a specimen of his poetical abilities, and which the people are still accustomed to sing to a low monotonous air:—
"Ulin guba inkulu siambata tina Ulodali bom' unadali pezula, Umdala undala idala izula, Yebinza inquinquis zixeliela. Utika umkula gozizuline, Yebinza inquinquis nozilimele. Umze uakonana subiziele, Umkokeli ua sikokeli tina, Uenza infama zenza go bomi; Imali inkula subiziele, Wena wena q'aba inyaniza, Wena wena kaka linyaniza, Wena wena klati linyaniza; Invena inh'inani subiziele, Ugaze laku ziman' heba wena, Usanhla zaku ziman' heba wena, Umkokili ua, sikokeli tina: Ulodali bom' uadali pezula, Umdala uadala idala izula."
Translation.
"Mantle of comfort! God of love! The Ancient One on high! Who guides the firmament above, The heavens, and starry sky;
Creator, Ruler, Mighty One; The only Good, All-wise,— To him, the great eternal God, Our fervent prayers arise.
Giver of life, we call on him, On his high throne above, Our Rock of refuge still to be, Of safety and of love;
Our trusty shield, our sure defence, Our leader, still to be: We call upon our pitying God, Who makes the blind to see.

We supplicate the Holy Lamb Whose blood for us was shed, Whose feet were pierced for guilty man, Whose hands for us have bled;
Even our God who gave us life, From heaven, his throne above, The great Creator of the world, Father, and God of love."

When any person is sick, the priests and devout people consult their favorite spirits. At Goumbi, in Equatorial Africa, this ceremony is quite frequent. Once upon a time the king fell sick. Quengueza was the name of the afflicted monarch. Ilogo was a favorite spirit who inhabited the moon. The time to invoke the favor of this spirit is during the full moon. The moon, in the language of Equatorial Africa, is Ogouayli. Well, the people gathered in front of the king's house, and began the ceremony, which consisted chiefly in singing the following song:—

"Ilogo, we ask thee! Tell who has bewitched the king!
Ilogo, we ask thee, What shall we do to cure the king?
The forests are thine, Ilogo! The rivers are thine, Ilogo!
The moon is thine! O moon! O moon! O moon! Thou art the house of Ilogo! Shall the king die? Ilogo! O Ilogo! O moon! O moon!"

In African caravans or processions, there is a man chosen to go in front and sing, brandishing a stick somewhat after the manner of our band-masters. The song is rather an indifferent howl, with little or no relevancy. It is a position much sought after, and affords abundant opportunity for the display of the voice. Such a person feels the dignity of the position. The following is a sample:—

"Shove him on! But is he a good man? No, I think he's a stingy fellow; Shove him on! Let him drop in the road, then. No, he has a big stick: Shove him on! Oh, matta-bicho! matta-bicho! Who will give me matta-bicho?"

Of this song Mr. Reade says,—

The Griot, as we have already mentioned, sings for money. He is a most accomplished parasite and flatterer. He makes a study of the art. Here is one of his songs gotten up for the occasion.

The most beautiful nursery song ever sung by any mother, in any language, may be heard in the Balengi county, in Central Africa. There is wonderful tenderness in it,—tenderness that would melt the coldest heart. It reveals a bright spot in the heart-life of this people.

"Why dost than weep, my child? The sky is bright; the sun is shining: why dost than weep? Go to thy father: he loves thee; go, tell him why thou weepest. What! thou weepest still! Thy father loves thee; I caress thee: yet still thou art sad. Tell me then, my child, why dost thou weep?"

It is not so very remarkable, when we give the matter thought, that the African mother should be so affectionate and devoted in her relations to her children. The diabolical system of polygamy has but this one feeble apology to offer in Africa. The wives of one man may quarrel, but the children always find loving maternal arms ready to shelter their heads against the wrath of an indifferent and cruel father. The mother settles all the disputes of the children, and cares for them with a zeal and tenderness that would be real beautiful in many American mothers; and, in return, the children are very noble in their relations to their mothers. "Curse me, but do not speak ill of my mother," is a saying in vogue throughout nearly all Africa. The old are venerated, and when they become sick they are abandoned to die alone.

It is not our purpose to describe the religions and superstitions of Africa. To do this would occupy a book. The world knows that this poor people are idolatrous,—"bow down to wood and stone." They do not worship the true God, nor conform their lives unto the teachings of the Saviour. They worship snakes, the sun, moon, and stars, trees, and water-courses. But the bloody human sacrifice which they make is the most revolting feature of their spiritual degradation. Dr. Prichard has gone into this subject more thoroughly than our time or space will allow.

The false religions of Africa are but the lonely and feeble reaching out of the human soul after the true God.

FOOTNOTES:

Stanley's Through the Dark Continent, vol. ii. pp. 320, 321; see, also, pp. 3, 78, 123, 245, 414.
Western Africa, p. 455.
Western Africa, p. 456.
Western Africa, p. 470.
Equatorial Africa, p. 531.
Savage Africa, p. 212.
Through the Dark Continent, vol. ii. pp, 470, 471.
Through the Dark Continent, vol. ii. pp. 482, 483.
History of English Literature, vol i. pp. 48. 49.
Equatorial Africa, pp. 448, 449.
On the intellectual faculties of the Negro, see Prichard, third ed., 1837, vol. ii. p. 346, sect. iii. Peschel's Races of Men, p. 462, sq., especially Blumenbach's Life and Works, p. 305, sq Western Africa, p. 379,—all of chap. xi.
See Prichard, fourth ed., 1841, vol. 1. p. 197, sect. v. Moffat's Southern Africa; Uncivilized Races of Men, vol 1. pp. 183-219.
Savage Africa, p. 287, sq.

CHAPTER IX.: SIERRA LEONE.

Its Discovery and Situation.—Natural Beauty.—Founding of a Negro Colony.—The Sierra Leone Company.—Fever and Insubordination.—It becomes an English Province—Character of its Inhabitants.—Christian Missions, etc.

SIERRA LEONE was discovered and named by Piedro de Cintra. It is a peninsula, about thirty miles in length by about twenty-five in breadth, and is situated 8° and 30' north latitude, and is about 13½° west longitude. Its topography is rather queer. On the south and west its mountains bathe their feet in the Atlantic Ocean, and on the east and north its boundaries are washed by the river and bay of Sierra Leone. A range of mountains, co-extensive with the peninsula,—forming its backbone,—rises between the bay of Sierra Leone and the Atlantic Ocean, from two to three thousand feet in altitude. Its outlines are as severe as Egyptian architecture, and the landscape view from east or west is charming beyond the power of description. Freetown is the capital, with about twenty thousand inhabitants, situated on the south side of Sierra Leone River, and hugged in by an amphitheatre of beautiful hills and majestic mountains.

In 1772 Lord Mansfield delivered his celebrated opinion on the case of the Negro man Sommersett, whose master, having abandoned him in a sick condition, afterwards sought to reclaim him. The decision was to the effect that no man, white or black, could set foot on British soil and remain a slave. The case was brought at the instance of Mr. Granville Sharp. The decision created universal comment. Many Negroes in New England, who had found shelter under the British flag on account of the proclamation of Sir Henry Clinton, went to England. Free Negroes from other parts—Jamaica, St. Thomas, and San Domingo—hastened to breathe the free air of the British metropolis. Many came to want, and wandered about the streets of London, strangers in a strange land. Granville Sharp, a man of great humanity, was deeply affected by the sad condition of these people. He consulted with Dr. Smeathman, who had spent considerable time in Africa; and they conceived the plan of transporting them to the west coast of Africa, to form a colony. The matter was agitated in London by the friends of the blacks, and finally the government began to be interested. A district of about twenty square miles was purchased by the government of Naimbanna, king of Sierra Leone, on which to locate the proposed colony. About four hundred Negroes and sixty white persons, the greater portion of the latter being "women of the town," were embarked on "The Nautilus," Capt. Thompson, and landed at Sierra Leone on the 9th of May, 1787. The climate was severe, the sanitary condition of the place vile, and the habits of the people immoral. The African fever, with its black death-stroke, reaped a harvest; while the irregularities and indolence of the majority of the colonists, added to the deeds of plunder perpetrated by predatory bands of savages, reduced the number of the colonists to about sixty-four souls in 1791.

The dreadful news of the fate of the colony was borne to the philanthropists in England. But their faith in colonization stood as unblanched before the revelation as the Iron Duke at Waterloo. An association was formed under the name of "St. George's Bay," but afterwards took the name of the "Sierra Leone Company," with a capital stock of one million two hundred and fifty thousand dollars, with such humanitarians as Granville Sharp, Thornton, Wilberforce, and Clarkson among its directors. The object of the company was to push forward the work of colonization. One hundred Europeans landed at Sierra Leone in the month of February, 1792, and were followed in March by eleven hundred and thirty-one Negroes. A large number of them had served in the British army during the Revolutionary War in America, and, accepting the offer of the British Government, took land in this colony as a reward for services performed in the army. Another fever did its hateful work; and fifty or sixty Europeans, and many blacks, fell under its parching and consuming touch. Jealous feuds rent the survivors, and idleness palsied every nerve of industry in the colony. In 1794 a French squadron besieged the place, and the people sustained a loss of about two hundred and fifty thousand dollars. Once more an effort was made to revive the place, and get its drowsy energies aroused in the discharge of necessary duties. Some little good began to show itself; but it was only the tender bud of promise, and was soon trampled under the remorseless heel of five hundred and fifty insurrectionary maroons from Jamaica and Nova Scotia.

The indifferent character of the colonists, and the hurtful touch of the climate, had almost discouraged the friends of the movement in England. It was now the year 1800. This vineyard planted by good men yielded "nothing but leaves." No industry had been developed, no substantial improvement had been made, and the future was veiled in harassing doubts and fears. The money of the company had almost all been expended. The company barely had the signs of organic life in it, but the light of a beautiful Christian faith had not gone out across the sea in stalwart old England. The founders of the colony believed that good management would make the enterprise succeed: so they looked about for a master hand to guide the affair. On the 8th of August, 1807, the colony was surrendered into the hands of the Crown, and was made an English colony. During the same year in which this transfer was made, Parliament declared the slave-trade piracy; and a naval squadron was stationed along the coast for the purpose of suppressing it. At the first, many colored people of good circumstances, feeling that they would be safe under the English flag, moved from the United States to Sierra Leone. But the chief source of supply of population was the captured slaves, who were always unloaded at this place. When the English Government took charge of Sierra Leone, the population was 2,000, the majority of whom were from the West Indies or Nova Scotia. In 1811 it was nearly 5,000; in 1820 it was 12,000; it 1833 it was 30,000; in 1835 it was 35,000; in 1844 it was 40,000; in 1869 it was 55,374, with but 129 white men. On the 31st of March, 1827, the slaves that had been captured and liberated by the English squadron numbered 11,878; of which there were 4,701 males above, and 1,875 under, fourteen years of age. There were 2,717 females above, and 1,517 under, the age of fourteen, besides 1,068 persons who settled in Freetown, working in the timber-trade.

With the dreadful scourge of slavery driven from the sea, the sanitary condition of the place greatly improved; and with a vigorous policy of order and education enforced, Sierra Leone began to bloom and blossom as a rose. When the slaver disappeared, the merchant-vessel came on her peaceful mission of commerce.

The annual trade-returns presented to Parliament show that the declared value of British and

Irish produce and manufactures exported to the West Coast of Africa, arranged in periods of five years each, has been as follows:—

EXPORTS FROM GREAT BRITAIN.

1846-50 . . . £2,773,408; or a yearly average of £554,6811851-55 . . . 4,314,752; " " "   862,9501856-60 . . . 5,582,941; " " " 1,116,5881861-63 . . . 4,216,045; " " " 1,405,348

IMPORTS

The same trade-returns show that the imports of African produce from the West Coast into Great Britain have been as follows. The "official value" is given before 1856, after that date the "computed real value" is given.

Official value, 1851-55 . . . £4,154,725; average, £830,945Computed real value, 1856-60 . . 9,376,251; " 1,875,250 " " " 1861-63 . . 5,284,611; " 1,761,537

The value of African produce has decreased during the last few years in consequence of the discovery of the petroleum or rock-oil in America. In 1864 between four and five thousand bales of cotton were shipped to England.

It is to be borne in mind, that under the system which existed when Sierra Leone, the Gambia, and Gold Coast settlements were maintained for the promotion of the slave-trade, the lawful commerce was only £20,000 annually, and that now the amount of tonnage employed in carrying legal merchandise is greater than was ever engaged in carrying slaves. W. Winwood Reade visited Sierra Leone during the Rebellion in America; but, being somewhat prejudiced against the Negro, we do not expect any thing remarkably friendly. But we quote from him the view he took of the people he met there:—

When England abolished the slave-trade on the West Coast of Africa, Christianity arose with healing in her wings. Until slavery was abolished in this colony, missionary enterprises were abortive; but when the curse was put under the iron heel of British prohibition, the Lord did greatly bless the efforts of the missionary. The Episcopal Church—"the Church of England"—was the first on the ground in 1808; but it was some years before any great results were obtained. In 1832 this Church had 638 communicants, 294 candidates for baptism, 684 sabbath-school pupils, and 1,388 children in day-schools. This Church carried its missionary work beyond its borders to the tribes that were "sitting in darkness;" and in 1850 had built 54 seminaries and schools, had 6,600 pupils, 2,183 communicants, and 7,500 attendants on public worship. It is pleasant to record that out of 61 teachers, 56 were native Africans! In 1865 there were sixteen missionary societies along the West Coast of Africa. Seven were American, six English, two German, and one West-Indian. These societies maintained 104 European or American missionaries, had 110 mission-stations, 13,000 scholars, 236 schools, 19,000 registered communicants; representing a Christian population of 60,000 souls.

The Wesleyan Methodists began their work in 1811; and in 1831 they had two missionaries, 294 members in their churches, and 160 pupils in school. They extended their missions westward to the Gambia, and eastward toward Cape Coast Castle, Badagry, Abbeokuta, and Kumasi; and in this connection, in 1850, had 44 houses of worship, 13 out-stations, 42 day-schools, 97 teachers, 4,500 pupils in day and sabbath schools, 6,000 communicants, 560 on probation, and 14,600 in attendance on public worship. In 1850 the population of Sierra Leone was 45,000; of which 36,000 were Christians, against 1,734 Mohammedans.

Sierra Leone represents the most extensive composite population in the world for its size. About one hundred different tribe are represented, with as many different languages or dialects. Bishop Vida, under direction of the British Parliament, gave special attention to this matter, and found not less than one hundred and fifty-one distinct languages, besides several dialects spoken in Sierra Leone. They were arranged under twenty-six groups, and yet fifty-four are unclassified that are distinct as German and French. "God makes the wrath of man to praise him, and the remainder thereof he will restrain." Through these numerous languages, poor benighted Africa will yet hear the gospel.

Some years ago Dr. Ferguson, who was once governor of the Sierra Leone colony, and himself a colored man, wrote and an extended account of the situation there, which was widely circulated in England and America at the time. It is so manifestly just and temperate in tone, so graphic and minute in description, that we reproduce it in extenso:—

But this account was written at the early sunrise of civilization in Sierra Leone. Now civilization is at its noonday tide, and the hopes of the most sanguine friends of the liberated Negro have been more than realized. How grateful this renewed spot on the edge of the Dark Continent would be to the weary and battle-dimmed vision of Wilberforce, Sharp, and other friends of the colony! And if they still lived, beholding the wonderful results, would they not gladly say, "Lord, now lettest thou thy servant depart in peace, according to thy word: for mine eyes have seen thy salvation which thou hast prepared before the face of all people; a light to lighten the Gentiles, and the glory of thy people Israel"?

FOOTNOTES:

Savage Africa, p. 25.

Précis sur l'Établissement des Colonies de Sierra Léona et de Boulama, etc. Par C.B. Wadström, pp. 3-28.

Wadström Essay on Colonization, p. 220.

This led to the sending of 119 whites, along with a governor, as counsellors, physicians, soldiers, clerks, overseers, artificers, settlers, and servants. Of this company 57 died within the year, 22 returned, and 40 remained. See Wadström, pp. 121, sq.

See Livingstone's Zambesi, pp. 633, 634.

CHAPTER X.: THE REPUBLIC OF LIBERIA.

Liberia.—Its Location.—Extent.—Rivers and Mountains.—History of the First Colony.—The Noble Men who laid the Foundation of the Liberian Republic.—Native Tribes.—Translation of the New Testament into the Vei Language.—The Beginning and Triumph of Christian Missions to Liberia.—History of the Different Denominations on the Field.—A Missionary Republic of Negroes.—Testimony of Officers of the Royal Navy as to the Efficiency of the Republic in suppressing the Slave-Trade.—The Work of the Future.

THAT section of country on the West Coast of Africa known as Liberia, extending from Cape Palmas to Cape Mount, is about three hundred miles coastwise. Along this line there are six colonies of Colored people, the majority of the original settlers being from the United States. The settlements are Cape Palmas, Cape Mesurado, Cape Mount, River Junk, Basa, and Sinon. The distance between them varies from thirty-five to one hundred miles, and the only means of communication is the coast-vessels. Cape Palmas, though we include it under the general title of Liberia, was founded by a company of intelligent Colored people from Maryland. This movement was started by the indefatigable J.H.B. Latrobe and Mr. Harper of the Maryland Colonization Society. This society purchased at Cape Palmas a territory of about twenty square miles, in which there was at that time—more than a half-century ago—a population of about four thousand souls. Within two years from the time of the first purchase, this enterprising society held deeds from friendly proprietors for eight hundred square miles, embracing the dominions of nine kings, who bound themselves to the colonists in friendly alliance. This territory spread over both banks of the Cavally River, and from the ocean to the town of Netea, which is thirty miles from the mouth of the river. In the immediate vicinity of Cape Palmas,—say within an area of twenty miles,—there was a native population of twenty-five thousand. Were we to go toward the interior from the Cape about forty-five or fifty miles, we should find a population of at least seventy thousand natives, the majority of whom we are sure are anxious to enjoy the blessings of education, trade, civilization, and Christianity. The country about Cape Palmas is very beautiful and fertile. The cape extends out into the sea nearly a mile, the highest place being about one hundred and twenty-five feet. Looking from the beach, the ground rises gradually until its distant heights are crowned with heavy, luxuriant foliage and dense forest timber. And to plant this colony the Maryland Legislature appropriated the sum of two hundred thousand dollars! And the colony has done worthily, has grown rapidly, and at present enjoys all the blessings of a Christian community. Not many years ago it declared its independence.

But Liberia, in the proper use of the term, is applied to all the settlements along the West Coast of Africa that were founded by Colored people from the United States. It is the most beautiful spot on the entire coast. The view is charming in approaching this country, Rev. Charles Rockwell says,—

The physical, social, and political bondage of the Colored people in America before the war was most discouraging. They were mobbed in the North, and sold in the South. It was not enough that they were isolated and neglected in the Northern States: they were proscribed by the organic law of legislatures, and afflicted by the most burning personal indignities. They had a few friends; but even their benevolent acts were often hampered by law, and strangled by caste-prejudice. Following the plans of Granville Sharp and William Wilberforce, Liberia was founded as a refuge to all Colored men who would avail themselves of its blessings.

Colonization societies sprang into being in many States, and large sums of money were contributed to carry out the objects of these organizations. Quite a controversy arose inside of anti-slavery societies, and much feeling was evinced; but the men who believed colonization to be the solution of the slavery question went forward without wavering or doubting. In March, 1820, the first emigrants sailed for Africa, being eighty-six in number; and in January, 1822, founded the town of Monrovia, named for President Monroe. Rev. Samuel J. Mills, while in college in 1806, was moved by the Holy Spirit to turn his face toward Africa as a missionary. His zeal for missionary labor touched the hearts of Judson, Newell, Nott, Hall, and Rice, who went to mission-fields in the East as early as 1812. The American Colonization Society secured the services of the Rev. Samuel J. Mills and Rev. Ebenezer Burgess to locate the colony at Monrovia. Mr. Mills found an early, watery grave; but the report of Mr. Burgess gave the society great hope, and the work was carried forward.

The first ten years witnessed the struggles of a noble band of Colored people, who were seeking a new home on the edge of a continent given over to the idolatry of the heathen. The funds of the society were not as large as the nature and scope of the work demanded. Emigrants went slowly, not averaging more than 170 per annum,—only 1,232 in ten years: but the average from the first of January, 1848, to the last of December, 1852, was 540 yearly; and, in the single year of 1853, 782 emigrants arrived at Monrovia. In 1855 the population of Monrovia and Cape Palmas had reached about 8,000.

Going south from Monrovia for about one hundred miles, and inland about twenty, the country was inhabited by the Bassa tribe and its branches; numbering about 130,000 souls, and speaking a common language. "They were peaceful, domestic, and industrious; and, after fully supplying their own wants, furnish a large surplus of rice, oil, cattle, and other articles of common use, for exportation." This tribe, like the Veis, of whom we shall make mention subsequently, have reduced their language to a written system. The New Testament has been translated into their language by a missionary, and they have had the gospel these many years in their own tongue.

The "Greybo language," spoken in and about Cape Palmas, has been reduced to a written form; and twenty thousand copies of eleven different works have been printed and distributed. There are about seventy-five thousand natives within fifty miles of Cape Palmas; and, as a rule, they desire to avail themselves of the blessings of civilization. The Veis occupy about fifty miles of seacoast; extending from Gallinas River, one hundred miles north of Monrovia, and extending south to Grand Mount. Their territory runs back from the seacoast about thirty miles, and they are about sixteen thousand strong.

This was a grand place to found a Negro state,—a missionary republic, as Dr. Christy terms it. When the republic rose, the better, wealthier class of free Colored people from the United States embarked for Liberia. Clergymen, physicians, merchants, mechanics, and school-teachers turned their faces toward the new republic, with an earnest desire to do something for themselves and race; and history justifies the hopes and players of all sincere friends of Liberia. Unfortunately, at the first, many white men were more anxious to get the Negro out of the country than to have him do well when out; and, in many instances, some unworthy Colored people got transportation to Liberia, of whom Americans were rid, but of whom Liberians could not boast. But the law of the survival of the fittest carried the rubbish to the bottom. The republic grew and expanded in every direction. From year to year new blood and fresh energy were poured into the social and business life of the people; and England, America, and other powers acknowledged the republic by sending resident ministers there.

The servants of Christ saw, at the earliest moment of the conception to build a black government in Africa, that the banner of the cross must wave over the new colony, if good were to be expected. The Methodist Church, with characteristic zeal and aggressiveness, sent with the first colonists several members of their denomination and two "local preachers;" and in March, 1833, the Rev. Melville B. Cox, an ordained minister of this church, landed at Monrovia. The mission experienced many severe trials; but the good people who had it in charge held on with great tenacity until the darkness began to give away before the light of the gospel. Nor did the Board of the Methodist Missionary Society in America lose faith. They appropriated for this mission, in 1851, $22,000; in 1852, $26,000; in 1853, $32,957; and in 1854, $32,957. In the report of the board of managers for 1851, the following encouraging statement occurs:—

At this time (1851) they had an annual Conference, with three districts, with as many presiding elders, whose duty it was to visit all the churches and schools in their circuit. The Conference had 21 members, all of whom were colored men. The churches contained 1,301 members, of whom 115 were on probation, and 116 were natives. There were 20 week-day schools, with 839 pupils, 50 of whom were natives. Then there Were seven schools among the natives, with 127 faithful attendants.

Bishop Scott, of the General Conference of the Methodist Episcopal Church, was, by order of his Conference, sent on an official visit to Liberia. He spent more than two months among the missions, and returned in 1853 much gratified with the results garnered in that distant field.

The above is certainly re-assuring, and had its due influence among Christian people at the time it appeared. At an anniversary meeting of the Methodist Church, held in Cincinnati, O., in the same year, 1853, Bishop Ames gave utterance to sentiments in regard to the character of the government of Liberia that quite shocked some pro-slavery people who held "hired pews" in the Methodist Church. His utterances were as brave as they were complimentary.

The Presbyterian Board of Missions sent Rev. J.B. Pinny into the field in 1833. In 1837, missions were established among the natives, and were blessed with very good results. In 1850 there were, under the management of this denomination, three congregations, with 116 members, two ordained ministers, and a flourishing sabbath school. A high-school was brought into existence in 1852, with a white gentleman, the Rev D.A. Wilson, as its principal. It was afterward raised into a college, and was always crowded.

The American Protestant-Episcopal Church raised its missionary standard in Liberia in 1836.

The Rev John Payne was at the head of this enterprise, assisted by six other clergymen, until 1850, when he was consecrated missionary bishop for Africa. He was a white gentleman of marked piety, rare scholarship, and large executive ability. The station at Monrovia was under the care of the Rev. Alexander Crummell, an educated and eloquent preacher of the Negro race. There was an excellent training-school for religious and secular teachers; there are several boarding-schools for natives, with an average attendance of a hundred; and up to 1850 more than a thousand persons had been brought into fellowship with this church.

The Foreign Missionary Board of the Southern Baptist Convention in 1845 turned its attention to this fruitful field. In 1855, ten years after they began work, they had 19 religious and secular teachers, 11 day-schools, 400 pupils, and 484 members in their churches. There were 13 mission-stations, and all the teachers were colored men.

We have said, a few pages back in this chapter, that the Methodist Church was first on the field when the colony of Liberia was founded. We should have said one of the first; because we find, in "Gammell's History of the American Baptist Missions," that the Baptists were in this colony as missionaries in 1822, that under the direction of the Revs. Lot Carey and Collin Teage, two intelligent Colored Baptists, a church was founded. Mr. Carey was a man of most exemplary character. He had received an education in Virginia, where he had resided as a freeman for some years, having purchased his freedom by his personal efforts, and where also he was ordained in 1821.

We regret that statistics on Liberia are not as full as desirable; but we have found enough to convince us that the cause of religion, education, and republican government are in safe hands, and on a sure foundation. There are now more than three thousand and eighteen hundred children, seven hundred of whom are natives; and in the day-schools are gathered about two thousand bright and promising pupils.

Many noble soldiers of the cross have fallen on this field, where a desperate battle has been waged between darkness and light, heathenism and religion, the wooden gods of men and the only true God who made heaven and earth. Many have been mortally touched by the poisonous breath of African fever, and, like the sainted Gilbert Haven, have staggered back to home and friends to die. Few of the white teachers have been able to remain on the field. During the first thirty years of missionary effort in the field, the mortality among the white missionaries was terrible. Up to 1850 the Episcopal Church had employed twenty white teachers, but only three of them were left. The rest died, or were driven home by the climate. Of nineteen missionaries sent out by the Presbyterian Church up to 1850, nine died, seven returned home, and but three remained. The Methodist Church sent out thirteen white teachers: six died, six returned home, and but one remained. Among the colored missionaries the mortality was reduced to a minimum. Out of thirty-one in the employ of the Methodist Church, only seven died natural deaths, and fourteen remained in the service. On this subject of mortality, Bishop Payne says,—

In thirty-three years Liberia gained wonderfully in population, and, at the breaking-out of the Rebellion in the United States, had about a hundred thousand souls, besides the three hundred thousand natives in the vast territory over which her government is recognized. Business of every kind has grown up. The laws are wholesome; the law-makers intelligent and upright; the army and navy are creditable, and the republic is in every sense a grand success. Mr. Wilson says,—

Liberia had its first constitution in 1825. It was drawn at the instance of the Colonization Society in the United States. It set forth the objects of the colony, defined citizenship, and declared the objects of the government. It remained in force until 1836. In 1839 a "Legislative Council" was created, and the constitution amended to meet the growing wants of the government. In 1847 Liberia declared herself an independent republic. The first article of the constitution of 1847 reads as follows:—

This section meant a great deal to a people who had abandoned their homes in the United States, where a chief justice of the Supreme Court had declared that "a Negro has no rights which a white man is bound to respect,"—a country where the Federal Congress had armed every United-States marshal in all the Northern States with the inhuman and arbitrary power to apprehend, load with chains, and hurl back into the hell of slavery, every poor fugitive who sought to find a home in a professedly free section of "the land of the free and the home of the brave." These brave black pilgrims, who had to leave "the freest land in the world" in order to get their freedom, did not intend that the solemn and formal declaration of principles contained in their constitution should be reduced to a reductio ad absurdum, as those in the American Constitution were by the infamous Fugitive-slave Law. And in section 4 of their constitution they prohibit "the sum of all villanies"—slavery! The article reads:—

They had no measure of compromise by which slavery could be carried on beyond certain limits "for highly commercial and business interests of a portion of their fellow-citizens." Liberians might have grown rich by merely suffering the slave-trade to be carried on among the natives. The constitution fixed a scale of revenue, and levied a tariff on all imported articles. A customs-service was introduced, and many reforms enforced which greatly angered a few avaricious white men whose profession as men-stealers was abolished by the constitution. Moreover, there were others who for years had been trading and doing business along the coast, without paying any duties on the articles they exported. The new government incurred their hostility.

In April, 1850, the republic of Liberia entered into a treaty with England, and in article nine of said treaty bound herself to the suppression of the slave-trade in the following explicit language:—

Notwithstanding the above treaty, the enemies of the republic circulated the report in England and America that the Liberian government was secretly engaged in the slave-trade. The friends of colonization in both countries were greatly alarmed by the rumor, and sought information in official quarters,—of men on the ground. The following testimony will show that the charge was malicious:—

The government was firmly and wisely administered, and its friends everywhere found occasion for great pleasure in its marked success. While the government had more than a quarter of a million of natives under its care, the greatest caution was exercised in dealing with them legally. The system was not so complicated as our Indian system, but the duties of the officers in dealing with the uncivilized tribes were as delicate as those of an Indian agent in the United States.

The republic did a vast amount of good before the Great Rebellion in the United States, but since emancipation its population has been fed by the natives who have been educated and converted to Christianity. Professor David Christy, the great colonizationist, said in a lecture delivered in 1855,—

The circumstances that led to the founding of the Negro Republic in the wilds of Africa perished in the fires of civil war. The Negro is free everywhere; but the republic of Liberia stands, and should stand until its light shall have penetrated the gloom of Africa, and until the heathen shall gather to the brightness of its shining. May it stand through the ages as a Christian Republic, as a faithful light-house along the dark and trackless sea of African paganism!

FOOTNOTES:

Ethiope, p. 197.
Foreign Travel and Life at Sea, vol. ii. p. 359.
Bishop Scott's Letter in the Colonization Herald, October, 1853.
In Methodist Missionary Advocate, 1853.
Gammell's History of the American Baptist Missions, pp. 248, 249.

Edward W. Blyden, L.L.D., president of Liberia College, a West Indian, is a scholar of marvellous erudition, a writer of rare abilities, a subtle reasoner, a preacher of charming graces, and one of the foremost Negroes of the world. He is himself the best argument in favor of the Negro's capacity for Christian civilization. He ranks amongst the world's greatest linguists.

Report of Bishop Payne, June 6, 1853.
Colonization Herald, December, 1852.
Ethiope, pp. 207, 208.

CHAPTER XI.: RÉSUMÉ.

The Unity of the Human Family re-affirmed.—God gave all Races of Men Civilization.—The Antiquity of the Negro beyond Dispute.—Idolatry the Cause of the Degradation of the American Races.—He has always had a Place in History, though Incidental.—Negro Type caused by Degradation.—Negro Empires an Evidence of Crude Ability for Self-Government.— Influence of the Two Christian Governments on the West Coast upon the Heathen.—Oration on Early Christianity in Africa.—The Duty of Christianity to evangelize Africa.

THE preceding ten chapters are introductory in their nature. We felt that they were necessary to a history of the Colored race in the United States. We desired to explain and explode two erroneous ideas,—the curse of Canaan, and the theory that the Negro is a distinct species,—that were educated into our white countrymen during the long and starless night of the bondage of the Negro. It must appear patent to every honest student of God's word, that the slavery interpretation of the curse of Canaan is without warrant of Scripture, and at war with the broad and catholic teachings of the New Testament. It is a sad commentary on American civilization to find even a few men like Helper, "Ariel," and the author of "The Adamic Race" still croaking about the inferiority of the Negro; but it is highly gratifying to know that they no longer find an audience or readers, not even in the South. A man never hates his neighbors until he has injured them. Then, in justification of his unjustifiable conduct, he uses slander for argument.

During the late war thousands of mouths filled with vituperative wrath against the colored race were silenced as in the presence of the heroic deeds of "the despised race," and since the war the obloquy of the Negro's enemies has been turned into the most fulsome praise.

We stand in line and are in harmony with history and historians —modern and ancient, sacred and profane—on the subject of the unity of the human family. There are, however, a few who differ; but their wild, incoherent, and unscholarly theories deserve the mercy of our silence.

It is our firm conviction, and it is not wholly unsupported by history, that the Creator gave all the nations arts and sciences. Where nations have turned aside to idolatry they have lost their civilization. The Canaanites, Jebusites, Hivites, etc., the idolatrous nations inhabiting the land of Canaan, were the descendants of Canaan; and the only charge the Lord brought against them when he commanded Joshua to exterminate them was, that they were his enemies in all that that term implies. The sacred record tells us that they were a warlike, powerful people, living in walled cities, given to agriculture, and possessing quite a respectable civilization; but they were idolaters—God's enemies.

It is worthy of emphasis, that the antiquity of the Negro race is beyond dispute. This is a fact established by the most immutable historical data, and recorded on the monumental brass and marble of the Oriental nations of the most remote period of time. The importance and worth of the Negro have given him a place in all the histories of Egypt, Greece, and Rome. His position, it is true, in all history up to the present day, has been accidental, incidental, and collateral; but it is sufficient to show how he has been regarded in the past by other nations. His brightest days were when history was an infant; and, since he early turned from God, he has found the cold face of hate and the hurtful hand of the Caucasian against him. The Negro type is the result of degradation. It is nothing more than the lowest strata of the African race. Pouring over the venerable mountain terraces, an abundant stream from an abundant and unknown source, into the malarial districts, the genuine African has gradually degenerated into the typical Negro. His blood infected with the poison of his low habitation, his body shrivelled by disease, his intellect veiled in pagan superstitions, the noblest yearnings of his soul strangled at birth by the savage passions of a nature abandoned to sensuality,—the poor Negro of Africa deserves more our pity than our contempt.

It is true that the weaker tribes, or many of the Negroid type, were the chief source of supply for the slave-market in this country for many years; but slavery in the United States—a severe ordeal through which to pass to citizenship and civilization— had the effect of calling into life many a slumbering and dying attribute in the Negro nature. The cruel institution drove him from an extreme idolatry to an extreme religious exercise of his faith in worship. And now that he is an American citizen,—the condition and circumstances which rendered his piety appropriate abolished,—he is likely to move over to an extreme rationalism.

The Negro empires to which we have called attention are an argument against the theory that he is without government, and his career as a soldier would not disgrace the uniform of an American soldier. Brave, swift in execution, terrible in the onslaught, tireless in energy, obedient to superiors, and clannish to a fault,—the abilities of these black soldiers are worthy of a good cause.

On the edge of the Dark Continent, Sierra Leone and Liberia have sprung up as light-houses on a dark and stormy ocean of lost humanity. Hundreds of thousands of degraded Negroes have been snatched from the vile swamps, and Christianity has been received and appreciated by them. These two Negro settlements have solved two problems; viz., the Negro's ability to administer a government, and the capacity of the native for the reception of education and Christian civilization. San Domingo and Jamaica have their lessons too, but it is not our purpose to write the history of the Colored people of the world. The task may be undertaken some time in the future, however.

It must be apparent to the interested friends of languishing Africa, that there are yet two more problems presented for our solution; and they are certainly difficult of solution. First, we must solve the problem of African geography; second, we must redeem by the power of the gospel, with all its attending blessings, the savage tribes of Africans who have never heard the beautiful song of the angels: "Glory to God in the highest, and on earth peace, good-will toward men." That this work will be done we do not doubt. We have great faith in the outcome of the missionary work going on now in Africa; and we are especially encouraged by the wide and kindly interest awakened on behalf of Africa by the noble life-work of Dr. David Livingstone, and the thrilling narrative of Mr. Henry M. Stanley.

It is rather remarkable now, in the light of recent events, that we should have chosen a topic at the close of both our academic and theological course that we can see now was in line with this work so near our heart. The first oration was on "The Footsteps of the Nation," the second was

"Early Christianity in Africa." Dr. Livingstone had just fallen a martyr to the cause of geography, and the orators and preachers of enlightened Christendom were busy with the virtues and worth of the dead. It was on the tenth day of June, 1874, that we delivered the last-named oration; and we can, even at this distance, recall the magnificent audience that greeted it, and the feeling with which we delivered it. We were the first Colored man who had ever taken a diploma from that venerable and world-famed institution (Newton Seminary, Newton Centre, Mass.), and therefore there was much interest taken in our graduation. We were ordained on the following evening at Watertown, Mass.; and the original poem written for the occasion by our pastor, the Rev. Granville S. Abbott, D.D., contained the following significant verses:—

> "Ethiopia's hands long stretching, Mightily have plead with God; Plead not vainly: time is fetching Answers, as her faith's reward. God is faithful, Yea, and Amen is his word. Countless prayers, so long ascending, Have their answer here and now; Threads of purpose, wisely meeting In an ordination vow. Afric brother, To thy mission humbly bow."

The only, and we trust sufficient, apology we have to offer to the reader for mentioning matters personal to the author is, that we are deeply touched in reading the oration, after many years, in the original manuscript, preserved by accident. It is fitting that it should be produced here as bearing upon the subject in hand.

It is our earnest desire and prayer, that the friends of missions in all places where God in his providence may send this history will give the subject of the civilization and Christianization of Africa prayerful consideration. The best schools the world can afford should be founded on the West Coast of Africa The native should be educated at home, and mission stations should be planted under the very shadow of the idol-houses of the heathen. The best talent and abundant means have been sent to Siam, China, and Japan. Why not send the best talent and needful means to Liberia, Sierra Leone, and Cape Palmas, that native missionaries may be trained for the outposts of the Lord? There is not a more promising mission-field in the world than Africa, and yet our friends in America take so little interest in this work! The Lord is going to save that Dark Continent, and it behooves his servants here to honor themselves in doing something to hasten the completion of this inevitable work! Africa is to be redeemed by the African, and the white Christians of this country can aid the work by munificent contributions. Will you do it, brethren? God help you!

FOOTNOTES:

Deut. xii. 2, 3, also 30th verse.
Deut. vi. 19.
Deut. vii. 7.
News comes to us from Egypt that Arabi Pacha's best artillerists are Negro soldiers.

Part II.

SLAVERY IN THE COLONIES.

CHAPTER XII.: THE COLONY OF VIRGINIA.: 1619-1775.

Introduction of the First Slaves.—"The Treasurer" and the Dutch Man-of-War.—The Correct Date.—The Number of Slaves.—Were there Twenty, or Fourteen?—Litigation about the Possession of the Slaves.—Character of the Slaves imported, and the Character of the Colonists.—Race Prejudices.—Legal Establishment of Slavery. Who are Slaves for Life.—Duties on Imported Slaves.—Political and Military Prohibitions against Negroes.—Personal Rights.—Criminal Laws against Slaves. Emancipation.—How brought about.—Free Negroes.—Their Rights.—Moral and Religious Training.—Population.—Slavery firmly established.

VIRGINIA was the mother of slavery as well as "the mother of Presidents." Unfortunate for her, unfortunate for the other colonies, and thrice unfortunate for the poor Colored people, who from 1619 to 1863 yielded their liberty, their toil,—unrequited,—their bodies and intellects to an institution that ground them to powder. No event in the history of North America has carried with it to its last analysis such terrible forces. It touched the brightest features of social life, and they faded under the contact of its poisonous breath. It affected legislation, local and national; it made and destroyed statesmen; it prostrated and bullied honest public sentiment; it strangled the voice of the press, and awed the pulpit into silent acquiescence; it organized the judiciary of States, and wrote decisions for judges; it gave States their political being, and afterwards dragged them by the fore-hair through the stormy sea of civil war; laid the parricidal fingers of Treason against the fair throat of Liberty,—and through all time to come no event will be more sincerely deplored than the introduction of slavery into the colony of Virginia during the last days of the month of August in the year 1619!

The majority of writers on American history, as well as most histories on Virginia, from Beverley to Howison, have made a mistake in fixing the date of the introduction of the first slaves. Mr. Beverley, whose history of Virginia was printed in London in 1772, is responsible for the error, in that nearly all subsequent writers—excepting the laborious and scholarly Bancroft and the erudite Campbell—have repeated his mistake. Mr. Beverley, speaking of the burgesses having "met the Governor and Council at James Town in May 1620," adds in a subsequent paragraph, "In August following a Dutch Man of War landed twenty Negroes for sale; which were the first of that kind that were carried into the country." By "August following," we infer that Beverley would have his readers understand that this was in 1620. But Burk, Smith, Campbell, and Neill gave 1619 as the date. But we are persuaded to believe that the first slaves were landed at a still earlier date. In Capt. John Smith's history, printed in London in 1629, is a mere incidental reference to the introduction of slaves into Virginia. He mentions, under date of June 25, that the "governor and councell caused Burgesses to be chosen in all places," which is one month later than the occurrence of this event as fixed by Beverley. Smith speaks of a vessel named "George" as having been "sent to Newfoundland" for fish, and, having started in May, returned after a voyage of "seven weeks." In the next sentence he says, "About the last of August came in a dutch man of warre that sold us twenty Negars." Might not he have meant "about the end of last August" came the Dutch man-of-war, etc.? All historians, except two, agree that these slaves were landed in August, but disagree as to the year. Capt. Argall, of whom so much complaint was made by the Virginia Company to Lord Delaware, fitted out the ship "Treasurer" at the expense of the Earl of Warwick, who sent him "an olde commission of hostility from the Duke of Savoy against the Spanyards," for a "filibustering" cruise to the West Indies. And, "after several acts of hostility committed, and some purchase gotten, she returns to Virginia at the end of ten months or thereabouts." It was in the early autumn of 1618, that Capt. Edward (a son of William) Brewster was sent into banishment by Capt. Argall; and this, we think, was one of the last, if not the last official act of that arbitrary governor. It was certainly before this that the ship "Treasurer," manned "with the ablest men in the colony," sailed for "the Spanish dominions in the Western hemisphere." Under date of June 15, 1618, John Rolfe, speaking of the death of the Indian Powhatan, which took place in April, says, "Some private differences happened betwixt Capt. Bruster and Capt. Argall," etc. Capt. John Smith's information, as secured from Master Rolfe, would lead to the conclusion that the difficulty which took place between Capt. Edward Brewster and Capt. Argall occurred in the spring instead of the autumn, as Neill says. If it be true that "The Treasurer" sailed in the early spring of 1618, Rolfe's statement as to the time of the strife between Brewster and Argall would harmonize with the facts in reference to the length of time the vessel was absent as recorded in Burk's history. But if Neill is correct as to the time of the quarrel,—for we maintain that it was about this time that Argall left the colony,—then his statement would tally with Burk's account of the time the vessel was on the cruise. If, therefore, she sailed in October, 1618, being absent ten months, she was due at Jamestown in August, 1619.

But, nevertheless, we are strangely moved to believe that 1618 was the memorable year of the landing of the first slaves in Virginia. And we have one strong and reliable authority on our side. Stith, in his history of Virginia, fixes the date in 1618. On the same page there is an account of the trial and sentence of Capt. Brewster. The ship "Treasurer" had evidently left England in the winter of 1618. When she reached the Virginia colony, she was furnished with a new crew and abundant supplies for her cruise. Neill says she returned with booty and "a certain number of negroes." Campbell agrees that it was some time before the landing of the Dutch man-of-war that "The Treasurer" returned to Virginia. He says, "She returned to Virginia after some ten months with her booty, which consisted of captured negroes, who were not left in Virginia, because Capt. Argall had gone back to England, but were put on the Earl of Warwick's plantation in the Somer Islands."

During the last two and one-half centuries the readers of the history of Virginia have been mislead as to these two vessels, the Dutch man-of-war and "The Treasurer." The Dutch man-of-war did land the first slaves; but the ship "Treasurer" was the first to bring them to this country, in 1618.

When in 1619 the Dutch man-of-war brought the first slaves to Virginia, Capt. Miles Kendall was deputy-governor. The man-of-war claimed to sail under commission of the Prince of Orange. Capt. Kendall gave orders that the vessel should not land in any of his harbors: but the vessel was without provisions; and the Negroes, fourteen in number, were tendered for supplies.

Capt. Kendall accepted the slaves, and, in return, furnished the man-of-war with the coveted provisions. In the mean while Capt. Butler came and assumed charge of the affairs of the Virginia Company, and dispossessed Kendall of his slaves, alleging that they were the property of the Earl of Warwick. He insisted that they were taken from the ship "Treasurer," "with which the said Holland man-of-war had consorted." Chagrined, and wronged by Gov. Butler, Capt. Kendall hastened back to England to lay his case before the London Company, and to seek equity. The Earl of Warwick appeared in court, and claimed the Negroes as his property, as having belonged to his ship, "The Treasurer." Every thing that would embarrass Kendall was introduced by the earl. At length, as a final resort, charges were formally preferred against him, and the matter referred to Butler for decision. Capt. Kendall did not fail to appreciate the gravity of his case, when charges were preferred against him in London, and the trial ordered before the man of whom he asked restitution! The case remained in statu quo until July, 1622, when the court made a disposition of the case. Nine of the slaves were to be delivered to Capt. Kendall, "and the rest to be consigned to the company's use." This decision was reached by the court after the Earl of Warwick had submitted the case to the discretion and judicial impartiality of the judges. The court gave instructions to Capt. Bernard, who was then the governor, to see that its order was enforced. But while the order of the court was in transitu, Bernard died. The earl, learning of the event, immediately wrote a letter, representing that the slaves should not be delivered to Kendall; and an advantage being taken—purely technical—of the omission of the name of the captain of the Holland man-of-war, Capt. Kendall never secured his nine slaves.

It should be noted, that while Rolfe, in Capt. Smith's history, fixes the number of slaves in the Dutch vessel at twenty,—as also does Beverley,—it is rather strange that the Council of Virginia, in 1623, should state that the commanding officer of the Dutch man-of-war told Capt. Kendall that "he had fourteen Negroes on board!" Moreover, it is charged that the slaves taken by "The Treasurer" were divided up among the sailors; and that they, having been cheated out of their dues, asked judicial interference. Now, these slaves from "The Treasurer" "were placed on the Earl of Warwick's lands in Bermudas, and there kept and detained to his Lordship's use." There are several things apparent; viz., that there is a mistake between the statement of the Virginia Council in their declaration of May 7, 1623, about the number of slaves landed by the man-of-war, and the statements of Beverley and Smith. And if Stith is to be relied upon as to the slaves of "The Treasurer" having been taken to the "Earl of Warwick's lands in Bermudas, and there kept," his lordship's claim to the slaves Capt. Kendall got from the Dutch man-of-war was not founded in truth or equity!

Whether the number was fourteen or twenty, it is a fact, beyond historical doubt, that the Colony of Virginia purchased the first Negroes, and thus opened up the nefarious traffic in human flesh. It is due to the Virginia Colony to say, that these slaves were forced upon them; that they were taken in exchange for food given to relieve the hunger of famishing sailors; that white servitude was common, and many whites were convicts from England; and the extraordinary demand for laborers may have deadened the moral sensibilities of the colonists as to the enormity of the great crime to which they were parties. Women were sold for wives, and sometimes were kidnapped in England and sent into the colony. There was nothing in the moral atmosphere of the colony inimical to the spirit of bondage that was manifest so early in the history of this people. England had always held her sceptre over slaves of some character: villeins in the feudal era, stolen Africans under Elizabeth and under the house of the Tudors; Caucasian children—whose German blood could be traced beyond the battle of Hastings—in her mines, factories, and mills; and vanquished Brahmans in her Eastern possessions. How, then, could we expect less of these "knights" and "adventurers" who "degraded the human race by an exclusive respect for the privileged classes"?

The institution of slavery once founded, it is rather remarkable that its growth was so slow. According to the census of Feb. 16, 1624, there were but twenty-two in the entire colony. There were eleven at Flourdieu Hundred, three in James City, one on James Island, one on the plantation opposite James City, four at Warisquoyak, and two at Elizabeth City. In 1648 the population of Virginia was about fifteen thousand, with a slave population of three hundred. The cause of the slow increase of slaves was not due to any colonial prohibition. The men who were engaged in tearing unoffending Africans from their native home were some time learning that this colony was at this time a ready market for their helpless victims. Whatever feeling or scruple, if such ever existed, the colonists had in reference to the subject of dealing in the slave-trade, was destroyed at conception by the golden hopes of large gains. The latitude, the products of the soil, the demand for labor, the custom of the indenture of white servants, were abundant reasons why the Negro should be doomed to bondage for life.

The subjects of slavery were the poor unfortunates that the strong push to the outer edge of organized African society, where, through neglect or abuse, they are consigned to the mercy of avarice and malice. We have already stated that the weaker tribes of Africa are pushed into the alluvial flats of that continent; where they have perished in large numbers, or have become the prey of the more powerful tribes, who consort with slave-hunters. Disease, tribal wars in Africa, and the merciless greed of slave-hunters, peopled the colony of Virginia with a class that was expected to till the soil. African criminals, by an immemorial usage, were sold into slavery as the highest penalty, save death; and often this was preferred to bondage. Many such criminals found their way into the colony. To be bondmen among neighboring tribes at home was dreaded beyond expression; but to wear chains in a foreign land, to submit to the dehumanizing treatment of cruel taskmasters, was an ordeal that fanned into life the last dying ember of manhood and resentment.

The character of the slaves imported, and the pitiable condition of the white servants, produced rather an anomalous result. "Male servants, and slaves of both sex" were bound together by the fellowship of toil. But the distinction "made between them in their clothes and food" drew a line, not between their social condition,—for it was the same,—but between their nationality. First, then, was social estrangement, next legal difference, and last of all political disagreement and strife. In order to oppress the weak, and justify the unchristian distinction between God's creatures, the persons who would bolster themselves into respectability must have the aid of law. Luther could march fearlessly to the Diet of Worms if every tile on the houses were a devil; but

Macbeth was conquered by the remembrance of the wrong he had done the virtuous Duncan and the unoffending Banquo, long before he was slain by Macduff. A guilty conscience always needs a multitude of subterfuges to guard against dreaded contingencies. So when the society in the Virginia Colony had made up its mind that the Negroes in their midst were mere heathen, they stood ready to punish any member who had the temerity to cross the line drawn between the races. It was not a mitigating circumstance that the white servants of the colony who came into natural contact with the Negroes were "disorderly persons," or convicts sent to Virginia by an order of the king of England. It was fixed by public sentiment and law that there should be no relation between the races. The first prohibition was made "September 17th, 1630." Hugh Davis, a white servant, was publicly flogged "before an assembly of Negroes and others," for defiling himself with a Negro. It was also required that he should confess as much on the following sabbath.

   In the winter of 1639, on the 6th of January, during the incumbency of Sir Francis Wyatt, the General Assembly passed the first prohibition against Negroes. "All persons," doubtless including fraternizing Indians, "except Negroes," were required to secure arms and ammunition, or be subject to a fine, to be imposed by "the Governor and Council." The records are too scanty, and it is impossible to judge, at this remote day, what was the real cause of this law. We have already called attention to the fact that the slaves were but a mere fraction of the summa summarum of the population. It could not be that the brave Virginians were afraid of an insurrection! Was it another reminder that the "Negroes were heathen," and, therefore, not entitled to the privileges of Christian freemen? It was not the act of that government, which in its conscious rectitude "can put ten thousand to flight," but was rather the inexcusable feebleness of a diseased conscience, that staggers off for refuge "when no man pursueth."

Mr. Bancroft thinks that the "special tax upon female slaves" was intended to discourage the traffic. It does not so seem to us. It seems that the Virginia Assembly was endeavoring to establish friendly relations with the Dutch and other nations in order to secure "trade." Tobacco was the chief commodity of the colonists. They intended by the act of March, 1659, to guarantee the most perfect liberty "to trade with" them. They required, however, that foreigners should "give bond and pay the impost of tenn shillings per hogshead laid upon all tobacco exported to any fforreigne dominions." The same act recites, that whenever any slaves were sold for tobacco, the amount of imposts would only be "two shillings per hogshead," which was only the nominal sum paid by the colonists themselves. This act was passed several years before the one became a law that is cited by Mr. Bancroft. It seems that much trouble had been experienced in determining who were taxable in the colony. It is very clear that the LIV. Act of March, 1662, which Mr. Bancroft thinks was intended to discourage the importation of slaves by taxing female slaves, seeks only to determine who shall be taxable. It is a general law, declaring "that all male persons, of what age soever imported into this country shall be brought into lysts and be liable to the payment of all taxes, and all negroes, male and female being imported shall be accopted tythable, and all Indian servants male or female however procured being adjudged sixteen years of age shall be likewise tythable from which none shall be exempted." Beverley says that "the male servants, and slaves of both sexes," were employed together. It seems that white women were so scarce as to be greatly respected. But female Negroes and Indians were taxable; although Indian children, unlike those of Negroes, were not held as slaves. Under the LIV. Act there is but one class exempted from tax,—white females, and, we might add, persons under sixteen years of age. So what Mr. Bancroft mistakes as repressive legislation against the slave-trade is only an exemption of white women, and intended to encourage their coming into the colony.

The legal distinction between slaves and servants was, "slaves for life, and servants for a time." Slavery existed from 1619 until 1662, without any sanction in law. On the 14th of December, 1662, the foundations of the slave institution were laid in the old law maxim, "Partus sequitur ventrum,"—that the issue of slave mothers should follow their condition. Two things were accomplished by this act; viz., slavery received the direct sanction of statutory law, and it was also made hereditary. On the 6th of March, 1655,—seven years before the time mentioned above,—an act was passed declaring that all Indian children brought into the colony by friendly Indians should not be treated as slaves, but be instructed in the trades. By implication, then, slavery existed legally at this time; but the act of 1662 was the first direct law on the subject. In 1670 a question arose as to whether Indians taken in war were to be servants for a term of years, or for life. The act passed on the subject is rather remarkable for the language in which it is couched; showing, as it does, that it was made to relieve the Indian, and fix the term of the Negro's bondage beyond a reasonable doubt. "It is resolved and enacted that all servants not being Christians imported into this colony by shipping shall be slaves for their lives; but what shall come by land shall serve, if boyes or girles, until thirty yeares of age, if men or women twelve yeares and no longer." This remarkable act was dictated by fear and policy. No doubt the Indian was as thoroughly despised as the Negro; but the Indian was on his native soil, and, therefore, was a more dangerous subject. Instructed by the past, and fearful of the future, the sagacious colonists declared by this act, that those who "shall come by land" should not be assigned to servitude for life. While this act was passed to define the legal status of the Indian, at the same time, and with equal force, it determines the fate of the Negro who is so unfortunate as to find his way into the colony. "All servants not being Christians imported into this colony by shipping shall be slaves for their lives." Thus, in 1670, Virginia, not abhorring the institution, solemnly declared that "all servants not christians"—heathen Negroes—coming into her "colony by shipping"—there was no other way for them to come!—should "be slaves for their lives!"

In 1682 the colony was in a flourishing condition. Opulence generally makes men tyrannical, and great success in business makes them unmerciful. Although Indians, in special acts, had not been classed as slaves, but only accounted "servants for a term of years," the growing wealth and increasing number of the colonists seemed to justify them in throwing off the mask. The act of the 3d of October, 1670, defining who should be slaves, was repealed at the November session of the General Assembly of 1682. Indians were now made slaves, and placed upon the same legal footing with the Negroes. The sacred rite of baptism did not alter the condition of children—Indian or Negro—when born in slavery. And slavery, as a cruel and inhuman institution, flourished and magnified with each returning year.

Encouraged by friendly legislation, the Dutch plied the slave-trade with a zeal equalled only by the enormous gains they reaped from the planters. It was not enough that faith had been broken with friendly Indians, and their children doomed by statute to the hell of perpetual slavery; it was not sufficient that the Indian and Negro were compelled to serve, unrequited, for their lifetime. On the 4th of October, 1705, "an act declaring the Negro, Mulatto, and Indian slaves, within this dominion, to be real estate," was passed without a dissenting voice. Before this time they had been denominated by the courts as chattels: now they were to pass in law as real estate. There were, however, several provisos to this act. Merchants coming into the colony with slaves, not sold, were not to be affected by the act until the slaves had actually passed in a bonâ-fide sale. Until such time their slaves were contemplated by the law as chattels. In case a master died without lawful heirs, his slaves did not escheat, but were regarded as other personal estate or property. Slave property was liable to be taken in execution for the payment of debts, and was recoverable by a personal action.

The only apology for enslaving the Negroes we can find in all the records of this colony is, that they "were heathen." Every statute, from the first to the last, during the period the colony was under the control of England, carefully mentions that all persons—Indians and Negroes—who "are not Christians" are to be slaves. And their conversion to Christianity afterwards did not release them from their servitude.

The act making Indian, Mulatto, and Negro slaves real property, passed in October, 1705, under the reign of Queen Anne, and by her approved, was "explained" and "amended" in February, 1727, during the reign of King George II. Whether the act received its being out of a desire to prevent fraud, like the "Statutes of Frauds," is beyond finding out. But it was an act that showed that slavery had grown to be so common an institution as not to excite human sympathy. And the attempt to "explain" and "amend" its cruel provisions was but a faint precursor of the evils that followed. Innumerable lawsuits grew out of the act, and the courts and barristers held to conflicting interpretations and constructions. Whether complaints were made to his Majesty, the king, the records do not relate; or whether he was moved by feelings of humanity is quite as difficult to understand. But on the 31st of October, 1751, he issued a proclamation repealing the act declaring slaves real estate. The proclamation abrogated nine other acts, and quite threw the colony into confusion. It is to be hoped that the king was animated by the noblest impulses in repealing one of the most dehumanizing laws that ever disgraced the government of any civilized people. The General Assembly, on the 15th of April, 1752, made an appeal to the king, "humbly" protesting against the proclamation. The law-makers in the colony were inclined to doubt the king's prerogative in this matter. They called the attention of his Majesty to the fact that he had given the "Governor" "full power and authority with the advice and consent of the council" to make needful laws; but they failed to realize fully that his Majesty, in accordance with the proviso contained in the grant of authority made to the governor and council of the colony, was using his veto. They recited the causes which induced them to enact the law, recounted the benefits accruing to his Majesty's subjects from the conversion of human beings into real property, and closed with a touching appeal for the retention of the act complained of, so that slaves "might not at the same time be real estate in some respects, personal in others, and bothe in others!" History does not record that the brusque old king was at all moved by this earnest appeal and convincing argument of the Virginia Assembly.

In 1699 the government buildings at James City were destroyed. The General Assembly, in an attempt to devise means to build a new Capitol, passed an act on the 11th of April of the aforesaid year, fixing a "duty on servants and slaves imported" into the colony. Fifteen shillings was the impost tax levied upon every servant imported, "not born in England or Wales, and twenty shillings for every Negro or other slave" thus imported. The revenue arising from this tax on servants and slaves was to go to the building of a new Capitol. Every slave-vessel was inspected by a customs-officer. The commanding officer of the vessel was required to furnish the names and number of the servants and slaves imported, the place of their birth, and pay the duty imposed upon each before they were permitted to be landed. This act was to be in force for the space of "three years from the publication thereof, and no longer." But, in the summer of 1701, it was continued until the 25th day of December, 1703. The act was passed as a temporary measure to secure revenue with which to build the Capitol. Evidently it was not intended to remain a part of the code of the colony. In 1732 it was revived by an act, the preamble of which leads us to infer that the home government was not friendly to its passage. In short, the act is preceded by a prayer for permission to pass it. Whatever may have been the feeling in England in reference to levying imposts upon servants and slaves, it is certain the colonists were in hearty accord with the spirit and letter of the act. It must be clear to every honest student of history, that there never was, up to this time, an attempt made to cure the growing evils of slavery. When a tax was imposed upon slaves imported, the object in view was the replenishing of the coffers of the colonial government. In 1734 another act was passed taxing imported slaves, because it had "been found very easy to the subjects of this colony, and no ways burthensome to the traders in slaves." The additional reason for continuing the law was, "that a competent revenue" might be raised "for preventing or lessening a poll-tax." And in 1738, this law being "found, by experience, to be an easy expedient for raising a revenue towards the lessening a pooll-tax, always grievous to the people of this colony, and is in no way burthensom to the traders in slaves," it was re-enacted. In every instance, through all these years, the imposition of a tax on slaves imported into the colony had but one end in view,—the raising of revenue. In 1699 the end sought through the taxing of imported slaves was the building of the Capitol; in 1734 it was to lighten the burden of taxes on the subjects in the colony; but, in 1740, the object was to get funds to raise and transport troops in his Majesty's service. The original duty remained; and an additional levy of five per centum was required on each slave imported, over and above the twenty shillings required by previous acts.

In 1742 the tax was continued, because it was "necessary" "to discharge the public debts." And again, in 1745, it was still believed to be necessary "for supporting the public expense." The act, in a legal sense, expired by limitation, but in spirit remained in full force until revived by the acts of 1752-53. In the spring of 1755 the General Assembly increased the tax on imported slaves above the amount previously fixed by law. The duty at this time was ten per centum on each slave sold into the colony. The same law was reiterated in 1757, and, when it had expired by limitation, was revived in 1759, to be in force for "the term of seven years from thence next following."

Encouraged by the large revenue derived from the tax imposed on servants and slaves imported into the colony from foreign parts, the General Assembly stood for the revival of the impost-tax. The act of 1699 required the tax at the hands of "the importer," and from as many persons as engaged in the slave-trade who were subjects of Great Britain, and residents of the colony; but the tax at length became a burden to them. In order to evade the law and escape the tax, they frequently went into Maryland and the Carolinas, and bought slaves, ostensibly for their own private use, but really to sell in the local market. To prevent this, an act was passed imposing a tax of twenty per centum on all such sales; but there was a great outcry made against this act. Twenty per centum of the gross amount on each slave, paid by the person making the purchase, was a burden that planters bore with ill grace. The question of the reduction of the tax to ten per centum was vehemently agitated. The argument offered in favor of the reduction was three-fold; viz., "very burthensom to the fair purchaser," inimical "to the settlement and improvement of the lands" in the colony, and a great hinderance to "the importation of slaves, and thereby lessens the fund arising upon the duties upon slaves." The reduction was made in May, 1760; and, under additional pressure, the additional duty on imported slaves to be "paid by the buyer" was taken off altogether. But in 1766 the duty on imported slaves was revived; and in 1772 an act was passed reviving the "additional duty" on "imported slaves, and was continued in force until the colonies threw off the British yoke in 1775."

In all this epoch, from 1619 down to 1775, there is not a scrap of history to prove that the colony of Virginia ever sought to prohibit in any manner the importation of slaves. That she encouraged the traffic, we have abundant testimony; and that she enriched herself by it, no one can doubt.

During the period of which we have just made mention above, the slaves in this colony had no political or military rights. As early as 1639, the Assembly excused them from owning or carrying arms; and in 1705 they were barred by a special act from holding or exercising "any office, ecclesiastical, civil, or military, or any place of publick trust or power," in the colony. If found with a "gun, sword, club, staff, or other weopon," they were turned over to the constable, who was required to administer "twenty lashes on his or her bare back." There was but one exception made. Where Negro and Indian slaves lived on the border or the colony, frequently harassed by predatory bands of hostile Indians, they could bear arms by first getting written license from their master; but even then they were kept under surveillance by the whites.

Personal rights, we cannot see that the slaves had any. They were not allowed to leave the plantation on which they were held as chattel or real estate, without a written certificate or pass from their master, which was only granted under the most urgent circumstances. If they dared lift a hand against any white man, or "Christian" (?) as they loved to call themselves, they were punished by thirty lashes; and if a slave dared to resist his master while he was correcting him, he could be killed; and the master would be guiltless in the eyes of the law. If a slave remained on another plantation more than four hours, his master was liable to a fine of two hundred pounds of tobacco. And if any white person had any commercial dealings with a slave, he was liable to imprisonment for one month without bail, and compelled to give security in the sum of ten pounds. If a slave had earned and owned a horse and buggy, it was lawful to seize them; and the church-warden was charged with the sale of the articles. Even with the full permission of his master, if a slave were found going about the colony trading any articles for his or master's profit, his master was liable to a fine of ten pounds; which fine went to the church-warden, for the benefit of the poor of the parish in which the slave did the trading.

   In all the matters of law, civil and criminal, the slave had no rights. Under an act of 1705, Catholics, Indian and Negro slaves, were denied the right to appear as "witnesses in any cases whatsoever," "not being Christians;" but this was modified somewhat in 1732, when Negroes, Indians, and Mulattoes were admitted as witnesses in the trial of slaves. In criminal causes the slave could be arrested, cast into prison, tried, and condemned, with but one witness against him, and sentenced without a jury. The solemnity and dignity of "trial by jury," of which Englishmen love to boast, was not allowed the criminal slave. And, when a slave was executed, a value was fixed upon him; and the General Assembly was required to make an appropriation covering the value of the slave to indemnify the master. More than five slaves meeting together, "to rebel or make insurrection" was considered "felony;" and they were liable to "suffer death, and be utterly excluded the benefit of clergy;" but, where one slave was guilty of manslaughter in killing another slave, he was allowed the benefit of clergy. In case of burglary by a slave, he was not allowed the benefit of the clergy, except "said breaking, in the case of a freeman, would be burglary." And the only humane feature in the entire code of the colony was an act passed in 1772, providing that no slave should be condemned to suffer "unless four of the judges" before whom he is tried "concur."

   The free Negroes of the colony of Virginia were but little removed by law from their unfortunate brothers in bondage. Their freedom was the act of individuals, with but one single exception. In 1710 a few recalcitrant slaves resolved to offer armed resistance to their masters, whose treatment had driven them to the verge of desperation. A slave of Robert Ruffin, of Surry County, entered into the plot, but afterwards revealed it to the masters of the rebellious slaves. As a reward for his services, the General Assembly, on the 9th of October, 1710, gave him his manumission papers, with the added privilege to remain in the colony. For the laws of the colony required "that no negro, mulatto, or indian slaves" should be set free "except for some meritorious services." The governor and council were to decide upon the merits of the services, and then grant a license to the master to set his slave at liberty. If any master presumed to emancipate a slave without a license granted according to the act of 1723, his slave thus emancipated could be taken up by the church-warden for the parish in which the master of the slave resided, and sold "by public outcry." The money accruing from such sale was to be used for the benefit of the parish. But if a slave were emancipated according to law, the General Assembly paid the master so much for him, as in the case of slaves executed by the authorities. But it was seldom that emancipated persons were permitted to remain in the colony. By the act of

1699 they were required to leave the colony within six months after they had secured their liberty, on pain of having to pay a fine of "ten pounds sterling to the church-wardens of the parish;" which money was to be used in transporting the liberated slave out of the country. If slave women came in possession of their freedom, the law sought them out, and required of them to pay taxes; a burden from which their white sisters, and even Indian women, were exempt.

If free Colored persons in the colony ever had the right of franchise, there is certainly no record of it. We infer, however, from the act of 1723, that previous to that time they had exercised the voting privilege. For that act declares "that no free negro shall hereafter have any vote at the election." Perhaps they had had a vote previous to this time; but it is mere conjecture, unsupported by historical proof. Being denied the right of suffrage did not shield them from taxation. All free Negroes, male and female, were compelled to pay taxes. They contributed to the support of the colonial government, and yet they had no voice in the government. They contributed to the building of schoolhouses, but were denied the blessings of education.

Free Negroes were enlisted in the militia service, but were not permitted to bear arms. They had to attend the trainings, but were assigned the most servile duties. They built fortifications, pitched and struck tents, cooked, drove teams, and in some instances were employed as musicians. Where free Negroes were acting as housekeepers, they were allowed to have fire-arms in their possession; and if they lived on frontier plantations, as we have made mention already, they were permitted to use arms under the direction of their employers.

In a moral and religious sense, the slaves of the colony of Virginia received little or no attention from the Christian Church. All intercourse was cut off between the races. Intermarrying of whites and blacks was prohibited by severe laws. And the most common civilities and amenities of life were frowned down when intended for a Negro. The plantation was as religious as the Church, and the Church was as secular as the plantation. The "white christians" hated the Negro, and the Church bestowed upon him a most bountiful amount of neglect. Instead of receiving religious instruction from the clergy, slaves were given to them in part pay for their ministrations to the whites,—for their "use and encouragement." It was as late as 1756 before any white minister had the piety and courage to demand instruction for the slaves. The prohibition against instruction for these poor degraded vassals is not so much a marvel after all. For in 1670, when the white population was forty thousand, servants six thousand, and slaves two thousand, Sir William Berkeley, when inquired of by the home government as to the condition of education in the colony, replied:—

Thus was the entire colony in ignorance and superstition, and it was the policy of the home government to keep out the light. The sentiments of Berkeley were applauded in official circles in England, and most rigorously carried out by his successor who, in 1682, with the concurrence of the council, put John Buckner under bonds for introducing the art of printing into the colony. This prohibition continued until 1733. If the whites of the colony were left in ignorance, what must have been the mental and moral condition of the slaves? The ignorance of the whites made them the pliant tools of the London Company, and the Negroes in turn were compelled to submit to a condition "of rather rigorous servitude." This treatment has its reflexive influence on the planters. Men fear most the ghosts of their sins, and for cruel deeds rather expect and dread "the reward in the life that now is." So no wonder Dinwiddie wrote the father of Charles James Fox in 1758: "We dare not venture to part with any of our white men any distance, as we must have a watchful eye over our negro slaves."

In 1648, as we mentioned some pages back, there were about three hundred slaves in the colony. Slow coming at first, but at length they began to increase rapidly, so that in fifty years they had increased one hundred per cent. In 1671 they were two thousand strong, and all, up to that date, direct from Africa. In 1715 there were twenty-three thousand slaves against seventy-two thousand whites. By the year 1758 the slave population had increased to the alarming number of over one hundred thousand, which was a little less than the numerical strength of the whites.

During this period of a century and a half, slavery took deep root in the colony of Virginia, and attained unwieldy and alarming proportions. It had sent its dark death-roots into the fibre and organism of the political, judicial, social, and religious life of the people. It was crystallized now into a domestic institution. It existed in contemplation of legislative enactment, and had high judicial recognition through the solemn forms of law. The Church had proclaimed it a "sacred institution," and the clergy had covered it with the sanction of their ecclesiastical office. There it stood, an organized system,—the dark problem of the uncertain future: more terrible to the colonists in its awful, spectral silence during the years of the Revolution than the victorious guns of the French and Continental armies, which startled the English lion from his hurtful hold at the throat of white men's liberties—black men had no country, no liberty—in this new world in the West. But, like the dead body of the Roman murderer's victim, slavery was a curse that pursued the colonists evermore.

FOOTNOTES:

A Flemish favorite of Charles V. having obtained of his king a patent, containing an exclusive right of importing four thousand Negroes into America, sold it for twenty-five thousand ducats to some Genoese merchants, who first brought into a regular form the commerce for slaves between Africa and America.--Holmes's American Annals, vol. i. p. 35.

R. Beverley's History of Virginia, pp. 35, 36.

See Campbell, p. 144; Burk, vol. i. p. 326.

Smith, vol. ii pp. 38, 39.

Smith's History of Virginia, vol. ii. p. 39.

Virginia Company of London, p. 117, sq.

Campbell, p. 144.

Burk, vol. I. p. 319.

Neill, p. 120.

Smith, vol. II. p. 37.

There were two vessels, The Treasurer and the Dutch man-of-war; but the latter, no doubt, put the first slaves ashore.

Campbell, p. 144.

Burk, Appendix, p. 316, Declaration of Virginia Company, 7th May, 1623.

See Burk, vol. i. p. 326.

Stith, Book III. pp. 153, 154.

Beverley, 235, sq.

Campbell, 147.

Beverley, p. 248.

Court and Times of James First, ii. p. 108; also, Neill p. 121.

Bancroft, vol. i. p. 468.

Neill, p. 121.

Hist. Tracts, vol. ii. Tract viii.

Beverley, p. 236.

Campbell, p. 145.

Hening, vol. i. p. 146; also p. 552.

Hening, vol. i. p 226.

Bancroft, vol. i. p. 178.

Hening, vol. i. p. 540.

Ibid., vol. ii. p. 84.

Hening, vol. i. p. 396.

Burk, vol. ii. Appendix, p. xxiii.

Beverley, p. 235.

Hening, vol. ii. p. 170; see, also, vol. iii. p. 140.

Beverley, p. 195.

Hening, vol. i. p. 396.
Ibid., vol. ii. p. 283.
Campbell, p. 160; also Bacon's Rebellion.
Hening, vol. ii. pp. 490, 491.
Ibid., vol. ii. p. 260; see, also, vol. iii. p. 460.
Ibid., vol. iii. p. 333.
Hening, vol. iii. pp. 334, 335.
Ibid., vol. iii. p. 448; see, also, vol. v. p. 548.
Hildreth, in his History of the United States, says that the law making "Negroes, Mulattoes, and Indians" real estate "continued to be the law so long as Virginia remained a British colony." This is a mistake, as the reader can see. The law was repealed nearly a quarter of a century before Virginia ceased to be a British colony.
Hening, vol. v. p. 432, sq.
Beverley, p. 98.
Hening, vol. iii, pp. 193, 194.
Hening, vol. iii. p. 195.
Burk, vol. ii. Appendix, p. xxii.
Hening, vol. iv. p. 394.
Ibid., vol, v. pp. 92, 93.
Ibid., vol. v. pp. 160, 161.
Ibid., vol. v. pp. 318, 319.
Ibid., vol. vi. pp. 217, 218.
Ibid., vol. vii. p. 466.
Ibid., vol. vii. p. 81.
Ibid., vol. vii. p. 281.
Hening, vol. vii, p. 338.
Ibid., vol. vii. p. 363.
Ibid., vol. vii. p. 383.
Ibid., vol. viii. pp. 190, 191, 237, 336, 337.
Ibid., vol. viii, pp. 530, 532.
Ibid., vol. i. p. 226.
Ibid., vol. iii. p. 251.
Ibid., vol. iii. p. 459; also vol. iv. p. 131, vol. vi. p. 109, and vol. ii. p. 481.
Hening., vol. vi. p. 110.
Ibid., vol. ii. p. 481.
Ibid., vol. ii p. 270.
Ibid., vol. ii. p. 493.
Ibid., vol. iii, p. 451.
Ibid., vol. iii. pp. 459, 460.
Ibid., vol. viii. p. 360.

Ibid., vol. iii. p. 298.
Ibid., vol. iv. p. 327.
Ibid., vol. iii. p. 103.
Ibid., vol. iii, p. 270, and vol. iv. p. 128.
Hening, vol. iv. p. 126, and vol. vi. p. 104, sq.
Ibid., vol. viii. p. 139.
Ibid., vol. viii. p. 522.
Ibid., vol. viii. p. 523.
Ibid., vol. viii. pp. 536, 537.
Ibid., vol. iv. p. 132.
Ibid., vol. vi, p. 112.
Hening, vol. iii. pp. 87, 88.
Ibid., vol. ii. p. 267.
Ibid., vol. iv. pp. 133, 134.
Ibid., vol. iv, p. 133.
Ibid., vol. vii. p. 95; and vol. vi. p. 533.
Ibid., vol. iv. p. 131.
Ibid., vol. iii. p. 87.
Campbell, p. 529.
Burk, vol. ii. Appendix, p. xiii.
Foot's Sketches, First Series, p. 291.
Hening, vol. ii. p. 517.
Hening, vol. ii. p. 518.
Campbell, p. 383.
Chalmers's American Colonies, vol. ii. p. 7.

CHAPTER XIII.: THE COLONY OF NEW YORK.: 1628-1775.

Settlement of New York by the Dutch in 1609.—Negroes introduced into the Colony, 1628.—The Trade in Negroes increased.—Tobacco exchanged for Slaves and Merchandise. Government of the Colony.—New Netherland falls into the Hands of the English, Aug. 27, 1664.—Various Changes.—New Laws adopted.—Legislation.—First Representatives elected in 1683.—In 1702 Queen Anne instructs the Royal Governor in Regard to the Importation of Slaves.—Slavery Restrictions.—Expedition to effect the Conquest of Canada unsuccessful.—Negro Riot.—Suppressed by the Efficient Aid of Troops.—Fears of the Colonists.—Negro Plot of 1741.—The Robbery of Hogg's House.—Discovery of a Portion of the Goods.—The Arrest of Hughson, his Wife, and Irish Peggy.—Crimination and Recrimination.—The Breaking-out of Numerous Fires.—The Arrest of Spanish Negroes.—The Trial of Hughson.—Testimony of Mary Burton.—Hughson hanged.—The Arrest of Many Others implicated in the Plot.—The Hanging of Cæsar and Prince.—Quack and Cuffee burned at the Stake.—The Lieutenant-Governor's Proclamation.—Many White Persons accused of being Conspirators.—Description of Hughson's Manner of Swearing those having Knowledge of the Plot.—Conviction and Hanging of the Catholic Priest Ury.—The Sudden and Unexpected Termination of the Trial.—New Laws more Stringent toward Slaves adopted.

FROM the settlement of New York by the Dutch in 1609, down to its conquest by the English in 1664, there is no reliable record of slavery in that colony. That the institution was coeval with the Holland government, there can be no historical doubt. During the half-century that the Holland flag waved over the New Netherlands, slavery grew to such proportions as to be regarded as a necessary evil. As early as 1628 the irascible slaves from Angola, Africa, were the fruitful source of wide-spread public alarm. A newly settled country demanded a hardy and energetic laboring class. Money was scarce, the colonists poor, and servants few. The numerous physical obstructions across the path of material civilization suggested cheap but efficient labor. White servants were few, and the cost of securing them from abroad was a great hinderance to their increase. The Dutch had possessions on the coast of Guinea and in Brazil, and hence they found it cheap and convenient to import slaves to perform the labor of the colony.

The early slaves went into the pastoral communities, worked on the public highways, and served as valets in private families. Their increase was stealthy, their conduct insubordinate, and their presence a distressing nightmare to the apprehensive and conscientious.

The West India Company had offered many inducements to its patroons. And its pledge to furnish the colonists with "as many blacks as they conveniently could," was scrupulously performed. In addition to the slaves furnished by the vessels plying between Brazil and the coast of Guinea, many Spanish and Portuguese prizes were brought into the Netherlands, where the slaves were made the chattel property of the company. An urgent and extraordinary demand for labor, rather than the cruel desire to traffic in human beings, led the Dutch to encourage the bringing of Negro slaves. Scattered widely among the whites, treated often with the humanity that characterized the treatment bestowed upon the white servants, there was little said about slaves in this period. The majority of them were employed upon the farms, and led quiet and sober lives. The largest farm owned by the company was "cultivated by the blacks;" and this fact was recorded as early as the 19th of April, 1638, by "Sir William Kieft, Director-General of New Netherland." And, although the references to slaves and slavery in the records of Amsterdam are incidental, yet it is plainly to be seen that the institution was purely patriarchal during nearly all the period the Hollanders held the Netherlands.

Manumission of slaves was not an infrequent event. Sometimes it was done as a reward for meritorious services, and sometimes it was prompted by the holy impulses of humanity and justice. The most cruel thing done, however, in this period, was to hold as slaves in the service of the company the children of Negroes who were lawfully manumitted. "All their children already born, or yet to be born, remained obligated to serve the company as slaves." In cases of emergency the liberated fathers of these bond children were required to serve "by water or by land" in the defence of the Holland government. It is gratifying, however, to find the recorded indignation of some of the best citizens of the New Netherlands against the enslaving of the children of free Negroes. It was severely denounced, as contrary to justice and in "violation of the law of nature." "How any one born of a free Christian mother" could, notwithstanding, be a slave, and be obliged to remain such, passed their comprehension. It was impossible for them to explain it." And, although "they were treated just like Christians," the moral sense of the people could not excuse such a flagrant crime against humanity.

Director-General Sir William Kieft's unnecessary war, "without the knowledge, and much less the order, of the XIX., and against the will of the Commonality there," had thrown the Province into great confusion. Property was depreciating, and a feeling of insecurity seized upon the people. Instead of being a source of revenue, New Netherlands, as shown by the books of the Amsterdam Chamber, had cost the company, from 1626 to 1644, inclusive, "over five hundred and fifty thousand guilders, deducting the returns received from there." It was to be expected that the slaves would share the general feeling of uneasiness and expectancy. Something had to be done to stay the panic so imminent among both classes of the colonists, bond and free. The Bureau of Accounts made certain propositions to the company calculated to act as a tonic upon the languishing hopes of the people. After reciting many methods by which the Province was to be rejuvenated, it was suggested "that it would be wise to permit the patroons, colonists, and other farmers to import as many Negroes from the Brazils as they could purchase for cash, to assist them on their farms; as (it was maintained) these slaves could do more work for their masters, and were less expensive, than the hired laborers engaged in Holland, and conveyed to New Netherlands, "by means of much money and large promises."

Nor was the substitution of slave labor for white a temporary expedient. Again in 1661 a loud call for more slaves was heard. In the October treaty of the same year, the Dutch yielded to the seductive offer of the English, "to deliver two or three thousand hogsheads of tobacco annually ... in return for negroes and merchandise." At the first the Negro slave was regarded as a cheap laborer,—a blessing to the Province; but after a while the cupidity of the English induced the Hollanders to regard the Negro as a coveted, marketable chattel.

The Dutch colony was governed by the Dutch and Roman law. The government was tripartite,—executive, legislative, and judicial,—all vested in, and exercised by, the governor and council. There seemed to be but little or no necessity for legislation on the slavery question. The Negro seemed to be a felt need in the Province, and was regarded with some consideration by the kind-hearted Hollanders. Benevolent and social, they desired to see all around them happy. The enfranchised African might and did obtain a freehold; while the Negro who remained under an institution of patriarchal simplicity, scarcely knowing he was in bondage, danced merrily at the best, in "kermis," at Christmas and Pinckster. There were, doubtless, a few cases where the slaves received harsh treatment from their masters; but, as a rule, the jolly Dutch fed and clothed their slaves as well as their white servants. There were no severe rules to strip the Negroes of their personal rights,—such as social amusements or public feasts when their labors had been completed. During this entire period, they went and came among their class without let or hinderance. They were married, and given in marriage; they sowed, and, in many instances, gathered an equitable share of the fruits of their labors. If there were no schools for them, there were no laws against an honest attempt to acquire knowledge at seasonable times. The Hollanders built their government upon the hearthstone, believing it to be the earthly rock of ages to a nation that would build wisely for the future. And while it is true that they regarded commerce as the life-blood of the material existence of a people, they nevertheless found their inspiration for multifarious duties in the genial sunshine of the family circle. A nation thus constituted could not habilitate slavery with all the hideous features it wore in Virginia and Massachusetts. The slaves could not escape the good influences of the mild government of the New Netherlands, nor could the Hollanders withhold the brightness and goodness of their hearts from their domestic slaves.

On the 27th of August, 1664, New Netherlands fell into the hands of the English; and the city received a new name,—New York, after the famous Duke of York. When the English colors were run up over Fort Amsterdam, it received a new name, "Fort James." In the twenty-four articles in which the Hollanders surrendered their Province, there is no direct mention of slaves or slavery. The only clause that might be construed into a reference to the slaves is as follows: "IV. If any inhabitant have a mind to remove himself, he shall have a year and six weeks from this day to remove himself, wife, children, servants, goods, and to dispose of his lands here." There was nothing in the articles of capitulation hostile to slavery in the colony.

During the reign of Elizabeth, the English government gave its royal sanction to the slave-traffic. "In 1562 Sir John Hawkins, Sir Lionel Duchet, Sir Thomas Lodge, and Sir William Winter"—all "honorable men"—became the authors of the greatest curse that ever afflicted the earth. Hawkins, assisted by the aforenamed gentlemen, secured a ship-load of Africans from Sierra Leone, and sold them at Hispaniola. Many were murdered on the voyage, and cast into the sea. The story of this atrocity coming to the ears of the queen, she was horrified. She summoned Hawkins into her presence, in order to rebuke him for his crime against humanity. He defended his conduct with great skill and eloquence. He persuaded her Royal Highness that it was an act of humanity to remove the African from a bad to a better country, from the influences of idolatry to the influences of Christianity. Elizabeth afterwards encouraged the slave-trade.

So when New Netherlands became an English colony, slavery received substantial official encouragement, and the slave became the subject of colonial legislation.

The first laws under the English Government were issued under the patent to the Duke of York, on the 1st of March, 1665, and were known as "the Duke's Laws." It is rather remarkable that they were fashioned after the famous "Massachusetts Fundamentals," adopted in 1641. These laws have the following caption: "Laws collected out of the several laws now in force in his majesty's American colonies and plantations." The first mention of slavery is contained in a section under the caption of "Bond Slavery."

By turning to the first chapter on Massachusetts, the reader will observe that the above is the Massachusetts law of 1641 with but a very slight alteration. We find no reference to slavery directly, and the word slave does not occur in this code at all. Article 7, under the head of "Capital Laws," reads as follows: "If any person forcibly stealeth or carrieth away any mankind he shall be put to death."

On the 27th of January, 1683, Col. Thomas Dongan was sent to New York as its governor, and charged with carrying out a long list of instructions laid down by his Royal Highness the Duke of York. Gov. Dongan arrived in New York during the latter part of August; and on the 13th of September, 1683, the council sitting at Fort James promulgated an order calling upon the people to elect representatives. On the 17th October, 1683, the General Assembly met for the first time at Fort James, in the city of New York. It is a great misfortune that the journals of both houses are lost. The titles of the Acts passed have been preserved, and so far we are enabled to fairly judge of the character of the legislation of the new assembly. On the 1st November, 1683, the Assembly passed "An Act for naturalizing all those of foreign nations at present inhabiting within this province and professing Christianity, and for encouragement for others to come and settle within the same." This law was re-enacted in 1715, and provided, that "nothing contained in this Act is to be construed to discharge or set at liberty any servant, bondman or slave, but only to have relation to such persons as are free at the making hereof."

So the mild system of domestic slavery introduced by the Dutch now received the sanction of positive British law. Most of the slaves in the Province of New York, from the time they were first introduced, down to 1664, had been the property of the West-India Company. As such they had small plots of land to work for their own benefit, and were not without hope of emancipation some day. But under the English government the condition of the slave was clearly defined by law and one of great hardships. On the 24th of October, 1684, an Act was passed in which slavery was for the first time regarded as a legitimate institution in the Province of New York under the English government.

The slave-trade grew. New York began to feel the necessity of a larger number of slaves. In 1702 her "most gracious majesty," Queen Anne, among many instructions to the royal governor, directed that the people "take especial care, that God Almighty be devoutly and duly served," and that the "Royal African Company of England" "take especial care that the said Province may have a constant and sufficient supply of merchantable Negroes, at moderate rates." It was a marvellous zeal that led the good queen to build up the Church of England alongside of the institution of human slavery. It was an impartial zeal that sought their mutual growth,—the one intended by our divine Lord to give mankind absolute liberty, the other intended by man to rob mankind of the great boon of freedom! But with the sanction of statutory legislation, and the silent acquiescence of the Church, the foundations of the institution of slavery were firmly laid in the approving conscience of a selfish public. Dazzled by prospective riches, and unscrupulous in the methods of accumulations, the people of the Province of New York clamored for more exacting laws by which to govern the slaves. Notwithstanding Lord Cornbury had received the following instructions from the crown, "you shall endeavor to get a law passed for the restraining of any inhuman severity ... to find out the best means to facilitate and encourage the conversion of Negroes and Indians to the Christian religion," the Colonial Assembly (the same year, 1702) passed severe laws against the slaves. It was "An Act for regulating slaves," but was quite lengthy and specific. It was deemed "not lawful to trade with negro slaves," and the violation of this law was followed by fine and imprisonment. "Not above three slaves may meet together:" if they did they were liable to be whipped by a justice of the peace, or sent to jail. "A common whipper to be appointed," showed that the justices had more physical exercise than they cared for. "A slave not to strike a freeman," indicated that the slaves in New York as in Virginia were accounted as heathen. "Penalty for concealing slaves," and the punishment of Negroes for stealing, etc., were rather severe, but only indicated the temper of the people at that time.

The recommendations to have Negro and Indian slaves baptized gave rise to considerable discussion and no little alarm. As was shown in the chapter on Virginia, the proposition to baptize slaves did not meet with a hearty indorsement from the master-class. The doctrine had obtained in most of the colonies, that a man was a freeman by virtue of his membership in a Christian church, and hence eligible to office. To escape the logic of this position, the dealer in human flesh sought to bar the door of the Church against the slave. But in 1706 "An Act to encourage the baptizing of Negro, Indian, and mulatto slaves," was passed in the hope of quieting the public mind on this question.

So when the door of the Christian Church was opened to the Negro, he was to appear at the sacred altar with his chains on. Though emancipated from the bondage of Satan, he nevertheless remained the abject slave of the Christian colonists. Claiming spiritual kinship with Christ, the Negro could be sold at the pleasure of his master, and his family hearthstone trodden down by the slave-dealer. The humane feature of the system of slavery under the simple Dutch government, of allowing slaves to acquire an interest in the soil, was now at an end. The tendency to manumit faithful slaves called forth no approbation. The colonists grew cold and hard-fisted. They saw not God's image in the slave,—only so many dollars. There were no strong men in the pulpits of the colony who dared brave the avaricious spirit of the times. Not satisfied with colonial legislation, the municipal government of the city of New York passed, in 1710, an ordinance forbidding Negroes, Indians, and Mulatto slaves from appearing "in the streets after nightfall without a lantern with a lighted candle in it." The year before, a slave-market was erected at the foot of Wall Street, where slaves of every description were for sale. Negroes,

Indians, and Mulattoes; men, women, and children; the old, the middle-aged, and the young,—all, as sheep in shambles, were daily declared the property of the highest cash-bidder. And what of the few who secured their freedom? Why, the law of 1712 declared that no Negro, Indian, or Mulatto that shall hereafter be set free "shall hold any land or real estate, but the same shall escheat." There was, therefore, but little for the Negro in either state,—bondage or freedom. There was little in this world to allure him, to encourage him, to help him. The institution under which he suffered was one huge sepulchre, and he was buried alive.

The poor grovelling worm turns under the foot of the pedestrian. The Negro winched under his galling yoke of British colonial oppression.

A misguided zeal and an inordinate desire of conquest had led the Legislature to appropriate ten thousand pounds sterling toward an expedition to effect the conquest of Canada. Acadia had just fallen into the hands of Gov. Francis Nicholson without firing a gun, and the news had carried the New Yorkers off their feet. "On to Canada!" was the shibboleth of the adventurous colonists; and the expedition started. Eight transports, with eight hundred and sixty men, perished amid the treacherous rocks and angry waters of the St. Lawrence. The troops that had gone overland returned in chagrin. The city was wrapped in gloom: the Legislature refused to do any thing further; and here the dreams of conquest vanished. The city of New York was thrown on the defensive. The forts were repaired, and every thing put in readiness for an emergency. Like a sick man the colonists started at every rumor. On account of bad faith the Iroquois were disposed to mischief.

In the feeble condition of the colonial government, the Negro grew restless. At the first, as previously shown, the slaves were very few, but now, in 1712, were quite numerous. The Negro, the Quaker, and the Papist were a trinity of evils that the colonists most dreaded. The Negro had been badly treated; and an attempt on his part to cast off the yoke was not improbable, in the mind of the master-class. The fears of the colonists were at length realized. A Negro riot broke out. A house was burned, and a number of white persons killed; and, had it not been for the prompt and efficient aid of the troops, the city of New York would have been reduced to ashes.

Now, what was the condition of the slaves in the Christian colony of New York? They had no family relations: for a long time they lived together by common consent. They had no property, no schools, and, neglected in life, were abandoned to burial in a common ditch after death. They dared not lift their hand to strike a Christian or a Jew. Their testimony was excluded by the courts, and the power of their masters over their bodies extended sometimes to life and limb. This condition of affairs yielded its bitter fruit at length.

The Negro plot of 1741 furnishes the most interesting and thrilling chapter in the history of the colony of New York. Unfortunately for the truth of history, there was but one historian of the affair, and he an interested judge; and what he has written should be taken cum grano salis. His book was intended to defend the action of the court that destroyed so many innocent lives, but no man can read it without being thoroughly convinced that the decision of the court was both illogical and cruel. There is nothing in this country to equal it, except it be the burning of the witches at Salem. But in stalwart old England the Popish Plot in 1679, started by Titus Oates, is the only occurrence in human history that is so faithfully reproduced by the Negro plot. Certainly history repeats itself. Sixty-two years of history stretch between the events. One tragedy is enacted in the metropolis of the Old World, the other in the metropolis of the New World. One was instigated by a perjurer and a heretic, the other by an indentured servant, in all probability from a convict ship. The one was suggested by the hatred of the Catholics, and the other by hatred of the Negro. And in both cases the evidence that convicted and condemned innocent men and women was wrung from the lying lips of doubtful characters by an overwrought zeal on the part of the legal authorities.

Titus Oates, who claimed to have discovered the "Popish Plot," was a man of the most execrable character. He was the son of an Anabaptist, took orders in the Church, and had been settled in a small living by the Duke of Norfolk. Indicted for perjury, he effected an escape in a marvellous manner. While a chaplain in the English navy he was convicted of practices not fit to be mentioned, and was dismissed from the service. He next sought communion with the Church of Rome, and made his way into the Jesuit College of St. Omers. After a brief residence among the students, he was deputed to perform a confidential mission to Spain, and, upon his return to St. Omers, was dismissed to the world on account of his habits, which were very distasteful to Catholics. He boasted that he had only joined them to get their secrets. Such a man as this started the cry of the Popish Plot, and threw all England into a state of consternation. A chemist by the name of Tongue, on the 12th of August, 1678, had warned the king against a plot that was directed at his life, etc. But the king did not attach any importance to the statement until Tongue referred to Titus Oates as his authority. The latter proved himself a most arrant liar while on the stand: but the people were in a credulous state of mind, and Oates became the hero of the hour; and under his wicked influence many souls were hurried into eternity. Read Hume's account of the Popish Plot, and then follow the bloody narrative of the Negro plot of New York, and see how the one resembles the other.

On the 28th of February, 1741, the house of one Robert Hogg, Esq., of New-York City, a merchant, was robbed of some fine linen, medals, silver coin, etc. Mr. Hogg's house was situated on the corner of Broad and Mill Streets, the latter sometimes being called Jew's Alley. The case was given to the officers of the law to look up.

The population of New-York City was about ten thousand, about two thousand of whom were slaves. On the 18th of March the chapel in the fort took fire from some coals carelessly left by an artificer in a gutter he had been soldering. The roof was of shingles; and a brisk wind from the south-east started a fire, that was not observed until it had made great headway. In those times the entire populace usually turned out to assist in extinguishing fires; but this fire being in the fort, the fear of an explosion of the magazine somewhat checked their usual celerity on such occasions. The result was, that all the government buildings in the fort were destroyed. A militia officer by the name of Van Horne, carried away by the belief that the fire was purposely set by the Negroes, caused the beating of the drums and the posting of the "night watch." And for his vigilance he was nicknamed "Major Drum." The "Major's" apprehensions, however, were contagious. The fact that the governor reported the true cause of the fire to the Legislature had but little influence in dispossessing the people of their fears of a Negro plot. The next week the chimney of Capt. Warren's house near the fort took fire, but was saved with but slight damage. A few days after this the storehouse of a Mr. Van Zandt was found to be on fire, and it was said at the time to have been occasioned by the carelessness of a smoker. In about three days after, two fire alarms were sounded. One was found to be a fire in some hay in a cow-stable near a Mr. Quick's house. It was soon extinguished. The other alarm was on account of a fire in the kitchen loft of the dwelling of a Mr. Thompson. On the next day coals were discovered under the stables of a Mr. John Murray on Broadway. On the next morning an alarm called the people to the residence of Sergeant Burns, near the fort; and in a few hours the dwelling of a Mr. Hilton, near Fly Market, was found to be on fire. But the flames in both places were readily extinguished. It was thought that the fire was purposely set at Mr. Hilton's, as a bundle of tow was found near the premises. A short time before these strange fires broke out, a Spanish vessel, partly manned by Spanish Catholic Negroes, had been brought into the port of New York as a prize. All the crew that were Negroes were hurried into the Admiralty Court; where they were promptly condemned to slavery, and an order issued for their sale. The Negroes pleaded their freedom in another country, but had no counsel to defend them. A Capt. Sarly purchased one of these Negroes. Now, Capt. Sarly's house adjoined that of Mr. Hilton's; and so, when the latter's house was discovered to be on fire, a cry was raised, "The Spanish Negroes! The Spanish! Take up the Spanish Negroes!" Some persons took it upon themselves to question Capt. Sarly's Negro about the fires, and it is said that he behaved in an insolent manner; whereupon he was sent to jail. A magistrate gave orders to the constables to arrest and incarcerate the rest of the Spanish Negroes. The magistrates held a meeting the same day, in the afternoon; and, while they were deliberating about the matter, another fire broke out in Col. Phillipes's storehouse. Some of the white people cried "Negro! Negro!" and "Cuff Phillipes!" Poor Cuff, startled at the cry, ran to his master's house, from whence he was dragged to jail by an excited mob. Judge Horsemanden says,—

Let the reader return now to the robbery committed in Mr. Hogg's house on the 28th of February. The officers thought they had traced the stolen goods to a public house on the North River, kept by a person named John Hughson. This house had been a place of resort for Negroes; and it was searched for the articles, but nothing was found. Hughson had in his service an indentured servant,—a girl of sixteen years,—named Mary Burton. She intimated to a neighbor that the goods were concealed in Hughson's house, but that it would be at the expense of her life to make this fact known. This information was made known to the sheriff, and he at once apprehended the girl and produced her before Alderman Banker. This benevolent officer promised the girl her freedom on the ground that she should tell all she knew about the missing property. For prudential reasons the Alderman ordered Mary Burton to be taken to the City Hall, corner Wall and Nassua Streets. On the 4th of March the justices met at the City Hall. In the mean while John Hughson and his wife had been arrested for receiving stolen goods. They were now examined in the presence of Mary Burton. Hughson admitted that some goods had been brought to his house, produced them, and turned them over to the court. It appears from the testimony of the Burton girl that another party, dwelling in the house of the Hughson's, had taken part in receiving the stolen articles. She was a girl of bad character, called Margaret Sorubiero, alias Solinburgh, alias Kerry, but commonly called Peggy Carey. This woman had lived in the home of the Hughsons for about ten months, but at one time during this period had remained a short while at the house of John Rommes, near the new Battery, but had returned to Hughson's again. The testimony of Mary Burton went to show that a Negro by the name of Cæsar Varick, but called Quin, on the night in which the burglary was committed, entered Peggy's room through the window. The next morning Mary Burton saw "speckled linen" in Peggy's room, and that the man Varick gave the deponent two pieces of silver. She further testified that Varick drank two mugs of punch, and bought of Hughson a pair of stockings, giving him a lump of silver; and that Hughson and his wife received and hid away the linen. Mr. John Varick (it was spelled Vaarck then), a baker, the owner of Cæsar, occupied a house near the new Battery, the kitchen of which adjoined the yard of John Romme's house. He found some of Robert Hogg's property under his kitchen floor, and delivered it to the mayor. Upon this revelation Romme fled to New Jersey, but was subsequently captured at Brunswick. He had followed shoemaking and tavern-keeping, and was, withal, a very suspicious character.

Up to this time nothing had been said about a Negro plot. It was simply a case of burglary. Hughson had admitted receiving certain articles, and restored them; Mr. Varick had found others, and delivered them to the mayor.

The reader will remember that the burglary took place on the 28th of February; that the justices arraigned the Hughsons, Mary Burton, and Peggy Carey on the 4th of March; that the first fire broke out on the 18th, the second on the 25th, of March, the third on the 1st of April, and the fourth and fifth on the 4th of April; that on the 5th of April coals were found disposed so as to burn a haystack, and that the day following two houses were discovered to be on fire.

On the 11th of April the Common Council met. The following gentlemen were present: John Cruger, Esq., mayor; the recorder, Daniel Horsemanden; aldermen, Gerardus Stuyvesant, William Romaine, Simon Johnson, John Moore, Christopher Banker, John Pintard, John Marshall; assistants, Henry Bogert, Isaac Stoutenburgh, Philip Minthorne, George Brinckerhoff, Robert Benson, and Samuel Lawrence. Recorder Horsemanden suggested to the council that the governor be requested to offer rewards for the apprehension of the incendiaries and all persons implicated, and that the city pay the cost, etc. It was accordingly resolved that the lieutenant-governor be requested to offer a reward of one hundred pounds current money of the Province to any white person, and pardon, if concerned; and twenty pounds, freedom, and, if concerned, pardon to any slave (the master to be paid twenty-five pounds); and to any free Negro, Mulatto, or Indian, forty-five pounds and pardon, if concerned. The mayor and the recorder (Horsemanden), called upon Lieut.-Gov. Clark, and laid the above resolve before him.

The city was now in a state of great excitement. The air was peopled with the wildest rumors.

On Monday the 13th of April each alderman, assistant, and constable searched his ward. The militia was called out, and sentries posted at the cross-streets. While the troops were patrolling the streets, the aldermen were examining Negroes in reference to the origin of the fires. Nothing was found. The Negroes denied all knowledge of the fires or a plot.

On the 21st of April, 1741, the Supreme Court convened. Judges Frederick Phillipse and Daniel Horsemanden called the grand jury. The members were as follows: Robert Watts, merchant, foreman; Jeremiah Latouche, Joseph Read, Anthony Rutgers, John M'Evers, John Cruger, jun., John Merrit, Adoniah Schuyler, Isaac DePeyster, Abraham Ketteltas, David Provoost, Rene Hett, Henry Beeckman, jun., David van Horne, George Spencer, Thomas Duncan, and Winant Van Zandt,—all set down as merchants,—a respectable, intelligent, and influential grand jury! Judge Phillipse informed the jury that the people "have been put into many frights and terrors," in regard to the fires; that it was their duty to use "all lawful means" to discover the guilty parties, for there was "much room to suspect" that the fires were not accidental. He told them that there were many persons in jail upon whom suspicion rested; that arson was felony at common law, even though the fire is extinguished, or goes out itself; that arson was a deep crime, and, if the perpetrators were not apprehended and punished, "who can say he is safe, or where will it end?" The learned judge then went on to deliver a moral lecture against the wickedness of selling "penny drams" to Negroes, without the consent of their masters. In conclusion, he charged the grand jury to present "all conspiracies, combinations and other offences."

It should be kept in mind that Mary Burton was only a witness in the burglary case already mentioned. Up to that time there had been no fires. The fires, and wholesale arrests of innocent Negroes, followed the robbery. But the grand jury called Mary Burton to testify in reference to the fires. She refused to be sworn. She was questioned concerning the fires, but gave no answer. Then the proclamation of the mayor, offering protection, pardon, freedom, and one hundred pounds, was read. It had the desired effect. The girl opened her mouth, and spake all the words that the jury desired. At first she agreed to tell all she knew about the stolen goods, but would say nothing about the fires. This declaration led the jury to infer that she could, but would not say any thing about the fires. After a moral lecture upon her duty in the matter in the light of eternal reward, and a reiteration of the proffered reward that then awaited her wise decision, her memory brightened, and she immediately began to tell all she knew. She said that a Negro named Prince, belonging to a Mr. Auboyman, and Prince (Varick) brought the goods, stolen from Mr. Hogg's house, to the house of her master, and that Hughson, his wife, and Peggy (Carey) received them; further, that Cæsar, Prince, and Cuffee (Phillipse) had frequently met at Hughson's tavern, and discoursed about burning the fort; that they had said they would go down to the Fly (the east end of the city), and burn the entire place; and that Hughson and his wife had assented to these insurrectionary remarks, and promised to assist them. She added, by way of fulness and emphasis, that when a handful of wretched slaves, seconded by a miserable and ignorant white tavern-keeper, should have lain the city in ashes, and murdered eight or nine thousand persons,— then Cæsar should be governor, Hughson king, and Cuffee supplied with abundant riches! The loquacious Mary remembered that this intrepid trio had said, that when they burned the city it would be in the night, so they could murder the people as they came out of their homes. It should not be forgotten that all the fires broke out in the daytime!

It is rather remarkable and should be observed, that this wonderful witness stated that her master, John Hughson, had threatened to poison her if she told anybody that the stolen goods were in his house; that all the Negroes swore they would burn her if she told; and that, when they talked of burning the town during their meetings, there were no white persons present save her master, mistress, and Peggy Carey.

The credulous Horsemanden tells us that "the evidence of a conspiracy," not only to burn the city, but also "to destroy and murder the people," was most "astonishing to the grand jury!" But that any white person should confederate with slaves in such a wicked and cruel purpose was astounding beyond measure! And the grand jury was possessed of the same childlike faith in the ingenious narrative of the wily Mary. In their report to the judges, they set forth in strong terms their faith in the statements of the deponent, and required the presence of Peggy Carey. The extent of the delusion of the judges, jury, and people may be seen in the fact, that, immediately upon the report of the jury, the judges summoned the entire bar of the city of New York to meet them. The following gentlemen responded to the call: Messrs. Murray, Alexander, Smith, Chambers, Nichols, Lodge, and Jameson. All the lawyers were present except the attorney-general. By the act of 1712, "for preventing, suppressing and punishing the conspiracy and insurrection of negroes and other slaves," a justice of the peace could try the refractory slaves at once. But here was a deep, dark, and bloody plot to burn the city and murder its inhabitants, in which white persons were implicated. This fact led the learned judges to conclude it wise and prudent to refer this whole matter to the Supreme Court. And the generous offer of the entire bar of New-York City to assist, in turns, in every trial, should remain evermore an indestructible monument to their unselfish devotion to their city, the existence of which was threatened by less than a score of ignorant, penniless Negro slaves!

By the testimony of Mary Burton, Peggy Carey stood convicted as one of the conspirators. She had already languished in jail for more than a month. The judges thought it advisable to examine her in her cell. They tried to cajole her into criminating others; but she stoutly denied all knowledge of the fires, and said "that if she should accuse anybody of any such thing, she must accuse innocent persons, and wrong her own soul."

On the 24th of April, Cæsar Varick, Prince Auboyman, John Hughson, his wife, and Peggy Carey were arraigned for felony, and pleaded not guilty. Cæsar and Prince were first put on trial. As they did not challenge the jury, the following gentlemen were sworn: Messrs. Roger French, John Groesbeck, John Richard, Abraham Kipp, George Witts, John Thurman, Patrick Jackson, Benjamin Moore, William Hammersley, John Lashiere, Joshua Sleydall, and John Shurmer. "Guilty!" as charged in the indictment. They had committed the robbery, so said the jury.

On the 3d of May one Arthur Price, a common thief, was committed to jail for theft. He occupied a cell next to the notorious Peggy Carey. In order to bring himself into favor with the judges, he claimed to have had a conversation with Peggy through the hole in the door. Price says she told him that "she was afraid of those fellows" (the Negroes); that if they said any thing in any way involving her she would hang every one of them; that she did not care to go on the stand again unless she was called; that when asked if she intended to set the town on fire she said no; but she knew about the plot; that Hughson and his wife "were sworn with the rest;" that she was not afraid of "Prince, Cuff, Cæsar, and Fork's Negro—not Cæsar, but another," because they "were all true-hearted fellows." This remarkable conversation was flavored throughout with the vilest species of profanity. Notwithstanding this interview was between a common Irish prostitute and a wretched sneak-thief, it had great weight with the solemn and upright judges.

   In the midst of this trial, seven barns were burnt in the town of Hackinsack. Two Negroes were suspected of the crime, but there was not the slightest evidence that they were guilty. But one of them said that he had discharged a gun at the party who set his master's barn on fire, but did not kill any one. The other one was found loading a gun with two bullets. This was enough to convict. They were burnt alive at a stake. This only added fuel to the flame of public excitement in New York.

   On the 6th of May (Wednesday) two more arrests were made,—Hughson's daughter Sarah, suspected of being a confederate, and Mr. Sleydall's Negro Jack,—on suspicion of having put fire to Mr. Murray's haystack. On the same day the judges arraigned the white persons implicated in the case,—John Hughson, his wife, and Peggy Carey. The jury promptly found them guilty of "receiving stolen goods." "Peggy Carey," says Recorder Horsemanden, "seeming to think it high time to do something to recommend herself to mercy, made a voluntary confession." This vile, foul-mouthed prostitute takes the stand, and gives a new turn to the entire affair. She removes the scene of the conspiracy to another tavern near the new Battery, where John Romme had made a habit of entertaining, contrary to law, Negro slaves. Peggy had seen many meetings at this place, particularly in December, 1740. At that time she mentioned the following Negroes as being present: Cuff, Brash, Curacoa, Cæsar, Patrick, Jack, Cato; but her especial Cæsar Varick was not implicated! Romme administered an oath to all these Negroes, and then made a proposition to them; viz., that they should destroy the fort, burn the town, and bring the spoils to him. He engaged to divide with them, and take them to a new country, where he would give them their freedom. Mrs. Romme was present during this conversation; and, after the Negroes had departed, she and the deponent (Peggy) were sworn by Romme to eternal secrecy. Mrs. Romme denied swearing to the conspiracy, but acknowledged that her husband had received stolen goods, that he sold drams to Negroes who kept game-fowls there; but that never more than three Negroes came at a time. She absconded in great fright. It has been mentioned that Peggy Carey had lived at the tavern of John Romme for a short time, and that articles belonging to Mr. Hogg had been found under the kitchen floor of the house next to Romme's.

   The judges evidently reasoned that all Negroes would steal, or that stealing was incident upon or implied by the condition of the slave. Then Romme kept a "tippling-house," and defied the law by selling "drams" to Negroes. Now, a man who keeps a "tippling-house" was liable to encourage a conspiracy.

   A full list of the names of the persons implicated by Peggy was handed to the proper officers, and those wicked persons apprehended. They were brought before the redoubtable Peggy for identification. She accused them of being sworn conspirators. They all denied the charge. Then they were turned over to Mary Burton; and she, evidently displeased at Peggy's attempt to rival her in the favor of the powerful judges, testified that she knew them not. But it was vain. Peggy had the ear of the court, and the terror-stricken company was locked up in the jail. Alarmed at their helpless situation, the ignorant Negroes began "to accuse one another, as it would seem, by way of injuring an enemy and guarding themselves."

Cæsar and Prince, having been tried and convicted of felony, were sentenced to be hanged. The record says,—

On the 13th of May, 1741, a solemn fast was observed; "because many houses and dwellings had been fired about our ears, without any discovery of the cause or occasion of them, which had put us into the utmost consternation." Excitement ran high. Instead of getting any light on the affair, the plot thickened.

On the 6th of May, Hughson, his wife, and Peggy Carey had been tried and found guilty, as has already been stated. Sarah Hughson, daughter of the Hughsons, was in jail. Mary Burton was the heroine of the hour. Her word was law. Whoever she named was produced in court. The sneak-thief, Arthur Price, was employed by the judges to perform a mission that was at once congenial to his tastes and in harmony with his criminal education. He was sent among the incarcerated Negroes to administer punch, in the desperate hope of getting more "confessions!" Next, he was sent to Sarah Hughson to persuade her to accuse her father and mother of complicity in the conspiracy. He related a conversation he had with Sarah, but she denied it to his teeth with great indignation. This vile and criminal method of securing testimony of a conspiracy never brought the blush to the cheek of a single officer of the law. "None of these things moved" them. They were themselves so completely lost in the general din and excitement, were so thoroughly convinced that a plot existed, and that it was their duty to prove it in some manner or other,—that they believed every thing that went to establish the guilt of any one.

Even a feeble-minded boy was arrested, and taken before the grand jury. He swore that he knew nothing of the plot to burn the town, but the kind magistrates told him that if he would tell the truth he should not be hanged. Ignorant as these helpless slaves were, they now understood "telling the truth" to mean to criminate some one in the plot, and thus gratify the inordinate hunger of the judges and jury for testimony relating to a "conspiracy." This Negro imbecile began his task of telling "what he knew," which was to be rewarded by allowing him to leave without being hung! He deposed that Quack desired him to burn the fort; that Cuffee said he would fire one house, Curacoa Dick another, and so on ad infinitum. He was asked by one of the learned gentlemen, "what the Negroes intended by all this mischief?" He answered, "To kill all the gentlemen and take their wives; that one of the fellows already hanged, was to be an officer in the Long Bridge Company, and the other, in the Fly Company."

On the 25th of May a large number of Negroes were arrested. The boy referred to above (whose name was Sawney, or Sandy) was called to the stand again on the 26th, when he grew very talkative. He said that "at a meeting of Negroes he was called in and frightened into undertaking to burn the slip Market;" that he witnessed some of the Negroes in their attempts to burn certain houses; that at the house of one Comfort, he, with others, was sworn to secrecy and fidelity to each other; said he was never at either tavern, Hughson's nor Romme's; and ended his revelations by accusing a woman of setting fire to a house, and of murdering her child. As usual, after such confessions, more arrests followed. Quack and Cuffee were tried and convicted of felony, "for wickedly and maliciously conspiring with others to burn the town and murder the inhabitants." This was an occasion to draw forth the eloquence of the attorney-general; and in fervid utterance he pictured the Negroes as "monsters, devils, etc." A Mr. Rosevelt, the master of Quack, swore that his slave was home when the fire took place in the fort; and Mr. Phillipse, Cuffee's master, testified as much for his servant. But this testimony was not what the magistrates wanted: so they put a soldier on the stand who swore that Quack did come to the fort the day of the fire; that his wife lived there, and when he insisted on going in he (the sentry) knocked him down, but the officer of the guard passed him in. Lawyer Smith, "whose eloquence had disfranchised the Jews," was called upon to sum up. He thought too much favor had been shown the Negroes, in that they had been accorded a trial as if they were freemen; that the wicked Negroes might have been proceeded against in a most summary manner; that the Negro witnesses had been treated with too much consideration; that "the law requires no oath to be administered to them; and, indeed, it would be a profanation of it to administer it to a heathen in a legal form;" that "the monstrous ingratitude of this black tribe is what exceedingly aggravates their guilt;" that their condition as slaves was one of happiness and peace; that "they live without care; are commonly better fed and clothed than the poor of most Christian countries; they are indeed slaves," continued the eloquent and logical attorney, "but under the protection of the law: none can hurt them with impunity; but notwithstanding all the kindness and tenderness with which they have been treated among us, yet this is the second attempt of this same kind that this brutish and bloody species of mankind have made within one age!" Of course the jury knew their duty, and merely went through the form of going out and coming in immediately with a verdict of "guilty." The judge sentenced them to be chained to a stake and burnt to death,—"and the Lord have mercy upon your poor wretched souls." His Honor told them that "they should be thankful that their feet were caught in the net; that the mischief had fallen upon their own pates." He advised them to consider the tenderness and humanity with which they had been treated; that they were the most abject wretches, the very outcasts of the nations of the earth; and, therefore, they should look to their souls, for as to their bodies, they would be burnt.

These poor fellows were accordingly chained to the stake the next Sunday; but, before the fuel was lighted, Deputy Sheriff More and Mr. Rosevelt again questioned Quack and Cuffee, and reduced their confessions to paper, for they had stoutly protested their innocence while in court, in hope of being saved they confessed, in substance, that Hughson contrived to burn the town, and kill the people; that a company of Negroes voted Quack the proper person to burn the fort, because his wife lived there; that he did set the chapel on fire with a lighted stick; that Mary Burton had told the truth, and that she could implicate many more if she would, etc. All this general lying was done with the understanding that the confessors were to be reprieved until the governor could be heard from. But a large crowd had gathered to witness the burning of these poor Negroes, and they compelled the sheriff to proceed with the ceremonies. The convicted slaves were burned.

On the 1st of June the boy Sawney was again put upon the witness-stand. His testimony led to the arrest of more Negroes. He charged them with having been sworn to the plot, and with having sharp penknives with which to kill white men. One Fortune testified that he never knew of houses where conspirators met, nor did he know Hughson, but accuses Sawney, and Quack who had been burnt. The next witness was a Negro girl named Sarah. She was frightened out of her senses. She foamed at the mouth, uttered the bitterest imprecations, and denied all knowledge of a conspiracy. But the benevolent gentlemen who conducted the trial told her that others had said certain things in proof of the existence of a conspiracy, that the only way to save her life was to acknowledge that there had been a conspiracy to burn the town and kill the inhabitants. She then assented to all that was told her, and thereby implicated quite a number of Negroes; but, when her testimony was read to her, she again denied all. She was without doubt a fit subject for an insane-asylum rather than for the witness-stand, in a cause that involved so many human lives.

It will be remembered that John Hughson, his wife, and daughter had been in the jail for a long time. He now desired to be called to the witness-stand. He begged to be sworn, that in the most solemn manner he might deny all knowledge of the conspiracy, and exculpate his wife and child. But the modest recorder reminded him of the fact that he stood convicted as a felon already, that he and his family were doomed to be hanged, and that, therefore, it would be well for him to "confess all." He was sent back to jail unheard. Already condemned to be hung, the upright magistrates had Hughson tried again for "conspiracy" on the 4th of June! The indictments were three in number: First, that Hughson, his wife, his daughter, and Peggy Carey, with three Negroes, Cæsar, Prince, and Cuffee, conspired in March last to set fire to the house in the fort. Second, That Quack (already burnt) did set fire to and burn the house, and that the prisoners, Hughson, his wife, daughter Sarah, and Peggy, encouraged him so to do. Third, That Cuffee (already burnt) did set fire to Phillipse's house, and burnt it; and they, the prisoners, procured and encouraged him so to do. Hughson, his family, and Peggy pleaded not guilty to all the above indictments. The attorney-general delivered a spirited address to the jury, which was more forcible than elegant. He denounced the unlucky Hughson as "infamous, inhuman, an arch-rebel against God, his king, and his country,—a devil incarnate," etc. He was ably assisted by eminent counsel for the king,—Joseph Murray, James Alexander, William Smith, and John Chambers. Mary Burton was called again. She swore that Negroes used to go to Hughson's at night, eat and drink, and sometimes buy provisions; that Hughson did swear the Negroes to secrecy in the plot; that she herself had seen seven or eight guns and swords, a bag of shot, and a barrel of gunpowder at Hughson's house; that the prisoner told her he would kill her if she ever revealed any thing she knew or saw; wanted her to swear like the rest, offered her silk gowns, and gold rings,—but none of those tempting things moved the virtuous Mary. Five other witnesses testified that they heard Quack and Cuffee say to Hughson while in jail, "This is what you have brought us to." The Hughsons had no counsel, and but three witnesses. One of them testified that he had lived in Hughson's tavern about three months during the past winter, and had never seen Negroes furnished entertainment there. The two others said that they had never seen any evil in the man nor in his house, etc.

"William Smith, Esq." now took the floor to sum up. He told the jury that it was "black and hellish" to burn the town, and then kill them all; that John Hughson, by his complicity in this crime, had made himself blacker than the Negroes; that the credit of the witnesses was good, and that there was nothing left for them to do but to find the prisoners guilty, as charged in the indictment. The judge charged the jury, that the evidence against the prisoners "is ample, full, clear, and satisfactory. They were found guilty in twenty minutes, and on the 8th of June were brought into court to receive sentence. The judge told them that they were guilty of a terrible crime; that they had not only made Negroes their equals, but superiors, by waiting upon, keeping company with, entertaining them with meat, drink, and lodging; that the most amazing part of their conduct was their part in a plot to burn the town, and murder the inhabitants,—to have consulted with, aided, and abetted the "black seed of Cain," was an unheard of crime,—that although "with uncommon assurance they deny the fact, and call on God, as a witness of their innocence, He, out of his goodness and mercy, has confounded them, and proved their guilt, to the satisfaction of the court and jury." After a further display of forensic eloquence, the judge sentenced them "to be hanged by the neck 'till dead," on Friday, the 12th of June, 1741.

The Negro girl Sarah, referred to above, who was before the jury on the 1st of June in such a terrified state of body and mind, was re-called on the 5th of June. She implicated twenty Negroes, whom she declared were present at the house of Comfort, whetting their knives, and avowing that "they would kill white people." On the 6th of June, Robin, Cæsar, Cook, Cuffee, and Jack, another Cuffee, and Jamaica were arrested, and put upon trial on the 8th of June. It is a sad fact to record, even at this distance, that these poor blacks, without counsel, friends, or money, were tried and convicted upon the evidence of a poor ignorant, hysterical girl, and the "dying confession" of Quack and Cuffee, who "confessed" with the understanding that they should be free! Tried and found guilty on the 8th, without clergy or time to pray, they were burned at the stake the next day! Only Jack found favor with the court, and that favor was purchased by perjury. He was respited until it "was found how well he would deserve further favor." It was next to impossible to understand him, so two white gentlemen were secured to act as interpreters. Jack testified to having seen Negroes at Hughson's tavern; that "when they were eating, he said they began to talk about setting the houses on fire:" he was so good as to give the names of about fourteen Negroes whom he heard say that they would set their masters' houses on fire, and then rush upon the whites and kill them; that at one of these meetings there were five or six Spanish Negroes present, whose conversation he could not understand; that they waited a month and a half for the Spaniards and French to come, but when they came not, set fire to the fort. As usual, more victims of these confessors swelled the number already in the jail; which was, at this time, full to suffocation.

On the 19th of June the lieutenant-governor issued a proclamation of freedom to all who would "confess and discover" before the 1st of July. Several Indians were in the prison, charged with conspiracy. The confessions and discoveries were numerous. Every Negro charged with being an accomplice of the unfortunate wretches that had already perished at the stake began to accuse some one else of complicity in the plot. They all knew of many Negroes who were going to cut the white people's throats with penknives; and when the town was in flames they were to "meet at the end of Broadway, next to the fields!" And it must be recorded, to the everlasting disgrace of the judiciary of New York, that scores of ignorant, helpless, and innocent Negroes—and a few white people too—were convicted upon the confessions of the terror-stricken witnesses! There is not a court to-day in all enlightened Christendom that would accept as evidence—not even circumstantial—the incoherent utterances of these Negro "confessors." And yet an intelligent (?) New-York court thought the evidence "clear (?), and satisfactory!"

But the end was not yet reached. A new turn was to be given to the notorious Mary Burton. The reader will remember that she said that there never were any white persons present when the burning of the town was the topic of conversation, except her master and mistress and Peggy Carey. But on the 25th of June the budding Mary accused Rev. John Ury, a reputed Catholic priest, and a schoolmaster in the town, and one Campbell, also a school-teacher, of having visited Hughson's tavern with the conspirators.

On the 26th of June, nine more Negroes were brought before the court and arraigned. Seven pleaded guilty in the hope of a reprieve: two were tried and convicted upon the testimony of Mary Burton. Eight more were arraigned, and pleaded guilty; followed by seven more, some of whom pleaded guilty, and some not guilty. Thus, in one day, the court was enabled to dispose of twenty-four persons.

On the 27th of June, one Adam confessed that he knew of the plot, but said he was enticed into it by Hughson, three years before; that Hughson told him that he knew a man who could forgive him all his sins. So between John Hughson's warm rum, and John Ury's ability to forgive sin, the virtuous Adam found all his scruples overcome; and he took the oath. A Dr. Hamilton who lodged at Holt's, and the latter also, are brought into court as accused of being connected with the plot. It was charged that Holt directed his Negro Joe to set fire to the play-house at the time he should indicate. At the beginning of the trial only four white persons were mentioned; but now they began to multiply, and barrels of powder to increase at a wonderful rate. The confessions up to this time had been mere repetitions. The arrests were numerous, and the jail crowded beyond its capacity. The poor Negroes implicated were glad of an opportunity to "confess" against some one else, and thereby save their own lives. Recorder Horsemanden says, "Now many negroes began to squeak, in order to lay hold of the benefit of the proclamation." He deserves the thanks of humanity for his frankness! For before the proclamation there were not more than seventy Negroes in jail; but, within eight days after it was issued, thirty more frightened slaves were added to the number. And Judge Horsemanden says, "'Twas difficult to find room for them, nor could we see any likelihood of stopping the impeachments." The Negroes turned to accusing white persons, and seven or eight were arrested. The sanitary condition of the prison now became a subject of grave concern. The judges and lawyers consulted together, and agreed to pardon some of the prisoners to make room in the jail. They also thought it prudent to lump the confessions, and thereby facilitate their work; but the confessions went on, and the jail filled up again.

The Spanish Negroes taken by an English privateer, and adjudged to slavery by the admiralty court, were now taken up, tried, convicted, and sentenced to be hung. Five others received sentence the same day.

The bloody work went on. The poor Negroes in the jail, in a state of morbid desperation, turned upon each other the blistering tongue of accusation. They knew that they were accusing each other innocently,—as many confessed afterwards,—but this was the last straw that these sinking people could see to catch at, and this they did involuntarily. "Victims were required; and those who brought them to the altar of Moloch, purchased their own safety, or, at least, their lives."

On the 2d of July, one Will was produced before Chief-Justice James DeLancy. He plead guilty, and was sentenced to be burnt to death on the 4th of July. On the 6th of July, eleven plead guilty. One Dundee implicates Dr. Hamilton with Hughson in giving Negroes rum and swearing them to the plot. A white man by the name of William Nuill deposed that a Negro—belonging to Edward Kelly, a butcher—named London swore by God that if he should be arrested and cast into the jail, he would hang or burn all the Negroes in New York, guilty or not guilty. On this same day five Negroes were hanged. One of them was "hung in chains" upon the same gibbet with Hughson. And the Christian historian says "the town was amused" on account of a report that Hughson had turned black and the Negro white! The vulgar and sickening description of the condition of the bodies, in which Mr. Horsemanden took evident relish, we withhold from the reader. It was rumored that a Negro doctor had administered poison to the convicts, and hence the change in the bodies after death.

In addition to the burning of the Negro Will, on the 4th of July, was the sensation created by his accusing two white soldiers, Kane and Kelly, with complicity in the conspiracy. Kane was examined the next day: said that he had never been to the house of John Romme; acknowledged that he had received a stolen silver spoon, given to his wife, and sold it to one Van Dype, a silversmith; that he never knew John Ury, etc. Knowing Mary Burton was brought forward,—as she always was when the trials began to lag,—and accused Kane. He earnestly denied the accusation at first, but finally confessed that he was at Hughson's in reference to the plot on two several occasions, but was induced to go there "by Corker, Coffin, and Fagan." After his tongue got limbered up, and his memory refreshed, he criminated Ury. He implicated Hughson's father and three brothers, Hughson's mother-in-law, an old fortune-teller, as being parties to the plot as sworn "to burn, and kill;" that Ury christened some of the Negroes, and even had the temerity to attempt to proselyte him, Kane; that Ury asked him if he could read Latin, could he read English; to both questions he answered no; that the man Coffin read to him, and descanted upon the benefits of being a Roman Catholic; that they could forgive sins, and save him from hell; and that if he had not gone away from their company they might have seduced him to be a Catholic; that one Conolly, on Governor's Island, admitted that he was "bred up a priest;" that one Holt, a dancing-master, also knew of the plot; and then described the mystic ceremony of swearing the plotters. He said, "There was a black ring made on the floor, about a foot and a half in diameter; and Hughson bid every one put off the left shoe and put their toes within the ring; and Mrs. Hughson held a bowl of punch over their heads, as the Negroes stood around the circle, and

Hughson pronounced the oath above mentioned, (something like a freemason's oath and penalties,) and every negro severally repeated the oath after him, and then Hughson's wife fed them with a draught out of the bowl."

This was "new matter," so to speak, and doubtless broke the monotony of the daily recitals to which their honors had been listening all summer. Kane was about to deprive Mary Burton of her honors; and, as he could not write, he made his mark. A peddler named Coffin was arrested and examined. He denied all knowledge of the plot, never saw Hughson, never was at his place, saw him for the first time when he was executed; had never seen Kane but once, and then at Eleanor Waller's, where they drank beer together. But the court committed him. Kane and Mary Burton accused Edward Murphy. Kane charged David Johnson, a hatter, as one of the conspirators; while Mary Burton accuses Andrew Ryase, "little Holt," the dancing-master, John Earl, and seventeen soldiers,—all of whom were cast into prison.

On the 16th of July nine Negroes were arraigned: four plead guilty, two were sentenced to be burnt, and the others to be hanged. On the next day seven Negroes plead guilty. One John Schultz came forward, and made a deposition that perhaps had some little influence on the court and the community at large. He swore that a Negro man slave, named Cambridge, belonging to Christopher Codwise, Esq., did on the 9th of June, 1741, confess to the deponent, in the presence of Codwise and Richard Baker, that the confession he had made before Messrs. Lodge and Nichols was entirely false; viz., that he had confessed himself guilty of participating in the conspiracy; had accused a Negro named Cajoe through fear; that he had heard some Negroes talking together in the jail, and saying that if they did not confess they would be hanged; that what he said about Horsefield Cæsar was a lie; that he had never known in what section of the town Hughson lived, nor did he remember ever hearing his name, until it had become the town talk that Hughson was concerned in a plot to burn the town and murder the inhabitants.

This did not in the least abate the zeal of Mary Burton and William Kane. They went on in their work of accusing white people and Negroes, receiving the approving smiles of the magistrates. Mary Burton says that John Earl, who lived in Broadway, used to come to Hughson's with ten soldiers at a time; that these white men were to command the Negro companies; that John Ury used to be present; and that a man near the Mayor's Market, who kept a shop where she (Mary Burton) got rum from, a doctor, by nationality a Scotchman, who lived by the Slip, and another dancing-master, named Corry, used to meet with the conspirators at Hughson's tavern.

On the 14th of July, John Ury was examined, and denied ever having been at Hughson's, or knowing any thing about the conspiracy; said he never saw any of the Hughsons, nor did he know Peggy Carey. But William Kane, the soldier, insisted that Ury did visit the house of Hughson. Ury was again committed. On the next day eight persons were tried and convicted upon the evidence of Kane and Mary Burton. The jail was filling up again, and the benevolent magistrates pardoned fourteen Negroes. Then they turned their judicial minds to the case of William Kane vs. John Ury. First, he was charged with having counselled, procured, and incited a Negro slave, Quack, to burn the king's house in the fort: to which he pleaded not guilty.

Second, that being a priest, made by the authority of the pretended See of Rome, he had come into the Province and city of New York after the time limited by law against Jesuits and Popish priests, passed in the eleventh year of William III., and had remained for the space of seven months; that he had announced himself to be an ecclesiastical person, made and ordained by the authority of the See of Rome; and that he had appeared so to be by celebrating masses and granting absolution, etc. To these charges Ury pleaded not guilty, and requested a copy of the indictments, but was only allowed a copy of the second; and pen, ink, and paper grudgingly granted him. His private journal was seized, and a portion of its contents used as evidence against him. The following was furnished to the grand jury:—

On the 21st of July, Sarah Hughson, who had been respited, was put on the witness-stand again. There were some legal errors in the indictments against Ury, and his trial was postponed until the next term; but he was arraigned on a new indictment. The energies of the jury and judges received new life. Here was a man who was a Catholic,—or had been a Catholic,—and the spirit of religious intolerance asserted itself. Sarah Hughson remembered having seen Ury at her father's house on several occasions; had seen him make a ring with chalk on the floor, make all the Negroes stand around it, while he himself would stand in the middle, with a cross, and swear the Negroes. This was also "new matter:" nothing of this kind was mentioned in the first confession. But this was not all. She had seen Ury preach to the Negroes, forgive their sins, and baptize some of them! She said that Ury wanted her to confess to him, and that Peggy confessed to him in French.

On the 24th of July, Elias Desbroses, confectioner, being called, swore that Ury had come to his shop with one Webb, a carpenter, and inquired for sugar-bits, or wafers, and asked him "whether a minister had not his wafers of him? or, whether that paste, which the deponent showed him, was not made of the same ingredients as the Luthern minister's?" or words to that effect: the deponent told Ury that if he desired such things a joiner would make him a mould; and that when he asked him whether he had a congregation, Ury "waived giving him an answer."

On the 27th of July, Mr. Webb, the carpenter, was called to the witness-stand and testified as follows: That he had met Ury at John Croker's (at the Fighting Cocks), where he became acquainted with him; that he had heard him read Latin and English so admirably that he employed him to teach his child; that finding out that he was a school-teacher, he invited him to board at his house without charge; that he understood from him that he was a non-juring minister, had written a book that had drawn the fire of the Church, was charged with treason, and driven out of England, sustaining the loss of "a living" worth fifty pounds a year; that on religious matters the deponent could not always comprehend him; that the accused said Negroes were only fit for slaves, and to put them above that condition was to invite them to cut your throats. The observing Horsemanden was so much pleased with the above declaration, that he gives Ury credit in a footnote for understanding the dispositions of Negroes! Farther on Mr. Webb says, that, after one Campbell removed to Hughson's, Ury went thither, and so did the deponent on three different times, and heard him read prayers after the manner of the Church of England; but in the prayer for the king he only mentioned "our sovereign lord the King," and not

"King George." He said that Ury pleaded against drunkenness, debauchery, and Deists; that he admonished every one to keep his own minister; that when the third sermon was delivered one Mr. Hildreth was present, when Ury found fault with certain doctrines, insisted that good works as well as faith were necessary to salvation; that he announced that on a certain evening he would preach from the text, "Upon this rock I will build my church, and the gates of hell shall not prevail against it; and whosoever sins ye remit, they are remitted, and whosoever sins ye retain, they are retained."

The judges, delighted with this flavor added to the usually dry proceedings, thought they had better call Sarah Hughson; that if she were grateful for her freedom she would furnish the testimony their honors desired. Sarah was accordingly called. She is recommended for mercy. She is, of course, to say what is put in her mouth, to give testimony such as the court desires. So the fate of the poor schoolmaster was placed in the keeping of the fateful Sarah.

On the 28th of July another grand jury was sworn, and, like the old one, was composed of merchants. The following persons composed it: Joseph Robinson, James Livingston, Hermanus Rutgers, jun., Charles LeRoux, Abraham Boelen, Peter Rutgers, Jacobus Roosevelt, John Auboyneau, Stephen Van Courtlandt, jun., Abraham Lynsen, Gerardus Duyckinck, John Provost, Henry Lane, jun., Henry Cuyler, John Roosevelt, Abraham DePeyster, Edward Hicks, Joseph Ryall, Peter Schuyler, and Peter Jay.

Sarah Hughson had been pardoned. John Ury was brought into court, when he challenged some of the jury. William Hammersley, Gerardus Beekman, John Shurmur, Sidney Breese, Daniel Shatford, Thomas Behenna, Peter Fresneau, Thomas Willett, John Breese, John Hastier, James Tucker, and Brandt Schuyler were sworn to try him. Barring formalities, he was arraigned upon the old indictment; viz., felony, in inciting and exciting the Negro slave Quack to set fire to the governor's house. The king's counsel were the attorney-general, Richard Bradley, and Messrs. Murray, Alexander, Smith, and Chambers. Poor Ury had no counsel, no sympathizers. The attorney-general, in an opening speech to the jury, said that certain evidence was to be produced showing that the prisoner at the bar was guilty as charged in the indictment; that he had a letter that he desired to read to them, which had been sent to Lieut.-Gov. Clark, written by Gen. Oglethorpe ("the visionary Lycurgus of Georgia"), bearing date of the 16th of May. The following is a choice passage from the letter referred to:—

The burden of his effort was the wickedness of Popery and the Roman-Catholic Church. The first witness called was the irrepressible Mary Burton. She began by rehearsing the old story of setting fire to the houses: but this time she varied it somewhat; it was not the fort that was to be burnt first, but Croker's, near a coffee-house, by the long bridge. She remembered the ring drawn with chalk, saw things in it that looked like rats (the good Horsemanden throws a flood of light upon this otherwise dark passage by telling his reader that it was the Negroes' black toes!); that she peeped in once and saw a black thing like a child, and Ury with a book in his hand, and at this moment she let a silver spoon drop, and Ury chased her, and would have caught her, had she not fallen into a bucket of water, and thus marvellously escaped! But the rule was to send this curious Mary to bed when any thing of an unusual nature was going on. Ury asked her some questions.

    She then says several kinds, but particularly, or chiefly, a riding-coat, and often a brown coat, trimmed with black.

    William Kane, the soldier, took the stand. He was very bold to answer all of Ury's questions. He saw him baptize a child, could forgive sins, and wanted to convert him! Sarah Hughson was next called, but Ury objected to her because she had been convicted. The judge informed him that she had been pardoned, and was, therefore, competent as a witness. Judge Horsemanden was careful to produce newspaper scraps to prove that the court of France had endeavored to create and excite revolts and insurrections in the English colonies, and ended by telling a pathetic story about an Irish schoolmaster in Ulster County who drank the health of the king of Spain! This had great weight with the jury, no doubt. Poor Ury, convicted upon the evidence of three notorious liars, without counsel, was left to defend himself. He addressed the jury in an earnest and intelligent manner. He showed where the evidence clashed; that the charges were not in harmony with his previous character, the silence of Quack and others already executed. He showed that Mr. Campbell took possession of the house that Hughson had occupied, on the 1st of May; that at that time Hughson and his wife were in jail, and Sarah in the house; that Sarah abused Campbell, and that he reproved her for the foul language she used; and that this furnished her with an additional motive to accuse him; that he never knew Hughson or any of the family. Mr. John Croker testified that Ury never kept company with Negroes, nor did he receive them at Croker's house up to the 1st of May, for all the plotting was done before that date; that he was a quiet, pious preacher, and an excellent schoolmaster; that he taught Webb's child, and always declared himself a non-juring clergyman of the Church of England. But the fatal revelation of this friend of Ury's was, that Webb made him a desk; and the jury thought they saw in it an altar for a Catholic priest! That was enough. The attorney-general told the jury that the prisoner was a Romish priest, and then proceeded to prove the exceeding sinfulness of that Church. Acknowledging the paucity of the evidence intended to prove him a priest, the learned gentleman hastened to dilate upon all the dark deeds of Rome, and thereby poisoned the minds of the jury against the unfortunate Ury. He was found guilty, and on the 29th of August, 1741, was hanged, professing his innocence, and submitting cheerfully to a cruel and unjust death as a servant of the Lord.

    The trials of the Negroes had continued, but were somewhat overshadowed by that of the reputed Catholic priest. On the 18th of July seven Negroes were hanged, including a Negro doctor named Harry. On the 23d of July a number of white persons were fined for keeping disorderly houses,—entertaining Negroes; while nine Negroes were, the same day, released from jail on account of a lack of evidence! On the 15th of August a Spanish Negro was hanged. On the 31st of August, Corry (the dancing-master), Ryan, Kelly, and Coffin—all white persons—were dismissed because no one prosecuted; while the reader must have observed that the evidence against them was quite as strong as that offered against any of the persons executed, by the lying trio Burton, Kane, and Sarah. But Mr. Smith the historian gives the correct reason why these trials came to such a sudden end.

The 24th of September was solemnly set apart for public thanksgiving for the escape of the citizens from destruction!

As we have already said, this "Negro plot" has but one parallel in the history of civilization. It had its origin in a diseased public conscience, inflamed by religious bigotry, accelerated by hired liars, and consummated in the blind and bloody action of a court and jury who imagined themselves sitting over a powder-magazine. That a robbery took place, there was abundant evidence in the finding of some of the articles, and the admissions of Hughson and others; but there was not a syllable of competent evidence to show that there was an organized plot. And the time came, after the city had gotten back to its accustomed quietness, that the most sincere believers in the "Negro plot" were converted to the opinion that the zeal of the magistrates had not been "according to knowledge." For they could not have failed to remember that the Negroes were considered heathen, and, therefore, not sworn by the court; that they were not allowed counsel; that the evidence was indirect, contradictory, and malicious, while the trials were hasty and unfair. From the 11th of May to the 29th of August, one hundred and fifty-four Negroes were cast into prison; fourteen of whom were burnt, eighteen hanged, seventy-one transported, and the remainder pardoned. During the same space of time twenty-four whites were committed to prison; four of whom were executed, and the remainder discharged. The number arrested was one hundred and seventy-eight, thirty-six executed, and seventy-one transported! What a terrible tragedy committed in the name of law and Christian government! Mary Burton, the Judas Iscariot of the period, received her hundred pounds as the price of the blood she had caused to be shed; and the curtain fell upon one of the most tragic events in all the history of New York or of the civilized world.

The legislature turned its attention to additional legislation upon the slavery question. Severe laws were passed against the Negroes. Their personal rights were curtailed until their condition was but little removed from that of the brute creation. We have gone over the voluminous records of the Province of New York, and have not found a single act calculated to ameliorate the condition of the slave. He was hated, mistrusted, and feared. Nothing was done, of a friendly character, for the slave in the Province of New York, until threatening dangers from without taught the colonists the importance of husbanding all their resources. The war between the British colonies in North America and the mother country gave the Negro an opportunity to level, by desperate valor, a mountain of prejudice, and wipe out with his blood the dark stain of 1741. History says he did it.

FOOTNOTES:

Brodhead's History of New York, vol. i. p. 184.
O'Callaghan's History of New Netherlands, pp. 384, 385.
Brodhead, vol. i. p. 194.
Ibid, vol. i. pp. 196, 197.
Dunlap's History of New York, vol. i. p, 58.
O'Callaghan, p. 385.
Van Tienhoven.
Hildreth, vol. i. p. 441; also Hol. Doc., III. p. 351.
Annals of Albany, vol. ii. pp. 55-60.
O'Callaghan, p. 353. N.Y. Col. Docs., vol. ii, pp. 368, 369.
Brodhead, vol. i. p. 697.
Brodhead, vol. i. p. 746.
Ibid., vol. i. p. 748.
Valentine's Manual for 1861, pp. 640-664.
New York Hist. Coll., vol. i. pp. 322, 323.
Journals of Legislative Council, vol. i. p xii.
Bradford's Laws, p. 125.
Journals, etc., N.Y., vol. i. p. xiii.
Dunlap's Hist, of N.Y., vol. i. p. 260,
Booth's Hist, of N.Y., vol. i. p, 270-272.

On the 22nd of March, 1680, the following proclamation was issued: "Whereas, several inhabitants within this city have and doe dayly harbour, entertain and countenance Indian and neger slaves in their houses, and to them sell and deliver wine, rum, and other strong liquors, for which they receive money or goods which by the said Indian and negro slaves is pilfered, purloyned, and stolen from their several masters, by which the publick peace is broken, and the damage of the master is produced, etc., therefore they are prohibited, etc.; and if neger or Indian slave make application for these forbidden articles, immediate information is to be given to his master or to the mayor or oldest alderman."—Dunlap, vol. ii. Appendix, p. cxxviii.

Bradford Laws, p. 81.

The ordinance referred to was re-enacted on the 22d of April, 1731, and reads as follows: "No Negro, Mulatto, or Indian slave, above the age of fourteen, shall presume to appear in any of the streets, or in any other place of this city on the south side of Fresh Water, in the night time, above an hour after sunset, without a lanthorn and candle in it (unless in company with his owner or some white belonging to the family). Penalty, the watch-house that night; next day, prison, until the owner pays 4s, and before discharge, the slave to be whipped not exceeding forty lashes."—Dunlap, vol. ii. Appendix, p. clxiii.

Booth, vol. i. p. 271.
Hurd's Bondage and Freedom, vol. i. p. 281.

Dunlap, vol. i. p. 323.
Judge Daniel Horsemanden.
Hume, vol. vi. pp. 171-212.
Ibid., vol. vi. p. 171.
Horsemanden's Negro Plot, p. 29.

As far back as 1684 the following was passed against the entertainment of slaves: "No person to countenance or entertain any negro or Indian slave, or sell or deliver to them any strong liquor, without liberty from his master, or receive from them any money or goods; but, upon any offer made by a slave, to reveal the same to the owner, or to the mayor, under penalty of £5."—

Dunlap, vol. ii. Appendix, p. cxxxiii.
Horsemanden's Negro Plot, p. 33.
Bradford's Laws, pp. 141-144.
Horsemanden's Negro Plot, p. 60.

The city of Now York was divided into parts at that time, and comprised two militia districts.

Dunlap, vol. i. p. 344.
Horsemanden's Negro Plot, p. 284.
Horsemanden's Negro Plot, p. 286.
Colonial Hist. of N.Y., vol. vi. p. 199.
Horsemanden's Negro Plot, pp. 292, 293.
Ibid., pp. 298, 299, note.
Horsemanden's Negro Plot, pp. 221, 222.
Smith's Hist. of N.Y., vol. ii. pp. 59, 60.

"On the 6th of March, 1742, the following order was passed by the Common Council: 'Ordered, that the indentures of Mary Burton be delivered up to her, and that she be discharged from the remainder of her servitude, and three pounds paid her, to provide necessary clothing.' The Common Council had purchased her indentures from her master, and had kept her and them, until this time."—Dunlap, vol. ii. Appendix, p. clxvii.

"On the 17th of November, 1767, a bill was brought into the House of Assembly "to prevent the unnatural and unwarrantable custom of enslaving mankind, and the importation of slaves into this province." It was changed into an act "for laying an impost on Negroes imported." This could not pass the governor and council; and it was afterward known that Benning I. Wentworth, the governor of New Hampshire, had received instructions not to pass any law "imposing duties on negroes imported into that province." Hutchinson of Massachusetts had similar instructions. The governor and his Majesty's council knew this at the time.

CHAPTER XIV.: THE COLONY OF MASSACHUSETTS.: 1633-1775.

The Earliest Mentions of Negroes in Massachusetts.—Pequod Indians exchanged for Negroes.—Voyage of the Slave-Ship "Desire" in 1638.—Fundamental Laws adopted.—Hereditary Slavery.—Kidnapping Negroes.—Growth of Slavery in the Seventeenth Century.—Taxation of Slaves.—Introduction of Indian Slaves prohibited.—The Position of the Church respecting the Baptism of Slaves.—Slave Marriage.—Condition of Free Negroes.—Phillis Wheatley the African Poetess.—Her Life.—Slavery recognized in England in Order to be maintained in the Colonies.—The Emancipation of Slaves.—Legislation favoring the Importation of White Servants, but prohibiting the Clandestine Bringing-in of Negroes.—Judge Sewall's Attack on Slavery.—Judge Saffin's Reply to Judge Sewall.

HAD the men who gave the colony of Massachusetts its political being and Revolutionary fame known that the Negro—so early introduced into the colony as a slave—would have been in the future Republic for years the insoluble problem, and at last the subject of so great and grave economic and political concern, they would have committed to the jealous keeping of the chroniclers of their times the records for which the historian of the Negro seeks so vainly in this period. Stolen as he was from his tropical home; consigned to a servitude at war with man's intellectual and spiritual, as well as with his physical, nature; the very lowest of God's creation, in the estimation of the Roundheads of New England; a stranger in a strange land,—the poor Negro of Massachusetts found no place in the sympathy or history of the Puritan,—Christians whose deeds and memory have been embalmed in song and story, and given to an immortality equalled only by the indestructibility of the English language. The records of the most remote period of colonial history have preserved a silence on the question of Negro slavery as ominous as it is conspicuous. What data there are concerning the introduction of slavery are fragmentary, uncertain, and unsatisfactory, to say the least. There is but one work bearing the luminous stamp of historical trustworthiness, and which turns a flood of light on the dark records of the darker crime of human slavery in Massachusetts. And we are sure it is as complete as the ripe scholarship, patient research, and fair and fearless spirit of its author, could make it.

The earliest mention of the presence of Negroes in Massachusetts is in connection with an account of some Indians who were frightened at a Colored man who had lost his way in the tangled path of the forest. The Indians, it seems, were "worse scared than hurt, who seeing a blackamore in the top of a tree looking out for his way which he had lost, surmised he was Abamacho, or the devil; deeming all devils that are blacker than themselves: and being near to the plantation, they posted to the English, and entreated their aid to conjure this devil to his own place, who finding him to be a poor wandering blackamore, conducted him to his master." This was in 1633. It is circumstantial evidence of a twofold nature; i.e., it proves that there were Negroes in the colony at a date much earlier than can be fixed by reliable data, and that the Negroes were slaves. It is a fair presumption that this "wandering blackamore" who was conducted "to his master" was not the only Negro slave in the colony. Slaves generally come in large numbers, and consequently there must have been quite a number at this time.

Negro slavery in Massachusetts was the safety-valve to the pent-up vengeance of the Pequod Indians. Slavery would have been established in Massachusetts, even if there had been no Indians to punish by war, captivity, and duplicity. Encouraged by the British authorities, avarice and gain would have quieted the consciences of Puritan slave-holders. But the Pequod war was the early and urgent occasion for the founding of slavery under the foster care of a free church and free government! As the Pequod Indians would "not endure the yoke," would not remain "as servants," they were sent to Bermudas and exchanged for Negroes, with the hope that the latter would "endure the yoke" more patiently. The first importation of slaves from Barbados, secured in exchange for Indians, was made in 1637, the first year of the Pequod war, and was doubtless kept up for many years.

But in the following year we have the most positive evidence that New England had actually engaged in the slave-trade.

"The Desire" was built at Marblehead in 1636; was of one hundred and twenty tons, and perhaps one of the first built in the colony. There is no positive proof that "The Mayflower," after landing the holy Pilgrim Fathers, was fitted out for a slave-cruise! But there is no evidence to destroy the belief that "The Desire" was built for the slave-trade. Within a few years from the time of the building of "The Desire," there were quite a number of Negro slaves in Massachusetts. "John Josselyn, Gen't" in his "Two Voyages to New England," made in "1638, 1663," and printed for the first time in 1674, gives an account of an attempt to breed slaves in Massachusetts.

It would appear, at first blush, that slavery was an individual speculation in the colony; but the voyage of the ship "Desire" was evidently made with a view of securing Negro slaves for sale. Josselyn says, in 1627, that the English colony on the Island of Barbados had "in a short time increased to twenty thousand, besides Negroes." And in 1637 he says that the New Englanders "sent the male children of Pequets to the Bermudus." It is quite likely that many individuals of large means and estates had a few Negro slaves quite early,—perhaps earlier than we have any record; but as a public enterprise in which the colony was interested, slavery began as early as 1638. "It will be observed," says Dr. Moore, "that this first entrance into the slave-trade was not a private, individual speculation. It was the enterprise of the authorities of the colony. And on the 13th of March, 1639, it was ordered by the General Court "that 3l 8s should be paid Lieftenant Davenport for the present, for charge disbursed for the slaves, which, when they have earned it, hee is to repay it back againe." The marginal note is "Lieft. Davenport to keep ye slaves." (Mass. Rec. i. 253.) So there can be no doubt as to the permanent establishment of the institution of slavery as early as 1639, while before that date the institution existed in a patriarchal condition. But there isn't the least fragment of history to sustain the haphazard statement of Emory Washburn, that slavery existed in Massachusetts "from the time Maverick was found dwelling on Noddle's Island in 1630." We are sure this assertion lacks the authority of historical data. It is one thing for a historian to think certain events happened at a particular time, but it is quite another thing to be able to cite reliable authority in proof of the assertion. But no doubt Mr. Washburn relies upon Mr. Palfrey, who refers his reader to Mr. Josselyn. Palfrey says, "Before Winthrop's arrival, there were two negro slaves in Massachusetts, held by Mr. Maverick, on Noddle's Island." Josselyn gives the only account we have of the slaves on Noddle's Island. The incident that gave rise to this scrap of history occurred on the 2d of October, 1639. Winthrop was chosen governor in the year 1637. It was in this year, on the 26th of February, that the slave-ship "Desire" landed a cargo of Negroes in the colony. Now, if Mr. Palfrey relies upon Josselyn for the historical trustworthiness of his statement that there were two Negroes in Massachusetts before Winthrop arrived, he has made a mistake. There is no proof for the assertion. That there were three Negroes on Noddle's Island, we have the authority of Josselyn, but nothing more. And if the Negro queen who kicked Josselyn's man out of bed had been as long in the island as Palfrey and Washburn indicate, she would have been able to explain her grief to Josselyn in English. We have no doubt but what Mr. Maverick got his slaves from the ship "Desire" in 1638, the same year Winthrop was inaugurated governor.

In Massachusetts, as in the other colonies, slavery made its way into individual families first; thence into communities, where it was clothed with the garment of usage and custom; and, finally, men longing to enjoy the fruit of unrequited labor gave it the sanction of statutory law. There was not so great a demand for slaves in Massachusetts as in the Southern States; and yet they had their uses in a domestic way, and were, consequently, sought after. As early as 1641 Massachusetts adopted a body of fundamental laws. The magistrates, armed with authority from the crown of Great Britain, had long exercised a power which well-nigh trenched upon the personal rights of the people. The latter desired a revision of the laws, and such modifications of the power and discretion of the magistrates as would be in sympathy with the spirit of personal liberty that pervaded the minds of the colonists. But while the people sought to wrest an arbitrary power from the unwilling hands of their judges, they found no pity in their hearts for the poor Negroes in their midst, who, having served as slaves because of their numerical weakness and the passive silence of justice, were now to become the legal and statutory vassals—for their life-time—of a liberty-loving and liberty-seeking people! In the famous "Body of Liberties" is to be found the first statute establishing slavery in the United States. It is as follows:—

We have omitted the old spelling, but none of the words, as they appeared in the original manuscript. There isn't the shadow of a doubt but what this law has been preserved inviolate.

There has been considerable discussion about the real bearing of this statute. Many zealous historians, in discussing it, have betrayed more zeal for the good name of the Commonwealth than for the truth of history. Able lawyers—and some of them still survive—have maintained, with a greater show of learning than of facts, that this statute abolished slavery in Massachusetts. But, on the other hand, there are countless lawyers who pronounce it a plain and unmistakable law, "creating and establishing slavery." An examination of the statute will help the reader to a clear understanding of it. To begin with, this law received its being from the existent fact of slavery in the colony. From the practice of a few holding Negroes as slaves, it became general and prodigious. Its presence in society called for lawful regulations concerning it. While it is solemnly declared "that there shall never be any bond slavery, villianage, or captivity" in the colony, there were three provisos; viz., "lawful captives taken in just wares," those who would "sell themselves or are sold to us," and such as "shall be judged thereto by authority." Under the foregoing conditions slavery was plainly established in Massachusetts. The "just wares" were the wars against the Pequod Indians. That these were made prisoners and slaves, we have the universal testimony of all writers on the history of Massachusetts. Just what class of people would "sell themselves" into slavery we are at a loss to know! We can, however, understand the meaning of the words, "or are sold to us." This was an open door for the traffic in human beings; for it made it lawful for to sell slaves to the colonists, and lawful for the latter to purchase them. Those who were "judged thereto by authority" were those in slavery already and such as should come into the colony by shipping.

This statute is wide enough to drive a load of hay through. It is not the work of a novice, but the labored and skilful product of great law learning.

The subject had been carefully weighed; and, lacking authority for legalizing a crime against man, the Mosaic code was cited, and in accordance with its humane provisions, slaves were to be treated. But it was authority for slavery that the cunning lawyer who drew the statute was seeking, and not precedents to determine the kind of treatment to be bestowed upon the slave. Under it "human slavery existed for nearly a century and a half without serious challenge;" and here, as well as in Virginia, it received the sanction of the Church and courts. It grew with its growth, and strengthened with its strength; until, as an organic institution, it had many defenders and few apologists.

And it is rather strange, in the light of this plain statute establishing and legalizing the purchase of slaves, that Mr. Washburn's statement, unsustained, should receive the public indorsement of so learned a body as the Massachusetts Historical Society!

No doubt Massachusetts was "inconsistent" in seeking liberty for her white citizens while forging legal chains for the Negro. And how far the colony "felt free to follow its own inclinations" Chief-Justice Parsons declares from the bench. Says that eminent jurist,—

So here we find an eminent authority declaring that slavery followed hard upon the heels of the Pilgrim Fathers, "and was tolerated" until 1780. Massachusetts "felt free" to tear from the iron grasp of the imperious magistrates the liberties of the people, but doubtless felt not "free" enough to blot out "the crime and folly of an evil time." And yet for years lawyers and clergymen, orators and statesmen, historians and critics, have stubbornly maintained, that, while slavery did creep into the colony, and did exist, it was "not probably by force of any law, for none such is found or known to exist."(?)

Slavery having been firmly established in Massachusetts, the next step was to make it hereditary. This was done under the sanction of the highest and most solemn forms of the courts of law. It is not our purpose to give this subject the attention it merits, in this place; but in a subsequent chapter it will receive due attention. We will, however, say in passing, that it was the opinion of many lawyers in the last century, some of whom served upon the bench in Massachusetts, that children followed the condition of their mothers. Chief-Justice Parsons held that "the issue of the female slave, according to the maxim of the civil law, was the property of her master." And, subsequently, Chief-Justice Parker rendered the following opinion:—

This decision is strengthened by the statement of Kendall in reference to the wide-spread desire of Negro slaves to secure free Indian wives, in order to insure the freedom of their children. He says,—

We refer the reader, with perfect confidence, to our friend Dr. George H. Moore, who, in his treatment of this particular feature of slavery in Massachusetts, has, with great research, put down a number of zealous friends of the colony who have denied, with great emphasis, that any child was ever born into slavery there. Neither the opinion of Chief-Justice Dana, nor the naked and barren assertions of historians Palfrey, Sumner, and Washburn,—great though the men were,—can dispose of the historical reality of hereditary slavery in Massachusetts, down to the adoption of the Constitution of 1780.

The General Court of Massachusetts issued an order in 1645 for the return of certain kidnapped or stolen Negroes to their native country. It has been variously commented upon by historians and orators. The story runs, that a number of ships, plying between New-England seaport towns and Madeira and the Canaries, made it their custom to call on the coast of Guinea "to trade for negroes." Thus secured, they were disposed of in the slave-markets of Barbadoes and the West Indies. The New-England slave-market did not demand a large supply. Situated on a cold, bleak, and almost sterile coast, Massachusetts lacked the conditions to make slave-trading as lucrative as the Southern States; but, nevertheless, she disposed of quite a number, as the reader will observe when we examine the first census. A ship from the town of Boston consorted with "some Londoners" with the object of gaining slaves. Mr. Bancroft says that "upon the Lord's day, invited the natives aboard one of their ships," and then made prisoners of such as came; which is not mentioned by Hildreth. The latter writer says, that "on pretence of some quarrel with the natives," landed a small cannon called a "murderer," attacked the village on Sunday; and having burned the village, and killed many, made a few prisoners. Several of these prisoners fell to the Boston ship. On account of a disagreement between the captain and under officers of the ship, as well as the owners, the story of the above affair was detailed before a Boston court. Richard Saltonstall was one of the magistrates before whom the case was tried. He was moved by the recital of the cruel wrong done the Africans, and therefore presented a petition to the court, charging the captain and mate with the threefold crime of "murder," "man-stealing," and "sabbath-breaking."

It seems that by the Fundamental Laws, adopted by the people in 1641, the first two offences were punishable by death, and all of them "capitall, by the law of God." The court doubted its jurisdiction over crimes committed on the distant coast of Guinea. But article ninety-one of "The Body of Liberties" determined who were lawful slaves,—those who sold themselves or were sold, "lawful captives taken in just wares," and those "judged thereto by authority." Had the unfortunate Negroes been purchased, there was no law in Massachusetts to free them from their owners; but having been kidnapped, unlawfully obtained, the court felt that it was its plain duty to bear witness against the "sin of man-stealing." For, in the laws adopted in 1641, among the "Capital Laws," at the latter part of article ninety-four is the following: "If any man stealeth a man, or mankind, he shall surely be put to death." There is a marginal reference to Exod. xxi. 16.

Dr. Moore does not refer to this in his elaborate discussion of statute on "bond slavery." And Winthrop says that the magistrates decided that the Negroes, "having been procured not honestly by purchase, but by the unlawful act of kidnaping," should be returned to their native country. That there was a criminal code in the colony, there can be no doubt; but we have searched for it in vain. Hildreth says it was printed in 1649, but that there is now no copy extant.

The court issued an order about the return of the kidnapped Negroes, which we will give in full, on account of its historical value, and because of the difference of opinion concerning it.

This "protest against man-stealing" has adorned and flavored many an oration on the "position of Massachusetts" on the slavery question. It has been brought out "to point a moral and adorn a tale" by the proud friends of the Commonwealth; but the law quoted above against "man-stealing," the language of the "protest," the statute on "bond servitude," and the practices of the colonists for many years afterwards, prove that many have gloried, but not according to the truth. When it came to the question of damages, the court said: "For the negars (they being none of his, but stolen) we thinke meete to allow nothing."

So the decision of the court was based upon law,—the prohibition against "man-stealing." And it should not be forgotten that many of the laws of the colony were modelled after the Mosaic code. It is referred to, apologetically, in the statute of 1641; and no careful student can fail to read between the lines the desire there expressed to refer to the Old Testament as authority for slavery. Now, slaves were purchased by Abraham, and the New-England "doctors of the law" were unwilling to have slaves stolen when they could be bought so easily. Dr. Moore says, in reference to the decision,—

And Dr. Moore is not alone in his opinion; for Mr. Hildreth says this case "in which Saltonstall was concerned has been magnified by too precipitate an admiration into a protest on the part of Massachusetts against the African slave-trade. So far, however, from any such protest being made, at the very birth of the foreign commerce of New England the African slave-trade became a regular business." There is now, therefore, no room to doubt but what the decision was rendered on a technical point of law, and not inspired by an anti-slavery sentiment.

As an institution, slavery had at first a stunted growth in Massachusetts, and did not increase its victims to any great extent until near the close of the seventeenth century. But when it did begin a perceptible growth, it made rapid and prodigious strides. In 1676 there were about two hundred slaves in the colony, and they were chiefly from Guinea and Madagascar. In 1680 Gov. Bradstreet, in compliance with a request made by the home government, said that the slave-trade was not carried on to any great extent. They were introduced in small lots, and brought from ten to forty pounds apiece. He thought the entire number in the colony would not reach more than one hundred and twenty-five. Few were born in the colony, and none had been baptized up to that time. The year 1700 witnessed an unprecedented growth in the slave-trade. From the 24th of January, 1698, to the 25th of December, 1707, two hundred Negroes were imported into the colony,—quite as many as in the previous sixty years. In 1708 Gov. Dudley's report to the board of trade fixed the number of Negroes at five hundred and fifty, and suggested that they were not so desirable as white servants, who could be used in the army, and in time of peace turn their attention to planting. The prohibition against the Negro politically and in a military sense, in that section of the country, made him almost valueless to the colonial government struggling for deliverance from the cruel laws of the mother country. The white servant could join the "minute-men," plough with his gun on his back, go to the church, and, having received the blessing of the parish minister, could hasten to battle with the proud and almost boastful feelings of a Christian freeman! But the Negro, bond and free, was excluded from all these sacred privileges. Wronged, robbed of his freedom,—the heritage of all human kind,—he was suspicioned and contemned for desiring that great boon. On the 17th of February, 1720, Gov. Shute placed the number of slaves—including a few Indians—in Massachusetts at two thousand. During the same year thirty-seven males and sixteen females were imported into the colony. We are unable to discover whether these were counted in the enumeration furnished by Gov. Shute or not. We are inclined to think they were included. In 1735 there were two thousand six hundred bond and free in the colony; and within the next seventeen years the Negro population of Boston alone reached 1,541.

In 1754 the colonial government found it necessary to establish a system of taxation. Gov. Shirley was required to inform the House of Representatives as to the different kinds of taxable property. And from a clause in his message, Nov. 19, 1754, on the one hundred and nineteenth page of the Journal, we infer two things; viz., that slaves were chattels or real estate, and, therefore, taxable. The governor says, "There is one part of the Estate, viz., the Negro slaves, which I am at a loss how to come at the knowledge of, without your assistance." In accordance with the request for assistance on this matter, the Legislature instructed the assessors of each town and district within the colony to secure a correct list of all Negro slaves, male and female, from sixteen years old and upwards, to be deposited in the office of the secretary of state. The result of this enumeration was rather surprising; as it fixed the Negro population at 4,489,—quite an increase over the last enumeration. Again, in 1764-65, another census of the Negroes was taken; and they were found to be 5,779.

Here, as in Virginia, an impost tax was imposed upon all Negro slaves imported into the colony. We will quote section 3 of the Act of October, 1705, requiring duty upon imported Negroes; because many are disposed to discredit some historical statements about slavery in Massachusetts.

A fine of eight pounds was imposed upon any person refusing or neglecting to make a proper entry of each slave imported, in the "Impost Office." If a Negro died within six weeks after his arrival, a drawback was allowed. If any slave was sold again into another Province or plantation within a year after his arrival, a drawback was allowed to the person who paid the impost duty. A subsequent and more stringent law shows that there was no desire to abate the traffic. In August, 1712, a law was passed "prohibiting the importation or bringing into the province any Indian servants or slaves;" but it was only intended as a check upon the introduction of the Tuscaroras and other "revengeful" Indians from South Carolina. Desperate Indians and insubordinate Negroes were the occasion of grave fears on the part of the colonists. Many Indians had been cruelly dealt with in war; in peace, enslaved and wronged beyond their power of endurance. Their stoical nature led them to the performance of desperate deeds. There is kinship in suffering. There is an unspoken language in sorrow that binds hearts in the indissoluble fellowship of resolve. Whatever natural and national differences existed between the Indian and the Negro—one from the bleak coasts of New England, the other from the tropical coast of Guinea—were lost in the commonality of degradation and interest. The more heroic spirits of both races began to grow restive under the yoke. The colonists were not slow to observe this, and hence this law was to act as a restraint upon and against "their rebellion and hostilities." And the reader should understand that it was not an anti-slavery measure. It was not "hostile to slavery" as a system: it was but the precaution of a guilty and ever-gnawing public conscience.

Slavery grew. There was no legal obstacle in its way. It had the sanction of the law, as we have already shown, and what was better still, the sympathy of public sentiment. The traffic in slaves appears to have been more an object in Boston than at any period before or since. For a time dealers had no hesitation in advertising them for sale in their own names. At length a very few who advertised would refer purchasers to "inquire of the printer, and know further." This was in 1727, fifteen years after the afore-mentioned Act became a law, and which many apologists would interpret as a specific and direct prohibition against slavery; but there is no reason for such a perversion of so plain an Act.

Slavery in Massachusetts, as elsewhere, in self-defence had to claim as one of its necessary and fundamental principles, that the slave was either naturally inferior to the other races, or that, by some fundamentally inherent law in the institution itself, the master was justified in placing the lowest possible estimate upon his slave property. "Property" implied absolute control over the thing possessed. It carried in its broad meaning the awful fact, not alone of ownership, but of the supremacy of the will of the owner. Mr. Addison says,—

None whatever! And yet the Puritans put the Negro slaves in their colony on a level with "horses and hogs." Let the intelligent American of to-day read the following remarkable note from Judge Sewall's diary, and then confess that facts are stranger than fiction.

It had been sent to the deputies, and was by them rejected, and then returned to the judge by Col. Thaxter. The House was "just going to make a New Valuation" of the property in the colony, and hence did not care to exclude slaves from the list of chattels, in which they had always been placed.

On the 22d of April, 1728, the following notice appeared in a Boston newspaper:—

So the "likely Negro girls" were mixed up in the sale of "women's stays" and "hoop-coats"! It was bad enough to "rate Negroes with Horses and Hogs," but to sell them with second-hand clothing was an incident in which is to be seen the low depth to which slavery had carried the Negro by its cruel weight. A human being could be sold like a cast-off garment, and pass without a bill of sale. The announcement that a "likely Negro woman about nineteen years and a child about six months of age to be sold together or apart" did not shock the Christian sensibilities of the people of Massachusetts. A babe six months old could be torn from the withered and famishing bosom of the young mother, and sold with other articles of merchandise. How bitter and how cruel was such a separation, mothers only can know; and how completely lost a community and government are that regard with complacency a hardship so diabolical, the

Christians of America must be able to judge.

The Church has done many cruel things in the name of Christianity. In the dark ages it filled the minds of its disciples with fear, and their bodies with the pains of penance. It burned Michael Servetus, and it strangled the scientific opinions of Galileo. And in stalwart old Massachusetts it thought it was doing God's service in denying the Negro slave the right of Christian baptism."

On the 25th of October, 1727, Matthias Plant wrote, in answer to certain questions put to him by "the secretary of the Society for the Propagation of the Gospel," as follows:—

It was nothing to her master that she was "desirous of baptism," "of wonderful sense," "prudent in matters," and "of equal knowledge in religion with most of her sex!" She was a Negro slave, and as such was denied the blessings of the Christian Church.

And those who were so fortunate as to secure baptism were not freed thereby. In Massachusetts no Negro ever had the courage to seek his freedom through this door, and, therefore, there was no necessity for legislation there to define the question, but in the Southern colonies the law declared that baptism did not secure the liberty of the subject. As early as 1631 a law was passed admitting no man to the rights of "freemen" who was not a member of some church within the limits of the jurisdiction of the colony. The blessings of a "freeman" were reserved for church-members only. Negroes were not admitted to the church, and, therefore, were denied the rights of a freeman. Even the mother country had no bowels of compassion for the Negro. In 1677 the English courts held that a Negro slave was property.

So as "infidels" the Negro slaves of Massachusetts were deprived of rights and duties belonging to a member of the Church and State.

But the deeper reason the colonists had for excluding slaves from baptism, and hence citizenship, was twofold; viz., to keep in harmony with the Mosaic code in reference to "strangers" and "Gentiles," and to keep the door of the Church shut in the face of the slave; because to open it to him was to emancipate him in course of time. Religious and secular knowledge were not favorable to slavery. The colonists turned to the narrow, national spirit of the Old Testament, rather than to the broad and catholic spirit of the New Testament, for authority to withhold the mercies of the Christian religion from the Negro slaves in their midst.

The rigorous system of domestic slavery established in the colony of Massachusetts bore its bitter fruit in due season. It was impossible to exclude the slaves from the privileges of the Church and State without inflicting a moral injury upon the holy marriage relation. In the contemplation of the law the slave was a chattel, an article of merchandise. The custom of separating parent and child, husband and wife, was very clear proof that the marriage relation was either positively ignored by the institution of slavery, or grossly violated under the slightest pretext. All well-organized society or government rests upon this sacred relation. But slavery, with lecherous grasp and avaricious greed, trailed the immaculate robes of marriage in the moral filth of the traffic in human beings. True, there never was any prohibition against the marriage of one slave to another slave,—for they tried to breed slaves in Massachusetts!—but there never was any law encouraging the lawful union of slaves until after the Revolutionary War, in 1786. We rather infer from the following in the Act of October, 1705, that the marriage relation among slaves had been left entirely to the caprices of the master.

We have not been able to discover "any law" positively prohibiting marriage among slaves; but there was a custom denying marriage to the Negro, that at length received the weight of positive law. Mr. Palfrey says,—

We have searched faithfully to find the slightest justification for this inference of Mr. Palfrey, but have not found it. There is not a line in any newspaper of the colony, until 1710, that indicates the concern of the people in the lawful union of slaves. And there was no legislation upon the subject until 1786, when an "Act for the orderly Solemnization of Marriage" passed. That Negro slaves were united in marriage, there is abundant evidence, but not many in this period. It was almost a useless ceremony when "the customs and usages" of slavery separated them at the convenience of the owner. The master's power over his slaves was almost absolute. If he wanted to sell the children and keep the parents, his decision was not subject to any court of law. It was final. If he wanted to sell the wife of his slave man into the rice-fields of the Carolinas or into the West India Islands, the tears of the husband only exasperated the master. "The fathers of New England" had no reverence for the "nuptial tie" among their slaves, and, therefore, tore slave families asunder without the least compunction of conscience. "Negro children were considered an incumbrance in a family, and, when weaned, were given away like puppies," says the famous Dr. Belknap. But after the Act of 1705; "their banns were published like those of white persons;" and public sentiment began to undergo a change on the subject. The following Negro marriage was prepared by the Rev. Samuel Phillips of Andover. His ministry did not commence until 1710; and, therefore, this marriage was prepared subsequent to that date. He realized the need of something, and acted accordingly.

Where a likely Negro woman was courted by the slave of another owner, and wanted to marry, she was sold, as a matter of humanity, "with her wearing apparel" to the owner of the man. "A Bill of Sale of a Negro Woman Servant in Boston in 1724, recites that 'Whereas Scipio, of Boston aforesaid, Free Negro Man and Laborer, proposes Marriage to Margaret, the Negro Woman Servant of the said Dorcas Marshall [a Widow Lady of Boston]: Now to the Intent that the said Intended Marriage may take Effect, and that the said Scipio may Enjoy the said Margaret without any Interruption,' etc., she is duly sold, with her apparel, for Fifty Pounds." Within the next twenty years the Governor and his Council found public opinion so modified on the question of marriage among the blacks, that they granted a Negro a divorce on account of his wife's adultery with a white man. But in Quincy's Reports, page 30, note, quoted by Dr. Moore, in 1758 the following rather loose decision is recorded: that the child of a female slave never married according to any of the forms prescribed by the laws of this land, by another slave, who "had kept her company with her master's consent," was not a bastard.

The Act of 1705 forbade any "christian" from marrying a Negro, and imposed a fine of fifty pounds upon any clergyman who should join a Negro and "christian" in marriage. It stood as the law of the Commonwealth until 1843, when it was repealed by an "Act relating to Marriage between Individuals of Certain Races."

As to the political rights of the Negro, it should be borne in mind, that, as he was excluded from the right of Christian baptism, hence from the Church; and as "only church-members enjoyed the rights of freemen, it is clear that the Negro was not admitted to the exercise of the duties of a freeman. Admitting that there were instances where Negroes received the rite of baptism, it was so well understood as not entitling them to freedom or political rights, that it was never questioned during this entire period. Free Negroes were but little better off than the slaves. While they might be regarded as owning their own labor, political rights and ecclesiastical privileges were withheld from them.

Though nominally free, they did not come under the head of "Christians." Neither freedom, nor baptism in the Church, could free them from the race-malice of the whites, that followed them like the fleet-footed "Furies." There were special regulations for free Negroes. The Act of 1703, forbidding slaves from being out at night after the hour of nine o'clock, extended to free Negroes. In 1707 an Act was passed "regulating of free negroes." It recites that "free negroes and mulattos, able of body, and fit for labor, who are not charged with trainings, watches, and other services," shall perform service equivalent to militia training. They were under the charge of the officer in command of the military company belonging to the district where they resided. They did fatigue-duty. And the only time, that, by law, the Negro was admitted to the trainings, was between 1652 and 1656. But there is no evidence that the Negroes took advantage of the law. Public sentiment is more potent than law. In May, 1656, the law of 1652, admitting Negroes to the trainings, was repealed.

And Gov. Bradstreet, in his report to the "Committee for Trade," made in May, 1680, says,—

The law of 1707—which is the merest copy of the Virginia law on the same subject—requires free Negroes to answer fire-alarms with the company belonging to their respective precincts. They were not allowed to entertain slave friends at their houses, without the permission of the owner of the slaves. To all prohibitions there was affixed severe fines in large sums of money. In case of a failure to pay these fines, the delinquent was sent to the House of Correction; where, under severe discipline, he was constrained to work out his fine at the rate of one shilling per day! If a Negro "presume to smite or strike any person of the English, or other Christian nation," he was publicly flogged by the justice before whom tried, at the discretion of that officer.

During this period the social condition of the Negroes, bond and free, was very deplorable. The early records of the town of Boston preserve the fact that one Thomas Deane, in the year 1661, was prohibited from employing a Negro in the manufacture of hoops, under a penalty of twenty shillings; for what reason is not stated. No churches or schools, no books or teachers, they were left to the gloom and vain imaginations of their own fettered intellects. John Eliot "had long lamented it with a Bleeding and Burning Passion, that the English used their Negroes but as their Horses or their Oxen, and that so little care was taken about their immortal souls; he looked upon it as a Prodigy, that any wearing the Name of Christians should so much have the Heart of Devils in them, as to prevent and hinder the Instruction of the poor Blackamores, and confine the souls of their miserable Slaves to a Destroying Ignorance, merely for fear of thereby losing the Benefit of their Vassalage; but now he made a motion to the English within two or three Miles of him, that at such a time and place they would send their Negroes once a week unto him: For he would then Catechise them, and Enlighten them, to the utmost of his power in things of their Everlasting Peace; however, he did not live to make much progress in this undertaking." The few faint voices of encouragement, that once in a great while reached them from the pulpit and forum, were as strange music, mellowed and sweetened by the distance. The free and slave Negroes were separated by law, were not allowed to communicate together to any great extent. They were not allowed in numbers greater than three, and then, if not in the service of some white person, were liable to be arrested, and sent to the House of Correction.

With but small means the free Negroes of the colony were unable to secure many comforts in their homes. They were hated and dreaded more than their brethren in bondage. They could judge, by contrast, of the abasing influences of slavery. They were only nominally free; because they were taxed without representation,—had no voice in the colonial government.

But, notwithstanding the obscure and neglected condition of the free Negroes, some of them by their industry, frugality, and aptitude won a place in the confidence and esteem of the more humane of the white population. Owning their own time, many of the free Negroes applied themselves to the acquisition of knowledge. Phillis Wheatley, though nominally a slave for some years, stood at the head of the intellectual Negroes of this period. She was brought from Africa to the Boston slave-market, where, in 1761, she was purchased by a benevolent white lady by the name of Mrs. John Wheatley. She was naked, save a piece of dirty carpet about her loins, was delicate of constitution, and much fatigued from a rough sea-voyage. Touched by her modest demeanor and intelligent countenance, Mrs. Wheatley chose her from a large company of slaves. It was her intention to teach her the duties of an ordinary domestic; but clean clothing and wholesome diet effected such a radical change in the child for the better, that Mrs. Wheatley changed her plans, and began to give her private instruction. Eager for learning, apt in acquiring, though only eight years old, she greatly surprised and pleased her mistress. Placed under the instruction of Mrs. Wheatley's daughter, Phillis learned the English language sufficiently well as to be able to read the most difficult portions of the Bible with ease and accuracy. This she accomplished in less than a year and a half. She readily mastered the art of writing; and within four years from the time she landed in the slave-market in Boston, she was able to carry on an extensive correspondence on a variety of topics.

Her ripening intellectual faculties attracted the attention of the refined and educated people of Boston, many of whom sought her society at the home of the Wheatleys. It should be remembered, that this period did not witness general culture among the masses of white people, and certainly no facilities for the education of Negroes. And yet some cultivated white persons gave Phillis encouragement, loaned her books, and called her out on matters of a literary character. Having acquired the principles of an English education, she turned her attention to the study of the Latin language, and was able to do well in it. Encouraged by her success, she translated one of Ovid's tales. The translation was considered so admirable that it was published in Boston by some of her friends. On reaching England it was republished, and called forth the praise of many of the reviews.

Her manners were modest and refined. Her nature was sensitive and affectionate. She early gave signs of a deep spiritual experience, which gave tone and character to all her efforts in composition and poetry. There was a charming vein of gratitude in all her private conversations and public utterances, which her owners did not fail to recognize and appreciate. Her only distinct recollection of her native home was, that every morning early her mother poured out water before the rising sun. Her growing intelligence and keen appreciation of the blessings of civilization overreached mere animal grief at the separation from her mother. And as she knew more of the word of God, she became more deeply interested in the condition of her race.

At the age of twenty her master emancipated her. Naturally delicate, the severe climate of New England, and her constant application to study, began to show on her health. Her friend and mother, for such she proved herself to be, Mrs. Wheatley, solicitous about her health, called in eminent medical counsel, who prescribed a sea-voyage. A son of Mrs. Wheatley was about to visit England on mercantile business, and therefore took Phillis with him. For the previous six years she had cultivated her taste for poetry; and, at this time, her reputation was quite well established. She had corresponded with persons in England in social circles, and was not a stranger to the English. She was heartily welcomed by the leaders of the society of the British metropolis, and treated with great consideration. Under all the trying circumstances of high social life, among the nobility and rarest literary genius of London, this redeemed child of the desert, coupled to a beautiful modesty the extraordinary powers of an incomparable conversationalist. She carried London by storm. Thoughtful people praised her; titled people dined her; and the press extolled the name of Phillis Wheatley, the African poetess.

Prevailed upon by admiring friends, in 1773 she gave her poems to the world. They were published in London in a small octavo volume of about one hundred and twenty pages, comprising thirty-nine pieces. It was dedicated to the Countess of Huntingdon, with a picture of the poetess, and a letter of recommendation signed by the governor and lieutenant-governor, with many other "respectable citizens of Boston."

The volume has passed through several English and American editions, and is to be found in all first-class libraries in the country. Mrs. Wheatley sickened, and grieved daily after Phillis. A picture of her little ward, sent from England, adorned her bedroom; and she pointed it out to visiting friends with all the sincere pride of a mother. On one occasion she exclaimed to a friend, "See! Look at my Phillis! Does she not seem as though she would speak to me?" Getting no better, she sent a loving request to Phillis to come to her at as early a moment as possible. With a deep sense of gratitude to Mrs. Wheatley for countless blessings bestowed upon her, Phillis hastened to return to Boston. She found her friend and benefactor just living, and shortly had the mournful satisfaction of closing her sightless eyes. The husband and daughter followed the wife and mother quickly to the grave. Young Mr. Wheatley married, and settled in England. Phillis was alone in the world.

Her married life was brief. She was the mother of one child, that died early. Ignorant of the duties of domestic life, courted and flattered by the cultivated, Peters's jealousy was at length turned into harsh treatment. Tenderly raised, and of a delicate constitution, Phillis soon went into decline, and died Dec. 5, 1784, in the thirty-first year of her life, greatly beloved and sincerely mourned by all whose good fortune it had been to know of her high mental endowments and blameless Christian life.

Her influence upon the rapidly growing anti-slavery sentiment of Massachusetts was considerable. The friends of humanity took pleasure in pointing to her marvellous achievements, as an evidence of what the Negro could do under favorable circumstances. From a state of nudity in a slave-market, a stranger to the English language, this young African girl had won her way over the rough path of learning; had conquered the spirit of caste in the best society of conservative old Boston; had brought two continents to her feet in admiration and amazement at the rare poetical accomplishments of a child of Africa!

She addressed a poem to Gen. Washington that pleased the old warrior very much. We have never seen it, though we have searched diligently. Mr. Sparks says of it,—

Gen. Washington, in a letter to Joseph Reed, bearing date of the 10th of February, 1776, from Cambridge, refers to the letter and poem as follows:—

This gives the world an "inside" view of the brave old general's opinion of the poem and poetess, but the "outside" view, as expressed to Phil's, is worthy of reproduction at this point.

This letter is a handsome compliment to the poetess, and does honor to both the head and heart of the general. His modesty, so characteristic, has deprived history of its dues. But it is consoling to know that the sentiments of the poem found a response in the patriotic heart of the first soldier of the Revolution, and the Father of his Country!

While Phillis Wheatley stands out as one of the most distinguished characters of this period, and who, as a Colored person, had no equal, yet she was not the only individual of her race of intellect and character. A Negro boy from Africa was purchased by a Mr. Slocum, who resided near New Bedford, Mass. After he acquired the language, he turned his thoughts to freedom, and in a few years, by working beyond the hours he devoted to his master, was enabled to buy himself from his master. He married an Indian woman named Ruth Moses, and settled at Cutterhunker, in the Elizabeth Islands, near New Bedford. In a few years, through industry and frugality, John Cuffe—the name he took as a freeman—was enabled to purchase a good farm of one hundred (100) acres. Every year recorded new achievements, until John Cuffe had a wide reputation for wealth, honesty, and intelligence. He applied himself to books, and secured, as the ripe fruit of his studious habits, a fair business education. Both himself and wife were Christian believers; and to lives of industry and increasing secular knowledge, they added that higher knowledge which makes alive to "everlasting life." Ten children were born unto them,—four boys and six girls. One of the boys, Paul Cuffe, became one of the most distinguished men of color Massachusetts has produced. The reader will be introduced to him in the proper place in the history. John Cuffe died in 1745, leaving behind, in addition to considerable property, a good name, which is of great price.

Richard Dalton, Esq., of Boston, owned a Negro boy whom he taught to read any Greek writer without hesitancy. Mr. Dalton was afflicted with weak eyes; and his fondness for the classics would not allow him to forego the pleasure of them, and hence his Negro boy Cæsar was instructed in the Greek. "The Boston Chronicle" of Sept. 21, 1769, contains the following advertisement: "To be sold, a Likely Little negroe boy, who can speak the French language, and very fit for a Valet."

With increasing evidence of the Negro's capacity for mental improvement, and fitness for the duties and blessings of a freeman, and the growing insolence and rigorous policy of the mother country, came a wonderful change in the colony. The Negroes were emboldened to ask for and claim rights as British subjects, and the more humane element among the whites saw in a relaxation of the severe treatment of the blacks security and immunity in war. But anti-slavery sentiment in Massachusetts was not born of a genuine desire to put down a wicked and cruel traffic in human beings. Two things operated in favor of humane treatment of the slaves,—an impending war, and the decision of Lord Mansfield in the Sommersett case. The English government was yearly increasing the burdens of the colonists. The country was young, its resources little known. The people were largely engaged in agricultural pursuits. There were no tariff laws encouraging or protecting the labor or skill of the people. Civil war seemed inevitable. Thoughtful men began to consider the question as to which party the Negroes of the colony would contribute their strength. It was no idle question to determine whether the Negroes were Tories or Whigs. As early as 1750 the questions as to the legality of holding Negroes in slavery in British colonies began to be discussed in England and New England. "What, precisely, the English law might be on the subject of slavery, still remained a subject of doubt." Lord Holt held that slavery was a condition unknown to English law,—that the being in England was evidence of freedom. This embarrassed New-England planters in taking their slaves to England. The planters banded for their common cause, and secured the written opinion of Yorke and Talbot, attorney and solicitor general of England. They held that slaves could be held in England as well as in America; that baptism did not confer freedom: and the opinion stood as sound law for nearly a half-century. The men in England who lived on the money wrung from the slave-trade, the members of the Royal African Company, came to the rescue of the institution of slavery. In order to maintain it by law in the American colonies, it had to be recognized in England. The people of Massachusetts took a lively interest in the question. In 1761, at a meeting "in the old court-house," James Otis, in a speech against the "writs of assistance," struck a popular chord on the questions of "The Rights of the Colonies," afterwards published (1764) by order of the Legislature. He took the broad ground, "that the colonists, black and white, born here, are free-born British subjects and entitled to all the essential rights of such." In 1766 Nathaniel Appleton and James Swan distinguished themselves in their defence of the doctrines of "liberty for all." It became the general topic of discussion in private and public, and country lyceums and college societies took it up as a subject of forensic disputation. In the month of May, 1766, the representatives of the people were instructed to advocate the total abolition of slavery. And on the 16th of March, 1767, a resolution was offered to see whether the instructions should be adhered to, and was unanimously carried in the affirmative. But it should be remembered that British troops were in the colony, in the streets of Boston. The mutterings of the distant thunder of revolution could be heard. Public sentiment was greatly tempered toward the Negroes. On the 31st of May, 1609, the House of Representatives of Massachusetts resolved against the presence of troops, and besought the governor to remove them. His Excellency disclaimed any power under the circumstances to interfere. The House denounced a standing army in time of peace, without the consent of the General Court, as "without precedent, and unconstitutional." In 1769 one of the courts of Massachusetts gave a decision friendly to a slave, who was the plaintiff. This stimulated the Negroes to an exertion for freedom. The entire colony was in a feverish state of excitement. An anonymous Tory writer reproached Bostonians for desiring freedom when they themselves enslaved others.

These trying and exasperating circumstances were but the friendly precursors of a spirit of universal liberty.

In England the decision of Lord Mansfield in the Sommersett case had encouraged the conscientious few who championed the cause of the slave. Charles Stewart, Esq., of Boston, Mass., had taken to London with him his Negro slave, James Sommersett. The Negro was seized with a sickness in the British metropolis, and was thereupon abandoned by his master. He afterwards regained his health, and secured employment. His master, learning of his whereabouts, had him arrested, and placed in confinement on board the vessel "Ann and Mary," Capt. John Knowls, commander, then lying in the Thames, but soon to sail for Jamaica, where Sommersett was to be sold.

The influence of this decision was wide-spread, and hurtful to slavery in the British colonies in North America. It poured new life into the expiring hopes of the Negroes, and furnished a rule of law for the advocates of "freedom for all." It raised a question of law in all the colonies as to whether the colonial governments could pass an Act legalizing that which was "contrary to English law."

Notwithstanding the general and generous impulse for liberty, the indissoluble ties of avarice, and the greed for the unearned gains of the slave-trade, made public men conservate to conserve the interests of those directly interested in the inhuman traffic.

Humane masters who desired to emancipate their slaves were embarrassed by a statute unfriendly to manumission. The Act of 1703 deterred many persons from emancipating their slaves on account of its unjust and hard requirements. And under it quite a deal of litigation arose. It required every master who desired to liberate his slave, before doing so, to furnish a bond to the treasurer of the town or place in which he resided, in a sum not less than fifty pounds. This was to indemnify the town or place in case the Negro slave thus emancipated should, through lameness or sickness, become a charge. In case a master failed to furnish such security, his emancipated slaves were still contemplated by the law as in bondage, "notwithstanding any manumission or instrument of freedom to them made or given." Judge Sewall, in a letter to John Adams, cites a case in point.

Mr. Adams replied as follows:—

It is pleaded in extenuation of this Act, that it was passed to put a stop to the very prevalent habit of emancipating old and decrepit Negroes after there was no more service in them. If this be true, it reveals a practice more cruel than slavery itself.

In 1702 the representatives of the town of Boston were "desired to promote the encouraging the bringing of White servants and to put a period to Negroes being slaves." This was not an anti-slavery measure, as some have wrongly supposed. It was not a resolution or an Act: it was simply a request; and one that the "Representatives" did not grant for nearly a century afterwards.

It was read in Council a first time on the 16th of June, and "sent down recommended" to the House; where it was also read a first time on the same day. The next day it was read a second time, and, "on the question for a third reading, decided in the negative." In 1706 an argument or "Computation that the Importation of Negroes is not so profitable as that of White Servants," was published in Boston. It throws a flood of light upon the Act mentioned above, and shows that the motives that inspired the people who wanted a period put to the holding of Negroes as slaves were grossly material and selfish. It was the first published article on the subject, and is worthy of reproduction in full. It is reprinted from "The Boston News-Letter," No. 112, June 10, 1706, in the New-York Historical Society.

Comment would be superfluous. It is only necessary for the reader to note that there is not a humane sentiment in the entire article.

But universal liberty was not without her votaries. All had not bowed the knee to Baal. The earliest friend of the Indian and the Negro was the scholarly, pious, and benevolent Samuel Sewall, at one time one of the judges of the Superior Court of Massachusetts, and afterwards the chief justice. He hated slavery with a righteous hatred, and early raised his voice and used his pen against it. He contributed the first article against slavery printed in the colony. It appeared as a tract, on the 24th of June, 1700, and was "Printed by Bartholomew Green and John Allen." It is withal the most remarkable document of its kind we ever saw. It is reproduced here to show the reader what a learned Christian judge thought of slavery one hundred and eighty-two years ago.

Judge Sewall's attack on slavery created no little stir in Boston; and the next year, 1701, Judge John Saffin, an associate of Judge Sewall, answered it in quite a lengthy paper. Having furnished Judge Sewall's paper, it is proper that Judge Saffin's reply should likewise have a place here.

Judge Sewall had dealt slavery a severe blow, and opened up an agitation on the subject that was felt during the entire Revolutionary struggle. He became the great apostle of liberty, the father of the anti-slavery movement in the colony. He was the bold and stern John the Baptist of that period, "the voice of one crying in the wilderness" of bondage, to prepare the way for freedom.

The Quakers, or Friends as they were called, were perhaps the earliest friends of the slaves, but, like Joseph of Arimathæa, were "secretly" so, for fear of the "Puritans." But they early recorded their disapprobation of slavery as follows:—

Considering the prejudice and persecution that pursued this good people, their testimony against slavery is very remarkable. In 1729-30 Elihu Coleman of Nantucket, a minister of the society of Friends, wrote a book against slavery, published in 1733, entitled, "A Testimony against that Anti-Christian Practice of making Slaves of men. It was well written, and the truth fearlessly told for the conservative, self-seeking period he lived in. He says,—

He examined and refuted the arguments put forth in defence of slavery, charged slaveholders with idleness, and contended that slavery was the mother of vice, at war with the laws of nature and of God. Others caught the spirit of reform, and the agitation movement gained recruits and strength every year. Felt says, "1765. Pamphlets and newspapers discuss the subjects of slavery with increasing zeal." The colonists were aroused. Men were taking one side or the other of a question of great magnitude. In 1767 an anonymous tract of twenty octavo pages against slavery made its appearance in Boston. It was written by Nathaniel Appleton, a co-worker with Otis, and an advanced thinker on the subject of emancipation. It was in the form of a letter addressed to a friend, and was entitled, "Considerations on Slavery." The Rev. Samuel Webster Salisbury published on the 2d of March, 1769, "An Earnest Address to my Country on Slavery." He opened his article with an argument showing the inconsistency of a Christian people holding slaves, pictured the evil results of slavery, and then asked,—

Begun among the members of the bar and the pulpit, the common folk at length felt a lively interest in the subject of emancipation. An occasional burst of homely, vigorous eloquence from the pulpit on the duties of the hour inflamed the conscience of the pew with a noble zeal for a righteous cause. The afflatus of liberty sat upon the people as cloven tongues. Every village, town, and city had its orators whose only theme was emancipation. "The pulpit and the press were not silent, and sermons and essays in behalf of the enslaved Africans were continually making their appearance." The public conscience was being rapidly educated, and from the hills of Berkshire to the waters of Massachusetts Bay the fires of liberty were burning.

FOOTNOTES:

George H. Moore, LL.D., for many years librarian of the New-York Historical Society, but at present the efficient superintendent of the Lenox Library, in his "Notes on the History of Slavery in Massachusetts," has summoned nearly all the orators and historians of Massachusetts to the bar of history. He leaves them open to one of three charges, viz., evading the truth, ignorance of it, or falsifying the record. And in addition to this work, which is authority, his "Additional Notes" glow with an energy and perspicuity of style which lead me to conclude that Dr. Moore works admirably under the spur, and that his refined sarcasm, unanswerable logic, and critical accuracy give him undisputed place amongst the ablest writers of our times.

Wood's New-England Prospect, 1634, p. 77.

Slavery in Mass., p. 7.

Ibid., pp. 4, 5, and 6.

Elliott's New-England Hist., pp. 167-205.

Winthrop's Journal, Feb. 26, 1638, vol. i. p. 254; see, also, Felt, vol. ii. p. 230.

Dr. Moore backs his statement as to the time The Desire was built by quoting from Winthrop, vol. i. p. 193. But there is a mistake somewhere as to the correct date. Winthrop says she was built in 1636; but I find in Mr. Drake's "Founders of New England," pp. 31, 32, this entry: "More (June) XXth, 1635. In the Desire de Lond. Pearce, and bond for New Eng. p'r cert, fro ij Justices of Peace and ministers of All Saints lionian in Northampton." If she sailed in 1635, she must have been built earlier.

Dr. George H. Moore says Josselyn's Voyages were printed in 1664. This is an error. They were not published until ten years later, in 1674. In 1833 the Massachusetts Historical Society printed the work in the third volume and third series of their collection.

Josselyn, p. 28.

Ibid., p. 250.

Ibid., p. 258.

Slavery in Mass., p. 9.

Mass. Hist Coll., vol. iv. 4th Series, p. 333, sq.

Mr. Bancroft (Centenary Edition, vol. i. p. 137) says, "The earliest importation of Negro slaves into New England was made in 1637, from Providence Isle, in the Salem ship Desire." But Winthrop (vol. i. p. 254, under date of the 26th of February, 1638) says, "The Desire returned from the West Indies after seven months." He also states (ibid., p. 193) that The Desire was "built at Marblehead in 1636." But this may or may not be true according to the old method of keeping time.

Palfrey's Hist. of N.E., vol. ii. p. 30, note.

Josselyn, p. 257.

Elliott's New-England Hist., vol. ii. pp. 57, 58.

Hildreth, vol. i, p. 270, sq.

Ancient Charters and Laws of Mass., pp. 52, 23.

Slavery in Mass., p. 13, note.
Slavery in Mass., pp. 18, 19.
Ibid., p. 12.
Elliott's New-England Hist., vol. i. p. 383.
Hildreth, vol. i. p. 278.
Mass. Hist. Coll., vol. iv. 4th Series, p. 334.
Quoted by Dr. Moore, p. 20.
Commonwealth vs. Aves, 18 Pickering, p. 208.
Andover vs. Canton, Mass. Reports, 551, 552, quoted by Dr. Moore.
Kendall's Travels, vol. ii. p. 179.

The following note, if it refers to the kidnapped Negroes, gives an earlier date,—"29th May, 1644. Mr. Blackleach his petition about the Mores was consented to, to be committed to the eldrs, to enforme us of the mind of God herein, & then further to consider it."—Mass. Records,
vol. ii. p. 67.
Bancroft, Centennial edition, vol. i. p. 137.
Hildreth, vol. i. p. 282.

To the honored general court. The oath I took this yeare att my enterance upon the place of assistante was to this effect: That I would truly endeavour the advancement of the gospell and the good of the people of this plantation (to the best of my skill) dispencing justice equally and impartially (according to the laws of God and this land) in all cases wherein I act by virtue of my place. I conceive myself called by virtue of my place to act (according to this oath) in the case concerning the negers taken by captain Smith and Mr. Keser; wherein it is apparent that Mr. Keser gave chace to certaine negers; and upon the same day tooke divers of them; and at another time killed others; and burned one of their townes. Omitting several misdemeanours, which accompanied these acts above mentioned, I conceive the acts themselves to bee directly contrary to these following laws (all of which are capitall by the word of God; and two of them by the lawes of this jurisdiction). The act (or acts) of murder (whether by force or fraude) are expressly contrary both to the law of God, and the law of this country. The act of stealing negers, or taking them by force (Whether it be considered as theft or robbery) is (as I conceive) expressly contrary, both to the law of God, and the law of this country. The act of chaceing the negers (as aforesayde) upon the sabbath day (being a servile worke and such as cannot be considered under any other heade) is expressly capitall by the law of God. These acts and outrages being committed where there was noe civill government, which might call them to accompt, and the persons, by whom they were committed beeing of our jurisdiction, I conceive this court to bee the ministers of God in this case, and therefore my humble request is that the severall offenders may be imprisoned by the order of this court, and brought into their deserved censure in convenient time; and this I humbly crave that soe the sinn they have committed may be upon their own heads, and not upon ourselves (as otherwise it will.) Yrs in all christean observance, Richard Saltonstall. The house of deputs thinke meete that this petition shall be granted, and desire our honored magistrats concurrence herein. Edward Rawson. —Coffin's Newbury, pp.

335, 336.
Laws Camb., 1675, p. 15.
Hildreth, vol. i. p. 368.
Coffin, p. 335.
Drake (p. 288) says, "This act, however, was afterwards repealed or disregarded."
Mass. Records, vol ii. p 129.
Moore, Appendix, 251, sq.
Slavery in Mass., p. 30.
Hildreth, vol. i. p, 282.
Slavery in Mass., p. 49. See, also, Drake's Boston, p. 441, note.
Mass. Hist. Coll., vol. viii. 3d Series, p. 337.
Slavery in Mass., p. 50.
Coll. Amer. Stat. Asso., vol. i. p. 586.
Douglass's British Settlements, vol. i. p. 531.
Drake, p. 714. I cannot understand how Dr. Moore gets 1,514 slaves in Boston in 1742, except from Douglass. His "1742" should read 1752, and his "1,514" slaves should read 1,541 slaves. "There is a curious illustration of 'the way of putting it' in Massachusetts, in Mr. Felt's account of this 'census of slaves,' in the Collections of the American Statistical Association, vol. i. p, 208. He says that the General Court passed this order 'for the purpose of having an accurate account of slaves in our Commonwealth, as a subject in which the people were becoming much interested, relative to the cause of liberty!" There is not a particle of authority for this suggestion—such a motive for their action never existed anywhere but in the imagination of the writer himself!"—Slavery in Mass., p. 51, note.
Ancient Charters and Laws of Mass., p. 748.
Ibid.
Slavery in Mass., p. 61.
Hildreth, vol. ii. pp. 269, 270.
Drake's Boston, p. 574.
Spectator, No. 215, Nov. 6, 1711.
Slavery in Mass., p. 64.
'Item, three negroes £133, 6s., 8d. Item, flax £12, 2s., 8.'
Slavery in Mass., pp. 64, 65.
Drake, 583, note.
Here is a sample of the sales of those days: "In 1716, Rice Edwards, of Newbury, shipwright, sells to Edmund Greenleaf 'my whole personal estate with all my goods and chattels as also one negro man, one cow, three pigs with timber, plank, and boards."—Coffin, p. 337.
New-England Weekly Journal, No. 267, May 1, 1732.
A child one year and a half old—a nursing child sold from the bosom of its mother!—and for life!—Coffin, p. 337.
Slavery in Mass., p. 96. Note.

Eight years after this, on the 22d of June, 1735, Mr. Plant records in his diary: "I wrote Mr. Salmon of Barbadoes to send me a Negro." (Coffin, p. 338.) It doesn't appear that the reverend gentleman was opposed to slavery!

Note quoted by Dr. Moore, p. 58.

Hildreth, vol. i. p. 44.

"For they tell the Negroes, that they must believe in Christ, and receive the Christian faith, and that they must receive the sacrament, and be baptized, and so they do; but still they keep them slaves for all this."—MACY'S Hist. of Nantucket, pp. 280, 281.

Ancient Charters and Laws of Mass., p. 117.

Mr. Palfrey relies upon a single reference in Winthrop for the historical trustworthiness of his statement that a Negro slave could be a member of the church. He thinks, however, that this "presents a curious question," and wisely reasons as follows: "As a church-member, he was eligible to the political franchise, and, if he should be actually invested with it, he would have a part in making laws to govern his master,—laws with which his master, if a non-communicant, would have had no concern except to obey them. But it is improbable that the Court would have made a slave—while a slave—a member of the Company, though he were a communicant.—

Palfrey, vol. ii. p. 30. Note.

Butts vs. Penny, 2 Lev., p. 201; 3 Kib., p. 785.

Hildreth, vol. ii. p. 426.

Ancient Charters and Laws of Mass., p. 748.

Palfrey, vol. ii. p. 30. Note.

Hist. Mag., vol. v., 2d Series, by Dr. G.H. Moore.

Slavery in Mass., p. 57, note.

I use the term freeman, because the colony being under the English crown, there were no citizens. All were British subjects.

Ancient Charters and Laws of Mass., p. 746.

Ibid., p. 386.

Mr. Palfrey is disposed to hang a very weighty matter on a very slender thread of authority. He says, "In the list of men capable of bearing arms, at Plymouth, in 1643, occurs the name of 'Abraham Pearse, the Black-moore,' from which we infer ... that Negroes were not dispensed from military service in that colony" (History of New England, vol. ii. p. 30, note). This single case is borne down by the laws and usages of the colonists on this subject. Negroes as a class were absolutely excluded from the military service, from the commencement of the colony down to the war with Great Britain.

Slavery in Mass., Appendix, p. 243.

Mass. Hist. Soc. Coll., vol. viii. 3d Series, p. 336.

Lyman's Report, 1822.

Mather's Magnalia, Book III., p. 207. Compare also p. 209.

Elliott's New-England Hist., vol. ii. p. 165.

Mr. Palfrey comes again with his single and exceptional case, asking us to infer a rule

therefrom. See History of New England, note, p. 30.
Chief-Justice Parker, in Andover vs. Canton, 13 Mass. p. 550.
Slavery in Mass., p. 62.
Mott's Sketches, p. 17.
At the early age of sixteen, in the year 1770, Phillis was baptized into the membership of the society worshipping in the "Old South Meeting-House." The gifted, eloquent, and noble Dr. Sewall was the pastor. This was an exception to the rule, that slaves were not baptized into the Church.
All writers I have seen on this subject—and I think I have seen all—leave the impression that Miss Wheatley's poems were first published in London. This is not true. The first published poems from her pen were issued in Boston in 1770. But it was a mere pamphlet edition, and has long since perished.
All the historians but Sparks omit the given name of Peters. It was John.
The date usually given for her death is 1780, while her age is fixed at twenty-six. The best authority gives the dates above, and I think they are correct.
"Her correspondence was sought, and it extended to persons of distinction even in England, among whom may be named the Countess of Huntingdon, Whitefield, and the Earl of Dartmouth."—Sparks's Washington, vol. iii. p. 298, note.
Sparks's Washington, vol iii. p. 299, note.
This destroys the last hope I have nursed for nearly six years that the poem might yet come to light. Somehow I had overlooked this note.
Sparks's Washington, vol iii. p. 288.
Ibid., vol. iii. pp. 297, 298.
Armistead's A Tribute to the Negro, pp. 460, 461.
Douglass, vol. ii. p. 345, note.
Hildreth, vol. ii. p. 426.
Pearce vs. Lisle, Ambler, 76.
It may sound strangely in the ears of some friends and admirers of the gifted John Adams to hear now, after the lapse of many years, what he had to say of the position Otis took. His mild views on slavery were as deserving of scrutiny as those of the elder Quincy. Mr. Adams says: "Nor were the poor negroes forgotten. Not a Quaker in Philadelphia, or Mr. Jefferson, of Virginia, ever asserted the rights of negroes in stronger terms. Young as I was, and ignorant as I was, I shuddered at the doctrine he taught; and I have all my lifetime shuddered, and still shudder, at the consequences that may be drawn from such premises. Shall we say, that the rights of masters and servants clash, and can be decided only by force? I adore the idea of gradual abolitions! But who shall decide how fast or how slowly these abolitions shall be made?"
Hildreth, vol. ii. pp. 564, 565.
Coffin says, "In October of 1773, an action was brought against Richard Greenleaf, of Newburyport, by Cæsar [Hendrick], a colored man, whom he claimed as his slave, for holding him in bondage. He laid the damages at fifty pounds. The council for the plaintiff, in whose favor

the jury brought in their verdict and awarded him eighteen pounds' damages and costs, was John Lowell, Esq., afterward Judge Lowell. This case excited much interest, as it was the first, if not the only one of the kind, that ever occurred in the county."

Hildreth, vol. ii, pp. 550, 551.

Drake, p. 729, note.

I use the English spelling,—Sommersett.

Hildreth, vol. ii. p. 567.

Bancroft, 12th ed. vol. iii. p. 412.

Ancient Charters and Laws of Mass., pp. 745, 746.

The following is from Felt's Salem, vol. ii. pp. 415, 416, and illustrates the manner in which the law was complied with: "1713. Ann, relict of Governor Bradstreet, frees Hannah, a negro servant. 1717, Dec. 21. William and Samuel Upton, of this town, liberate Thomas, who has faithfully served their father, John Upton, of Reading. They give security to the treasurer, that they will meet all charges, which may accrue against the said black man. 1721, May 27. Elizur Keyser does the same for his servant, Cato, after four years more, and then the latter was to receive two suits of clothes.... 1758, June 5. The heirs of John Turner, having freed two servants, Titus and Rebeckah, give bonds to the selectmen, that they shall be no public charge."

John Adams's Works, vol. i. p. 51.

Adams's Works, vol. i. p. 55.

Drake, p. 525.

The late Senator Sumner, in a speech delivered on the 28th of June, 1854, refers to this as "the earliest testimony from any official body against negro slavery." Even the weight of the senator's assertion cannot resist the facts of history. The "resolve" instructing the "representatives" was never carried; but, on the contrary, the next Act was the law of 1703 restricting manumission!

Journal H. of R., 15, 16. General Court Records, x. 282.

Slavery in Mass., p. 106.

It was thought to be lost for some years, until Dr. George H. Moore secured a copy from George Brinley, Esq., of Hartford, Conn., and reproduced it in his Notes.

History of Nantucket, p. 281.

Coffin, p. 338; also History of Nantucket, pp. 279, 280.

Coffin, p. 338.

CHAPTER XV.: THE COLONY OF MASSACHUSETTS,—CONTINUED.: 1633-1775.

The Era of Prohibitory Legislation against Slavery.—Boston instructs her Representatives to vote against the Slave-Trade.—Proclamation issued by Gov. Dummer against the Negroes, April 13, 1723.—Persecution of the Negroes.—"Suing for Liberty."—Letter of Samuel Adams to John Pickering, jun., on Behalf of Negro Memorialists.—A Bill for the Suppression of the Slave-Trade passes.—Is vetoed by Gov. Gage, and fails to become a Law.

THE time to urge legislation on the slavery question had come. Cultivated at the first as a private enterprise, then fostered as a patriarchal institution, slavery had grown to such gigantic proportions as to be regarded as an unwieldy evil, and subversive of the political stability of the colony. Men winked at the "day of its small things," and it grew. Little legislation was required to regulate it, and it began to take root in the social and political life of the people. The necessities for legislation in favor of slavery increased. Every year witnessed the enactment of laws more severe, until they appeared as scars upon the body of the laws of the colony. To erase these scars was the duty of the hour.

It was now 1755. More than a half-century of agitation and discussion had prepared the people for definite action. Manumission and petition were the first methods against slavery. On the 10th of March, 1755, the town of Salem instructed their representative, Timothy Pickering, to petition the General Court against the importation of slaves. The town of Worcester, in June, 1765, instructed their representative to "use his influence to obtain a law to put an end to that unchristian and impolitic practice of making slaves of the human species, and that he give his vote for none to serve in His Majesty's Council, who will use their influence against such a law." The people of Boston, in the month of May, 1766, instructed their representatives as follows:—

And in the following year, 1767, on the 16th of March, the question was put as to whether the town should adhere to its previous instructions in favor of the suppression of the slave-trade, and passed in the affirmative. Nearly all the towns, especially those along the coast, those accessible by mails and newspapers, had recorded their vote, in some shape or other, against slavery. The pressure for legislation on the subject was great. The country members of the Legislature were almost a unit in favor of the passage of a bill prohibiting the further importation of slaves. The opposition came from the larger towns, but the opposers were awed by the determined bearing of the enemies of the slave-trade. The scholarship, wealth, and piety of the colony were steadily ranging to the side of humanity.

On the 13th of March, 1767, a bill was introduced in the House of Representatives "to prevent the unwarrantable and unlawful Practice or Custom of inslaving Mankind in this Province, and the importation of slaves into the same." It was read the first time, when a dilatory motion was offered that the bill lie over to the next session, which was decided in the negative. An amendment was offered to the bill, limiting it "to a certain time," which was carried; and the bill made a special order for a second reading on the following day. It was accordingly read on the 14th, when a motion was made to defer it for a third reading to the next "May session." The friends of the bill voted down this dilatory motion, and had the bill made the special order of the following Monday,—it now being Saturday. On Sunday there must have been considerable lobbying done, as can be seen by the vote taken on Monday. After it was read, and the debate was concluded, it was "Ordered that the Matter subside, and that Capt. Sheaffe, Col. Richmond, and Col. Bourne, be a Committee to bring in a Bill for laying a Duty of Impost on slaves importing into this Province." This was a compromise, that, as will be seen subsequently, impaired the chances of positive and wholesome legislation against slavery. The original bill dealt a double blow: it struck at the slave-trade in the Province, and levelled the institution already in existence. But some secret influences were set in operation, that are forever hidden from the searching eye of history; and the friends of liberty were bullied or cheated. There was no need of a bill imposing an impost tax on slaves imported, for such a law had been in existence for more than a half-century. If the tax were not heavy enough, it could have been increased by an amendment of a dozen lines. On the 17th the substitute was brought in by the special committee appointed by the Speaker the previous day. The rules requiring bills to be read on three several days were suspended, the bill ordered to a first and second reading, and then made the special order for eleven o'clock on the next day, Wednesday, the 18th. The motion to lie on the table until the "next May" was defeated. An amendment was then offered to limit the life of the bill to one year, which was carried, and the bill recommitted. On the afternoon of the same day it was read a third time, and placed on its passage with the amendment. It passed, was ordered engrossed, and was "sent up by Col. Bowers, Col. Gerrish, Col. Leonard, Capt. Thayer, and Col. Richmond." On the 19th of March it was read a first time in the council. On the 20th it was read a second time, and passed to be engrossed "as taken into a new draft." When it reached the House for concurrence, in the afternoon of the same day, it was "Read and unanimously non-concurred, and the House adhere to their own vote, sent up for concurrence."

Massachusetts has gloried much and long in this Act to prohibit "the Custom of enslaving mankind;" but her silver-tongued orators and profound statesmen have never possessed the courage to tell the plain truth about its complete failure. From the first it was harassed by dilatory motions and amendments directed to its life; and the substitute, imposing an impost tax on imported slaves for one year, showed plainly that the friends of the original bill had been driven from their high ground. It was like applying for the position of a major-general, and then accepting the place of a corporal. It was as though they had asked for a fish, and accepted a serpent instead. It seriously lamed the cause of emancipation. It filled the slaves with gloom, and their friends with apprehension. On the other hand, those who profited by barter in flesh and blood laughed secretly to themselves at the abortive attempt of the anti-slavery friends to call a halt on the trade. They took courage. For ten weary years the voices lifted for the freedom of the slave were few, faint, and far between. The bill itself has been lost. What its subject-matter was, is left to uncertain and unsatisfactory conjecture. All we know is from the title just quoted. But it was, nevertheless, the only direct measure offered in the Provincial Legislature against slavery during the entire colonial period, and came nearest to passage of any. But "a miss is as good as a mile!"

It was now the spring season of 1771. Ten years had flown, and no one in all the Province of

Massachusetts had had the courage to attempt legislation friendly to the slave. The scenes of the preceding year were fresh in the minds of the inhabitants of Boston. The blood of the martyrs to liberty was crying from the ground. The "red coats" of the British exasperated the people. The mailed hand, the remorseless steel finger, of English military power was at the throat of the rights of the people. The colony was gasping for independent political life. A terrible struggle for liberty was imminent. The colonists were about to contend for all that men hold dear,—their wives, their children, their homes, and their country. But while they were panting for an untrammelled existence, to plant a free nation on the shores of North America, they were robbing Africa every year of her sable children, and condemning them to a bondage more cruel than political subjugation. This glaring inconsistency imparted to reflecting persons a new impulse toward anti-slavery legislation.

In the spring of 1771 the subject of suppressing the slave-trade was again introduced into the Legislature. On the 12th of April a bill "To prevent the Importation of slaves from Africa" was introduced, and read the first time, and, upon the question "When shall the bill be read again?" was ordered to a second reading on the day following at ten o'clock. Accordingly, on the 13th, the bill was read a second time, and postponed till the following Tuesday morning. On the 16th it was recommitted. On the 19th of the same month a "Bill to prevent the Importation of Negro slaves into this Province" was read a first time, and ordered to a second reading "to-morrow at eleven o'clock." On the following day it was read a second time, and made the special order for three o'clock on the following Monday. On the 22d, Monday, it was read a third time, and placed upon its passage and engrossed. On the 24th it passed the House. When it reached the Council James Otis proposed an amendment, and a motion prevailed that the bill lie upon the table. But it was taken from the table, and the amendment of Otis was concurred in by the House. It passed the Council in the latter part of April, but failed to receive the signature of the governor, on the ground that he was "not authorized by Parliament." The same reason for refusing his signature was set up by Gen. Gage. Thus the bill failed. Gov. Hutchinson gave his reasons to Lord Hillsborough, secretary of state for the colonies. The governor thought himself restrained by "instructions" to colonial governors "from assenting to any laws of a new and unusual nature." In addition to the foregoing, his Excellency doubted the lawfulness of the legislation to which the "scruple upon the minds of the people in many parts of the province" would lead them; and that he had suggested the propriety of transmitting the bill to England to learn "his Majesty's pleasure" thereabouts. Upon these reasons Dr. Moore comments as follows:—

Discouraged by the failure of the House and General Court to pass measures hostile to the slave-trade, the people in the outlying towns began to instruct their representatives, in unmistakable language, to urge the enactment of repressive legislation on this subject. At a town meeting in Salem on the 18th of May, 1773, the representatives were instructed to prevent, by appropriate legislation, the further importation of slaves into the colony, as "repugnant to the natural rights of mankind, and highly prejudicial to the Province." On the very next day, May 19, 1773, at a similar meeting in the town of Leicester, the people gave among other instructions to Thomas Denny, their representative, the following on the question of slavery:—

Medford instructed the representative to "use his utmost influence to have a final period put to that most cruel, inhuman and unchristian practice, the slave-trade." At a town meeting the people of Sandwich voted, on the 18th of May, 1773, "that our representative is instructed to endeavor to have an Act passed by the Court, to prevent the importation of slaves into this country, and that all children that shall be born of such Africans as are now slaves among us, shall, after such Act, be free at 21 yrs. of age."

This completes the list of towns that gave instructions to their representatives, as far as the record goes. But there doubtless were others; as the towns were close together, and as the "spirit of liberty was rife in the land."

The Negroes did not endure the yoke without complaint. Having waited long and patiently for the dawn of freedom in the colony in vain, a spirit of unrest seized them. They grew sullen and desperate. The local government started, like a sick man, at every imaginary sound, and charged all disorders to the Negroes. If a fire broke out, the "Negroes did it,"—in fact, the Negroes, who were not one-sixth of the population, were continually committing depreciations against the whites! On the 13th of April, 1723, Lieut.-Gov. Dummer issued a proclamation against the Negroes, which contained the following preamble:—

On Sunday, the 18th of April, 1723, the Rev. Joseph Sewall preached a sermon suggested "by the late fires yt have broke out in Boston, supposed to be purposely set by ye negroes." The town was greatly exercised. Everybody regarded the Negroes with distrust. Special measures were demanded to insure the safety of the town. The selectmen of Boston passed "nineteen articles" for the regulation of the Negroes. The watch of the town was increased, and the military called out at the sound of every fire-alarm "to keep the slaves from breaking out"! In August, 1730, a Negro was charged with burning a house in Malden; which threw the entire community into a panic. In 1755 two Negro slaves were put to death for poisoning their master, John Codman of Charlestown. One was hanged, and the other burned to death. In 1766 all slaves who showed any disposition to be free were "transported and exchanged for small negroes." In 1768 Capt. John Willson, of the Fifty-ninth Regiment, was accused of exciting the slaves against their masters; assuring them that the soldiers had come to procure their freedom, and that, "with their assistance, they should be able to drive the Liberty Boys to the Devil." The following letter from Mrs. John Adams to her husband, dated at the Boston Garrison, 22d September, 1774, gives a fair idea of the condition of the public pulse, and her pronounced views against slavery.

The Negroes of Massachusetts were not mere passive observers of the benevolent conduct of their white friends. They were actively interested in the agitation going on in their behalf. Here, as in no other colony, the Negroes showed themselves equal to the emergencies that arose, and capable of appreciating the opportunities to strike for their own rights. The Negroes in the colony at length struck a blow for their liberty. And it was not the wild, indiscriminate blow of Turner, nor the military measure of Gabriel; not the remorseless logic of bludgeon and torch,—but the sober, sensible efforts of men and women who believed their condition abnormal, and slavery prejudicial to the largest growth of the human intellect. The eloquence of Otis, the impassioned appeals of Sewall, and the zeal of Eliot had rallied the languishing energies of the Negroes, and charged their hearts with the divine passion for liberty. They had learned to spell out the letters of freedom, and the meaning of the word had quite ravished their fainting souls. They had heard that the royal charter declared all the colonists British subjects; they had devoured the arguments of their white friends, and were now prepared to act on their own behalf. The slaves of Greece and Rome, it is true, petitioned the authorities for a relaxation of the severe laws that crushed their manhood; but they were captives from other nations, noted for government and a knowledge of the science of warfare. But it was left to the Negroes of Massachusetts to force their way into counts created only for white men, and win their cause!

On Wednesday, Nov. 5, 1766, John Adams makes the following record in his diary:—

So as early as 1766 Mr. Adams records a case of "suing for liberty;" and though it was the first he had known of, nevertheless, he had "heard there have been many." How many of these cases were in Massachusetts it cannot be said with certainty, but there were "many." The case to which Mr. Adams makes reference was no doubt that of Jenny Slew vs. John Whipple, jun., cited by Dr. Moore. It being the earliest case mentioned anywhere in the records of the colony, great interest attaches to it.

The next of the "freedom cases," in chronological order, was the case of Newport vs. Billing, and was doubtless the one in which John Adams was engaged in the latter part of September, 1768. It was begun in the Inferior Court, where the decision was against the slave, Amos Newport. The plaintiff took an appeal to the highest court in the colony; and that court gave as its solemn opinion, "that the said Amos [Newport] was not a freeman, as he alleged, but the proper slave of the said Joseph [Billing]." It should not be lost sight of, that not only the Fundamental laws of 1641, but the highest court in Massachusetts, held, as late as 1768, that there was property in man!

The case of James vs. Lechmere is the one "which has been for more than half a century the grand cheval de bataille of the champions of the historic fame of Massachusetts." Richard Lechmere resided in Cambridge, and held to servitude for life a Negro named "James." On the 2d of May, 1769, this slave began an action in the Inferior Court of Common Pleas. The action was "in trespass for assault and battery, and imprisoning and holding the plaintiff in servitude from April 11, 1758, to the date of the writ." The judgment of the Inferior Court was adverse to the slave; but on the 31st of October, 1769, the Superior Court of Suffolk had the case settled by compromise. A long line of worthies in Massachusetts have pointed with pride to this decision as the legal destruction of slavery in that State. But it "is shown by the records and files of Court to have been brought up from the Inferior Court by sham demurrer, and, after one or two continuances, settled by the parties." The truth of history demands that the facts be given to the world. It will not be pleasant for the people of Massachusetts to have this delusion torn from their affectionate embrace. It was but a mere historical chimera, that ought not to have survived a single day; and, strangely enough, it has existed until the present time among many intelligent people. This case has been cited for the last hundred years as having settled the question of bond servitude in Massachusetts, when the fact is, there was no decision in this instance! And the claim that Richard Lechmere's slave James was adjudged free "upon the same grounds, substantially, as those upon which Lord Mansfield discharged Sommersett," is absurd and baseless. For on the 27th of April, 1785 (thirteen years after the famous decision), Lord Mansfield himself said, in reference to the Sommersett case, "that his decision went no farther than that the master cannot by force compel the slave to go out of the kingdom." Thirty-five years of suffering and degradation remained for the Africans after the decision of Lord Mansfield. His lordship's decision was rendered on the 22d of June, 1772; and in 1807, thirty-five years afterwards, the British government abolished the slave-trade. And then, after twenty-seven years more of reflection, slavery was abolished in English possessions. So, sixty-two years after Lord Mansfield's decision, England emancipated her slaves! It took only two generations for the people to get rid of slavery under the British flag. How true, then, that "facts are stranger than fiction"!

In 1770 John Swain of Nantucket brought suit against Elisha Folger, captain of the vessel "Friendship," for allowing a Mr. Roth to receive on board his ship a Negro boy named "Boston," and for the recovery of the slave. This was a jury-trial in the Court of Common Pleas. The jury brought in a verdict in favor of the slave, and he was "manumitted by the magistrates." John Swain took an appeal from the decision of the Nantucket Court to the Supreme Court of Boston, but never prosecuted it. In 1770, in Hanover, Plymouth County, a Negro asked his master to grant him his freedom as his right. The master refused; and the Negro, with assistance of counsel, succeeded in obtaining his liberty.

This case is mentioned in full by Mr. Dane in his "Abridgment and Digest of American Law," vol. ii. p. 426.

In the Inferior Court of Common Pleas, in the county of Essex, July term in 1774, a Negro slave of one Caleb Dodge of Beverly brought an action against his master for restraining his liberty. The jury gave a verdict in favor of the Negro, on the ground that there was "no law of the Province to hold a man to serve for life." This is the only decision we have been able to find based upon such a reason. The jury may have reached this conclusion from a knowledge of the provisions of the charter of the colony; or they may have found a verdict in accordance with the charge of the court. The following significant language in the charter of the colony could not have escaped the court:—

The Rev. Dr. Belknap, speaking of these cases which John Adams speaks of as "suing for liberty," gives an idea of the line of argument used by the Negroes:—

The argument pursued by the masters was,—

It is well that posterity should know the motives that inspired judges and juries to grant these Negroes their prayer for liberty.

And Chief-Justice Parsons, in the case of Winchendon vs. Hatfield, in error, says,—

Thus did the slaves of Massachusetts fill their mouths with arguments, and go before the courts. The majority of them, aged and infirm, were allowed to gain their cause in order that their masters might be relieved from supporting their old age. The more intelligent, and, consequently, the more determined ones, were allowed to have their freedom from prudential reasons, more keenly felt than frankly expressed by their masters. In some instances, however, noble, high-minded Christians, on the bench and on juries, were led to their conclusions by broad ideas of justice and humanity. But the spirit of the age was cold and materialistic. With but a very few exceptions, the most selfish and constrained motives conspired to loose the chains of the bondmen in the colony.

The slaves were not slow to see that the colonists were in a frame of mind to be persuaded on the question of emancipation. Their feelings were at white heat in anticipation of the Revolutionary struggle, and the slaves thought it time to strike out a few sparks of sympathy.

On the 25th of June, 1773, a petition was presented to the House of Representatives, and read before that body during the afternoon session. It was the petition "of Felix Holbrook, and others, Negroes, praying that they may be liberated from a state of Bondage, and made Freemen of this Community, and that this Court would give and grant to them some part of the unimproved Lands belonging to the Province, for a settlement, or relieve them in such other Way as shall seem good and wise upon the Whole." After its reading, a motion prevailed to refer it to a select committee for consideration, with leave to report at any time. It was therefore "ordered, that Mr. Hancock, Mr. Greenleaf, Mr. Adams, Capt. Dix, Mr. Pain, Capt. Heath, and Mr. Pickering consider this Petition, and report what may be proper to be done." It was a remarkably strong committee. There were the patriotic Hancock, the scholarly Greenleaf, the philosophic Pickering, and the eloquent Samuel Adams. It was natural that the Negro petitioners should have expected something. Three days after the committee was appointed, on the 28th of June, they recommended "that the further Consideration of the Petition be referred till next session." The report was adopted, and the petition laid over until the "next session."

But the slaves did not lose heart. They found encouragement among a few noble spirits, and so were ready to urge the Legislature to a consideration of their petition at the next session, in the winter of 1774. The following letter shows that they were anxious and earnest.

It is rather remarkable, that on the afternoon of the first day of the session,—Jan. 26, 1774,— the "Petition of a number of Negro Men, which was entered on the Journal of the 25th of June last, and referred for Consideration to this session," was "read again, together with a Memorial of the same Petitioners, and Ordered, that Mr. Speaker, Mr. Pickering, Mr. Hancock, Mr. Adams, Mr. Phillips, Mr. Pain, and Mr. Greenleaf consider the same, and report." The public feeling on the matter was aroused. It was considered as important as, if not more important than, any measure before the Legislature.

The committee were out until March, considering what was best to do about the petition. On the 2d of March, 1774, they reported to the House "a Bill to prevent the Importation of Negroes and others as slaves into this Province," when it was read a first time. On the 3d of March it was read a second time in the morning session; in the afternoon session, read a third time, and passed to be engrossed. It was then sent up to the Council to be concurred in, by Col. Gerrish, Col. Thayer, Col. Bowers, Mr. Pickering and Col. Bacon. On the next day the bill "passed in Council with Amendments," and was returned to the House. On the 5th of March the House agreed to concur in Council amendments, and on the 7th of March passed the bill as amended. On the day following it was placed upon its passage in the Council, and carried. It was then sent down to the governor to receive his signature, in order to become the law of the Province. That official's approval was withheld, and the reason given was, "the secretary said (on returning the approved bills) that his Excellency had not had time to consider the other Bills that had been laid before him."

It is quite fortunate that the bill was preserved; for it is now, in the certain light of a better civilization, a document of great historic value.

Like all other measures for the suppression of the slave-trade, this bill failed to become a law. If Massachusetts desired to free herself from this twofold cross of woe,—even if her great jurists could trace the law that justified the abolition of the curse, in the pages of the royal charter,—were not the British governors of the Province but conserving the corporation interests of the home government and the members of the Royal African Company? By the Treaty of Utrecht, England had agreed to furnish the Spanish West Indies with Negroes for the space of thirty years. She had aided all her colonies to establish slavery, and had sent her navies to guard the vessels that robbed Africa of five hundred thousand souls annually. This was the cruel work of England. For all her sacrifices in the war, the millions of treasure she had spent, the blood of her children so prodigally shed, with the glories of Blenheim, of Ramillies, of Oudenarde and Malplaquet, England found her consolation and reward in seizing and enjoying, as the lion's share of results of the grand alliance against the Bourbons, the exclusive right for thirty years of selling African slaves to the Spanish West Indies and the coast of America! Why should Gov. Hutchinson sign a bill that was intended to choke the channel of a commerce in human souls that was so near the heart of the British throne?

Gov. Hutchinson was gone, and Gen. Gage was now governor. He convened the General Court at Salem, in June, 1774. On the 10th of June the same bill that Gov. Hutchinson had refused to sign was introduced, with a few immaterial changes, and pushed to a third reading, and engrossed the same day. It was called up on the 16th of June, and passed. It was sent up to the Council, where it was read a third time, and concurred in. But the next day the General Court was dissolved! And over the grave of this, the last attempt at legislation to suppress the slave-trade in Massachusetts, was written: "Not to have been consented to by the governor"!

These repeated efforts at anti-slavery legislation were strategic and politic. The gentlemen who hurried those bills through the House and Council, almost regardless of rules, knew that the royal governors would never affix their signatures to them. But the colonists, having put themselves on record, could appeal to the considerate judgment of the impatient Negroes; while the refusal of the royal governors to give the bills the force of law did much to drive the Negroes to the standard of the colonists. In the long night of darkness that was drawing its sable curtains about the colonial government, the loyalty of the Negroes was the lonely but certain star that threw its peerless light upon the pathway of the child of England so soon to be forced to lift its parricidal hand against its rapacious and cruel mother.

FOOTNOTES:

Felt, vol. ii. p. 416.
Newspaper Literature, vol. i. p. 31.
Lyman's Report, quoted by Dr. Moore.
House Journal, p. 387.
Ibid.
House Journals; see, also, Gen. Court Records, May, 1763, to May, 1767, p. 485.
Slavery in Mass., pp. 131, 132.
Felt, vol. ii. pp. 416, 417.
Hist. of Leicester, pp. 442, 443.
Freeman's Hist. of Cape Cod, vol. ii. pp. 114, 115.
Boston Gazette, Aug. 17, 1761.
Letters of Mrs. Adams, p. 20.
Adams's Works, vol. ii. p. 200.
Adams's Works, vol. ii, p. 213.
Records, 1768, fol., p. 284.
This is the case referred to by the late Charles Sumner in his famous speech in answer to Senator Butler of South Carolina; see also Slavery in Mass., p. 115, 116; Washburn's Judicial Hist. of Mass., p. 202; Mass. Hist. Soc. Proc., 1863-64, p. 322.
Records, 1769, fol. p. 196. Gray in Quincy's Reports, p. 30, note, quoted by Dr. Moore.
Slavery in Mass., pp. 115, 116, note.
Lyman's Report, 1822.
Slavery in Mass., p. 118.
Hist. of Newbury, p. 339.
The Watchman's Alarm, p. 28, note; also Slavery in Mass., p. 119.
Mass. Hist Soc. Coll., vol. iv. 1st Series, pp. 202, 203.
Hildreth, vol. ii. p. 564.
House Journal, p. 85, quoted by Dr. Moore.
House Journal, p. 94.
Slavery in Mass., p. 136.
House Journal, p. 104.
House Journal p. 224.
Ibid., p. 226.
House Journal, Gen Court Records, xxx. pp. 248, 264; also, Slavery in Mass, p. 137.
Mass. Archives, Domestic Relations, 1643-1774, vol. ix. p. 457.
Ethiope, p. 12.
Bolingbroke, pp. 346-348.

CHAPTER XVI.: THE COLONY OF MARYLAND.: 1634-1775.

Maryland under the Laws of Virginia until 1630.—First Legislation on the Slavery Question in 1637-38—Slavery established by Statute in 1663—The Discussion of Slavery.—An Act passed encouraging the Importation of Negroes and White Slaves in 1671.—An Act laying an Impost on Negroes and White Servants imported into the Colony.—Duties imposed on Rum and Wine.—Treatment of Slaves and Papists.—Convicts imported into the Colony—An Attempt to justify the Convict-Trade.—Spirited Replies.—The Laws of 1723, 1729, 1752.—Rights of Slaves—Negro Population in 1728.—Increase of Slavery in 1750—No Efforts made to prevent the Evils of Slavery.—The Revolution nearing.—New Life for the Negroes.

UP to the 20th of June, 1630, the territory that at present constitutes the State of Maryland was included within the limits of the colony of Virginia. During that period the laws of Virginia obtained throughout the entire territory.

In 1637 the first assembly of the colony of Maryland agreed upon a number of bills, but they never became laws. The list is left, but nothing more. The nearest and earliest attempt at legislation on the slavery question to be found is a bill that was introduced "for punishment of ill servants." During the earlier years of the existence of slavery in Virginia, the term "servant" was applied to Negroes as well as to white persons. The legal distinction between slaves and servants was, "servants for a term of years,"—white persons; and "servants for life,"—Negroes. In the first place, there can be no doubt but what Negro slaves were a part of the population of this colony from its organization; and, in the second place, the above-mentioned bill of 1637 for the "punishment of ill servants" was intended, doubtless, to apply to Negro servants, or slaves. So few were they in number, that they were seldom referred to as "slaves." They were "servants;" and that appellation dropped out only when the growth of slavery as an institution, and the necessity of specific legal distinction, made the Negro the only person that was suited to the condition of absolute property.

In 1638 there was a list of bills that reached a second reading, but never passed. There was one bill "for the liberties of the people," that declared "all Christian inhabitants (slaves only excepted) to have and enjoy all such rights, liberties, immunities, privileges and free customs, within this province, as any natural born subject of England hath or ought to have or enjoy in the realm of England, by force or virtue of the common law or statute law of England, saving in such cases as the same are or may be altered or changed by the laws and ordinances of this province." There is but one mention made of "slaves" in the above Act, but in none of the other Acts of 1638. There are certain features of the Act worthy of special consideration. The reader should keep the facts before him, that by the laws of England no Christian could be held in slavery; that in the Provincial governments the laws were made to conform with those of the home government; that, in specifying the rights of the colonists, the Provincial assemblies limited the immunities and privileges conferred by the Magna Charta upon British subjects, to Christians; that Negroes were considered heathen, and, therefore, denied the blessings of the Church and State; that even where Negro slaves were baptized, it was held by the courts in the colonies, and was the law-opinion of the solicitor-general of Great Britain, that they were not ipso facto free; and that, where Negroes were free, they had no rights in the Church or State. So, while this law of 1638 did not say that Negroes should be slaves, in designating those who were to enjoy the rights of freemen, it excludes the Negro, and thereby fixes his condition as a slave by implication. If he were not named as a freeman, it was the intention of the law-makers that he should remain a bondman,—the exception to an established rule of law.

In subsequent Acts reference was made to "servants," "fugitives," "runaways," etc.; but the first statute in this colony establishing slavery was passed in 1663. It was "An Act concerning negroes and other slaves." It enacts section one:—

Section two:—

Section three:—

Section one is the most positive and sweeping statute we have ever seen on slavery. It fixes the term of servitude for the longest time man can claim,—the period of his earthly existence,—and dooms the children to a service from which they were to find discharge only in death. Section two was called into being on account of the intermarriage of white women with slaves. Many of these women had been indentured as servants to pay their passage to this country, some had been sent as convicts, while still others had been apprenticed for a term of years. Some of them, however, were very worthy persons. No little confusion attended the fixing of the legal status of the issue of such marriages; and it was to deter Englishwomen from such alliances, and to determine the status of the children before the courts, that this section was passed. Section three was clearly an ex post facto law: but the public sentiment of the colony was reflected in it; and it stood, and was re-enacted in 1676.

Like Virginia, the colony of Maryland found the soil rich, and the cultivation of tobacco a profitable enterprise. The country was new, and the physical obstructions in the way of civilization numerous and formidable. Of course all could not pursue the one path that led to agriculture. Mechanic and trade folk were in great demand. Laborers were scarce, and the few that could be obtained commanded high wages. The Negro slave's labor could be made as cheap as his master's conscience and heart were small. Cheaper labor became the cry on every hand, and the Negro was the desire of nearly all white men in the colony. In 1671 the Legislature passed "An Act encouraging the importation of negroes and slaves into" the colony, which was followed by another and similar Act in 1692. Two motives inspired the colony to build up the slave-trade; viz., to have more laborers, and to get something for nothing. And, as soon as Maryland was known to be a good market for slaves, the traffic increased with wonderful rapidity. Slaves soon became the bone and sinew of the working-force of the colony. They were used to till the fields, to fell the forests, to assist mechanics, and to handle light crafts along the water-courses. They were to be found in all homes of opulence and refinement; and, unfortunately, their presence in such large numbers did much to lower honorable labor in the estimation of the whites, and to enervate women in the best white society. While the colonists persuaded themselves that slavery was an institution indispensable to the colony, its evil effects soon became apparent. It were impossible to engage the colony in the slave-trade, and escape the bad results of such an inhuman enterprise. It made men cruel and avaricious.

It was the motion of individuals to have legislative encouragement tendered the venders of human flesh and blood; but the time came when the government of the colony saw that an impost tax upon the slaves imported into the colony would not impair the trade, while it would aid the government very materially. In 1696 "An Act laying an imposition on negroes, slaves and while persons imported" into the colony was passed. It is plain from the reading of the caption of the above bill, that it was intended to reach three classes of persons; viz., Negro servants, Negro slaves, and white servants. The word "imported" means such persons as could not pay their passage, and were therefore indentured to the master of the vessel. When they arrived, their time was hired out, if they were free, for a term of years, at so much per year; but if they were slaves the buyer had to pay all claims against this species of property before he could acquire a fee simple in the slave. Some historians have too frequently misinterpreted the motive and aim of the colonial Legislatures in imposing an impost tax upon Negroes and other servants imported into their midst. The fact that the law applied to white persons does not aid in an interpretation that would credit the makers of the act with feelings of humanity. A people who could buy and sell wives did not hesitate to see in the indentured white servants property that ought to be taxed. Why not? These white servants represented so many dollars invested, or so many years of labor in prospect! So all persons imported into the colony of Maryland, "Negroes, slaves, and white persons," were taxed as any other marketable article. A swift and remorseless civilization against the stolid forces of nature made men indiscriminate and cruel in their impulses to obtain. Public sentiment had been formulated into law: the law contemplated "servants and slaves" as chattel property; and the political economists of the Province saw in this species of property rich gains for the government. It was condition, circumstances, that made the servant or slave; but at length it was nationality, color.

When, on the threshold of the eighteenth century, "white indentured" servants were rapidly ceasing to exist under color or sanction of law, religious bigotry and ecclesiastical intolerance joined hands with the supporters of Negro slavery in a crusade against the Irish Catholics. In 1704 the Legislature passed "An Act imposing three pence per gallon on rum and wine, brandy and spirits, and twenty shillings per poll for negroes, for raising a supply to defray the public charge of this province, and twenty shillings, per poll, on Irish servants, to prevent the importing too great a number of Irish papist into this province." Although this Act was intended to remain on the statute-books only three years, its life was prolonged by a supplemental Act, and it disgraced the colony for twenty-one years. As in New York, so here, the government regarded the slave and Papist with feelings of hatred and fear. The former was only suited to a condition of perpetual bondage, the latter to be ostracized and driven out from before the face of the exclusive Protestants of that period. Both were cruelly treated; one on account of his face, the other on account of his faith.

A knowledge of the antecedents of the master-class will aid the reader to a more accurate conception of the character of the institution of slavery in the colony of Maryland.

It is not very pleasing for the student of history at this time to remember that the British colonies in North America received into their early life the worst poison of European society,—the criminal element. From the first the practice of transporting convicts into the colonies obtained. And, during the reign of George I., statutes were passed "authorizing transportation as a commutation punishment for clergyable felonies." These convicts were transported by private shippers, and then sold into the colony; and thus it became a gainful enterprise. From 1700 until 1760 this nefarious and pestiferous traffic greatly increased. At length it became, as already indicated, the subject of a special impost tax. Three or four hundred convicts were imported into the colony annually, and the people began to complain. In "The Maryland Gazette" of the 30th of July, 1767, a writer attempted to show that the convict element was not to be despised, but was rather a desirable addition to the Province. He says,—

After answering some objections to their importation because of the contagious diseases likely to be communicated by them, he further remarks,—

This attempt to justify the convict trade elicited two able and spirited replies over the signatures of "Philanthropos" and "C.D." appearing in "Green's Gazette" of 20th of August, 1767, in which the writer of the first article is handled "with the gloves off."

In another part of his reply he remarks,—

The writer felt that a young country could not be settled "without people of some sort," and that it was better to secure "convicts than slaves." Upon what grounds precisely this defender of buying convict labor based his conclusion that he would rather have "convicts than slaves" is not known. It could not have been that he believed the convicts of England more industrious or skilful than Negro slaves? Or, had he theoretical objections to slavery as a permanent institution? Perhaps the writer had himself graduated from the criminal class! But there were gentlemen who differed with him, and couched their objections to the convict system of importation in very vigorous English. On the 20th of August, 1767, two articles appeared in "Greene's Gazette." Says one of these writers,—

There can be no doubt but that many of the convicts thus imported, having served out their time, in a brief season became slave-drivers and slave-owners. With hearts reduced to flinty hardness in the fires of unrestrained passions, the convict element, as it became absorbed in the great free white population of the Province, created a most positive sentiment in favor of a cruel code for the government of the Negro slave. There were two motives that inspired the ex-convict to cruelty to the Negro: to divert attention from himself, and to persuade himself, in his doubting mind, that the Negro was inferior to him by nature. It was, no doubt, a great undertaking; but the findings of such a court must have been comforting to an anxious conscience! The result can be judged. Maryland made a slave-code, which, for cruelty and general inhumanity, has no equal in the South. The Maryland laws of 1715 contained, in chapter forty-four, an act with one hundred and thirty-five sections relating to Negro slaves. A most rigorous pass-system was established. By section six, no Negro or other servant was allowed to leave the county without a pass under the seal of the county in which their master resided; for which pass the slave or other servant was compelled to pay ten pounds of tobacco, or one shilling in money. If such persons were apprehended, a justice of the peace could impose such fines and inflict such punishment as were fixed by the law applying to runaways. By the Act of 1723, chapter fifteen, under the caption of "An Act to prevent the tumultuous meeting and other irregularities of negroes and other slaves," the severity of the laws was increased tenfold. According to section four, a Negro or other slave who had the temerity to strike a white person, was to have his ears "cropt on order of a Justice." Section six denies slaves the right of possession of property: they could not own cattle. Section seven gave authority to any white man to kill a Negro who resisted an attempt to arrest him; and by a supplemental Act of 1751, chapter fourteen, the owner of a slave thus killed was to be paid out of the public treasury. In 1729 an Act was passed providing, that upon the conviction of certain crimes, Negroes and other slaves shall be not only hanged, but the body should be quartered, and exposed to public view. When slaves grew old and infirm in the service of their masters, and the latter were inspired by a desire to compliment the faithfulness of their servants by emancipation, the law came in and forbade manumission by the "last will or testament," or the making free in any way of Negro slaves. It was a temporary Act, passed in 1752, void of every element of humanity; and yet it stood as the law of the colony for twenty long years.

In 1748 the Negro population of Maryland was thirty-six thousand, and still rapidly increasing.

In 1756 the blacks had increased to 46,225, and in 1761 to 49,675. There was nothing in the laws to prohibit the instruction of Negroes, and yet no one dared to brave public sentiment on that point. The churches gave no attention or care to the slaves. During the first half or three-quarters of a century there was an indiscriminate mingling and marrying among the Negroes and white servants; and, although this was forbidden by rigid statutes, it went on to a considerable extent. The half-breed, or Mulatto, population increased; and so did the number of free Negroes. The contact of these two elements—of slaves and convicts—was neither prudent nor healthy. The Negroes suffered from the touch of the moral contagion of this effete matter driven out of European society. Courted as rather agreeable companions by the convicts at first, the Negro slaves were at length treated worse by the ex-convicts than by the most intelligent and opulent slave-dealers in all the Province. And with no rights in the courts, incompetent to hold an office of any kind, the free Negroes were in almost as disagreeable a situation as the slaves.

From the founding of the colony of Maryland in 1632 down to the Revolutionary War, there is no record left us that any effort was ever made to cure the most glaring evils of slavery. For the Negro this was one long, starless night of oppression and outrage. No siren's voice whispered to him of a distant future, propitious and gracious to hearts almost insensible to a throb of joy, to minds unconscious of the feeblest rays of light. Being absolute property, it was the right of the master to say how much food, or what quantity of clothing, his slave should have. There were no rules by which a slave could claim the privilege of ceasing from labor at the close of the day. No, the master had the same right to work his slaves after nightfall as to drive his horse morning, noon, and night. Poor clothes, rough and scanty diet, wretched quarters, overworked, neglected in body and mind, the Negroes of Maryland had a sore lot.

The Revolution was nearing. Public attention was largely occupied with the Stamp Act and preparations for hostilities. The Negro was left to toil on; and, while at this time there was no legislation sought for slavery, there was nothing done that could be considered hostile to the institution. The Negroes hailed the mutterings of the distant thunders of revolution as the precursor of a new era to them. It did furnish an opportunity for them in Maryland to prove themselves patriots and brave soldiers. And how far their influence went to mollify public sentiment concerning them, will be considered in its appropriate place. Suffice it now to say, that cruel and hurtful, unjust and immoral, as the institution of slavery was, it had not robbed the Negro of a lofty conception of the fundamental principles that inspired white men to resist the arrogance of England; nor did it impair his enthusiasm in the cause that gave birth to a new republic amid the shock of embattled arms.

FOOTNOTES:

Dr. Abiel Holmes, in his American Annals, vol. ii. p. 5, says, "Maryland now contained about thirty-six thousand persons, of white men from sixteen years of age and upwards, and negroes male, and female from sixteen to sixty." I infer from this statement that slavery was in existence in Maryland in 1634; and I cannot find any thing in history to lead me to doubt but that slavery was born with the colony.

Cabinet Cyclopædia, vol. i. p. 61.

See Bacon's Laws, also Holmes's Annals, vol. i. p. 250.

The following appeared in the Plantation Laws, printed in London in 1705: "Where any negro or slave, being in servitude or bondage, is or shall become Christian, and receive the sacrament of baptism, the same shall not nor ought not to be deemed, adjudged or construed to be a manumission or freeing of any such negro or slave, or his or her issue, from their servitude or bondage, but that notwithstanding they shall at all times hereafter be and remain in servitude and bondage as they were before baptism, any opinion, matter or thing to the contrary notwithstanding."

McSherry's Hist. of Maryland, p. 86.

Freedom and Bondage, vol. i. p. 249.

McMahon's Hist. of Maryland, vol. i. p. 274.

This Indenture made the —— day of —— in the —— yeere of our Soveraigne Lord King Charles, &c betweene —— of the one party, and —— on the other party, Witnesseth, that the said —— doth hereby covenant promise, and grant, to and with the said —— his Executors and Assignes, to serve him from the day of the date hereof, untill his first and next arrivall in Maryland: and after for and during the tearme of —— yeeres, in such service and imployment, as the said —— or his assignee shall there imploy him, according to the custome of the Countrey in the like kind. In consideration whereof, the said —— doth promise and grant, to and with the said —— to pay for his passing, and to find him with Meat, Drinke, Apparell and Lodging, with other necessaries during the said terme; and at the end of the said terme, to give him one whole yeeres provision of Corne, and fifty acres of Land, according to the order of the countrey. In witnesse whereof, the said —— hath hereunto put his hand and seate, the day and yeere above written. Sealed and delivered in the presence of —— —Relation of the state of Maryland, pp. 62, 63.

Modern Traveller, vol. i. pp. 122, 123.

McMahon's Maryland, vol. i. p. 278.

1st Pitkin's United States, p. 133.

McMahone says of this convict element: "The pride of this age revolts at the idea of going back to such as these, for the roots of a genealogical tree; and they, whose delight it would be, to trace their blood through many generations of stupid, sluggish, imbecile ancestors, with no claim to merit but the name they carry down, will even submit to be called 'novi homines,' if a convict stand in the line of ancestry."

With perhaps the single exception of South Carolina, of which the reader will learn more farther on.

American Annals.

Dr. Holmes says, "The total number of mulattoes in Maryland amounted to 3,592," in 1755.

CHAPTER XVII.: THE COLONY OF DELAWARE.: 1636-1775.

The Territory of Delaware settled in part by Swedes and Danes, anterior to the Year 1638.—The Duke of York transfers the Territory of Delaware to William Penn.—Penn grants the Colony the Privilege of Separate Government.—Slavery introduced on the Delaware as early as 1636.—Complaint against Peter Alricks for using Oxen and Negroes belonging to the Company.—The First Legislation on the Slavery Question in the Colony.—An Enactment of a Law for the Better Regulation of Servants.—An Act restraining Manumission.

ANTERIOR to the year 1638, the territory now occupied by the State of Delaware was settled in part by Swedes and Danes. It has been recorded of them that they early declared that it was "not lawful to buy and keep slaves." But the Dutch claimed the territory. When New Netherlands was ceded to the Duke of York, Delaware was occupied by his representatives. On the 24th of August, 1682, the Duke transferred that territory to William Penn. But in 1703 Penn surrendered the old form of government, and gave the Delaware counties the privilege of a separate administration under the Charter of Privileges. Delaware inaugurated a legislature, but remained under the Council and Governor of Pennsylvania. But slavery made its appearance on the Delaware as early as 1636.

And on the 15th of September, 1657, complaint was made that Peter Alricks had "used the company's oxen and negroes;" thus showing that there were quite a number of Negroes in the colony at the time mentioned. In September, 1661, there was a meeting between Calvert, D'Hinoyossa, Peter Alricks, and two Indian chiefs, to negotiate terms of peace. At this meeting the Marylanders agreed to furnish the Dutch annually three thousand hogsheads of tobacco, provided the Dutch would "supply them with negroes and other commodities." Negroes were numerous, and an intercolonial traffic in slaves was established.

The first legislation on the slavery question in the colony of Delaware was had in 1721. "An Act for the trial of Negroes" provided that two justices and six freeholders should have full power to try "negro and mulatto slaves" for heinous offences. In case slaves were executed, the Assembly paid the owner two-thirds the value of such slave. It forbade convocations of slaves, and made it a misdemeanor to carry arms. During the same year an Act was passed punishing adultery and fornication. In case of children of a white woman by a slave, the county court bound them out until they were thirty-one years of age. In 1739 the Legislature passed an Act for the better regulation of servants and slaves, consisting of sixteen articles. It provided that no indentured servant should be sold into another government without the approval of at least one justice. Such servant could not be assigned over except before a justice. If a person manumitted a slave, good security was required: if he failed to do this, the manumission was of no avail. If free Negroes did not care for their children, they were liable to be bound out. In 1767 the Legislature passed another Act restraining manumission. It recites:—

The remainder of the slave code in this colony was like unto those of the other colonies, and therefore need not be described. Negroes had no rights, ecclesiastical or political. They had no property, nor could they communicate a relation of any character. They had no religious or secular training, and none of the blessings of home life. Goaded to the performance of the most severe tasks, their only audible reply was an occasional growl. It sent a feeling of terror through their inhuman masters, and occasioned them many ugly dreams.

FOOTNOTES:

Dr. Stevens in his History of Georgia, vol. i. p. 288, says, "In the Swedish and German colony, which Gustavus Adolphus planted in Delaware, and which in many points resembled the plans of the Trustees, negro servitude was disallowed." But he gives no authority, I regret.

See Laws of Delaware, vol. i. Appendix, pp. 1-4.

Albany Records, vol. ii, p. 10.

Vincent's History of Delaware, p. 159.

Ibid., p. 381.

Laws of Delaware, vol. i. p. 436.

CHAPTER XVIII.: THE COLONY OF CONNECTICUT.: 1646-1775.

The Founding of Connecticut, 1631-36.—No Reliable Data given for the Introduction of Slaves.—Negroes were first introduced by Ship during the Early Years of the Colony.—"Committee for Trade and Foreign Plantations."—Interrogating the Governor as to the Number of Negroes in the Colony in 1680.—The Legislature (1690) passes a Law pertaining to the Purchase and Treatment of Slaves and Free Persons.—An Act passed by the General Court in 1711, requiring Persons manumitting Slaves to maintain them.—Regulating the Social Conduct of Slaves in 1723.—The Punishment of Negro, Indian, and Mulatto Slaves, for the Use of Profane Language, in 1630.—Lawfulness of Indian and Negro Slavery recognized by Code, Sept. 5, 1646.—Limited Rights of Free Negroes in the Colony.—Negro Population in 1762.—Act against Importation of Slaves, 1774.

ALTHOUGH the colony of Connecticut was founded between the years 1631 and 1636, there are to be found no reliable data by which to fix the time of the introduction of slavery there. Like the serpent's entrance into the Garden of Eden, slavery entered into this colony stealthily; and its power for evil was discovered only when it had become a formidable social and political element. Vessels from the West Coast of Africa, from the West Indies, and from Barbadoes, landed Negroes for sale in Connecticut during the early years of its settlement. And for many years slavery existed here, without sanction of law, it is true, but perforce of custom. Negroes were bought as laborers and domestics, and it was a long time before their number called for special legislation. But, like a cancer, slavery grew until there was not a single colony in North America that could boast of its ability to check the dreadful curse. When the first slaves were introduced into this colony, can never be known; but, that there were Negro slaves from the beginning, we have the strongest historical presumption. For nearly two decades there was no reference made to slavery in the records of the colony.

In 1680 "the Committee for Trade and Foreign Plantations" addressed to the governors of the North-American plantations or colonies a series of questions. Among the twenty-seven questions put to Gov. Leete of Connecticut, were two referring to Negroes. The questions were as follows:—

To these the governor replied as follows:—

It is evident that the number of slaves was not great at this time, and that they were few and far between. The sullen and ofttimes revengeful spirit of the Indians had its effect upon the few Negro slaves in the colony. Sometimes they were badly treated by their masters, and occasionally they would run away. The country was new, the settlements scattered; and slavery as an institution, at this time and in this colony, in its infancy. The spirit of insubordination among the slave population seemed to call aloud for legislative restriction. In October, 1690, the Legislature passed the following bill:—

The general air of complaint that pervades the above bill leads to the conclusion that it was required by an alarming state of affairs. The pass-system was a copy from the laws of the older colonies where slavery had long existed. By implication free Negroes had to secure from the proper authorities a certificate of freedom; and the bill required them to carry it, or pay the cost of arrest.

One of the most palpable evidences of the humanity of the Connecticut government was the following act passed in May, 1702:—

Massachusetts had acted and did act very cowardly about this matter. But Connecticut showed great wisdom and humanity in making a just and equitable provision for such poor and decrepit slaves as might find themselves turned out to charity after a long life of unrequited toil. Slavery was in itself "the sum of all villanies,"—the blackest curse that ever scourged the earth. To buy and sell human beings; to tear from the famishing breast of the mother her speechless child; to separate the husband from the wife of his heart; to wring riches from the unpaid toil of human beings; to tear down the family altar, and let lecherous beasts, who claim the name of "Christian," run over defenceless womanhood as swine over God's altar!—is there any thing worse, do you ask? Yes! To work a human being from youth to old age, to appropriate the labor of that being exclusively, to rob it of the blessings of this life, to poison every domestic charity, to fetter the intellect by the power of fatal ignorance, to withhold the privileges of the gospel of love; and then, when the hollow cough comes under an inclement sky, when the shadows slant, when the hand trembles, when the gait is shuffling, when the ear is deaf, the eye dim, when desire faileth,—then to turn that human being out to die is by far the profoundest crime man can be guilty of in his dealings with mankind! And slavery had so hardened men's hearts, that the above act was found to be necessary to teach the alphabet of human kindness. No wonder human forbearance was strained to its greatest tension when masters, thus liberating their slaves, assumed the lofty air of humanitarians who had actually done a noble act in manumitting a slave!

In 1708 the General Court was called upon to legislate against the commercial communion that had gone on between the slaves and free persons in an unrestricted manner for a long time. Slaves would often steal articles of household furniture, wares, clothing, etc., and sell them to white persons. And, in order to destroy the ready market this wide-spread kleptomania found, an Act was passed making it a misdemeanor for a free person to purchase any article from slaves. It is rather an interesting law, and is quoted in full.

On the same day another act was passed, charging that as Mulatto and Negro slaves had become numerous in parts of the colony, destined to become insubordinate, abusive of white people, etc., and is as follows:—

In 1711 the General Court of Connecticut Colony signally distinguished itself by the passage of an act in harmony with that of 1702. It was found that indentured servants as well as slaves had been made the victims of the cruel policy of turning slaves and servants out into the world without means of support after they had become helpless, or had served out their time. This class of human beings had been cast aside, like a squeezed lemon, to be trodden under the foot of men. The humane and thoughtful men of the colony demanded a remedy at law, and it came in the following admirable bill:—

In 1723 an Act was passed regulating the social conduct, and restricting the personal rights, of slaves. The slaves were quite numerous at this time, and hence the colonists deemed it proper to secure repressive legislation. It is strange how anticipatory the colonies were during the zenith of the slavery institution! They were always expecting something of the slaves. No doubt they thought that it would be but the normal action of goaded humanity if the slaves should rise and cut their masters' throats. The colonists lived in mortal dread of their slaves, and the character of the legislation was but the thermometer of their fear. This Act was a slight indication of the unrest of the people of this colony on the slavery question:—

The laws regulating slavery in the colony of Connecticut, up to this time, had stood, and been faithfully enforced. There had been a few infractions of the law, but the guilty had been punished. And in addition to statutory regulation of slaves, the refractory ones were often summoned to the bar of public opinion and dealt with summarily. Individual owners of slaves felt themselves at liberty to use the utmost discretion in dealing with this species of their property. So on every hand the slave found himself scrutinized, suspicioned, feared, hated, and hounded by the entire community of whites who were by law a perpetual posse comitatus. The result of too great vigilance and severe censorship was positive and alarming. It made the slave desperate. It intoxicated him with a malice that would brook no restraint. It is said that the use of vigorous adjectives and strong English is a relief to one in moments of trial. But even this was denied the oppressed slaves in Connecticut; for in May, 1730, a bill was passed punishing them for using strong language.

The above act is the most remarkable document in this period of its kind. And yet there are two noticeable features in it: viz., the slave is to be proceeded against the same as if he were a free person; and he was to be entitled to offer evidence, enter his plea, and otherwise defend himself against the charge. This was more than was allowed in any of the other colonies.

On the 9th of September, 1730, Gov. J. Talcott, in a letter to the "Board of Trade," said that there were "about 700 Indian and Negro slaves" in the colony. The most of these were Negro slaves. For on the 8th of July, 1715, a proclamation was issued by the governor against the importation of Indians; and on the 13th of October, 1715, a bill was passed "prohibiting the Importation or bringing into" the colony any Indian slaves. It was an exact copy of the Act of May, 1712, passed in the colony of Massachusetts.

The colony of Connecticut never established slavery by direct statute; but in adopting a code which was ordered by the General Court of Hartford to be "copied by the secretary into the book of public records," it gave the institution legal sanction. This code was signed on the 5th of September, 1646. It recognized the lawfulness of Indian and Negro slavery. This was done under the confederacy of the "United Colonies of New England." For some reason the part of the code recognizing slavery is omitted from the revised laws of 1715. In this colony, as in Massachusetts, only members of the church, "and living within the jurisdiction," could be admitted to the rights of freemen. In 1715 an Act was passed requiring persons who desired to become "freemen of this corporation," to secure a certificate from the selectmen that they were "persons of quiet and peaceable behavior and civil conversation, of the age of twenty-one years, and freeholders." This provision excluded all free Negroes. It was impossible for one to secure such a certificate. Public sentiment alone would have frowned upon such an innovation upon the customs and manners of the Puritans. On the 17th of May, 1660, the following Act was passed: "It is ordered by this court, that neither Indian nor negar servts shall be required to traine, watch or ward in the Collo:"

To determine the status of the Negro here, this Act was necessary. He might be free, own his own labor; but if the law excluded him from the periodical musters and trainings, from the church and civil duties, his freedom was a mere misnomer. It is difficult to define the rights of a free Negro in this colony. He was restricted in his relations with the slaves, and in his intercourse with white people was regarded with suspicion. If he had, in point of law, the right to purchase property, the general prejudice that confronted him on every hand made his warmest friends judiciously conservative. There were no provisions made for his intellectual or spiritual growth. He was regarded by both the religious and civil government, under which he lived, as a heathen. Even his accidental conversion could not change his condition, nor mollify the feelings of the white Christians (?) about him. Like the wild animal, he was possessed with the barest privilege of getting something to eat. Beyond this he had nothing. Everywhere he turned, he felt the withering glance of a suspicious people. Prejudice and prescriptive legislation cast their dark shadows on his daily path; and the conscious superiority of the whites consigned him to the severest drudgery for his daily bread. The recollection of the past was distressing, the trials and burdens of the present were almost unbearable, while the future was one shapeless horror to him.

Perhaps the lowly and submissive acquiescence of the Negroes, bond and free, had a salutary effect upon the public mind. There is something awfully grand in an heroic endurance of undeserved pain. The white Christians married, and were given in marriage; they sowed and gathered rich harvests; they bought and built happy homes; beautiful children were born unto them; they built magnificent churches, and worshipped the true God: the present was joyous, and the future peopled with sublime anticipation. The contrast of these two peoples in their wide-apart conditions must have made men reflective. And added to this came the loud thunders of the Revolution. Connecticut had her orators, and they touched the public heart with the glowing coals of patriotic resolve. They felt the insecurity of their own liberties, and were now willing to pronounce in favor of the liberty of the Negroes. The inconsistency of asking for freedom, praying for freedom, fighting for freedom, and dying for freedom, when they themselves held thousands of human beings in bondage the most cruel the world ever knew, helped the cause of the slave. In 1762 the Negro population of this colony was four thousand five hundred and ninety. Public sentiment was aroused on the slavery question; and in October, 1774, the following prohibition was directed at slavery:—

The above bill was brief, but pointed; and showed that Connecticut was the only one of the New-England colonies that had the honesty and courage to legislate against slavery. And the patriotism and incomparable valor of the Negro soldiers of Connecticut, who proudly followed the Continental flag through the fires of the Revolutionary War, proved that they were worthy of the humane sentiment that demanded the Act of 1774.

FOOTNOTES:

In the Capital Laws of Connecticut, passed on the 1st of December, 1642, the te nth law reads as follows. "10. If any man stealeth a man or mankind, he shall be put to death. Ex. 21 16." But this was the law in Massachusetts, and yet slavery existed there for one hundred and forty-three (143) years.
Conn. Col. Recs., 1678-89, p. 293.
Ibid., p. 298.
Conn Col Recs., 1689-1706, p. 40
Ibid. 1689-1706, pp. 375, 376.
Conn. Col. Recs., 1706-16, p. 52.
Ibid., pp 51, 53.
Conn. Col. Recs., 1706-16, p. 233.
Conn. Col. Recs., 1717-25, pp. 390, 391.
Ibid., 1726-35, p. 290.
Conn. Col. Recs., 1706-16, pp. 515, 516.
Hazard, State Papers, vol. ii. pp. 1-6.
Conn. Col. Recs., vol. i. p. 349.
Pres. Stiles's MSS.
Freedom and Bondage, vol. i. pp. 272, 273.

CHAPTER XIX.: THE COLONY OF RHODE ISLAND.: 1647-1775.

Colonial Government in Rhode Island, May, 1647.—An Act passed to abolish Slavery in 1652, but was never enforced.—An Act specifying what Times Indian and Negro Slaves should not appear in the Streets.—An Impost-Tax on Slaves (1708).—Penalties imposed on Disobedient Slaves.—Anti Slavery Sentiment in the Colonies receives Little Encouragement.—Circular Letter from the Board of Trade to the Governor of the English Colonies, relative to Negro Slaves.—Governor Cranston's Reply.—List of Militia-Men, including White and black Servants.—Another Letter from the Board of Trade.—An Act preventing Clandestine Importations and Exportations of Passengers, Negroes, or Indian Slaves.—Masters of Vessels required to report the Names and Number of Passengers to the Governor.—Violation of the Impost-Tax Law on Slaves punished by Severe Penalties.—Appropriation by the General Assembly, July 5, 1715, from the Fund derived from the Impost Tax, for the paving of the Streets of Newport.—An Act passed disposing of the Money raised by Impost-Tax.—Impost-Law repealed, May, 1732.—An Act relating to freeing Mulatto and Negro Slaves passed 1728—An Act passed preventing Masters of Vessels from carrying Slaves out of the Colony, June 17, 1757.—Eve of the Revolution.—An Act prohibiting Importation of Negroes into the Colony in 1774.—The Population of Rhode Island in 1730 and 1774.

INDIVIDUAL Negroes were held in bondage in Rhode Island from the time of the formation of the colonial government there, in May, 1647, down to the close of the eighteenth century. Like her sister colonies, she early took the poison of the slave-traffic into her commercial life, and found it a most difficult political task to rid herself of it. The institution of slavery was never established by statute in this colony; but it was so firmly rooted five years after the establishment of the government, that it required the positive and explicit prohibition of law to destroy it. On the 19th of May, 1652, the General Court passed the following Act against slavery. It is the earliest positive prohibition against slavery in the records of modern nations.

The above law was admirable, but there was lacking the public sentiment to give it practical force in the colony. It was never repealed, and yet slavery flourished under it for a century and a half. Mr. Bancroft says, "The law was not enforced, but the principle lived among the people." No doubt the principle lived among the people; but, practically, they did but little towards emancipating their slaves until the Revolutionary War cloud broke over their homes. There is more in the statement Mr. Bancroft makes than the casual reader is likely to discern.

The men who founded Rhode Island, or Providence Plantation as it was called early, were of the highest type of Christian gentlemen. They held advanced ideas on civil government and religious liberty. They realized, to the full, the enormity of the sinfulness of slavery; but while they hesitated to strike down what many men pronounced a necessary social evil, it grew to be an institution that governed more than it could be governed. The institution was established. Slaves were upon the farms, in the towns, and in the families, of those who could afford to buy them. The population of the colony was small; and to manumit the slaves in whom much money was invested, or to suddenly cut off the supply from without, was more than the colonists felt able to perform. The spirit was willing, but the flesh was weak.

For a half-century there was nothing done by the General Court to check or suppress the slave-trade, though the Act of 1652 remained the law of the colony. The trade was not extensive. No vessels from Africa touched at Newport or Providence. The source of supply was Barbadoes; and, occasionally, some came by land from other colonies. Little was said for or against slavery during this period. It was a question difficult to handle. The sentiment against it was almost unanimous. It was an evil; but how to get rid of it, was the most important thing to be considered. During this period of perplexity, there was an ominous silence on slavery. The conservatism of the colonists produced the opposite in the Negro population. They began to think and talk about their "rights." The Act of 1652 had begun to bear fruit. At the expiration of ten years' service, slaves began to demand their freedom-papers. This set the entire Negro class in a state of expectancy. Their eagerness for liberty was interpreted by the more timid among the whites as the signal for disorder. A demand was made for legislation that would curtail the personal liberties of the Negroes in the evenings. It is well to produce the Act of Jan. 4, 1703, that the reader may see the similarity of the laws passed in the New-England colonies against Negroes:—

It is rather remarkable that this Act should prohibit free Negroes and free Indians from walking the streets after nine o'clock. In this particular this bill had no equal in any of the other colonies. This act seemed to be aimed with remarkable precision at the Negroes as a class, both bond and free. The influence of free Negroes upon the slaves had not been in harmony with the condition of the latter; and the above Act was intended as a reminder, in part, to free Negroes and Indians. It went to show that there was but little meaning in the word "free," when placed before a Negro's name. No such restriction could have been placed upon the personal rights of a white colonist; for, under the democratical government of the colony, a subject was greater than the government. No law could stand that was inimical to his rights as a freeman. But the free Negro had no remedy at law. He was literally between two conditions, bondage and freedom.

Attention has been called to the fact, that the Act of 1652 was never enforced. In April, 1708, an Act, laying an impost-tax upon slaves imported into the colony, was passed which really gave legal sanction to the slave-trade. The following is the Act referred to:—

The Act referred to as having passed "in February last past," cannot be found. But, from the one quoted above, it is to be inferred that two objects were aimed at, viz.: First, under the codes of Massachusetts and Virginia, a drawback was allowed to an importer of a Negro who exported him within a stated time: the Rhode-Island Act of "February" had allowed importers this privilege. Second, notwithstanding the loud-sounding Act of 1652, this colony was not only willing to levy an impost-tax upon all slaves imported, but, in her greed for "blood money," even denied the importer the mean privilege, in exporting his slave, of drawing his rebate! The consistency of Rhode Island must have been a jewel that the other colonies did not covet.

The last section of the Act of 1703 was directed against "house keepers," who were to be fined for entertaining Negro or Indian slaves after nine o'clock. In 1708 another Act was passed, supplemental to the one of 1703, and added stripes as a penalty for non-payment of fines. Many white persons in the larger towns had grown rather friendly towards the slaves; and, even where they did not speak out in public against the enslavement of human beings, their hearts led them to the performance of many little deeds of kindness. They discovered many noble attributes in the Negro character, and were not backward in expressing their admiration. When summoned before a justice, and fined for entertaining Negroes after nine o'clock, they paid the penalty with a willingness and alacrity that alarmed the slave-holding caste. This was regarded as treason. Some could not pay the fine, and, hence, went free. The new Act intended to remedy this. It was as follows:—

It is certain that what little anti-slavery sentiment there was in the British colonies in North America during the first century of their existence received no encouragement from Parliament. From the beginning, the plantations in this new world in the West were regarded as the hotbeds in which slavery would thrive, and bring forth abundant fruit, to the great gain of the English government. All the appointments made by the crown were expected to be in harmony with the plans to be carried out in the colonies. From the settlement of Jamestown down to the breaking out of the war, and the signing of the Declaration of Independence, not a single one of the royal governors ever suffered his sense of duty to the crowned heads to be warped by local views on "the right of slavery." The Board of Trade was untiring in its attention to the colonies. And no subject occupied greater space in the correspondence of that colossal institution than slavery. The following circular letter, addressed to the governors of the colonies, is worthy of reproduction here, rather than in the Appendix. It is a magnificent window, that lets the light in upon a dark subject. It gives a very fair idea of the profound concern that the home government had in foreign and domestic slavery.

The good Queen of England was interested in the traffic in human beings; and although the House of Commons was too busy to give attention to "a matter of so great weight," the "Board of Trade" felt that it was "absolutely necessary that a trade so beneficial to the kingdom should be carried on to the greatest advantage." England never gave out a more cruel document than the above circular letter. To read it now, under the glaring light of the nineteenth century, will almost cause the English-speaking people of the world to doubt even "the truth of history." Slavery did not exist at sufferance. It was a crime against the weak, ignorant, and degraded children of Africa, systematically perpetrated by an organized Christian government, backed by an army that grasped the farthest bounds of civilization, and a navy that overshadowed the oceans.

The reply of the governor of Rhode Island was not as encouraging as their lordships could have wished.

So in nine years there had been no Negro slaves imported into the colony; that in 1696 fourteen had been sold to the colonists for between thirty pounds and thirty-five pounds apiece; that this was the only time a vessel direct from the coast of Africa had touched in this colony; that the supply of Negro slaves came from Barbadoes, and that the colonists who would purchase slaves were supplied by the offspring of those already in the plantation; and that the colonists preferred white servants to black slaves. The best that can be said of Gov. Cranston's letter is, it was very respectful in tone. The following table was one of the enclosures of the letter. It is given in full on account of its general interest:—

The Board of Trade replied to Gov. Cranston, under date of "Whitehall, January 16th, 1709-10.," saying they should be glad to hear from him "in regard to Negroes," etc.

The letter of inquiry from the Board of Trade imparted to slave-dealers an air of importance and respectability. The institution was not near so bad as it had been thought to be; the royal family were interested in its growth; it was a gainful enterprise; and, more than all, as a matter touching the conscience, the Bible and universal practice had sanctified the institution. To attempt to repeal the Act of 1652 would have been an occasion unwisely furnished for anti-slavery men to use to a good purpose. The bill was a dead letter, and its enemies concluded to let it remain on the statute-book of the colony.

The experiment of levying an impost-tax upon Negro slaves imported into the colony had proved an enriching success. After 1709 the slave-trade became rather brisk. As the population increased, public improvements became necessary,—there were new public buildings in demand, roads to be repaired, bridges to be built, and the poor and afflicted to be provided for. To do all this, taxes had to be levied upon the freeholders. A happy thought struck the leaders of the government. If men would import slaves, and the freemen of the colony would buy them, they should pay a tax as a penalty for their sin. And the people easily accommodated their views to the state of the public treasury.

Attention has been called already to the impost Act of 1708. On the 27th of February, 1712, the General Assembly passed "An Act for preventing clandestine importations and exportations of passengers, or negroes, or Indian slaves into or out of this colony," etc. The Act is quite lengthy. It required masters of vessels to report to the governor the names and number of all passengers landed into the colony, and not to carry away any person without a pass or permission from the governor, upon pain of a fine of fifty pounds current money of New England. Persons desiring to leave the colony had to give public notice for ten days in the most public place in the colony; and it specifies the duties of naval officers, and closes with the following in reference to Negro slaves, calling attention to the impost Act of 1708.—

We have omitted a large portion of the bill, because of its length; but have quoted sufficient to give an excellent idea of the marvellous caution taken by the good Christians of Rhode Island to get every cent due them on account of the slave trade, which their prohibition did not prohibit. It was a carefully drawn bill for those days.

The diligence of the public officers in the seaport town of Newport was richly rewarded. The slave-trade now had the sanction and regulation of colonial law. The demand for Negro laborers was not affected in the least, while traders did not turn aside on account of three pounds per head tax upon every slave sold into Rhode Island. On the 5th of July, 1715, the General Assembly appropriated a portion of the fund derived from the impost-tax on imported Negroes to repairing the streets; and then strengthened and amplified the original law on impost-duties, etc. The following is the Act:—

And in October, 1717, the following order passed the assembly:—

The fund accruing from the impost-duty on slaves was regarded with great favor everywhere, especially in Newport. It had cleaned her streets and lightened the burdens of taxation which rested so grievously upon the freeholders. There was no voice lifted against the iniquitous traffic, and the conscience of the colony was at rest. In June, 1729, the following Act was passed:—

It is wonderful how potential the influence of money is upon mankind. The sentiments of the good people had been scattered to the winds; and they had found a panacea for the violated convictions of the wrong of slavery in the reduction of their taxes, new bridges, and cleansed streets. Conscience had been bribed into acquiescence, and the iniquity thrived. There were those who still endeavored to escape the vigilance of the naval officers, and save the three pounds on each slave. But the diligence and liberality of the authorities were not to be outdone by the skulking stinginess of Negro-smugglers. On the 18th of June, 1723, the General Assembly passed the following order:—

The above illustrates the spirit of the times. There was a mania for this impost-tax upon stolen Negroes, and the law was to be enforced against all who sought to evade its requirements. But the Assembly had a delicate sense of equity, as well as an inexorable opinion of the precise demands of the law in its letter and spirit. On the 19th of June, 1716, the following was passed:—

It was not below the dignity of the Legislature of the colony of Rhode Island to pass a bill of relief for Col. Vaughan, and refund to him the six pounds he had paid to land his two sucking Negro baby slaves! In June, 1731, the naval officer, James Cranston, called the attention of the Assembly to the case of one Mr. Royall,—who had imported forty-five Negroes into the colony, and after a short time sold sixteen of them into the Province of Massachusetts Bay, where there was also an impost-tax,—and asked directions. The Assembly replied as follows:—

But the zeal of the colony in seeking the enforcement of the impost-law created a strong influence against it from without; and by order of the king the entire law was repealed in May, 1732.

The cruel practice of manumitting aged and helpless slaves became so general in this plantation, that the General Assembly passed a law regulating it, in February, 1728. It was borrowed very largely from a similar law in Massachusetts, and reads as follows:—

It is very remarkable that there were no lawyers to challenge the legality of such laws as the above, which found their way into the statute books of all the New-England colonies. There could he no conditional emancipation. If a slave were set at liberty, why he was free, and, if he afterwards became a pauper, was entitled to the same care as a white freeman. But it is not difficult to see that the status of a free Negro was difficult of definition. When the Negro slave grew old and infirm, his master no longer cared for him, and the public was protected against him by law. Death was his most beneficent friend.

In October, 1743, a widow lady named Comfort Taylor, of Bristol County, Massachusetts Bay, sued and obtained judgment against a Negro named Cuff Borden for two hundred pounds, and cost of suit "for a grievous trespass." Cuff was a slave. An ordinary execution would have gone against his person: he would have been imprisoned, and nothing more. In view of this condition of affairs, Mrs. Taylor petitioned the General Assembly of Rhode Island, praying that authority be granted the sheriff to sell Cuff, as other property, to satisfy the judgment. The Assembly granted her prayer as follows:—

This case goes to show that in Rhode Island Negro slaves were rated, at law, as chattel property, and could be taken in execution to satisfy debts as other personal property.

A great many slaves availed themselves of frequent opportunities of going away in privateers and other vessels. With but little before them in this life, they were even willing to risk being sold into slavery at some other place, that they might experience a change. They made excellent seamen, and were greatly desired by masters of vessels. This went on for a long time. The loss to the colony was great; and the General Assembly passed the subjoined bill as a check to the stampede that had become quite general:—

The education of the Negro slave in this colony was thought to be inimical to the best interests of the master class. Ignorance was the sine qua non of slavery. The civil government and ecclesiastical establishment ground him, body and spirit, as between "the upper and nether millstones." But the Negro was a good listener, and was not unconscious of what was going on around him. He was neither blind nor deaf.

The fires of the Revolutionary struggle began to melt the frozen feelings of the colonists towards the slaves. When they began to feel the British lion clutching at the throat of their own liberties, the bondage of the Negro stared them in the face. They knew the Negro's power of endurance, his personal courage, his admirable promptitude in the performance of difficult tasks, and his desperate spirit when pressed too sharply. The thought of such an ally for the English army, such an element in their rear, was louder in their souls than the roar of the enemy's guns. The act of June, 1774, shows how deeply the people felt on the subject.

In 1730 the population of Rhode Island was, whites, 15,302; Indians, 985; Negroes, 1,648; total, 17,935. In 1749 there were 28,439 whites, and 3,077 Negroes. Indians were not given this year. In 1756 the whites numbered 35,939, the Negroes 4,697. In 1774 Rhode Island contained 9,439 families, Newport had 9,209 inhabitants. The whites in the entire colony numbered 54,435, the Negroes, 3,761, and the Indians, 1,482. It will be observed that the Negro population fell off between the years 1749 and 1774. It is accounted for by the fact mentioned before,—that many ran away on ships that came into the Province.

The Negroes received better treatment at this time than at any other period during the existence of the colony. There was a general relaxation of the severe laws that had been so rigidly enforced. They took great interest in public meetings, devoured with avidity every scrap of news regarding the movements of the Tory forces, listened with rapt attention to the patriotic conversations of their masters, and when the storm-cloud of war broke were as eager to fight for the independence of North America as their masters.

FOOTNOTES:

R.I. Col. Recs., vol. i. p. 243.
Bancroft, vol. i. 5th ed. p. 175.
R.I. Col. Recs., vol. iii. pp. 492, 493.

There is no law making the manufacturing of whiskey legal in the United States; and yet the United-States government makes laws to regulate the business, and collects a revenue from it. It exists by and with the consent of the government, and, in a sense, is legal.

R.I. Col. Recs., vol. iv. p. 34.

I have searched diligently for the Act of February, among the Rhode-Island Collections and Records, but have not found it. It was evidently more comprehensive than the above Act.

R.I. Col. Recs., vol iv. p. 50.
R.I. Col. Recs, vol. iv. pp. 53, 54.
R.I. Coll. Recs., vol. iv. pp. 54, 55.
R.I. Col. Recs., vol iv. p. 59.
J. Carter Brown's Manuscripts, vol. viii. Nos. 506, 512.

It was a specious sort of reasoning. I learn that the bank over on the corner is to be robbed to-night at twelve o'clock. Shall I go and rob it at ten o'clock; because, if I do not do so, another person will, two hours later?

R.I. Col. Recs., vol. iv. pp. 133-135.
R.I. Col. Recs., vol. iv. pp. 191-193.
R.I. Col. Recs., vol. iv p. 225.
R.I. Col. Recs., vol. iv. pp. 423, 424.
Ibid., p. 330.
Ibid., vol. iv. p. 209.
R.I. Col. Recs., vol. iv. p. 454.
Ibid., vol. iv. p. 471.
Ibid., vol. iv. pp. 415, 416.
R.I. Col. Recs., vol. v. pp. 72, 73.
R.I. Col. Recs., vol vi. pp. 64, 65.
R.I. Col. Recs., vol. vii. pp. 251, 252.
American Annals, vol ii. pp. 107, 155, 156, 184, and 265.

CHAPTER XX.: THE COLONY OF NEW JERSEY.: 1664-1775.

New Jersey passes into the Hands of the English.—Political Powers conveyed to Berkeley and Carteret.—Legislation on the Subject of Slavery during the Eighteenth Century.—The Colony divided into East and West Jersey.—Separate Governments.—An Act concerning Slavery by the Legislature of East Jersey.—General Apprehension respecting the rising of Negro and Indian Slaves.—East and West Jersey surrender their Rights of Government to the Queen.—An Act for regulating the Conduct of Slaves.—Impost-Tax of Ten Pounds levied upon each Negro imported into the Colony.—The General Court passes a Law regulating the Trial of Slaves.—Negroes ruled out of the Militia Establishment upon Condition.—Population of the Jerseys in 1738 and 1745.

THE colony of New Jersey passed into the control of the English in 1664; and the first grant of political powers, upon which the government was erected, was conveyed by the Duke of York to Berkeley and Carteret during the same year. In the "Proprietary Articles of Concession," the words servants, slaves, and Christian servants occur. It was the intention of the colonists to draw a distinction between "servants for a term of years," and "servants for life," between white servants and black slaves, between Christians and pagans.

When slavery was introduced into Jersey is not known. There is no doubt but that it made its appearance there almost as early as in New Netherlands. The Dutch, the Quakers, and the English held slaves. But the system was milder here than in any of the other colonies. The Negroes were scattered among the families of the whites, and were treated with great humanity. Legislation on the subject of slavery did not begin until the middle of the eighteenth century, and it was not severe. Before this time, say three-quarters of a century, a few Acts had been passed calculated to protect the slave element from the sin of intoxication. In 1675 an Act passed, imposing fines and punishments upon any white person who should transport, harbor, or entertain "apprentices, servants, or slaves." It was perfectly natural that the Negroes should be of a nomadic disposition. They had no homes, no wives, no children,—nothing to attach them to a locality. Those who resided near the seacoast watched, with unflagging interest, the coming and going of the mysterious white-winged vessels. They hung upon the storied lips of every fugitive, and dreamed of lands afar where they might find that liberty for which their souls thirsted as the hart for the water-brook. Far from their native country, without the blessings of the Church, or the warmth of substantial friendship, they fell into a listless condition, a somnolence that led them to stagger against some of the regulations of the Province. Their wandering was not inspired by any subjective, inherent, generic evil: it was but the tossing of a weary, distressed mind under the dreadful influences of a hateful dream. And what little there is in the early records of the colony of New Jersey is at once a compliment to the humanity of the master, and the docility of the slave.

In 1676 the colony was divided into East and West Jersey, with separate governments. The laws of East Jersey, promulgated in 1682, contained laws prohibiting the entertaining of fugitive servants, or trading with Negroes. The law respecting fugitive servants was intended to destroy the hopes of runaways in the entertainment they so frequently obtained at the hands of benevolent Quakers and other enemies of "indenture" and slavery. The law-makers acted upon the presumption, that as the Negro had no property, did not own himself, he could not sell any article of his own. All slaves who attempted to dispose of any article were regarded with suspicion. The law made it a misdemeanor for a free person to purchase any thing from a slave, and hence cut off a source of revenue to the more industrious slaves, who by their frugality often prepared something for sale.

In 1694 "an Act concerning slaves" was passed by the Legislature of East Jersey. It provided, among other things, for the trial of "negroes and other slaves, for felonies punishable with death, by a jury of twelve persons before three justices of the peace; for theft, before two justices; the punishment by whipping." Here was the grandest evidence of the high character of the white population in East Jersey. In every other colony in North America the Negro was denied the right of "trial by jury," so sacred to Englishmen. In Virginia, Maryland, Massachusetts, Connecticut,—in all the colonies,—the Negro went into court convicted, went out convicted, and was executed, upon the frailest evidence imaginable. But here in Jersey the only example of justice was shown toward the Negro in North America. "Trial by jury" implied the right to be sworn, and give competent testimony. A Negro slave, when on trial for his life, was accorded the privilege of being tried by twelve honest white colonists before three justices of the peace. This was in striking contrast with the conduct of the colony of New York, where Negroes were arrested upon the incoherent accusations of dissolute whites and terrified blacks. It gave the Negroes a new and an anomalous position in the New World. It banished the cruel theory of Virginia, New York, and Connecticut, that the Negro was a pagan, and therefore should not be sworn in courts of justice, and threw open a wide door for his entrance into a more hopeful state than he had, up to that time, dared to anticipate. It allowed him to infer that his life was a little more than that of the brute that perisheth; that he could not be dragged by malice through the forms of a trial, without jury, witness, counsel, or friend, to an ignominious death, that was to be regretted only by his master, and his regrets to be solaced by the Legislature paying "the price;" that the law regarded him as a man, whose life was too dear to be committed to the disposition of irascible men, whose prejudices could be mollified only in extreme cruelty or cold-blooded murder. It had much to do toward elevating the character of the Negro in New Jersey. It first fired his heart with the noble impulse of gratitude, and then led him to hope. And how much that little word means! It causes the soul to spread its white pinions to every favoring breeze, and hasten on to a propitious future. And then the fact that Negroes had rights acknowledged by the statutes, and respectfully accorded them by the courts, had its due influence upon the white colonists. The men, or class of men, who have rights not challenged, command the respect of others. The fact clothes them with dignity as with a garment. And then, by the inevitable logic of the position of the courts of East Jersey, the colonists were led to the conclusion that the Negroes among them had other rights. And, as it has been said already, they received better treatment here than in any other colony in the country.

In West Jersey happily the word "slave" was omitted from the laws. Only servants and runaway servants were mentioned, and the selling of rum to Negroes and Indians was strictly forbidden.

The fear of insurrection among Indians and Negroes was general throughout all of the colonies. One a savage, and the other untutored, they knew but two manifestations,—gratitude and revenge. It was deemed a wise precaution to keep these unfortunate people as far removed from the exciting influences of rum as possible. Chapter twenty-three of a law passed in West Jersey in 1676, providing for publicity in judicial proceedings, concludes as follows:—

In 1702 the proprietors of East and West Jersey surrendered their rights of government to the queen. The Province was immediately placed with New York, and the government committed to the hands of Lord Cornbury. In 1704 "An Act for regulating negroe, Indian and mulatto slaves within the province of New Jersey," was introduced, but was tabled and disallowed. The Negroes had just cause for the fears they entertained as to legislation directed at the few rights they had enjoyed under the Jersey government. Their fellow-servants over in New York had suffered under severe laws, and at that time had no privilege in which they could rejoice. In 1713 the following law was passed:—

Nearly all the humane features of the Jersey laws were supplanted by severe prohibitions, requirements, and penalties. The trial by jury was construed to mean that one Negro's testimony was good against another Negro in a trial for a felony, allowing the owner of the slave to demand a jury. Humane masters were denied the right to emancipate their slaves, and the latter were prohibited from owning real property in fee simple or fee tail. Having stripped the Negro of the few rights he possessed, the General Court, during the same year, went on to reduce him to absolute property, and levied an impost-tax of ten pounds upon every Negro imported into the colony, to remain in force for seven years.

In 1754 an Act provided, that in the borough of Elizabeth any white servant or servants, slave or slaves, which shall "be brought before the Mayor, &c., by their masters or other inhabitant of the Borough, for any misdemeanor rude or disorderly behavior, may be committed to the workhouse to hard labor and receive correction not exceeding thirty lashes." This Act was purely local in character, and indiscriminate in its application to every class of servants. It was nothing more than a police regulation, and as such was a wholesome law.

In 1768 the General Court passed An Act to regulate the trial of slaves for murder and other crimes and to repeal so much of an act, &c. Sections one and two provided for the trial of slaves by the ordinary higher criminal courts. Section three provided that the expenses incurred in the execution of slaves should be levied upon all the owners of able-bodied slaves in the county, by order of the justices presiding at the trial. Section four repealed sections four, five, six, and seven of the Act of 1713. This was significant. It portended a better feeling toward the Negroes, and illumined the dark horizon of slavery with the distant light of hope. A strong feeling in favor of better treatment for Negro slaves made itself manifest at this time. When the Quaker found the prejudice against himself subsiding, he turned, like a good Samaritan, to pour the wine of human sympathy into the lacerated feelings of the Negro. Private instruction was given to them in many parts of Jersey. The gospel was expounded to them in its beauty and simplicity, and produced its good fruit in better lives.

The next year, 1769, a mercenary spirit inspired and secured the passage of another Act levying a tax upon imported slaves, and requiring persons manumitting slaves to give better securities. It reads,—

How an impost-tax upon imported slaves would be "beneficial in the introduction of sober industrious foreigners," is not easily perceived; and how it would promote "a spirit of industry among the inhabitants in general," is a problem most difficult of solution. But these were the lofty reasons that inspired the General Court to seek to fill the coffers of the Province with money drawn from the slave-lottery, where human beings were raffled off to the highest bidders in the colony. The cautious language in which the Act was couched indicated the sensitive state of the public conscience on slavery at that time. They were afraid to tell the truth. They did not dare to say to the people: We propose to repair the streets of your towns, the public roads, and lighten the burden of taxation, by saying to men-stealers, we will allow you to sell your cargoes of slaves into this colony provided you share the spoils of your superlative crime! No, they had to tell the people that the introduction of Negro slaves, upon whom there was a tax, would entice sober and industrious white people to come among them, and would quicken the entire Province with a spirit of thrift never before witnessed!

In 1760 the Negro was ruled out of the militia establishment upon a condition. The law provided against the enlistment of any "young man under the age of twenty-one years, or any slaves who are so for terms of life, or apprentices," without leave of their masters. This was the mildest prohibition against the entrance of the slave into the militia service in any of the colonies. There is nothing said about the employment of the free Negroes in this service; and it is fair to suppose, in view of the mild character of the laws, that they were not excluded. In settlements where the German and Quaker elements predominated, the Negro found that his "lines had fallen unto him in pleasant places, and that he had a goodly heritage." In the coast towns, and in the great centres of population, the white people were of a poorer class. Many were adventurers, cruel and unscrupulous in their methods. The speed with which the people sought to obtain a competency wore the finer edges of their feeling to the coarse grain of selfishness; and they not only drew themselves up into the miserable rags of their own selfish aggrandizements as far as all competitors were concerned, but regarded slavery with imperturbable complacency.

In 1738 the population of the Jerseys was, whites, 43,388; blacks, 3,981. In 1745 the whites numbered 56,797, and the blacks, 4,606.

FOOTNOTES:

It is unfortunate that there is no good history of New Jersey. The records of the Historical Society of that State are not conveniently printed, nor valuable in colonial data.

Freedom and Bondage, vol. i. p. 283.

The following were the instructions his lordship received, concerning the treatment of Negro slaves: "You shall endeavour to get a law past for the restraining of any inhuman severity, which by ill masters or overseers may be used towards their Christian servants and their slaves, and that provision be made therein that the wilfull killing of Indians and negroes may be punished with death, and that a fit penalty be emposed for the maiming of them."—Freedom and Bondage, vol. i. p. 280, note.

Freedom and Bondage, vol. i. p. 284.

Hurd, vol. i. p. 285.

Hurd, vol. i. p 285.

American Annals, vol. ii. pp. 127, 143.

CHAPTER XXI.: THE COLONY OF SOUTH CAROLINA.: 1665-1775.

The Carolinas receive two Different Charters from the Crown of Great Britain.—Era of Slavery Legislation.—Law establishing Slavery.—The Slave Population of this Province regarded as Chattel Property.—Trial of Slaves.—Increase of Slave Population.—The Increase in the Rice-Trade.—Severe Laws regulating the Private and Public Conduct of Slaves.—Punishment of Slaves for running away.—The Life of Slaves regarded as of Little Consequence by the Violent Master Class.—An Act empowering two Justices of the Peace to investigate Treatment of Slaves.—An Act prohibiting the Overworking of Slaves.—Slave-Market at Charleston.—Insurrection.—A Law authorizing the carrying of Fire-Arms among the Whites.—The Enlistment of Slaves to serve in Time of Alarm.—Negroes admitted to the Militia Service.—Compensation to Masters for the Loss of Slaves killed by the Enemy or who desert.—Few Slaves manumitted.—From 1754-76, Little Legislation on the Subject of Slavery.—Threatening War between England and her Provincial Dependencies.—The Effect upon Public Sentiment.

THE Carolinas received two different charters from the crown of Great Britain. The first was witnessed by the king at Westminster, March 24, 1663; the second, June 30, 1665. The last charter was surrendered to the king by seven of the eight proprietors on the 25th July, 1729. The government became regal; and the Province was immediately divided into North and South Carolina by an order of the British Council, and the boundaries between the two governments fixed.

There were Negro slaves in the Carolinas from the earliest days of their existence. The era of slavery legislation began about the year 1690. The first Act for the "Better Ordering of Slaves" was "read three times and passed, and ratified in open Parliament, the seventh day of February, Anno Domini, 1690." It bore the signatures of Seth Sothell, G. Muschamp, John Beresford, and John Harris. It contained fifteen articles of the severest character. On the 7th of June, 1712, the first positive law establishing slavery passed, and was signed. The entire Act embraced thirty-five sections. Section one is quoted in full because of the interest that centres in it in connection with the problem of slavery legislation in the colonies.

The above section was re-enacted into another law, containing forty-three sections, passed on the 23d of February, 1722. Virginia declared that children should follow the condition of their mothers, but never passed a law in any respect like unto this most remarkable Act. South Carolina has the unenviable reputation of being the only colony in North America where by positive statute the Negro was doomed to perpetual bondage. On the 10th of May, 1740, an act regulating slaves, containing fifty sections, recites:—

The first section of this Act was made more elaborate than any other law previously passed. It bore all the marks of ripe scholarship and profound law learning. The first section is produced here:—

The entire slave population of this Province was regarded as chattel property, absolutely. They could be seized in execution as in the case of other property, but not, however, if there were other chattels available. In case of "burglary, robbery, burning of houses, killing or stealing of any meat or other cattle, or other petty injuries, as maiming one of the other, stealing of fowls, provisions, or such like trespass or injuries," a justice of the peace was to be informed. He issued a warrant for the arrest of the offender or offenders, and summoned all competent witnesses. After examination, if found guilty, the offender or offenders were committed to jail. The justice then notified the justice next to him to be associated with him in the trial. He had the authority to fix the day and hour of the trial, to summon witness, and "three discreet and sufficient freeholders." The justices then swore the "freeholders," and, after they had tried the case, had the authority to pronounce the sentence of death, "or such other punishment" as they felt meet to fix. "The solemnity of a jury" was never accorded to slaves. "Three freeholders" could dispose of human life in such cases, and no one could hinder. The confession of the accused slave, and the testimony of another slave, were "held for good and convincing evidence in all petty larcenies or trespasses not exceeding forty shillings." In the case of a Negro on trial for his life, "the oath of Christian evidence" was required, or the "positive evidence of two Negroes or slaves," in order to convict.

The increase of slaves was almost phenomenal. The rice-trade had grown to enormous proportions. The physical obstruction gave away rapidly before the incessant and stupendous efforts of Negro laborers. The colonists held out most flattering inducements to Englishmen to emigrate into the Province. The home government applauded the zeal and executive abilities of the local authorities. Attention was called to the necessity of legislation for the government of the vast Negro population in the colony. The code of South Carolina was without an example among the civilized governments of modern times. It was unlawful for any free person to inhabit or trade with Negroes. Slaves could not leave the plantation on which they were owned, except in livery, or armed with a pass, signed by their master, containing the name of the possessor. For a violation of this regulation they were whipped on the naked back. No man was allowed to conduct a "plantation, cow-pen or stock," that shall be six miles distant from his usual place of abode, and wherein six Negroes were employed, without one or more white persons were residing on the place. Negro slaves found on another plantation than the one to which they belonged, "on the Lord's Day, fast days, or holy-days," even though they could produce passes, were seized and whipped. If a slave were found "keeping any horse, horses, or neat cattle," any white man, by warrant, could seize the animals, and sell them through the church-wardens; and the money arising from such sale was devoted to the poor of the parish in which said presumptuous slaves resided. If more than seven slaves were found travelling on the highway, except accompanied by a white man, it was lawful for any white man to apprehend each and every one of such slaves, and administer twenty lashes upon their bare back. No slave was allowed to hire out his time. Some owners of slaves were poor, and, their slaves being trusty and industrious, permitted them to go out and get whatever work they could, with the understanding that the master was to have the wages. An Act was passed in 1735, forbidding such transactions, and fining the persons who hired slaves who had no written certificate from their masters setting forth the terms upon which the work was to be done. No slave could hire a house or plantation.

No amount of industry could make him an exception to the general rule. If he toiled faithfully for years, amassed a fortune for his master, earned quite a competence for himself during the odd moments he caught from a busy life, and then, with acknowledged character and business tact, he sought to hire a plantation or buy a house, the law came in, and pronounced it a misdemeanor, for which both purchaser and seller had to pay in fines, stripes, and imprisonment. A slave could not keep in his own name, or that of his master, any kind of a house of entertainment. He was even prohibited by law from selling corn or rice in the Province. The penalty was a fine of forty shillings, and the forfeiture of the articles for sale. They could not keep a boat or canoe.

The cruelties of the code are without a parallel, as applied to the correction of Negro slaves.

As the penalties for the smallest breach of the slave-code grew more severe, the slaves grew more restless and agitated. Sometimes under great fear they would run away for a short time, in the hope that their irate masters would relent. But this, instead of helping, hindered and injured the cause of the slaves. Angered at the conduct of their slaves, the master element, having their representatives on the floor of the Assembly, secured the passage of the following brutal law:—

If any slave attempted to run away from his or her master, and go out of the Province, he or she could be tried before two justices and three freeholders, and sentenced to suffer a most cruel death. If it could be proved that any Negro, free or slave, had endeavored to persuade or entice any other Negro to run off out of the Province, upon conviction he was punished with forty lashes, and branded on the forehead with a red hot iron, "that the mark thereof may remain." If a white man met a slave, and demanded of him to show his ticket, and the slave refused, the law empowered the white man "to beat, maim, or assault; and if such Negro or slave" could not "be taken, to kill him," if he would not "shew his ticket."

The cruel and barbarous code of the slave-power in South Carolina produced, in course of time, a re-action in the opposite direction. The large latitude that the law gave to white people in their dealings with the hapless slaves made them careless and extravagant in the use of their authority. It educated them into a brood of tyrants. They did not care any more for the life of a Negro slave than for the crawling worm in their path. Many white men who owned no slaves poured forth their wrathful invectives and cruel blows upon the heads of innocent Negroes with the slightest pretext. They pushed, jostled, crowded, and kicked the Negro on every occasion. The young whites early took their lessons in abusing God's poor and helpless children; while an overseer was prized more for his brutal powers—to curse, beat, and torture—than for any ability he chanced to possess for business management. The press and pulpit had contemplated this state of affairs until they, too, were the willing abettors in the most cruel system of bondage that history has recorded. But no man wants his horse driven to death, if it is a beast. No one cares to have every man that passes kick his dog, even if it is not the best dog in the community. It is his dog, and that makes all the difference in the world. The men who did the most cruel things to the slaves they found in their daily path were, as a rule, without slaves or any other kind of property. They used their authority unsparingly. Common-sense taught the planters that better treatment of the slaves meant better work, and increased profits for themselves. A small value was finally placed upon a slave's life,—fifty pounds. Fifty pounds paid into the public treasury by a man who, "of wantonness, or only of bloody-mindedness, or cruel intention," had killed "a negro or other slave of his own," was enough to appease the public mind, and atone for a cold-blooded murder! If he killed another man's slave, the law demanded that he pay fifty pounds current money into the public treasury, and the full price of the slave to the owner, but was "not to be liable to any other punishment or forfeiture for the same." The law just referred to, passed in 1712, was re-enacted in 1722. One change was made in it: i.e., if a white servant, having no property, killed a slave, three justices could bind him over to the master whose slave he killed to serve him for five years. This law had a wholesome effect upon irresponsible white men, who often presumed upon their nationality, having neither brains, money, nor social standing, to punish slaves.

In 1740, May 10, the following Act became a law, showing that there had been a wonderful change in public sentiment rejecting the treatment of slaves:—

It may be said truthfully that the slaves in the colony of South Carolina were accorded treatment as good as that bestowed upon horses, in 1750. But their social condition was most deplorable. The law positively forbid the instruction of slaves, and the penalty was "one hundred pounds current money." For a few years Saturday afternoon had been allowed them as a day of recreation, but as early as 1690 it was forbidden by statute. In the same year an Act was passed declaring that slaves should "have convenient clothes, once every year; and that no slave" should "be free by becoming a christian, but as to payments of debts" were "deemed and taken as all other goods and chattels." Their houses were searched every fortnight "for runaway slaves" and "stolen goods." Druggists were not allowed to employ a Negro to handle medicines, upon pain of forfeiting twenty pounds current money for every such offence. Negroes were not allowed to practise medicine, nor administer drugs of any kind, except by the direction of some white person. Any gathering of Negroes could be broken up at the discretion of a justice living in the district where the meeting was in session.

Poor clothing and insufficient food bred wide-spread discontent among the slaves, and attracted public attention. Many masters endeavored to get on as cheaply as possible in providing for their slaves. In 1732 the Legislature passed an Act empowering two justices of the peace to inquire as to the treatment of slaves on the several plantations; and if any master neglected his slaves in food and raiment, he was liable to a fine of not more than fifty shillings. In May, 1740, an Act was passed requiring masters to see to it that their slaves were not overworked. The time set for them to work, was "from the 25th day of March to the 25th day of September," not "more than fifteen hours in four-and-twenty;" and "from the 25th day of September to the 25th day of March," not "more than fourteen hours in four-and-twenty."

The history of the impost-tax on slaves imported into the Province of South Carolina is the history of organized greed, ambition, and extortion. Many were the gold sovereigns that were turned into the official coffers at Charleston! With a magnificent harbor, and a genial climate, no city in the South could rival it as a slave-market. With an abundant supply from without, and a steady demand from within, the officials at Charleston felt assured that high impost-duties could not interfere with the slave-trade; while the city would be a great gainer by the traffic, both mediately and immediately.

Sudden and destructive insurrections were the safety-valves to the institution of slavery. A race long and cruelly enslaved may endure the yoke patiently for a season: but like the sudden gathering of the summer clouds, the pelting rain, the vivid, blinding lightning, the deep, hoarse thundering, it will assert itself some day; and then it is indeed a day of judgment to the task-masters! The Negroes in South Carolina endured a most cruel treatment for a long time; and, when "the day of their wrath" came, they scarcely knew it themselves, much less the whites. Florida was in the possession of the Spaniards. Its governor had sent out spies into Georgia and South Carolina, who held out very flattering inducements to the Negroes to desert their masters and go to Florida. Moreover, there was a Negro regiment in the Spanish service, whose officers were from their own race. Many slaves had made good their escape, and joined this regiment. It was allowed the same uniform and pay as the Spanish soldiers had. The colony of South Carolina was fearing an enemy from without, while behold their worst enemy was at their doors! In 1740 some Negroes assembled themselves together at a town called Stone, and made an attack upon two young men, who were guarding a warehouse, and killed them. They seized the arms and ammunition, effected an organization by electing one of their number captain; and, with boisterous drums and flying banners, they marched off "like a disciplined company." They entered the house of one Mr. Godfrey, slew him, his wife, and child, and then fired his dwelling. They next took up their march towards Jacksonburgh, and plundered and burnt the houses of Sacheveral, Nash, Spry, and others. They killed all the white people they found, and recruited their ranks from the Negroes they met. Gov. Bull was "returning to Charleston from the southward, met them, and, observing them armed, quickly rode out of their way." In a march of twelve miles, they had wrought a work of great destruction. News reached Wiltown, and the militia were called out. The Negro insurrectionists were intoxicated with their triumph, and drunk from rum they had taken from the houses they had plundered. They halted in an open field to sing and dance; and, during their hilarity, Capt. Bee, at the head of the troops of the district, fell upon them, and, having killed several, captured all who did not make their escape in the woods.

The Province was thrown into intense excitement. The Legislature called attention to the insurrection, and declared legal some very questionable and summary acts. In 1743 the people had not recovered from the fright they received from the insurrection. On the 7th of May, 1743, an Act was passed requiring every white male inhabitant, who resorted "to any church or any other public place of divine worship, within" the Province to "carry with him a gun or a pair of horse pistols, in good order and fit for service, with at least six charges of gun-powder and ball," upon pain of paying "twenty shillings."

As there was a law against teaching slaves to read and write, there were no educated preachers. If a Negro desired to preach to his fellow-slaves, he had to secure written permission from his master. While Negroes were sometimes baptized into the communion of the Church,—usually the Episcopal Church,—they were allowed only in the gallery, or organ-loft, of white congregations, in small numbers. No clergyman ventured to break unto this benighted people the bread of life. They were abandoned to the superstitions and religious fanaticisms incident to their condition.

In 1704 an Act was passed "for raising and enlisting such slaves as shalt be thought serviceable to this Province in time of Alarms." It required, within thirty days after the publication of the Act, that the commanders of military organizations throughout the Province should appoint "five freeholders," "sober and discreet men," who were to make a complete list of all the able-bodied slaves in their respective districts. Three of them were competent to decide upon the qualifications of a slave. After the completion of the list, the freeholders mentioned above notified the owners to appear before them upon a certain day, and show cause why their slaves should not be chosen for the service of the colony. The slaves were then enlisted, and their masters charged with the duty of arming them "with a serviceable lance, hatchet or gun, with sufficient amunition and hatchets, according to the conveniency of the said owners, to appear under the colours of the respective captains, in their several divisions, throughout" the Province, for the performance of such "public service" as required. If an owner refused to equip or permit his slave to respond to alarms, he was fined five pounds for each neglect, which was to be paid to the captain of the company to which the slave belonged. If a slave were killed by the enemy "in the line of duty," the owner of such slave was paid out of the public treasury such sum of money as three freeholders, under oath, should award. The Negroes did admirably; and four years later, on the 24th of April, 1708, the Legislature re-enacted the bill making them militia-men. The last Act contained ten sections, and bears evidence of the pleasure the whites took in the employment of Negroes as their defenders. If a Negro were taken prisoner by the enemy, and effected his escape back into the Province, he was emancipated. And if a Negro captured and killed an enemy, he was emancipated, but if wounded himself, was set free at the public expense. If he deserted to the enemy, his master was paid for his loss.

Few slaves were manumitted. The law required that masters who emancipated their slaves should make provisions for transporting them out of the Province. If they were found in the Province twelve months after they were set free, the manumission was considered void, except approved by the Legislature.

From 1754 till 1776 there was little legislation on the subject of slavery. The pressure from without made men conservative about slavery, and radical on the question of the rights and liberties of the colonies. The threatening war between England and her provincial dependencies made men humane and patriotic; and during these years of anxiety and excitement, the weary slaves breathed a better atmosphere, and enjoyed the rare sensation of confidence and benevolence.

FOOTNOTES:

An eminent lawyer, chief justice of the Supreme Court of the State of——, and a warm personal friend of mine, recently said to me, during an afternoon stroll, that he never knew that slavery was ever established by statute in any of the British colonies in North America.

Statutes of S.C., vol. vii. p. 352.

Virginia made slavery statutory as did other colonies, but we have no statute so explicit as the above. But slavery was slavery in all the colonies, cruel and hurtful.

Statutes of S.C., vol. vii. p. 397.

Statutes of S.C., vol. vii. pp. 397, 398.

Ibid., vol. vii. pp. 343, 344.

This Act, passed on the 16th of March, 1696, was made "perpetual" on the 12th of December, 1712. It remained throughout the entire period. See Statutes of S.C., vol. ii, p. 598.

Statutes of S.C., vol. vii. p. 363.

Statutes of S.C., vol. vii. pp. 359, 360.

Statutes of S.C., vol. vii. 363.

Ibid., vol vii. pp. 410. 411.

The following is the Act of the 7th of June, 1690. "XXXIV Since charity, and the christian religion, which we profess, obliges us to wish well to the souls of all men, and that religion may not be made a pretence to alter any man's property and right, and that no person may neglect to baptize their negroes or slaves, or suffer them to be baptized, for fear that thereby they should be manumitted and set free, Be it therefore enacted by the authority aforesaid, that it shall be, and is hereby declared, lawful for any negro or Indian slave, or any other slave or slaves whatsoever, to receive and profess the christian faith, and be thereinto baptized; but that notwithstanding such slave or slaves shall receive and profess the Christian religion, and be baptized, he or they shall not thereby be manumitted or set free, or his or their owner, master or mistress lose his or their civil right, property, and authority over such slave or slaves, but that the slave or slaves, with respect to his servitude shall remain and continue in the same state and condition that he or they was in before the making of this act."—Statutes of S.C., vol. vii. pp 364, 365.

In 1740 an Act was passed requiring masters to provide "sufficient clothing" for their slaves.

Hist. S.C. and Georgia, vol. ii. p. 73.

Statutes of S.C., vol. vii. p. 416.

CHAPTER XXII.: THE COLONY OF NORTH CAROLINA.: 1669-1775.

The Geographical Situation of North Carolina Favorable to the Slave-Trade.—The Locke Constitution adopted.—William Sayle commissioned Governor.—Legislative Career of the Colony.—The Introduction of the Established Church of England into the Colony.—The Rights of Negroes controlled absolutely by their Masters.—An Act respecting Conspiracies.—The Wrath of Ill-natured Whites visited upon their Slaves.—An Act against the Emancipation of Slaves.—Limited Rights of Free Negroes.

THE geographical situation of North Carolina was favorable to the slave-trade.

Through the genius of Shaftesbury, and the subtle cunning of John Locke, Carolina received, and for a time adopted, the most remarkable constitution ever submitted to any people in any age of the world. The whole affair was an insult to humanity, and in its fundamental elements bore the palpable evidences of the cruel conclusions of an exclusive philosophy. "No elective franchise could be conferred upon a freehold of less than fifty acres," while all executive power was vested in the proprietors themselves. Seven courts were controlled by forty-two counsellors, twenty-eight of whom held their places through the gracious favor of the proprietary and "the nobility." Trial by jury was concluded by the opinions of the majority.

The men who formed the rank and file of the yeomanry of the colony of North Carolina were ill prepared for a government launched upon the immense scale of the Locke Constitution. The hopes and fears, the feuds and debates, the vexatious and insoluble problems, of the political science of government which had clouded the sky of the most astute and ambitous statesmen of Europe, were dumped into this remarkable instrument. The distance between the people and the nobility was sought to be made illimitable, and the right to govern was based upon permanent property conditions. Hereditary wealth was to go arm in arm with political power.

The constitution was signed on the 21st of July, 1669, and William Sayle was commissioned as governor. The legislative career of the Province began in the fall of the same year; and history must record that it was one of the most remarkable and startling North America ever witnessed. The portions of the constitution which refer to the institution of slavery are as follows:—

Though the Locke Constitution was adopted by the proprietaries, March 1, 1669, it may be doubted whether it ever had the force of law, as it was never ratified by the local Legislature. Article one hundred and ten, granting absolute power and authority to a master over his Negro slave, is without a parallel in the legislation of the colonies. And while the slave might enter the Christian Church, and his humanity thereby be recognized, it was strangely inconsistent to place his life at the disposal of brutal masters, who "neither feared God nor regarded man."

The Negro slaves in North Carolina occupied the paradoxical position of being eligible to membership in the Christian Church, and the absolute property of their white brothers. In the second draught of the constitution, signed in March, 1670, against the eloquent protest of John Locke, the section on religion was amended so as, while tolerating every religious creed, to declare ,"the Church Of England" the only true Orthodox Church, and the national religion of the Province. This, in the face of the fact that the great majority of all the Christians who flocked to the New World were dissenters, separatists, and nonconformists, can only be explained in the light of the burning zeal of the Church of England to out-Herod Herod,—to carry the Negroes into the communion of the State church for political purposes. It was the most sordid motive that impelled the churchmen to open the church to the slave. His membership did not change his condition, nor secure him immunity from the barbarous treatment the institution of slavery bestowed upon its helpless victims.

In the eyes of the law the Negro, being absolute property, had no rights, except those temporarily delegated by the master; and he acted in the relation of an agent. Negro slaves were not allowed "to raise horses, cattle or hogs;" and if any stock were found in their possession six months after the passage of the Act of 1741, they were to be seized by the sheriff of the county, and sold by the church-wardens of the parish. The profits arising from such sales went, one half to the parish, the other half to the informer. A slave was not suffered to go off of the plantation where he was appointed to live, without a pass signed by his master or the overseer. There was an exception made in the case of Negroes wearing liveries. Negro slaves were not allowed the use of fire-arms or other weapons, except they were armed with a certificate from their master granting the coveted permission. If they hunted with arms, not having a certificate, any Christian could apprehend them, seize the weapons, deliver the slave to the first justice of the peace; who was authorized to administer, without ceremony, twenty lashes upon his or her bare back, and send him or her home. The master had to pay the cost of arrest and punishment. The one exception to this law was, that one Negro on each plantation or in each district could carry a gun to shoot game for his master and protect stock, etc.; but his certificate was to be in his possession all the time. If a Negro went from the plantation on which he resided, to another plantation or place, he was required by statute to travel in the most generally frequented road. If caught in another road, not much travelled, except in the company of a white man, it was lawful for the man who owned the land through which he was passing to seize him, and administer not more than forty lashes. If Negroes visited each other in the night season,—the only time they could visit,—the ones who were found on another plantation than their master's were punished with lashes on their naked back, not exceeding forty; while the Negroes who had furnished the entertainment received twenty lashes for their hospitality. In case any slave, who had not been properly fed and clothed by his master, was convicted of stealing cattle, hogs, or corn from another man, an action of trespass could be maintained against the master in the general or county court, and damages recovered.

Here, as in the other colonies, the greatest enemy of the colonists was an accusing conscience. The people started at every breath of rumor, and always imagined their slaves conspiring to cut their throats. There was nothing in the observed character of the slaves to justify the wide-spread consternation that filled the public mind. Nor was there any occasion to warrant the passage of the Act of 1741, respecting conspiracies among slaves. It is a remarkable document, and is produced here.

The manner of conducting the trials of Negroes charged with felony or misdemeanor was rather peculiar. Upon one or more white persons' testimony, or the evidence of Negroes and

Indians, bond or free, the unfortunate defendant, "without the solemnity of a jury," before three justices and four freeholders, could be hurried through a trial, convicted, sentenced to die a dreadful death, and then be executed without the officiating presence of a minister of the gospel.

The unprecedented discretion allowed to masters in the government led to the most tragic results. Men were not only reckless of the lives of their own slaves, but violent toward those belonging to others. If a Negro showed the least independence in conversation with a white man, he could be murdered in cold blood; and it was only a case of a contumacious slave getting his dues. But men became so prodigal in the exercise of this authority that the public became alarmed, and the Legislature called a halt on the master-class. At first the Legislature paid for the slaves who were destroyed by the consuming wrath of ill-natured whites, but finally allowed an action to lie against the persons who killed a slave. This had a tendency to reduce the number of murdered slaves; but the fateful clause in the Locke Constitution had educated a voracious appetite for blood, and the extremest cruel treatment continued without abatement.

The free Negro population was very small in this colony. The following act on manumission differs so widely from the law on this point in the other colonies, that it is given as an illustration of the severe character of the legislation of North Carolina against the emancipation of Negroes.

The free Negroes were badly treated. They were not allowed any communion with the slaves. A free Negro man was not allowed to marry a white woman, nor even a Negro slave woman without the consent of her master. If he formed an alliance with a white woman, her offspring were bound out, or sold by the church-wardens, until they obtained their majority. If the white woman were an indentured servant, she was constrained to serve an additional year. If she were a free woman, she was sold for two years by the church-wardens. Free Negroes were greatly despised and shunned by both slaves and white people.

As a conspicuous proof of the glaring hypocrisy of the "nobility," who, in the constitution, threw open the door of the Church to the Negro, it should be said, that, during the period from the founding of the Province down to the colonial war, no attempt was ever made, through the ecclesiastical establishment, to dissipate the dark clouds of ignorance that enveloped the Negro's mind. They were left in a state of ignorance and crime. The gravest social evils were winked at by masters, whose lecherous examples were the occasion for the most grievous offending of the slaves. The Mulattoes and other free Negroes were taxed. They had no place in the militia, nor could they claim the meanest rights of the humblest "leetman."

FOOTNOTES:

Bancroft, vol. ii., 5th ed. p. 148.
Statutes of S.C., vol. i. pp. 53-55.
Public Acts of N.C., vol. i. p. 64.
This is an instance of humanity in the North-Carolina code worthy of special note. It stands as the only instance of justice toward the over-worked and under-fed slaves of the colony.
Public Acts of N.C., p.65.
Public Acts of N.C., p. 66.
The Act of 1741 says, "until 31 years of age."

CHAPTER XXIII.: THE COLONY OF NEW HAMPSHIRE.: 1679-1775.

The Provincial Government of Massachusetts exercises Authority over the State of New Hampshire at its Organization.—Slavery existed from the Beginning.—The Governor releases a Slave from Bondage.—Instruction against Importation of Slaves.—Several Acts regulating the Conduct of Servants.—The Indifferent Treatment of Slaves.—The Importation of Indian Servants forbidden.—An Act checking the Severe Treatment of Servants and Slaves.—Slaves in the Colony until the Commencement of Hostilities.

ANTERIOR to the year 1679, the provincial government of Massachusetts exercised authority over the territory that now comprises the State of New Hampshire. It is not at all improbable, then, that slavery existed in this colony from the beginning of its organic existence. As early as 1683 it was set upon by the authorities as a wicked and hateful institution. On the 14th of March, 1684, the governor of New Hampshire assumed the responsibility of releasing a Negro slave from bondage. The record of the fact is thus preserved:—

It may be inferred from the above, that the royal governor of the Province felt the pressure of public sentiment on the question of anti-slavery. While this colony copied its criminal code from Massachusetts, its people seemed to be rather select, and, on the question of human rights, far in advance of the people of Massachusetts. The twelfth article was: "If any man stealeth mankind he shall be put to death or otherwise grievously punished." The entire code—the first one—was rejected in England as "fanatical and absurd." It was the desire of this new and feeble colony to throw every obstacle in the way of any legal recognition of slavery. The governors of all the colonies received instruction in regard to the question of slavery, but the governor of New Hampshire had received an order from the crown to have the tax on imported slaves removed. The royal instructions, dated June 30, 1761, were as follows:—

New Hampshire never passed any law establishing slavery, but in 1714 enacted several laws regulating the conduct of servants. One was An Act to prevent disorder in the night:—

The instructions against the importation of slaves were in harmony with the feelings of the great majority of the people. They felt that slavery would be a hinderance rather than a help to them, and in the selection of servants chose white ones. If the custom of holding men in bondage had become a part of the institutions of Massachusetts,—so like a cancer that it could not be removed without endangering the political and commercial life of the colony,—the good people of New Hampshire, acting in the light of experience, resolved, upon the threshold of their provincial life, to oppose the introduction of slaves into their midst. The first result was, that they learned quite early that they could get on without slaves; and, second, the traders in human flesh discovered that there was no demand for slaves in New Hampshire. Even nature fought against the crime; and Negroes were found to be poorly suited to the climate, and, of course, were an expensive luxury in that colony.

But, nevertheless, there were slaves in New Hampshire. The majority of them had gone in during the time the colony was a part of the territory of Massachusetts. They had been purchased by men who regarded them as indispensable to them. They had lived long in many families;

children had been born unto them, and in many instances they were warmly attached to their owners. But all masters were not alike. Some treated their servants and slaves cruelly. The neglect in some cases was worse than stripes or over-work. Some were poorly clad and scantily fed; and, thus exposed to the inclemency of the severe climate, many were precipitated into premature graves. Even white and Indian servants shared this harsh treatment. The Indians endured greater hardships than the Negroes. They were more lofty in their tone, more sensitive in their feelings, more revengeful in their disposition. They were both hated and feared, and the public sentiment against them was very pronounced. A law, passed in 1714, forbid their importation into the colony under a heavy penalty.

In 1718 it was found necessary to pass a law to check the severe treatment inflicted upon servants and slaves. An Act for restraining inhuman severities recited,—

There were slaves in New Hampshire down to the breaking-out of the war in the colonies, but they were only slaves in name. Few in number, widely scattered, they felt themselves closely identified with the interests of the colonists.

FOOTNOTES:

Belknap's Hist. of N.H., vol. i. p. 333.
Hildreth, vol. i. p. 501.
Gordon's Hist. of Am. Rev., vol. v. Letter 2.
Freedom and Bondage, vol. i. p. 266.
Freedom and Bondage, vol. i. p. 267.

CHAPTER XXIV.: THE COLONY OF PENNSYLVANIA.: 1681-1775.

Organization of the Government of Pennsylvania.—The Swedes and Dutch plant Settlements on the Western Bank of the Delaware River.—The Governor of New York seeks to exercise Jurisdiction over the Territory of Pennsylvania.—The First Laws agreed upon in England.—Provisions of the Law.—Memorial against Slavery draughted and adopted by the Germantown Friends.—William Penn presents a Bill for the Better Regulation of Servants.—An Act preventing the Importation of Negroes and Indians.—Rights of Negroes.—A Duty laid upon Negroes and Mulatto Slaves.—The Quaker the Friend of the Negro.—England begins to threaten her Dependencies in North America.—The People of Pennsylvania reflect upon the Probable Outrages their Negroes might commit.

LONG before there was an organized government in Pennsylvania, the Swedes and Dutch had planted settlements on the western bank of the Delaware River. But the English crown claimed the soil; and the governor of New York, under patent from the Duke of York, sought to exercise jurisdiction over the territory. On the 11th of July, 1681, "Conditions and Concessions were agreed upon by William Penn, Proprietary," and the persons who were "adventurers and purchasers in the same province." Provision was made for the punishment of persons who should injure Indians, and that the planter injured by them should "not be his own judge upon the Indian." All controversies arising between the whites and the Indians were to be settled by a council of twelve persons,—six white men and six Indians.

The first laws for the government of the colony were agreed upon in England, and in 1682 went into effect. Provision was made for the registering of all servants, their full names, amount of wages paid, and the time when they received their remuneration. It was strictly required that servants should not be kept beyond the time of their indenture, should be kindly treated, and the customary outfit furnished at the time of their freedom.

The baneful custom of enslaving Negroes had spread through every settlement in North America, and was even "tolerated in Pennsylvania under the specious pretence of the religious instruction of the slave." In 1688 Francis Daniel Pastorius draughted a memorial against slavery, which was adopted by the Germantown Friends, and by them sent up to the Monthly Meeting, and thence to the Yearly Meeting at Philadelphia. The original document was found by Nathan Kite of Philadelphia in 1844. It was a remarkable document, and the first protest against slavery issued by any religious body in America. Speaking of the slaves, Pastorius asks, "Have not these negroes as much right to fight for their freedom as you have to keep them slaves?" He believed the time would come,—

"When, from the gallery to the farthest seat, Slave and slave-owner shall no longer meet, But all sit equal at the Master's feet."

He regarded the "buying, selling, and holding men in slavery, as inconsistent with the Christian religion." When his memorial came before the Yearly Meeting for action, it confessed itself "unprepared to act," and voted it "not proper then to give a positive judgment in the case." In 1696 the Yearly Meeting pronounced against the further importation of slaves, and adopted measures looking toward their moral improvement. George Keith, catching the holy inspiration of humanity, with a considerable following, denounced the institution of slavery "as contrary to the religion of Christ, the rights of man, and sound reason and policy."

While these efforts were, to a certain extent, abortive, yet, nevertheless, the Society of the Friends made regulations for the better treatment of the enslaved Negroes. The sentiment thus created went far toward deterring the better class of citizens from purchasing slaves. To his broad and lofty sentiments of humanity, the pious William Penn sought to add the force of positive law. The published views of George Fox, given at Barbadoes in 1671, in his "Gospel Family Order, being a short discourse concerning the ordering of Families, both of Whites, Blacks, and Indians," had a salutary effect upon the mind of Penn. In 1700 he proposed to the Council "the necessitie of a law [among others] about ye marriages of negroes." The bill was referred to a joint committee of both houses, and they brought in a bill "for regulating Negroes in their Morals and Marriages &c." It reached a second reading, and was lost. Penn regarded the teaching of Negroes the sanctity of the marriage relation as of the greatest importance to the colony, and the surest means of promoting pure morals. Upon what grounds it was rejected is not known. He presented, at the same session of the Assembly, another bill, which provided "for the better regulation of servants in this province and territories." He desired the government of slaves to be prescribed and regulated by law, rather than by the capricious whims of masters. No servant was to be sold out of the Province without giving his consent, nor could he be assigned over except before a justice of the peace. It provided for a regular allowance to servants at the expiration of their time, and required them to serve five days extra for every day's absence from their master without the latter's assent. A penalty was fixed for concealing runaway slaves, and a reward offered for apprehending them. No free person was allowed to deal with servants, and justices and sheriffs were to be punished for neglecting their duties in the premises.

In case a Negro was guilty of murder, he was tried by two justices, appointed by the governor, before six freeholders. The manner of procedure was prescribed, and the nature of the sentence and acquittal. Negroes were not allowed to carry a gun or other weapons. Not more than four were allowed together, upon pain of a severe flogging. An Act for raising revenue was passed, and a duty upon imported slaves was levied, in 1710. In 1711-12, an Act was passed "to prevent the importation of negroes and Indians" into the Province. A general petition for the emancipation of slaves by law was presented to the Legislature during this same year; but the wise law-makers replied, that "it was neither just nor convenient to set them at liberty." The bill passed on the 7th of June, 1712, but was disapproved by Great Britain, and was accordingly repealed by an Act of Queen Anne, Feb. 20, 1713. In 1714 and 1717, Acts were passed to check the importation of slaves. But the English government, instead of being touched by the philanthropic endeavors of the people of Pennsylvania, was seeking, for purposes of commercial trade and gain, to darken the continent with the victims of its avarice.

Negroes had no political rights in the Province. Free Negroes were prohibited from entertaining Negro or Indian slaves, or trading with them. Masters were required, when manumitting slaves, to furnish security, as in the other colonies. Marriages between the races were forbidden. Negroes were not allowed to be abroad after nine o'clock at night.

In 1773 the Assembly passed "An Act making perpetual the Act entitled, An Act for laying a duty on negroes and mulatto slaves," etc., and added ten pounds to the duty. The colonists did much to check the vile and inhuman traffic; but, having once obtained a hold, it did eat like a canker. It threw its dark shadow over personal and collective interests, and poisoned the springs of human kindness in many hearts. It was not alone hurtful to the slave: it transformed and blackened character everywhere, and fascinated those who were anxious for riches beyond the power of moral discernment. Here, however, as in New Jersey, the Negro found the Quaker his practical friend; and his upper and better life received the pruning advice, refining and elevating influence, of a godly people. But intelligence in the slave was an occasion of offending, and prepared him to realize his deplorable situation. So to enlighten him was to excite in him a deep desire for liberty, and, not unlikely, a feeling of revenge toward his enslavers. So there was really danger in the method the guileless Friends adopted to ameliorate the condition of the slaves.

When England began to breathe out threatenings against her contumacious dependencies in North America, the people of Pennsylvania began to reflect upon the probable outrages their Negroes would, in all probability, commit. They inferred that the Negroes would be their enemy because they were their slaves. This was the equitable findings of a guilty conscience. They did not dare expect less than the revengeful hate of the beings they had laid the yoke of bondage upon; and verily they found themselves with "fears within, and fightings without."

FOOTNOTES:

Gordon's History of Penn., p. 114.
Whittier's Penn. Pilgrim, p. viii.
The memorial referred to was printed in extenso in The Friend, vol. xviii. No 16.
Minutes of Yearly Meeting, Watson's MS. Coll. Bettle's notices of N.S. Minutes, Penn. Hist. Soc.
Colonial Rec., vol. i. pp. 598, 606. See also Votes of Assembly, vol. i. pp. 120-122.

CHAPTER XXV.: THE COLONY OF GEORGIA.: 1732-1775.

Georgia once included in the Territory of Carolina.—The Thirteenth Colony planted in North America by the English Government.—Slaves ruled out altogether by the Trustees.—The Opinion of Gen. Oglethorpe concerning Slavery.—Long and Bitter Discussion in Regard to the Admission of Slavery into the Colony.—Slavery introduced.—History of Slavery in Georgia.

GEORGIA was once included in the territory of Carolina, and extended from the Savannah to the St. John's River. A corporate body, under the title of "The Trustees for establishing the Colony of Georgia," was created by charter, bearing date of June 9, 1732. The life of their trust was for the space of twenty-one years. The rules by which the trustees sought to manage the infant were rather novel; but as a discussion of them would be irrelevant, mention can be made only of that part which related to slavery. Georgia was the last colony—the thirteenth—planted in North America by the English government. Special interest centred in it for several reasons, that will be explained farther on.

The trustees ruled out slavery altogether. Gen. John Oglethorpe, a brilliant young English officer of gentle blood, the first governor of the colony, was identified with "the Royal African Company, which alone had the right of planting forts and trading on the coast of Africa." He said that "slavery is against the gospel, as well as the fundamental law of England. We refused, as trustees, to make a law permitting such a horrid crime." Another of the trustees, in a sermon preached on Sunday, Feb. 17, 1734, at St. George's Church, Hanover Square, London, declared, "Slavery, the misfortune, if not the dishonor, of other plantations, is absolutely proscribed. Let avarice defend it as it will, there is an honest reluctance in humanity against buying and selling, and regarding those of our own species as our wealth and possessions." Beautiful sentiments! Eloquent testimony against the crime of the ages! At first blush the student of history is apt to praise the sublime motives of the "trustees," in placing a restriction against the slave-trade. But the declaration of principles quoted above is not borne out by the facts of history. On this point Dr. Stevens, the historian of Georgia, observes, "Yet in the official publications of that body [the trustees], its inhibition is based only on political and prudential, and not on humane and liberal grounds, and even Oglethorpe owned a plantation and negroes near Parachucla in South Carolina, about forty miles above Savannah." To this reliable opinion is added:—

The reasons that led the trustees to prohibit slavery in the colony are put thus tersely.—

It is clear, then, that the founders of the colony of Georgia were not moved by the noblest impulses to prohibit slavery within their jurisdiction. In the chapter on South Carolina, attention was called to the influence of the Spanish troops in Florida on the recalcitrant Negroes in the Carolinas, the Negro regiment with subalterns from their own class, and the work of Spanish emissaries among the slaves. The home government thought it wise to build up Georgia out of white men, who could develop its resources, and bear arms in defence of British possessions along an extensive border exposed to a pestiferous foe. But the Board of Trade soon found this an impracticable scheme, and the colonists themselves began to clamor "for the use of negroes." The first petition for the introduction and use of Negro slaves was offered to the trustees in 1735.

This prayer was promptly and positively denied, and for fifteen years they refused to grant all requests for the use of Negroes. They adhered to their prohibition in letter and spirit. Whenever and wherever Negroes were found in the colony, they were sold back into Carolina. In the month of December, 1738, a petition, addressed to the trustees, including nearly all the names of the foremost colonists, set forth the distressing condition into which affairs had drifted under the enforcement of the prohibition, and declared that "the use of negroes, with proper limitations, which, if granted, would both occasion great numbers of white people to come here, and also to render us capable to subsist ourselves, by raising provisions upon our lands, until we could make some produce fit for export, in some measure to balance our importations." But instead of securing a favorable hearing, the petition drew the fire of the friends of the prohibition against the use of Negroes. On the 3d of January, 1739, a petition to the trustees combating the arguments of the above-mentioned petition, and urging them to remain firm, was issued at Darien. This was followed by another one, issued from Ebenezer on the 13th of March, in favor of the position occupied by the trustees. A great many Scotch and German people had settled in the colony; and, familiar with the arts of husbandry, they became the ardent supporters of the trustees. James Habersham, the "dear fellow-traveller," of Whitefield, exclaimed,—

But the trustees stood firm against the subtle cunning of the politicians, and the eloquent pleadings of avarice.

On the 7th October, 1741, a large meeting was held at Savannah, and a petition drawn, in which the land-holders and settlers presented their grievances to the English authorities in London. On the 26th of March, 1742, Mr. Thomas Stephens, armed with the memorial, as the agent of the memorialists, sailed for London. While the document ostensibly set forth their wish for a definition of "the tenure of the lands," really the burden of the prayer was for "Negroes." He presented the memorial to the king, and his Majesty referred it to a committee of the "Lords of Council for Plantation Affairs." This committee transferred a copy of the memorial to the trustees, with a request for their answer. About this time Stephens presented a petition to Parliament, in which he charged the trustees with direliction of duty, improper use of the public funds, abuse of their authority, and numerous other sins against the public welfare. It created a genuine sensation. The House resolved to go into a "committee of the whole," to consider the petitions and the answer of the trustees. The answer of the trustees was drawn by the able pen of the Earl of Egmont, and by them warmly approved on the 3d of May, and three days later was read to the House of Commons. A motion prevailed "that the petitions do lie upon the table," for the perusal of the members, for the space of one week. At the expiration of the time fixed, Stephens appeared, and all the petitions of the people of Georgia to the trustees in reference to "the tenure of lands," and for "the use of negroes," were laid before the honorable body. In the committee of the whole the affairs of the colony were thoroughly investigated; and, after a few days session, Mr. Carew reported a set of resolutions, being the sense of the committee after due deliberation upon the matters before them:—

When the resolution making the importation of rum lawful reached a vote, it was amended by adding, "As also the use of negroes, who may be employed there with advantage to the colony, under proper regulations and restrictions." It was lost by a majority of nine votes. A resolution prevailed calling Thomas Stephens to the bar of the House, "to be reprimanded on his knees by Mr. Speaker," for his offence against the trustees.

On the next day Stephens, upon his bended knees at the bar of the House of Commons, before the assembled statesmen of Great Britain, was publicly reprimanded by the speaker, and discharged after paying his fees. Thus ended the attempt of the people of the colony of Georgia to secure permission, over the heads of the trustees, to introduce slaves into their service.

The dark tide of slavery influence was dashing against the borders of the colony. The people were discouraged. Business was stagnated. Internal dissatisfaction and factional strife wore hard upon the spirit of a people trying to build up and develop a new country. Then the predatory incursions of the Spaniards, and the threatening attitude of the Indians, unnerved the entire Province. In this state of affairs white servants grew insolent and insubordinate. Those whose term of service expired refused to work. In this dilemma many persons boldly put the rule of the trustees under foot, and hired Negroes from the Carolinas. At length the trustees became aware of the clandestine importation of Negroes into the colony, and thereupon gave the magistrates a severe reproval. On the 2d of October, 1747, they received the following reply:—

It was charged that the law-officers knew of the presence of Negroes in Georgia; that their standing and constant toast was, "the one thing needful" (Negroes); and that they themselves had surreptitiously aided in the procurement of Negroes for the colony. The supporters of the colonists grew less powerful as the struggle went forward. The most active grew taciturn and conservative. The advocates of Negro labor became bolder, and more acrimonious in debate; and at length the champions of exclusive white labor shrank into silence, appalled at the desperation of then opponents. The Rev. Martin Bolzius, one of the most active supporters of the trustees, wrote those gentlemen on May 3, 1748:—

The Rev. George Whitefield and James Habersham used their utmost influence upon the trustees to obtain a modification of the prohibition against "the use of negroes." On the 6th of December, 1748, Rev. Whitefield, speaking of a plantation and Negroes he had purchased, wrote the trustees:—

The sentiment in favor of the importation of Negro slaves had become well-nigh unanimous. The trustees began to waver. On the 10th of January, 1749, another petition was presented to the trustees. It was carefully drawn, and set forth the restrictions under which slaves should be introduced. On the 16th of May following, it was read to the trustees; and they resolved to have it "presented to His Majesty in council." They also asked that the prohibition against the introduction of Negroes, passed in "1735, be repealed." The Earl of Shaftesbury, at the head of a special committee, draughted a bill repealing the prohibition. On the 26th of October, 1749, a large and influential committee of twenty-seven drew up and signed a petition urging the immediate introduction of slavery, with certain limitations. The paper was duly attested, and returned to the trustees. The opposition to the introduction of slavery into the colony of Georgia had been conquered; and, after a long and bitter struggle, slavery was firmly and legally established in this the last Province of the English in the Western world. The colonists were jubilant.

The charter under which the trustees acted expired by limitation in 1752, and a new form of government was established under the Board of Trade. The royal commission appointed a governor and council. One of the first ordinances enacted by them was one whereby "all offences committed by slaves were to be tried by a single justice, without a jury, who was to award execution, and, in capital cases, to set a value on the slave, to be paid out of the public treasury." At the first session of the Assembly in 1755, a law was passed "for the regulation and government of slaves." In 1765 an Act was passed establishing a pass system, and the rest of the legislation in respect to slaves was a copy of the laws of South Carolina.

The history of slavery in Georgia during this period is unparalleled and incomparably interesting. It illustrates the power of the institution, and shows that there was no Province sufficiently independent of its influence so as to expel it from its jurisdiction. Like the Angel of Death that passed through Egypt, there was no colony that it did not smite with its dark and destroying pinions. The dearest, the sublimest, interests of humanity were prostrated by its defiling touch. It shut out the sunlight of human kindness; it paled the fires of hope; it arrested the development of the branches of men's better natures, and peopled their lower being with base and consuming desires; it placed the "Golden Rule" under the unholy heel of time-servers and self-seekers; it made the Church as secular as the Change, and the latter as pious as the former: it was a gigantic system, at war with the civilization of the Roundheads and Puritans, and an intolerable burden to a people who desired to build a new nation in this New World in the West.

FOOTNOTES:

Stephens's Journal, vol. iii. p. 281.
Freedom and Bondage, vol. i. p. 310, note.
Stevens's Hist. of Georgia, vol. i. p. 289.
Bancroft, vol. iii. 12th ed. p. 427.
Stevens's Hist. of Georgia, vol. i. p. 307.
Whitefield's Works, vol. ii. pp. 90, 105, 208.

Part III.

THE NEGRO DURING THE REVOLUTION.

CHAPTER XXVI.: MILITARY EMPLOYMENT OF NEGROES.: 1775-1780.

The Colonial States in 1715.—Ratification of the Non-Importation Act by the Southern Colonies.—George Washington presents Resolutions against Slavery, in a Meeting at Fairfax Court-House, Va.—Letter written by Benjamin Franklin to Dean Woodward, pertaining to Slavery.—Letter to the Freemen of Virginia from a Committee, concerning the Slaves brought from Jamaica.—Severe Treatment of Slaves in the Colonies modified.—Advertisement in "The Boston Gazette" of the Runaway Slave Crispus Attucks.—The Boston Massacre.—Its Results.—Crispus Attucks shows his Loyalty.—His Spirited Letter to the Tory Governor of the Province.—Slaves admitted into the Army.—The Condition of the Continental Army.—Spirited Debate in the Continental Congress, over the Draught of a Letter to Gen. Washington.—Instructions to discharge all Slaves and Free Negroes in his Army.—Minutes of the Meeting held at Cambridge.—Lord Dunmore's Proclamation.—Prejudice in the Southern Colonies.—Negroes in Virginia flock to the British Army.—Caution to the Negroes printed in a Williamsburg Paper.—The Virginia Convention answers the Proclamation of Lord Dunmore.—Gen. Greene, in a Letter to Gen. Washington, calls Attention to the raising of a Negro Regiment on Staten Island.—Letter from a Hessian Officer.—Connecticut Legislature on the Subject of Employment of Negroes as Soldiers.—Gen. Varnum's Letter to Gen. Washington, suggesting the Employment of Negroes, sent to Gov. Cooke.—The Governor refers Varnum's Letter to the General Assembly.—Minority Protest against enlisting Slaves to serve in the Army.—Massachusetts tries to secure Legal Enlistments of Negro Troops.—Letter of Thomas Kench to the Council and House of Representatives, Boston, Mass.—Negroes serve in White Organizations until the Close of the American Revolution.—Negro Soldiers serve in Virginia.—Maryland employs Negroes.—New York passes an Act providing for the Raising of two Colored Regiments.—War in the Middle and Southern Colonies.—Hamilton's Letter to John Jay.—Col. Laurens's Efforts to raise Negro Troops in South Carolina.—Proclamation of Sir Henry Clinton inducing Negroes to desert the Rebel Army.—Lord Cornwallis issues a Proclamation offering Protection to all Negroes seeking his Command,—Col. Laurens is called to France on Important Business.—His Plan for securing Black Levies for the South upon his Return.—His Letters to Gen. Washington in Regard to his Fruitless Plans.—Capt David Humphreys recruits a Company of Colored Infantry in Connecticut.—Return of Negroes in the Army in 1778.

THE policy of arming the Negroes early claimed the anxious consideration of the leaders of the colonial army during the American Revolution. England had been crowding her American plantations with slaves at a fearful rate; and, when hostilities actually began, it was difficult to tell whether the American army or the ministerial army would be able to secure the Negroes as allies. In 1715 the royal governors of the colonies gave the Board of Trade the number of the Negroes in their respective colonies. The slave population was as follows:—

Sixty years afterwards, when the Revolution had begun, the slave population of the thirteen colonies was as follows:—

Such a host of beings was not to be despised in a great military struggle. Regarded as a neutral element that could be used simply to feed an army, to perform fatigue duty, and build fortifications, the Negro population was the object of fawning favors of the white colonists. In the Non-Importation Covenant, passed by the Continental Congress at Philadelphia, on the 24th of October, 1774, the second resolve indicated the feeling of the representatives of the people on the question of the slave-trade:—

It, with the entire covenant, received the signatures of all the delegates from the twelve colonies. The delegates from the Southern colonies were greatly distressed concerning the probable attitude of the slave element. They knew that if that ignorant mass of humanity were inflamed by some act of strategy of the enemy, they might sweep their homes and families from the face of the earth. The cruelties of the slave-code, the harsh treatment of Negro slaves, the lack of confidence in the whites everywhere manifested among the blacks,—as so many horrid dreams, harassed the minds of slaveholders by day and by night. They did not even possess the courage to ask the slaves to remain silent and passive during the struggle between England and themselves. The sentiment that adorned the speeches of orators, and graced the writings of the colonists, during this period, was "the equality of the rights of all men." And yet the slaves who bore their chains under their eyes, who were denied the commonest rights of humanity, who were rated as chattels and real property, were living witnesses to the insincerity and inconsistency of this declaration. But it is a remarkable fact, that all the Southern colonies, in addition to the action of their delegates, ratified the Non-Importation Covenant. The Maryland Convention on the 8th of December, 1774; South Carolina Provincial Congress on the 11th January, 1775; Virginia Convention on the 22d March, 1775; North Carolina Provincial Congress on the 23d of August, 1775; Delaware Assembly on the 25th of March, 1775 (refused by Gov. John Penn); and Georgia,—passed the following resolves thereabouts:—

Meetings were numerous and spirited throughout the colonies, in which, by resolutions, the people expressed their sentiments in reference to the mother country. On the 18th of July, 1774, at a meeting held in Fairfax Court-House, Virginia, a series of twenty-four resolutions was presented by George Washington, chairman of the committee on resolutions, three of which were directed against slavery.

Mr. Sparks comments upon the resolutions as follows:—

Dr. Benjamin Franklin, in a letter to Dean Woodward, dated April 10, 1773, says,—

Virginia gave early and positive proof that she was in earnest on the question of non-importation. One John Brown, a merchant of Norfolk, broke the rules of the colony by purchasing imported slaves, and was severely rebuked in the following article:—

And the first delegation from Virginia to Congress in August, 1774, had instructions as follows, drawn by Thomas Jefferson:—

It is scarcely necessary to mention the fact, that there were several very cogent passages in the first draught of the Declaration of Independence that were finally omitted. The one most pertinent to this history is here given:—

The solicitude concerning the slavery question was not so great in the Northern colonies. The slaves were not so numerous as in the Carolinas and other Southern colonies. The severe treatment of slaves had been greatly modified, the spirit of masters toward them more gentle and conciliatory, and the public sentiment concerning them more humane. Public discussion of the Negro question, however, was cautiously avoided. The failure of attempted legislation friendly to the slaves had discouraged their friends, while the critical situation of public affairs made the supporters of slavery less aggressive. On the 25th of October, 1774, an effort was made in the Provincial Congress of Massachusetts to re-open the discussion, but it failed. The record of the attempt is as follows:—

Thus ended the attempt to call the attention of the people's representatives to the inconsistency of their doctrine and practice on the question of the equality of human rights. Further agitation of the question, followed by the defeat of just measures in the interest of the slaves, was deemed by many as dangerous to the colony. The discussions were watched by the Negroes with a lively interest; and failure led them to regard the colonists as their enemies, and greatly embittered them. Then it was difficult to determine just what would be wisest to do for the enslaved in this colony. The situation was critical: a bold, clear-headed, loyal-hearted man was needed.

On Tuesday, Oct. 2, 1750, "The Boston Gazette, or Weekly Journal," contained the following advertisement:—

During the month of November,—the 13th and 20th,—a similar advertisement appeared in the same paper; showing that the "Molatto Fellow" had not returned to his master.

Twenty years later "Crispas's" name once more appeared in the journals of Boston. This time he was not advertised as a runaway slave, nor was there reward offered for his apprehension. His soul and body were beyond the cruel touch of master; the press had paused to announce his apotheosis, and to write the name of the Negro patriot, soldier, and martyr to the ripening cause of the American Revolution, in fadeless letters of gold,—Crispus Attucks!

On March 5, 1770, occurred the Boston Massacre; and, while it was not the real commencement of the Revolutionary struggle, it was the bloody drama that opened the most eventful and thrilling chapter in American history. The colonists had endured, with obsequious humility, the oppressive acts of Britain, the swaggering insolence of the ministerial troops, and the sneers of her hired minions. The aggressive and daring men had found themselves hampered by the conservative views of a large class of colonists, who feared lest some one should take a step not exactly according to the law. But while the "wise and prudent" were deliberating upon a legal method of action, there were those, who, "made of sterner stuff," reasoned right to the conclusion, that they had rights as colonists that ought to be respected. That there was cause for just indignation on the part of the people towards the British soldiers, there is no doubt. But there is reason to question the time and manner of the assault made by the citizens. Doubtless they had "a zeal, but not according to knowledge." There is no record to controvert the fact of the leadership of Crispus Attucks. A manly-looking fellow, six feet two inches in height, he was a commanding figure among the irate colonists. His enthusiasm for the threatened interests of the Province, his loyalty to the teachings of Otis, and his willingness to sacrifice for the cause of equal rights, endowed him with a courage, which, if tempered with better judgment, would have made him a military hero in his day. But consumed by the sacred fires of patriotism, that lighted his path to glory, his career of usefulness ended at the beginning. John Adams, as the counsel for the soldiers, thought that the patriots Crispus Attucks led were a "rabble of saucy boys, negroes, mulattoes, &c.," who could not restrain their emotion. Attucks led the charge with the shout, "The way to get rid of these soldiers is to attack the main-guard; strike at the root: this is the nest." A shower of missiles was answered by the discharge of the guns of Capt. Preston's company. The exposed and commanding person of the intrepid Attucks went down before the murderous fire. Samuel Gray and Jonas Caldwell were also killed, while Patrick Carr and Samuel Maverick were mortally wounded.

The scene that followed beggared description. The people ran from their homes and places of business into the streets, white with rage. The bells rang out the alarm of danger. The bodies of Attucks and Caldwell were carried into Faneuil Hall, where their strange faces were viewed by the largest gathering of people ever before witnessed. Maverick was buried from his mother's house in Union Street, and Gray from his brother's residence in Royal Exchange Lane. But Attucks and Caldwell, strangers in the city, without relatives, were buried from Faneuil Hall, so justly called "the Cradle of Liberty." The four hearses formed a junction in King Street; and from thence the procession moved in columns six deep, with a long line of coaches containing the first citizens of Boston. The obsequies were witnessed by a very large and respectful concourse of people. The bodies were deposited in one grave, over which a stone was placed bearing this inscription:—

"Long as in Freedom's cause the wise contend, Dear to your country shall your fame extend; While to the world the lettered stone shall tell Where Caldwell, Attucks, Gray and Maverick fell."

Who was Crispus Attucks? A Negro whose soul, galling under the destroying influence of slavery, went forth a freeman, went forth not only to fight for his liberty, but to give his life as an offering upon the altar of American liberty. He was not a madcap, as some would have the world believe. He was not ignorant of the issues between the American colonies and the English government, between the freemen of the colony and the dictatorial governors. Where he was during the twenty years from 1750 to 1770, is not known; but doubtless in Boston, where he had heard the fiery eloquence of Otis, the convincing arguments of Sewall, and the tender pleadings of Belknap. He had learned to spell out the fundamental principles that should govern well-regulated communities and states; and, having come to the rapturous consciousness of his freedom in fee simple, the brightest crown God places upon mortal man, he felt himself neighbor and friend. His patriotism was not a mere spasm produced by sudden and exciting circumstances. It was an education; and knowledge comes from experience; and the experience of this black hero was not of a single day. Some time before the memorable 5th of March, Crispus addressed the following spirited letter to the Tory governor of the Province:—

This was the declaration of war. It was fulfilled. The world has heard from him; and, more, the English-speaking world will never forget the noble daring and excusable rashness of Attucks in the holy cause of liberty! Eighteen centuries before he was saluted by death and kissed by immortality, another Negro bore the cross of Christ to Calvary for him. And when the colonists were staggering wearily under their cross of woe, a Negro came to the front, and bore that cross to the victory of glorious martyrdom!

And the people did not agree with John Adams that Attucks led "a motley rabble," but a band of patriots. Their evidence of the belief they entertained was to be found in the annual commemoration of the "5th of March," when orators, in measured sentences and impassioned eloquence, praised the hero-dead. In March, 1775, Dr. Joseph Warren, who a few months later, as Gen. Warren, made Bunker Hill the shrine of New-England patriotism, was the orator. On the question of human liberty, he said,—

These noble sentiments were sealed by his blood at Bunker Hill, on the 17th of June, 1775, and are the amulet that will protect his fame from the corroding touch of centuries of time

The free Negroes of the Northern colonies responded to the call "to arms" that rang from the placid waters of Massachusetts Bay to the verdant hills of Berkshire, and from Lake Champlain to the upper waters of the Hudson. Every Northern colony had its Negro troops, not as separate organizations,—save the black regiment of Rhode Island,—but scattered throughout all of the white organizations of the army. At the first none but free Negroes were received into the army; but before peace came Negroes were not only admitted, they were purchased, and sent into the war, with an offer of freedom and fifty dollars bounty at the close of their service. On the 29th of May, 1775, the "Committee of Safety" for the Province of Massachusetts passed the following resolve against the enlistment of Negro slaves as soldiers:—

On Tuesday, the 6th of June, 1775, "A resolve of the committee of safety, relative to the [admission] of slaves into the army was read, and ordered to lie on the table for further consideration." But this was but another evidence of the cold, conservative spirit of Massachusetts on the question of other people's rights.

The Continental army was in bad shape. Its arms and clothing, its discipline and efficiency, were at such a low state as to create the gravest apprehensions and deepest solicitude. Gen. George Washington took command of the army in and around Boston, on the 3d of July, 1775, and threw his energies into the work of organization. On the 10th of July he issued instructions to the recruiting-officers of Massachusetts Bay, in which he forbade the enlistment of any "negro," or "any Person who is not an American born, unless such Person has a Wife and Family and is a settled resident in this Country." But, nevertheless, it is a curious fact, as Mr. Bancroft says, "the roll of the army at Cambridge had from its first formation borne the names of men of color." "Free negroes stood in the ranks by the side of white men. In the beginning of the war they had entered the provincial army; the first general order which was issued by Ward, had required a return, among other things, of the 'complexion' of the soldiers; and black men like others were retained in the service after the troops were adopted by the continent." There is no room to doubt. Negroes were in the army from first to last, but were there in contravention of law and positive prohibition.

On the 29th of September, 1775, a spirited debate occurred in the Continental Congress, over the draught of a letter to Gen. Washington, reported by Lynch, Lee, and Adams. Mr. Rutledge of South Carolina moved that the commander-in-chief be instructed to discharge all slaves and free

Negroes in his army. The Southern delegates supported him earnestly, but his motion was defeated. Public attention was called to the question, and at length the officers of the army debated it. The following minute of a meeting held at Cambridge preserves and reveals the sentiment of the general officers of the army on the subject:—

Ten days later, Oct. 18, 1775, a committee of conference met at Cambridge, consisting of Dr. Franklin, Benjamin Harrison, and Thomas Lynch, who conferred with Gen. Washington, the deputy-governors of Connecticut and Rhode Island, and the Committee of the Council of Massachusetts Bay. The object of the conference was the renovation and improvement of the army. On the 23d of October, the employment of Negroes as soldiers came before the conference for action, as follows:—

In his General Orders, issued from headquarters on the 12th of November, 1775, Washington said,—

But the general repaired this mistake the following month. Lord Dunmore had issued a proclamation declaring "all indented servants, negroes, or others (appertaining to rebels) free." Fearing lest many Negroes should join the ministerial army, in General Orders, 30th December, Washington wrote:—

Lord Dunmore's proclamation is here given:—

On account of this, on the 31st of December, Gen. Washington wrote the President of Congress as follows:—

This letter was referred to a committee consisting of Messrs. Wythe, Adams, and Wilson. On the 16th of January, 1776, they made the following report:—

This action on the part of Congress had reference to the army around Boston, but it called forth loud and bitter criticism from the officers of the army at the South. In a letter to John Adams, dated Oct. 24, 1775, Gen. Thomas indicated that there was some feeling even before the action of Congress was secured. He says,—

The Dunmore proclamation was working great mischief in the Southern colonies. The Southern colonists were largely engaged in planting, and, as they were Tories, did not rush to arms with the celerity that characterized the Northern colonists. At an early moment in the struggle, the famous Rev. Dr. Hopkins of Rhode Island wrote the following pertinent extract:—

On Sunday, the 24th of September, 1775, John Adams recorded the following conversation, that goes to show that Lord Dunmore's policy was well matured:—

The Negroes in Virginia sought the standards of the ministerial army, and the greatest consternation prevailed among the planters. On the 27th of November, 1775, Edmund Pendleton wrote to Richard Lee that the slaves were daily flocking to the British army.

But the dark stream of Negroes that had set in toward the English troops, where they were promised the privilege of bearing arms and their freedom, could not easily be stayed. The proclamation of Dunmore received the criticism of the press, and the Negroes were appealed to and urged to stand by their "true friends." A Williamsburg paper, printed on the 23d of November, 1775, contained the following well-written plea:—

But the Negroes had been demoralized, and it required an extraordinary effort to quiet them.

On the 13th of December, the Virginia Convention put forth an answer to the proclamation of Lord Dunmore. On the 14th of December a proclamation was issued "offering pardon to such slaves as shall return to their duty within ten days after the publication thereof." The following; was their declaration:—

Gen. Washington was not long in observing the effects of the Dunmore proclamation. He began to fully realize the condition of affairs at the South, and on Dec. 15 wrote Joseph Reed as follows:—

The slaves themselves were not incapable of perceiving the cunning of Lord Dunmore. England had forced slavery upon the colonists against their protest, had given instructions to the royal governors concerning the increase of the traffic, and therefore could not be more their friends than the colonists. The number that went over to the enemy grew smaller all the while, and finally the British were totally discouraged in this regard. Lord Dunmore was unwilling to acknowledge the real cause of his failure to secure black recruits, and so he charged it to the fever.

While the colonists felt, as Dr. Hopkins had written, that something ought to be done toward securing the services of the Negroes, yet their representatives were not disposed to legislate the Negro into the army. He was there, and still a conservative policy was pursued respecting him. Some bold officers took it upon themselves to receive Negroes as soldiers. Gen. Greene, in a letter to Gen. Washington, called attention to the raising of a Negro regiment on Staten Island.

To the evidence already produced as to the indiscriminate employment of Negroes as soldiers in the American army, the observations of a foreign officer are added. Under date of the 23d of October, 1777, a Hessian officer wrote:—

In the month of May, 1777, the Legislature of Connecticut sought to secure some action on the subject of the employment of Negroes as soldiers."

In the lower house the report was put over to the next session, but when it reached the upper house it was rejected.

Gen. Varnum, a brave and intelligent officer from Rhode Island, early urged the employment of Negro soldiers. He communicated his views to Gen. Washington, and he referred the correspondence to the governor of Rhode Island.

The letter of Gen. Varnum to Gen. Washington, in reference to the employment of Negroes as soldiers, is as follows:—

Gov. Cooke wrote Gen. Washington as follows:—

The governor laid the above letters before the General Assembly, at their February session; and the following act was passed:—

This measure met with some opposition, but it was too weak to effect any thing. The best thing the minority could do was to enter a written protest.

Upon the passage of the Act, Gov. Cooke hastened to notify Gen. Washington of the success of the project.

Where masters had slaves in the army, they were paid an annual interest on the appraised value of the slaves, out of the public treasury, until the end of the military service of such slaves. If owners presented certificates from the committee appointed to appraise enlisted Negroes, they were paid in part or in full in "Continental loan-office certificates."

The reader will remember, that it has been already shown that Negroes, both bond and free, were excluded from the militia of Massachusetts; and, furthermore, that both the Committee of Safety and the Provincial Congress had opposed the enlistment of Negroes. The first move in the colony to secure legal enlistments and separate organizations of Colored troops was a communication to the General Assembly of Massachusetts, 3d of April, 1778.

A few days later he addressed another letter to the same body.

On the 11th of April the first letter was referred to a joint committee, with instructions "to consider the same, and report." On the 17th of April, "a resolution of the General Assembly of Rhode Island for enlisting Negroes in the public service" was referred to the same committee. In the Militia Act of 1775, the exceptions were, "Negroes, Indians, and mulattoes." By the act of May, 1776, providing for the re-enforcement of the American army, it was declared that, "Indians, negroes, and mulattoes, shall not be held to take up arms or procure any person to do it in their room." By another act, passed Nov. 14, 1776, looking toward the improvement of the army, "Negroes, Indians, and mulattoes" were excluded. During the year 1776 an order was issued for taking the census of all males above sixteen, but excepted "Negroes, Indians, and mulattoes." But after some reverses to the American army, Massachusetts passed a resolve on Jan. 6, 1777, "for raising every seventh man to complete our quota," "without any exceptions, save the people called Quakers." This was the nearest Massachusetts ever got toward recognizing Negroes as soldiers. And on the 5th of March, 1778, Benjamin Goddard, for the selectmen, Committee of Safety, and militia officers of the town of Grafton, protested against the enlistment of the Negroes in his town.

It is not remarkable, in view of such a history, that Massachusetts should have hesitated to follow the advice of Thomas Kench. On the 28th of April, 1778, a law was draughted following closely the Rhode-Island Act. But no separate organization was ordered; and, hence, the Negroes served in white organizations till the close of the American Revolution.

There is nothing in the records of Virginia to show that there was ever any legal employment of Negroes as soldiers; but, from the following, it is evident that free Negroes did serve, and that there was no prohibition against them, providing they showed their certificates of freedom:—

Maryland employed Negroes as soldiers, and sent them into regiments with white soldiers. John Cadwalder of Annapolis, wrote Gen. Washington on the 5th of June, 1781, in reference to Negro soldiers, as follows:—

The legislature of New York, on the 20th of March, 1781, passed the following Act, providing for the raising of two regiments of blacks:—

The theatre of the war was now transferred from the Eastern to the Middle and Southern colonies. Massachusetts alone had furnished, and placed in the field, 67,907 men; while all the colonies south of Pennsylvania, put together, had furnished but 50,493,—or 8,414 less than the single colony of Massachusetts. It was a difficult task to get the whites to enlist at the South. Up to 1779, nearly all the Negro soldiers had been confined to the New-England colonies. The enemy soon found out that the Southern colonies were poorly protected, and thither he moved. The Hon. Henry Laurens of South Carolina, an intelligent and observing patriot, wrote Gen. Washington on the 16th of March, 1779, concerning the situation at the South:—

Gen. Washington sent the following conservative reply:—

The gifted and accomplished Alexander Hamilton, a member of Washington's military family, was deeply interested in the plan suggested by the Hon. Henry Laurens, whose son was on Washington's staff. Col. John Laurens was the bearer of the following remarkable letter from Hamilton to John Jay, President of Congress.

The condition of the Southern States became a matter of Congressional solicitude. The letter of Col. Hamilton was referred to a special committee on the 29th of March, 1779. It was represented that South Carolina especially was in great danger. The white population was small; and, while there were some in the militia service, it was thought necessary to keep as large a number of whites at home as possible. The fear of insurrection, the desertion of Negroes to the enemy, and the exposed condition of her border, intensified the anxiety of the people. The only remedy seemed to lie in the employment of the more fiery spirits among the Negroes as the defenders of the rights and interests of the colonists. Congress rather hesitated to act,—it was thought that that body lacked the authority to order the enlistment of Negroes in the States,—and therefore recommended to "the states of South Carolina and Georgia, if they shall think the same expedient, to take measures immediately for raising three thousand able-bodied negroes." After some consideration the following plan was recommended by the special committee, and adopted:—

Congress supplemented the foregoing measure by commissioning young Col. Laurens to carry forward the important work suggested. The gallant young officer was indeed worthy of the following resolutions:—

He repaired to South Carolina, and threw all his energies into his noble mission. That the people did not co-operate with him, is evidenced in the following extract from a letter he subsequently wrote to Col. Hamilton:—

The enemy was not slow in discovering the division of sentiment among the colonists as to the policy of employing Negroes as soldiers. And the suspicions of Gen. Washington, indicated to Henry Laurens, in a letter already quoted, were not groundless. On the 30th of June, 1779, Sir Henry Clinton issued a proclamation to the Negroes. It first appeared in "The Royal Gazette" of New York, on the 3d of July, 1779.

The proclamation had effect. Many Negroes, weary of the hesitancy of the colonists respecting acceptance of their services, joined the ministerial army. On the 14th of February, 1780, Col. Laurens wrote Gen. Washington, from Charleston, S.C., as follows:—

Lord Cornwallis also issued a proclamation, offering protection to all Negroes who should seek his command. But the treatment he gave them, as narrated by Mr. Jefferson in a letter to Dr. Gordon, a few years after the war, was extremely cruel, to say the least.

Col. Laurens was called from the South, and despatched to France on an important mission in 1780. But the effort to raise Negro troops in the South was not abandoned.

On the 13th of March, 1780, Gen. Lincoln, in a letter to Gov. Rutledge of South Carolina, dated at Charleston, urged the importance of raising a Negro regiment at once. He wrote,—

James Madison saw in the emancipation and arming of the Negroes the only solution of the vexatious Southern problem. On the 20th of November, 1780, he wrote Joseph Jones as follows:—

The struggle went on between Tory and Whig, between traitor and patriot, between selfishness and the spirit of noble consecration to the righteous cause of the Americans. Gen. Greene wrote from North Carolina on the 28th of February, 1781, to Gen. Washington as follows:—

Upon his return to America, Col. Laurens again espoused his favorite and cherished plan of securing black levies for the South. But surrounded and hindered by the enemies of the country he so dearly loved, and for the honor and preservation of which he gladly gave his young life, his plans were unsuccessful. In two letters to Gen. Washington, a few months before he fell fighting for his country, he gave an account of the trials that beset his path, which he felt led to honorable duty. The first bore date of May 19, 1782.

The second was dated June 12, 1782, and breathes a despondent air:—

Washington's reply showed that he, too, had lost faith in the patriotism of the citizens of the South to a great degree. He wrote his faithful friend:—

Although the effort of the Legislature of Connecticut to authorize the enlistment of Negroes in 1777 had failed, many Negroes, as has been shown, served in regiments from that State; and a Negro company was organized. When white officers refused to serve in it, the gallant David Humphreys volunteered his services, and became the captain.

The following was the roster of his company:—

But notwithstanding the persistent and bitter opposition to the employment of slaves, from the earliest hours of the Revolutionary War till its close, Negroes, bond and free, were in all branches of the service. It is to be regretted that the exact number cannot be known. Adjutant-Gen. Scammell made the following official return of Negro soldiers in the main army, under Washington's immediate command, two months after the battle of Monmouth; but the Rhode-Island regiment, the Connecticut, New York, and New-Hampshire troops are not mentioned. Incomplete as it is, it is nevertheless official, and therefore correct as far as it goes.

RETURN OF NEGROES IN THE ARMY, 24th Aug., 1778.

Alex. Scammell, Adj.-Gen.

It is gratifying to record the fact, that the Negro was enrolled as a soldier in the war of the American Revolution. What he did will be recorded in the following chapter.

FOOTNOTES:

Journal of the Continental Congress.
The Hon. Peter Force, in an article to The National Intelligencer, Jan. 16 and 18, 1855, says: "Southern colonies, jointly with all the others, and separately each for itself, did agree to prohibit the importation of slaves, voluntarily and in good faith." Georgia was not represented in this Congress, and, therefore, could not sign.
Sparks's Washington, vol. ii. pp. 488-495.
Sparks's Franklin, vol. viii, p. 42.
Jefferson's Works, vol. i. p. 135.
Ibid., pp. 23,24.
Journals of the Provincial Congress of Mass., p. 29.
Adams's Works, vol. ii. p. 322.
Journals of the Provincial Congress of Mass., p. 553.
Ibid., p. 302.
"You are not to enlist any deserter from the Ministerial Army, or any stroller, negro, or vagabond, or person suspected of being an enemy to the liberty of America, nor any under eighteen years of age. "As the cause is the best that can engage men of courage and principle to take up arms, so it is expected that none but such will be accepted by the recruiting officer. The pay, provision, &c., being so ample, it is not doubted but that the officers sent upon this service will, without delay, complete their respective corps, and march the men forthwith to camp. "You are not to enlist any person who is not an American born, unless such person has a wife and family, and is a settled resident in this country. The persons you enlist must be provided with good and complete arms." —Moore's Diary of the American Revolution, vol. i. p. 110.
The Provincial Congress of South Carolina, Nov 20, 1775, passed the following resolve:—"On motion,Resolved, That the colonels of the several regiments of militia throughout the Colony have leave to enroll such a number of able male slaves, to be employed as pioneers and laborers, as public exigencies may require; and that a daily pay of seven shillings and sixpence be allowed for the service of each such slave while actually employed." —American Archives, 4th Series, vol. iv p. 6.
Sparks's Washington, vol. iii. p. 155, note.
Force's American Archives, 4th Series, vol. iii. p. 1,385.
Spark's Washington, vol. iii. p. 218.
Journals of Congress, vol ii. p. 26.
Hopkins's Works, vol. ii. p. 584.
Works of John Adams, vol. ii p. 428.
Force's American Archives, 4th Series, vol. iv. p. 202.
Force's American Archives, 4th Series, vol. iii. p. 1,387.
Force's American Archives, 4th Series, vol. iv. pp. 84, 85.
Life and Correspondence of Joseph Reed, vol. i. p. 135.

Force's American Archives, 5th Series, vol. ii. pp 160, 162.
Force's American Archives, 5th Series, vol. i p. 486.
During a few months of study in New-York City, I came across the above in the library of the N.Y. Hist. Soc.
Schloezer's Briefwechsel, vol. iv. p. 365.
An Historical Research (Livermore), pp. 114-116.
R.I. Col. Recs., vol. viii. p. 640.
R.I. Col. Recs., vol. viii. p. 641.
Ibid., vol. viii. p. 524.
R.I. Col. Recs., vol viii. pp. 358-360.
R.I. Col. Recs., vol. viii. p. 361.
This is evidently a mistake, as Washington's letter was dated Jan. 2, as the reader will see.
R.I. Col. Recs., vol. viii. p. 526.
Ibid., p. 376.
Ibid., p. 465.
MSS. Archives of Mass., vol. cxcix. pp. 80, 84.
Hening, vol. ix. 280.
Sparks's Correspondence of the American Revolution, vol. iii. p. 331.
Laws of the State of New York, chap. xxxiii. (March 20, 1781, 4th Session).
The American Loyalist, p. 30, second edition.
Sparks's Washington, vol. vi p. 204, note.
Ibid., vol. vi. p. 204.
Life of John Jay, by William Jay, vol. II. pp. 31, 32.
Ramsay, the historian of South Carolina says, "It has been computed by good judges, that, between 1775 and 1783, the State of South Carolina lost twenty-five thousand negroes."
Secret Journals of Congress, vol. i. pp. 107-110.
Journals of Congress, vol. v. p. 123.
Works of Hamilton, vol. i. pp. 114, 115.
Sparks's Correspondence of the American Revolution, vol. ii. p. 402.
Jefferson's Works, vol ii. p. 426.
Madison Papers, p. 68.
Sparks's Correspondence of the American Revolution, vol. iii. p. 246.
Sparks's Correspondence of the American Revolution, vol. iii. p. 506.
Ibid., p. 515.
Sparks's Washington, vol. viii. pp. 322, 323.
Biographical Sketch in "The National Portrait Gallery of Distinguished Americans."
Colored Patriots of the Revolution, p. 134.
This return was discovered by the indefatigable Dr. George H. Moore. It is the only document of the kind in existence.

CHAPTER XXVII.: NEGROES AS SOLDIERS.: 1775-1783.

The Negro as a Soldier.—Battle of Bunker Hill—Gallantry of Negro Soldiers.—Peter Salem, the Intrepid Black Soldier.—Bunker-hill Monument.—The Negro Salem Poor distinguishes himself by Deeds of Desperate Valor.—Capture of Gen. Lee.—Capture of Gen. Prescott—Battle of Rhode Island.—Col. Greene commands a Negro Regiment.—Murder of Col. Greene in 1781.—The Valor of the Negro Soldiers.

AS soldiers the Negroes went far beyond the most liberal expectations of their stanchest friends. Associated with white men, many of whom were superior gentlemen, and nearly all of whom were brave and enthusiastic, the Negro soldiers of the American army became worthy of the cause they fought to sustain. Col. Alexander Hamilton had said, "their natural faculties are as good as ours;" and the assertion was supported by their splendid behavior on all the battle-fields of the Revolution. Endowed by nature with a poetic element, faithful to trusts, abiding in friendships, bound by the golden threads of attachment to places and persons, enthusiastic in personal endeavor, sentimental and chivalric, they made hardy and intrepid soldiers. The daring, boisterous enthusiasm with which they sprang to arms disarmed racial prejudice of its sting, and made friends of foes.

Their cheerfulness in camp, their celerity in the performance of fatigue-duty, their patient endurance of heat and cold, hunger and thirst, and their bold efficiency in battle, made them welcome companions everywhere they went. The officers who frowned at their presence in the army at first, early learned, from experience, that they were the equals of any troops in the army for severe service in camp, and excellent fighting in the field.

The battle of Bunker Hill was one of the earliest and most important of the Revolution. Negro soldiers were in the action of the 17th of June, 1775, and nobly did their duty. Speaking of this engagement, Bancroft says,—

Two Negro soldiers especially distinguished themselves, and rendered the cause of the colonists great service. Major Pitcairn was a gallant officer of the British marines. He led the charge against the redoubt, crying exultingly, "The day is ours!" His sudden appearance and his commanding air at first startled the men immediately before him. They neither answered nor fired, probably not being exactly certain what was next to be done. At this critical moment, a Negro soldier stepped forward, and, aiming his musket directly at the major's bosom, blew him through. Who was this intrepid black soldier, who at a critical moment stepped to the front, and with certain aim brought down the incarnate enemy of the colonists? What was his name, and whence came he to battle? His name was Peter Salem, a private in Col Nixon's regiment of the Continental Army.

Perhaps Salem was then a slave: probably he thought of the chains and stripes from whence he had come, of the liberty to be purchased in the ordeals of war, and felt it his duty to show himself worthy of his position as an American soldier. He proved that his shots were as effective as those of a white soldier, and that he was not wanting in any of the elements that go to make up the valiant soldier. Significant indeed that a Negro was the first to open the hostilities between Great

Britain and the colonies,—the first to pour out his blood as a precious libation on the altar of a people's rights; and that here, at Bunker Hill, when the crimson and fiery tide of battle seemed to be running hard against the small band of colonists, a Negro soldier's steady musket brought down the haughty form of the arch-rebel, and turned victory to the weak! England had loaded the African with chains, and doomed him to perpetual bondage in the North-American colonies; and when she came to forge political chains, in the flames of fratricidal war, for an English-speaking people, the Negro, whom she had grievously wronged, was first to meet her soldiers, and welcome them to a hospitable grave.

Bunker-hill Monument has a charm for loyal Americans; and the Negro, too, may gaze upon its enduring magnificence. It commemorates the deeds, not of any particular soldier, but all who stood true to the principles of equal rights and free government on that memorable "17th of June."

The other Negro soldier who won for himself rare fame and distinguished consideration in the action at Bunker Hill was Salem Poor. Delighted with his noble bearing, his superior officers could not refrain from calling the attention of the civil authorities to the facts that came under their personal observation. The petition that set forth his worth as a brave soldier is still preserved in the manuscript archives of Massachusetts:—

How many other Negro soldiers behaved with cool and determined valor at Bunker Hill, it is not possible to know. But many were there; they did their duty as faithful men, and their achievements are the heritage of the free of all colors under our one flag. Col. Trumbull, an artist as well as a soldier, who was stationed at Roxbury, witnessed the engagement from that elevation. Inspired by the scene, when it was yet fresh in his mind, he painted the historic picture of the battle in 1786. He represents several Negroes in good view, while conspicuous in the foreground is the redoubtable Peter Salem. Some subsequent artists—mere copyists—have sought to consign this black hero to oblivion, but 'tis vain. Although the monument at Bunker Hill "does not bear his name, the pencil of the artist has portrayed the scene, the pen of the impartial historian has recorded his achievement, and the voice of the eloquent orator has resounded his valor."

Major Samuel Lawrence "at one time commanded a company whose rank and file were all Negroes, of whose courage, military discipline, and fidelity he always spoke with respect. On one occasion, being out reconnoitring with this company, he got so far in advance of his command, that he was surrounded, and on the point of being made prisoner by the enemy. The men, soon discovering his peril, rushed to his rescue, and fought with the most determined bravery till that rescue was effectually secured. He never forgot this circumstance, and ever after took especial pains to show kindness and hospitality to any individual of the colored race who came near his dwelling."

Gen. Lee, of the American army, was captured by Col. Harcourt of the British army. It was regarded as a very distressing event; and preparations were made to capture a British officer of the same rank, so an exchange could be effected. Col. Barton of the Rhode-Island militia, a brave and cautious officer, was charged with the capture of Major-Gen. Prescott, commanding the royal army at Newport. On the night of the 9th of July, 1777, Col. Barton, with forty men, in two boats with muffled oars, evaded the enemy's boats, and, being taken for the sentries at Prescott's head-quarters, effected that officer's capture—a Negro taking him. The exploit was bold and successful.

Another account was published by a surgeon of the army, and is given here:—

Col. Barton evidently entertained great respect for the valor and trustworthiness of the Negro soldier whom he made the chief actor in a most hazardous undertaking. It was the post of honor; and the Negro soldier Prince discharged the duty assigned him in a manner that was entirely satisfactory to his superior officer, and crowned as one of the most daring and brilliant coups d'état of the American Revolution.

The battle of Rhode Island, fought on the 29th of August, 1778, was one of the severest of the Revolution. Newport was laid under siege by the British. Their ships-of-war moved up the bay on the morning of the action, and opened a galling fire upon the exposed right flank of the American army; while the Hessian columns, stretching across a chain of the "highland," attempted to turn Gen. Greene's flank, and storm the advanced redoubt. The heavy cannonading that had continued since nine in the morning was now accompanied by heavy skirmishing; and the action began to be general all along the lines. The American army was disposed in three lines of battle; the first extended in front of their earthworks on Butt's Hill, the second in rear of the hill, and the third as reserve a half-mile in the rear of the advance line. At ten o'clock the battle was at white heat. The British vessels kept up a fire that greatly annoyed the Americans, but imparted courage to the Hessians and British infantry. At length the foot columns massed, and swept down the slopes of Anthony's Hill with the impetuosity of a whirlwind. But the American columns received them with the intrepidity and coolness of veterans. The loss of the enemy was fearful.

A few years later the Marquis de Chastellux, writing of this regiment, said,—

On the 14th of May, 1781, the gallant Col. Greene was surprised and murdered at Point's Bridge, New York, but it was not effected until his brave black soldiers had been cut to pieces in defending their leader. It was one of the most touching and beautiful incidents of the war, and illustrates the self-sacrificing devotion of Negro soldiers to the cause of American liberty.

At a meeting of the Congregational and Presbyterian Anti-Slavery Society, at Francestown, N.H., the Rev. Dr. Harris, himself a Revolutionary soldier, spoke thus complimentarily of the Rhode-Island Negro regiment:—

From the opening to the closing scene of the Revolutionary War; from the death of Pitcairn to the surrender of Cornwallis; on many fields of strife and triumph, of splendid valor and republican glory; from the hazy dawn of unequal and uncertain conflict, to the bright morn of profound peace; through and out of the fires of a great war that gave birth to a new, a grand republic,—the Negro soldier fought his way to undimmed glory, and made for himself a magnificent record in the annals of American history. Those annals have long since been committed to the jealous care of the loyal citizens of the Republic black men fought so heroically to snatch from the iron clutches of Britain.

FOOTNOTES:

Bancroft, vol. vii., 6th ed., p. 421.
An Historical Research, p. 93.
History of Leicester, p. 267.
Orations and Speeches of Everett, vol. iii. p. 529.
MS. Archives of Massachusetts, vol. clxxx, p. 241.
Memoir of Samuel Lawrence, by Rev. S.K. Lothrop, D.D., pp. 8, 9.
Frank Moore's Diary of the American Revolution, vol. i. p. 468.
Thatcher's Military Journal, p. 87.
Arnold's History of Rhode Island, vol. ii. pp. 427, 428.
Chastellux' Travels, vol. i. p. 454; London, 1789.

CHAPTER XXVIII.: LEGAL STATUS OF THE NEGRO DURING THE REVOLUTION.: 1775-1783.

The Negro was Chattel or Real Property.—His Legal Status during his New Relation as a Soldier—Resolution introduced in the Massachusetts House of Representatives to prevent the selling of Two Negroes captured upon the High Seas—The Continental Congress appoints a Committee to consider what should be done with Negroes taken by Vessels of War in the Service of the United Colonies.—Confederation of the New States.—Spirited Debate in Congress respecting the Disposal of Recaptures.—The Spanish Ship "Victoria" captures an English Vessel having on Board Thirty-four Negroes taken from South Carolina.—The Negroes recaptured by Vessels belonging to the State of Massachusetts.—They are delivered to Thomas Knox, and conveyed to Castle Island.—Col. Paul Revere has Charge of the Slaves on Castle Island—Massachusetts passes a Law providing for the Security, Support, and Exchange of Prisoners brought into the State.—Gen Hancock receives a Letter from the Governor of South Carolina respecting the Detention of Negroes—In the Provincial Articles between the United States of America and His Britannic Majesty, Negroes were rated as Property.—And also in the Definite Treaty of Peace between the United States of America and His Britannic Majesty.—And also in the Treaty of Peace of 1814, between His Britannic Majesty and the United States, Negroes were designated as Property.—Gen. Washington's Letter to Brig-Gen Rufus Putnam in regard to a Negro in his Regiment claimed by Mr. Hobby.—Enlistment in the Army did not always work a Practical Emancipation.

WHEN the Revolutionary War began, the legal status of the Negro slave was clearly defined in the courts of all the colonies. He was either chattel or real property. The question naturally arose as to his legal status during his new relation as a soldier. Could he be taken as property, or as a prisoner of war? Was he booty, or was he entitled to the usage of civilized warfare,—a freeman, and therefore to be treated as such?

The Continental Congress, Nov. 25, 1775, passed a resolution recommending the several colonial legislatures to establish courts that should give jurisdiction to courts, already in existence, to dispose of "cases of capture." In fact, and probably in law, Congress exercised power in cases of appeal. Moreover, Congress had prescribed a rule for the distribution of prizes. But, curiously enough, Massachusetts, in 1776, passed an Act declaring, that, in case captures were made by the forces of the colony, the local authorities should have complete jurisdiction in their distribution; but, when prizes or captives were taken upon colonial territory by the forces of the United Colonies, the distributions should be made in accordance with the laws of Congress. This was but a single illustration of the divided sovereignty of a crude government. That there was need of a uniform law upon this question, there could be no doubt, especially in a war of the magnitude of the one that was then being waged.

On the 13th of September, 1776, a resolution was introduced into the Massachusetts House of Representatives, "to prevent the sale of two negro men lately brought into this state, as prisoners taken on the high seas, and advertised to be sold at Salem, the 17th inst., by public auction." The resolve in full is here given:—

On the Journal of the House, p. 106, appears the following record,—

The resolve, as it originally appeared, was dragged through a tedious debate, non-concurred in by the House, recommitted, remodelled, and sent back, when it finally passed.

It looked like a new resolve. The pronounced and advanced sentiment in favor of the equal rights of all created beings had been taken out, and it appeared now as a war measure, warranted upon military policy. This is the only chaplet that the most devout friends of Massachusetts can weave out of her acts on the Negro problem during the colonial period, to place upon her brow. It attracted wide-spread and deserved attention.

During the following month, on the 14th of October, 1776, the Continental Congress appointed a special committee, Messrs. Lee, Wilson, and Hall, "to consider what is to be done with Negroes taken by vessels of war, in the service of the United States." Here was a profound legal problem presented for solution. According to ancient custom and law, slaves came as the bloody logic of war. War between nations was of necessity international; but while this truth had stood through many centuries, the conversion of the Northern nations of Europe into organized society greatly modified the old doctrine of slavery. Coming under the enlightening influences of modern international law, war captives could not be reduced to slavery. This doctrine was thoroughly understood, doubtless, in the North-American colonies as in Europe. But the almost universal doctrine of property in the Negro, and his status in the courts of the colonies, gave the royal army great advantage in the appropriation of Negro captives, under the plea that they were "property," and hence legitimate "spoils of war;" while, on the part of the colonists, to declare that captured Negroes were entitled to the treatment of "prisoners of war," was to reverse a principle of law as old as their government. It was, in fact, an abandonment of the claim of property in the Negro. It was a recognition of his rights as a soldier, a bestowal of the highest favors known in the treatment of captives of war. But there was another difficulty in the way. Slavery had been recognized in the venerable memorials of the most remote nations. This condition was coeval with the history of all nations, but nowhere regarded as a relation of a local character. It grew up in social compacts, in organized communities of men, and in great and powerful states. It was recognized in private international law; and the relation of master and slave was guarded in their local habitat, and respected wherever found. And this relation, this property in man, did not cease because the slave sought another nation, for it was recognized in all the commercial transactions of nations. Now, upon this principle, the colonists were likely to claim their right to property in slaves captured.

The confederation of the new States was effected on the 1st of March, 1781. Art. IX. gave the "United States in Congress assembled" the exclusive authority of making laws to govern the disposal of all captures made by land or water; to decide which were legal; how prizes taken by the land or naval force of the government should be appropriated, and the right to establish courts of competent jurisdiction in such case, etc. The first legislation under this article was an Act establishing a court of appeals on the 4th of June, 1781. It was discussed on the 25th of June, and again, on the 17th of July, took up a great deal of time, but was recommitted. The committee were instructed to prepare an ordinance regulating the proceedings of the admiralty cases, in the several States, in instances of capture; to codify all resolutions and laws upon the subject; and to request the States to enact such provisions as would be in harmony with the reserved rights of the Congress in such cases as were specified in the Ninth Article. Accordingly, on the 21st of September, 1781, the committee reported to Congress the results of their labor, in a bill on the subject of captures. Upon the question of agreeing to the following section, the yeas and nays were demanded by Mr. Mathews of South Carolina:—

The delegates from North Carolina, Delaware, New Jersey, and Connecticut, refrained from voting; South Carolina voted in the negative: but it was carried by twenty-eight yeas, against two nays. After a spirited debate, continuing through several days, and having received several amendments, it finally passed on Dec. 4, 1781, as follows:—

It should be carefully observed that the above law refers only to recaptures. It would be interesting to know the views the committee entertained in reference to slaves captured by the ministerial army. Nothing was said about this interesting feature of the case. Why Congress did not claim proper treatment of the slaves captured by the enemy while in the service of the United Colonies, is not known. Doubtless its leaders saw where the logic of such a position would lead them. The word "another" was left out of the original measure, and was made to read, in the one that passed, "a State or citizen;" as if it were feared that, by implication, a Negro would be recognized as a citizen.

By the proclamation of Sir Henry Clinton, already mentioned in the preceding chapter, Negroes were threatened with sale for "the public service;" and Mr. Jefferson in his letter to Mr. Gordon (see preceding chapter), says the enemy sold the Negroes captured in Virginia into the West Indies. After the capture of Stony Point by Gen. Wayne, concerning two Negroes who fell into his hands, he wrote to Lieut.-Col. Meigs from New Windsor on the 25th of July, 1779, as follows:—

In June, 1779, a Spanish ship called "Victoria" sailed from Charleston, S.C., for Cadiz. During the first part of her voyage she was run down by a British privateer; but, instead of being captured, she seized her assailant, and found on board thirty-four Negroes, whom the English vessel had taken from plantations in South Carolina. The Spaniards got the Negroes on board their ship, disabled the English vessel, and then dismissed her. Within a few days she was taken by two British letters-of-marque, and headed for New York. During her passage thither she was re-captured by the "Hazard" and "Tyrannicide," armed vessels in the service of Massachusetts, and taken into the port of Boston. By direction of the Board of War she was ordered into the charge of Capt. Johnson, and was unloaded on the 21st of June. The Board of War reported to the Legislature that there were thirty-four Negroes "taken on the high seas and brought into the state." On the 23d of June [1780] the Legislature ordered "that Gen. Lovell, Capt. Adams, and Mr. Cranch, be a committee to consider what is proper to be done with a number of negroes brought into port in the prize ship called the Lady Gage." On the 24th of June, "the committee appointed to take into consideration the state and circumstances of a number of negroes lately brought into the port of Boston, reported a resolve directing the Board of War to inform our delegates in Congress of the state of facts relative to them, to put them into the barracks on Castle Island, and cause them to be supplied and employed." The resolve passed without opposition.

The Negroes were delivered to Thomas Knox on the 28th of June, and were conveyed "to Castle Island pr. Order of Court." The Board of War voted the "34 Negroes delivered" rations. Lieut.-Col. Paul Revere was instructed to "issue to the Negroes at Castle Island—1 lb. of Beef, 1 lb. of Rice pr. day." The following letter is not without interest:—

In accordance with the order of the Legislature, made on the 24th of June, the president of the Board of War, Samuel P. Savage, wrote a letter to the Massachusetts delegates in Congress, dated "War Office June 29th 1779," calling attention to the re-captured Negroes. The letter closed with the following:—

The writer was at pains to enumerate, in his letter, such slaves as he was enabled to locate.

Pending the action of the lawful owners of these captives, the council instructed the commandant of Castle Island, Col. Paul Revere, to place out to service, in different towns, some of the Negroes, with the understanding that they should be delivered up to the authorities on their order. Some were delivered to gentlemen who desired them as servants. But in the fall of 1779 quite a number were still on the island, as may be seen by the following touching letter:—

In the mean time some of the reputed owners of the Negroes at Castle Island had come from Charleston, S.C., to secure their property. When they arrived in Boston they secured the services of John Codman, Isaac Smith, and William Smith, who on the 15th of November, 1779, petitioned the Council for the "restitution" of slaves taken by a British privateer, and retaken by two armed vessels of Massachusetts. A committee was appointed to consider the petitions, and report what action should be taken in the matter. Two days later another petition was presented to the Council by one John Winthrop, "praying that certain negroes, who were brought into this state by the Hazard and Tyrannicide, may be delivered to him." It was referred to the committee appointed on the 15th of November. On the 18th of November, "Jabez Fisher, Esq., brought down a report of the Committee of both Houses on the petition of Isaac Smith, being by way of resolve, directing the Board of War to deliver so many of the negroes therein mentioned, as are now alive. Passed in Council, and sent down for concurrence." The order of the House is, "Read and concurred, as taken into a new draught. Sent up for concurrence."

It is printed among the resolves of November, 1779.

On the 12th of April, 1780, Massachusetts passed an Act providing more effectually "for the security, support, and exchange of prisoners of war brought into the State." It declares that

The above Act was passed in compliance with a resolution of Congress, Jan. 13, 1780; and it repealed an Act of 1777, that made no provisions for the capture of Negroes.

On the 23d of January, 1784, Gov. Hancock sent a message to the Legislature, transmitting correspondence received dining the adjournment of the Legislature from Oct 28, 1783, to Jan. 21, 1784. Calling the attention of the Legislature to this correspondence, he referred to a letter from "His Excellency the Governor of South Carolina, respecting the detention of some Negroes here, belonging to the subjects of that state. I have communicated it to the Judges of the Supreme

Judicial Court—their observations upon it are with the Papers. I have made no reply to the letter, judging it best to have your decision upon it." The same papers on the same day were read in the Senate, and a joint committee of both houses was appointed. The committee reported to both branches of the Legislature on the 23d of March, 1784, and the report was adopted. A request was made of the governor to furnish copies of the opinions of the judges, etc.

The papers referred to seem to have been lost, but extracts are here produced:—

By the Treaty of Peace in 1783, Negroes were put in the same category with horses and other articles of property.

On the 6th of May, 1783, Gen. Washington wrote Sir Guy Carleton:—

In his reply, dated New York, May 12, 1783, Sir Guy Carleton says,—

It is clear, that notwithstanding the Act of the Massachusetts Legislature, and in the face of the law of Congress on the question of recaptures, Gen. Washington, the Congress of the United Colonies, and subsequently of the United States, regarded Negroes as property from the beginning to the end of the war. The following treaties furnish abundant proof that Negroes were regarded as property during the war, by the American government:—

It was not a difficult matter to retake Negroes captured by the enemy, and then treat them as prisoners of war. But no officer in the American army, no member of Congress, had the moral courage to proclaim that property ceased in a man the moment he donned the uniform of a Revolutionary soldier, and that all Negro soldiers captured by the enemy should be treated as prisoners of war. So, all through the war with Britain, the Negro soldier was liable to be claimed as property; and every bayonet in the army was at the command of the master to secure his property, even though it had been temporarily converted into an heroic soldier who had defended the country against its foes. The unprecedented spectacle was to be witnessed, of a master hunting his slaves under the flag of the nation. And at the close of hostilities many Negro soldiers were called upon to go back into the service of their masters; while few secured their freedom as a reward for their valor. The following letter of Gen. Washington, addressed to Brig.-Gen. Rufus Putnam, afterwards printed at Marietta, O., from his papers, indicates the regard the Father of his Country had for the rights of the master, though those rights were pushed into the camp of the army where many brave Negroes were found; and it also illustrates the legal strength of such a claim:—

Enlistment in the army did not work a practical emancipation of the slave, as some have thought. Negroes were rated as chattel property by both armies and both governments during the entire war. This is the cold fact of history, and it is not pleasing to contemplate. The Negro occupied the anomalous position of an American slave and an American soldier. He was a soldier in the hour of danger, but a chattel in time of peace.

FOOTNOTES:

Felt says, in History of Salem, vol. ii. p. 278: "Sept. 17 [1776]. At this date two slaves, taken on board of a prize, were to have been sold here; but the General Court forbid the sale, and ordered such prisoners to be treated like all others."

Resolves, p. 14. Quoted by Dr. Moore from the original documents.

Mr. Motley, "Rise of Dutch Republic," vol. i. p. 151, says that in the sixteenth century, in wars between European states, the captor had a property in his prisoner, which was assignable.

Law of Fiefdom and Bondage, vol. i. p. 158.

Mr. Hurd says, "In ascribing slavery to the law of nations it is a very common error to use that term not in the sense of universal jurisprudence—the Roman jus gentium-but in the modern sense of public international law, and to give the custom of enslaving prisoners of war, in illustration: as if the legal condition of other slaves who had never been taken in war were not equally jure gentium according to the Roman jurisprudence" See Mr. Webster's speech, 7th March, 1830; Works, vol. v. p. 329.

Dawson's Stony Point, pp. 111, 118.

Dr. Moore thinks this the wrong name. The resolve proves it.

House Journal, p. 60.

Ibid, pp. 63, 64.

Resolves, p. 51.

Mass. Archives, vol. cli., pp. 202-294.

The indefatigable Dr. George H. Moore copied the letter from the original manuscript. The portions in Italics are in the handwriting of Hancock. I have been placed under many obligations to my friend Dr. Moore.

Resolves, p. 131.

Laws, 1780, chap. v. pp. 283, 284.

Journal, vol. iv. pp. 308, 309.

From Mr. Bancroft's MSS., America, 1783, vol. ii. Quoted by Dr. Moore.

Sparks's Washington, vol. viii. p. 428, note.

Works of Hamilton, vol. vii. p. 191.

Sparks's Washington, vol. viii. pp. 431,432.

Sparks's Washington, vol. viii, Appendix, p. 544.

U.S. Statutes at large, vol. viii, pp. 54, 57.

Ibid., pp. 80, 83.

U.S. Statutes at large, vol. viii. p. 218.

CHAPTER XXIX.: THE NEGRO INTELLECT.—BANNEKER THE ASTRONOMER.[611].— FULLER THE MATHEMATICIAN.—DERHAM THE PHYSICIAN.

Statutory Prohibition against the Education of Negroes.—Benjamin Banneker, the Negro Astronomer and Philosopher.—His Antecedents—Young Banneker as a Farmer and Inventor—The Mills of Ellicott & Co.—Banneker cultivates his Mechanical Genius and Mathematical Tastes.—Banneker's first Calculation of an Eclipse submitted for Inspection in 1789.—His Letter to Mr Ellicott.—The Testimony of a Personal Acquaintance of Banneker as to his Upright Character.—His Home becomes a Place of Interest to Visitors.—Record of his Business Transactions.—Mrs. Mason's Visit to him.—She addresses him in Verse.—Banneker replies by Letter to her.—Prepares his First Almanac for Publication in 1792.—Title of his Almanac—Banneker's Letter to Thomas Jefferson.—Thomas Jefferson's Reply.—Banneker invited to accompany the Commissioners to run the Lines of the District of Columbia.—Banneker's Habits of studying the Heavenly Bodies.—Minute Description given to his Sisters in Reference to the Disposition of his Personal Property after Death.—His Death.—Regarded as the most Distinguished Negro of his Time.—Fuller the Mathematician, or "The Virginia Calculator."—Fuller of African Birth, but stolen and sold as a Slave into Virginia.—Visited by Men of Learning.—He was pronounced to be a Prodigy in the Manipulation of Figures.—His Death.—Derham the Physician.—Science of Medicine regarded as the most Intricate Pursuit of Man.—Early Life of James Derham.—His Knowledge of Medicine, how acquired.—He becomes a Prominent Physician in New Orleans.—Dr. Rush gives an Account of an Interview with him.—What the Negro Race produced by their Genius in America.

FROM the moment slavery gained a foothold in North America until the direful hour that witnessed its dissolution amid the shock of embattled arms, learning was the forbidden fruit that no Negro dared taste. Positive and explicit statutes everywhere, as fiery swords, drove him away hungry from the tree of intellectual life; and all persons were forbidden to pluck the fruit for him, upon pain of severe penalties. Every yearning for intellectual food was answered by whips and thumb-screws.

But, notwithstanding the state of almost instinctive ignorance in which slavery held the Negro, there were those who occasionally astounded the world with the brightness of their intellectual genius. There were some Negroes whose minds ran the gauntlet of public proscription on one side and repressive laws on the other, and safely gained eminence in astronomy, mathematics, and medicine.

BANNEKER THE ASTRONOMER.

Benjamin Banneker, the Negro astronomer and philosopher, was born in Maryland, on the 9th of November, 1731. His maternal grandmother was a white woman, a native of England, named Molly Welsh. She came to Maryland in a shipload of white emigrants, who, according to the custom of those days, were sold to pay their passage. She served her master faithfully for seven years, when, being free, she purchased a small farm, at a nominal price. Soon after she bought two Negro slaves from a ship that had come into the Chesapeake Bay, and began life anew. Both of these Negroes proved to be men of more than ordinary fidelity, industry, and intelligence. One of them, it was said, was the son of an African king. She gave him his freedom, and then married him. His name was Banneker. Four children were the fruit of this union; but the chief interest centres in only one,—a girl, named Mary. Following the example of her mother, she also married a native of Africa: but both tradition and history preserve an unbroken silence respecting his life, with the single exception that, embracing the Christian religion, he was baptized "Robert Banneker;" and the record of his death is thus preserved, in the family Bible: "Robert Banneker departed this life, July ye 10th 1759." Thus it is evident that he took his wife's surname. Benjamin Banneker was the only child of Robert and Mary Banneker.

Young Benjamin was a great favorite with his grandmother, who taught him to read. She had a sincere love of the Sacred Scriptures, which she did not neglect to inculcate into the youthful heart of her grandson. In the neighborhood,—at that time an almost desolate spot,—a school was conducted where the master admitted several Colored children, with the whites, to the benefits of his instructions. It was a "pay school," and thither young Banneker was sent at a very tender age. His application to his studies was equalled by none. When the other pupils were playing, he found great pleasure in his books. How long he remained in school, is not known.

His father purchased a farm of one Richard Gist, and here he spent the remnant of his days.

When young Banneker had obtained his majority, he gave attention to the various interests of farm-life. He was industrious, intelligent in his labors, scrupulously neat in the management of his grounds, cultivated a valuable garden, was gentle in his treatment of stock,—horses, cows, etc.,—and was indeed comfortably situated. During those seasons of leisure which come to agriculturists, he stored his mind with useful knowledge. Starting with the Bible, he read history, biography, travels, romance, and such works on general literature as he was able to borrow. His mind seemed to turn with especial satisfaction to mathematics, and he acquainted himself with the most difficult problems.

He had a taste also for mechanics. He conceived the idea of making a timepiece, a clock, and about the year 1770 constructed one. With his imperfect tools, and with no other model than a borrowed watch, it had cost him long and patient labor to perfect it, to make the variation necessary to cause it to strike the hours, and produce a concert of correct action between the hour, the minute, and the second machinery. He confessed that its regularity in pointing out the progress of time had amply rewarded all his pains in its construction.

In 1773 Ellicott & Co. built flour-mills in a valley near the banks of the Patapsco River. Banneker watched the mills go up; and, when the machinery was set in motion, looked on with interest, as he had a splendid opportunity of observing new principles of mechanism. He made many visits to the mills, and became acquainted with their proprietors; and, till the day of his death, he found in the Ellicotts kind and helpful friends.

After a short time the Ellicotts erected a store, where, a little later, a post-office, was opened. To this point the farmers and gentlemen, for miles around, used to congregate. Banneker often called at the post-office, where, after overcoming his natural modesty and diffidence, he was frequently called out in conversations covering a variety of topics. His conversational powers, his inexhaustible fund of information, and his broad learning (for those times and considering his circumstances), made him the connoisseur of that section. At times he related, in modest terms, the difficulties he was constrained to encounter in order to acquire the knowledge of books he had, and the unsatisfied longings he still had for further knowledge. His fame as a mathematician was already established, and with the increasing facilities of communication his accomplishments and achievements were occupying the thought of many intelligent people.

The following question was propounded to Mr. George Ellicott, and was solved by Benjamin Hallowell of Alexandria.

"A Cooper and Vintner sat down for a talk, Both being so groggy, that neither could walk, Says Cooper to Vintner, 'I'm the first of my trade, There's no kind of vessel, but what I have made, And of any shape, Sir,—just what you will,— And of any size, Sir,—from a ton to a gill!' 'Then,' says the Vintner, 'you're the man for me,— Make me a vessel, if we can agree. The top and the bottom diameter define, To bear that proportion as fifteen to nine; Thirty-five inches are just what I crave, No more and no less, in the depth, will I have; Just thirty-nine gallons this vessel must hold,— Then I will reward you with silver or gold,— Give me your promise, my honest old friend?' 'I'll make it to-morrow, that you may depend!' So the next day the Cooper his work to discharge, Soon made the new vessel, but made it too large:— He took out some staves, which made it too small, And then cursed the vessel, the Vintner and all. He beat on his breast, 'By the Powers!'—he swore, He never would work at his trade any more! Now my worthy friend, find out, if you can, The vessel's dimensions and comfort the man!

"Benjamin Banneker.

The greater diameter of Banneker's tub must be 24.746 inches; the less diameter, 14.8476 inches.

He was described by a gentleman who had often met him at Ellicott's Mills as "of black complexion, medium stature, of uncommonly soft and gentlemanly manners and of pleasing colloquial powers."

Fortunately Mr. George Ellicott was a gentleman of exquisite literary taste and critical judgment. He discovered in Banneker the elements of a cultivated gentleman and profound scholar. He threw open his library to this remarkable Negro, loaded him with books and astronomical instruments, and gave him the emphatic assurance of sympathy and encouragement. He occasionally made Banneker a visit, when he would urge upon him the importance of making astronomical calculations for almanacs. Finally, in the spring of 1789, Banneker submitted to Mr. Ellicott his first projection of an eclipse. It was found to contain a slight error; and, having kindly pointed it out, Mr. Ellicott received the following reply from Banneker:—

His mother, an active, intelligent, slight-built Mulatto, with long black hair, had exercised a tender but positive influence over him. His character, so far as is known, was without blemish, with the single exception of an occasional use of ardent spirits. He found himself conforming too frequently to the universal habit of the times, social drinking. Liquors and wines were upon the tables and sideboards of the best families, and wherever Banneker went it confronted him. He felt his weakness in this regard, and resolved to abstain from the use of strong drink. Some time after returning from a visit to Washington, in company with the commissioners who laid out the District of Columbia, he related to his friends that during the entire absence from home he had abstained from the use of liquors; adding, "I feared to trust myself even with wine, lest it should steal away the little sense I have." On a leaf of one of his almanacs, appears the following in his own handwriting:—

He had a just appreciation of his own strength. He hated vice of every kind; and, while he did not connect himself to any church, he was deeply attached to the Society of Friends. He was frequently seen in their meeting-house. He usually occupied the rear bench, where he would sit with uncovered head, leaning upon his staff, wrapt in profound meditation. The following letter addressed to Mr. J. Saurin Norris shows that his character was upright:—

After the death of his mother, Banneker dwelt alone until the day of his death, having never married, his manners were gentle and engaging, his benevolence proverbial. His home became a place of great interest to visitors, whom he always received cordially, and treated hospitably all who called.

Within a few days after this visit Mrs. Mason addressed him in a poetical letter, which found its way into the papers of the section, and was generally read. The subjoined portions are sufficient to exhibit the character of the effusion. The admonitory lines at the end doubtless refer to his early addiction to strong drink.

During the following year Banneker sent the following letter to his good friend Mrs. Mason:—

With the use of Mayer's Tables, Ferguson's Astronomy, and Leadbeater's Lunar Tables, Banneker had made wonderful progress in his astronomical investigations. He prepared his first almanac for publication in 1792. Mr. James McHenry became deeply interested in him, and, convinced of his talent in this direction, wrote a letter to the firm of Goddard & Angell, publishers of almanacs, in Baltimore. They became the sole publishers of Banneker's almanacs till the time of his death. In an editorial note in the first almanac, they say,—

And they further say,—

The title of his almanac is given below as a matter of historic interest.

He had evidently read Mr. Jefferson's Notes on Virginia; and touched by the humane sentiment there exhibited, as well as saddened by the doubt expressed respecting the intellect of the Negro, Banneker sent him a copy of his first almanac, accompanied by a letter which pleaded the cause of his race, and in itself, was a refutation of the charge that the Negro had no intellectual outcome.

Mr. Jefferson, who was Secretary of State under President Washington, sent the great Negro the following courteous reply:—

The only time Banneker was ever absent from his home any distance was when "the Commissioners to run the lines of the District of Columbia"—then known as the "Federal Territory"—invited him to accompany them upon their mission. Mr. Norris says:—

His habits of study were rather peculiar. At nightfall, wrapped in a great cloak, he would lie prostrate upon the ground, where he spent the night in contemplation of the heavenly bodies. At sunrise he would retire to his dwelling, where he spent a portion of the day in repose. But as he seemed to require less sleep than most people, he employed the hours of the afternoons in the cultivation of his garden, trimming of fruit-trees, or in observing the habits and flight of his bees. When his service and attention were not required out-doors, he busied himself with his books, papers, and mathematical instruments, at a large oval table in his house. The situation of Banneker's dwelling was one which would be admired by every lover of nature, and furnished a fine field for the observation of celestial phenomena. It was about half a mile from the Patapsco River, and commanded a prospect of the near and distant hills upon its banks, which have been so justly celebrated for their picturesque beauty. A never-failing spring issued from beneath a large golden-willow tree in the midst of his orchard. The whole situation was charming, inspiring, and no doubt helped him in the solution of difficult problems.

There is no reliable data to enlighten us as to the day of his death; but it is the opinion of those who lived near him, and their descendants, that he died in the fall of 1804. It was a bright, beautiful day, and feeling unwell he walked out on the hills to enjoy the sunlight and air. During his walk he came across a neighbor, to whom he complained of being sick. They both returned to his house, where, after lying down upon his couch, he became speechless, and died peacefully. During a previous sickness he had charged his sisters, Minta Black and Molly Morten, that, so soon as he was dead, all the books, instruments, etc., which Mr. Ellicott had loaned him, should be taken back to the benevolent lender; and, as a token of his gratitude, all his manuscripts containing all his almanacs, his observations and writings on various subjects, his letter to Thomas Jefferson, and that gentleman's reply, etc., were given to Mr. Ellicott. On the day of his death, faithful to the instructions of their brother, Banneker's sisters had all the articles moved to Mr. Ellicott's house; and their arrival was the first sad news of the astronomer's death. To the promptness of these girls in carrying out his orders is the gratitude of the friends of science due for the preservation of the results of Banneker's labors. During the performance of the last sad rites at the grave, two days after his death, his house was discovered to be on fire. It burnt so rapidly that it was impossible to save any thing: so his clock and other personal property perished in the flames. He had given to one of his sisters a feather-bed, upon which he had slept for many years; and she, fortunately and thoughtfully, removed it when he died, and prized it as the only memorial of her distinguished brother. Some years after, she had occasion to open the bed, when she discovered a purse of money—another illustration of his careful habits and frugality.

Benjamin Banneker was known favorably on two continents, and at the time of his death was the most intelligent and distinguished Negro in the United States.

FULLER THE MATHEMATICIAN.

One of the standing arguments against the Negro was, that he lacked the faculty of solving mathematical problems. This charge was made without a disposition to allow him an opportunity to submit himself to a proper test. It was equivalent to putting out a man's eyes, and then asserting boldly that he cannot see; of manacling his ankles, and charging him with the inability to run. But notwithstanding all the prohibitions against instructing the Negro, and his far remove from intellectual stimulants, the subject to whom attention is now called had within his own untutored intellect the elements of a great mathematician.

Thomas Fuller, familiarly known as the Virginia Calculator, was a native of Africa. At the age of fourteen he was stolen, and sold into slavery in Virginia, where he found himself the property of a planter residing about four miles from Alexandria. He did not understand the art of reading or writing, but by a marvellous faculty was able to perform the most difficult calculations. Dr. Benjamin Rush of Philadelphia, Penn., in a letter addressed to a gentleman residing in Manchester, Eng., says that hearing of the phenomenal mathematical powers of "Negro Tom," he, in company with other gentlemen passing through Virginia, sent for him. One of the gentlemen asked him how many seconds a man of seventy years, some odd months, weeks, and days, had lived, he gave the exact number in a minute and a half. The gentleman took a pen, and after some figuring told Tom he must be mistaken, as the number was too great." 'Top, massa!" exclaimed Tom, "you hab left out de leap-years!" And sure enough, on including the leap-years in the calculation, the number given by Tom was correct.

That he was a prodigy, no one will question. He was the wonder of the age. The following appeared in several newspapers at the time of his death:—

DERHAM THE PHYSICIAN.

Through all time the science of medicine has been regarded as ranking among the most intricate and delicate pursuits man could follow. Our Saviour was called "the Great Physician," and St. Luke "the beloved physician." No profession brings a man so near to humanity, and no other class of men have a higher social standing than those who are consecrated to the "art of healing." Such a position demands of a man not only profound research in the field of medicine, but the rarest intellectual and social gifts and accomplishments. For a Negro to gain such a position in the nineteenth century would require merit of unusual order. But in the eighteenth century, when slavery had cast its long, dark shadows over the entire life of the nation, for a Negro, born and reared a slave, to obtain fame in medicine second to none on the continent, was an achievement that justly challenged the admiration of the civilized world.

Dr. James Derham was born a slave in Philadelphia in 1762. His master was a physician. James was taught to read and write, and early rendered valuable assistance to his master in compounding medicines. Endowed with more than average intelligence, he took a great liking to the science of medicine, and absorbed all the information that came within his observation. On the death of his master he was sold to the surgeon of the Sixteenth British Regiment, at that time stationed in Philadelphia. At the close of the war he was sold to Dr. Robert Dove of New Orleans, a humane and intelligent man, who employed him as his assistant in a large business. He grew in a knowledge of his profession every day, was prompt and faithful in the discharge of the trusts reposed in him, and thereby gained the confidence of his master. Dr. Dove was so much pleased with him, that he offered him his freedom upon very easy terms, requiring only two or three years' service. At the end of the time designated, Dr. Derham entered into the practice of medicine upon his own account. He acquired the English, French, and Spanish languages so as to speak them fluently, and built up a practice in a short time worth three thousand dollars a year. He married, and attached himself to the Episcopal Church, in 1788, and at twenty-six years of age was regarded as one of the most eminent physicians in New Orleans.

Dr. Rush of Philadelphia, in "The American Museum" for January, 1789, gave an interesting account of this distinguished "Negro physician." Says Dr. Rush,—

Phillis Wheatley has been mentioned already. So, in the midst of darkness and oppression, the Negro race in America, without the use of the Christian church, schoolhouse, or printing-press, produced a poetess, an astronomer, a mathematician, and a physician, who, had they been white, would have received monuments and grateful memorials at the hands of their countrymen. But even their color cannot rob them of the immortality their genius earned.

FOOTNOTES:

William Wells Brown, William C Nell, and all the Colored men whose efforts I have seen, have made a number of very serious mistakes respecting Banneker's parentage, age, accomplishments, etc. He was of mixed blood. His mother's name was not Molly Morton, but one of his sisters bore that name. I have used the Memoirs of Banneker, prepared by J.H.B. Latrobe and J. Saurin Norris, and other valuable material from the Maryland Historical Society.

In the most remote records the name was written Banneky.

J. Saurin Norris's sketch.

Jefferson's Works, vol. iii. p. 291.

See Norris, paper on Banneker.

All of Banneker's literary remains were published by J.H.B. Latrobe in the Maryland Historical Society, and in the Maryland Colonization Journal in 1845. The Memoir of Banneker was somewhat marred by a too precipitous and zealous attempt to preach the doctrine of colonization.

Needles's Hist. Memoir of the Penn. Society for Promoting the Abolition of Slavery, p 32.

J.P. Brissot de Warville's Travels in the U.S., vol. i p. 243.

Columbian Centinal of Boston, Dec. 29, 1790.

Brissot de Warville's New Travels in the U.S., ed. 1794, vol. i. p. 242.

For an account of Fuller and Derham, see De la Littérature des Nègres, ou Recherches sur leurs Facultés intellectuelles, leurs Qualités morales et leur Littérature; suivies de Notices sur la Vie et les Ouvrages des Nègres qui se sont distingués dans les Sciences, les Lettres et les Arts. Par H. Grégoire, ancien Évêque de Blois, membre du Sénat conservateur, de l'Institut national, de la Société royale des Sciences de Göttingue, etc. Paris: MDCCCVIII.

CHAPTER XXX.: SLAVERY DURING THE REVOLUTION.: 1775-1783.

Progress of the Slave-Trade.—A Great War for the Emancipation of the Colonies from Political Bondage.—Condition of the Southern States during the War.—The Virginia Declaration of Rights.—Immediate Legislation against Slavery demanded.—Advertisement from "The Independent Chronicle."—Petition of Massachusetts Slaves.—An Act preventing the Practice of holding Persons in Slavery.—Advertisements from "The Continental Journal."—A Law passed in Virginia limiting the Rights of Slaves.—Law emancipating all Slaves who served in the Army.—New York promises her Negro Soldiers Freedom.—A Conscientious Minority in Favor of the Abolition of the Slave-Trade.—Slavery flourishes during the Entire Revolutionary Period.

THE thunder of the guns of the Revolution did not drown the voice of the auctioneer. The slave-trade went on. A great war for the emancipation of the colonies from the political bondage into which the British Parliament fain would precipitate them did not depreciate the market value of human flesh. Those whose hearts were not enlisted in the war skulked in the rear, and gloated over the blood-stained shekels they wrung from the domestic slave-trade. While the precarious condition of the Southern States during the war made legislation in support of the institution of slavery impolitic, there were, nevertheless, many severe laws in force during this entire period. In the New England and Middle States there was heard an occasional voice for the oppressed; but it was generally strangled at the earliest moment of its being by that hell-born child, avarice. On the 21st of September, 1776, William Gordon of Roxbury, Mass., wrote,—

No one gave heed. Two months later, Nov. 14, there appeared in "The Independent Chronicle" of Boston a plan for gradual emancipation; and on the 28th of the same month, in the same paper there appeared a communication demanding specific and immediate legislation against slavery. But all seemed vain: there were few moral giants among the friends of "liberty for all;" and the comparative silence of the press and pulpit gave the advocates of human slavery an easy victory.

Boston, the home of Warren, and the city that witnessed the first holy offering to liberty, busied herself through all the perilous years of the war in buying and selling human beings. The following are but a few of the many advertisements that appeared in the papers of the city of Boston during the war:—

From "The Independent Chronicle," Oct. 3, 1776:—

From the same, Oct. 10:—

From the same, Nov. 28:—

From the same, Feb. 27, 1777:—

From "The Continental Journal," April 3, 1777:—

From "The Independent Chronicle," May 8, 1777:—

The strange and trying vicissitudes through which the colonies had passed exposed their hypocrisy, revealed the weakness of their government, and forced them to another attempt at the extirpation of slavery. The valorous conduct of the Negro soldiers in the army had greatly encouraged their friends and emboldened their brethren, who still suffered from the curse of slavery. The latter were not silent when an opportunity presented to claim the rights they felt their due. On the 18th of March, 1777, the following petition was addressed, by the slaves in Boston, to the Legislature:—

The following entry, bearing the same date, was made:—

There is no record of the action of the committee, if any were ever had; but at the afternoon session of the Legislature, Monday, June 9, 1777, a bill was introduced to prevent "the Practice of holding persons in Slavery." It was "read a first time, and ordered to be read again on Friday next, at 10 o'clock A.M." Accordingly, on the 13th of June, the bill was "read a second time, and after Debate thereon, it was moved and seconded, That the same lie upon the Table, and that Application be made to Congress on the subject thereof; and the Question being put, it passed in the affirmative, and Mr. Speaker, Mr. Wendell, and Col. Orne, were appointed a Committee to prepare a letter to Congress accordingly, and report." The last action, as far as indicated by the journal, was had on Saturday, June 14, when "the Committee appointed to prepare a Letter to Congress, on the subject of the Bill for preventing the Practice of holding Persons in Slavery, reported." It was "Read and ordered to lie." And so it did "lie," for that was the end of the matter.

Judge Sargent, who was chairman of the committee appointed on the 18th of March, 1777, was doubtless the author of the following bill:—

On the back of the bill the following indorsement was written by some officer of the Legislature: "Ordered to lie till the second Wednesday of the next Session of the General Court." This might have ended the struggle for the extinction of slavery in Massachusetts, had not the people at this time made an earnest demand for a State constitution. As the character of the constitution was discussed, the question of slavery divided public sentiment. If it were left out of the constitution, then the claims of the master would forever lack the force of law; if it were inserted as part of the constitution, it would evidence the insincerity of the people in their talk about the equality of the rights of man, etc. The Legislature—Convention of 1777-78—prepared, debated, and finally approved and submitted to the people, a draught of a constitution for the State, on the 28th of February, 1778. The framers of the constitution seemed to lack the courage necessary to declare in favor of the freedom of the faithful blacks who had rendered such efficient aid to the cause of the colonists. The prevailing sentiment of the people demanded an article in the constitution denying Negroes the right of citizens. It may be fortunate for the fame of the Commonwealth that the record of the debates on the article denying Negroes the right of suffrage has not been preserved. The article is here given:—

By this article three classes of inhabitants were excluded from the rights, blessings, and duties of citizenship; and the institution of slavery was recognized as existing by sanction of law. But the constitution was rejected by the people, by an overwhelming majority; not, however, on account of the fifth article, but because the instrument was obnoxious to them on general principles.

The defeat of the constitution did not temper public sentiment on the question of Negro slavery, for the very next year the domestic trade seemed to receive a fresh impetus. The following advertisements furnish abundant proof of the undiminished vigor of the enterprise.

From "The Continental Journal," Nov. 25, 1779:—
From the same, Dec. 16, 1779:—
From "The Independent Chronicle," March 9, 1780:—
From the same, March 30 and April 6, 1780:—
From "The Continental Journal," Aug. 17, 1780:—
From the same, Aug. 24 and Sept. 7:—
From the same, Oct. 19 and 26, and Nov. 2:—
From the same, Oct. 26, 1780:—
"Independent Chronicle," Dec. 14, 21, 28, 1780:—
"Continental Journal," Dec. 21, 1780, and Jan. 4, 1781:—
From *'The Continental Journal," March 1, 1781:—

It is evident, from the wording of the last advertisement quoted, that the Negroes were sniffing the air of freedom that occasionally blew from the victorious battle-fields, where many of their race had distinguished themselves by the most intrepid valor. They began to get "notions of freedom," and this depreciated their market value.

Dr. William Gordon, the steadfast, earnest, and intelligent friend of the Negro, was deposed as chaplain of both branches of the Legislature on account of his vehement protest against the adoption of the fifth article of the constitution by that body. But his zeal was not thereby abated. He continued to address able articles to the public, and wrought a good work upon the public conscience.

In Virginia, notwithstanding Negroes were among the State's most gallant defenders, a law was passed in October, 1776, "declaring tenants of lands or slaves in taille to hold the same in fee simple." Under the circumstances, after the war had begun, and after the declaration by the State of national independence, it was a most remarkable law.

But the valor of the Negro soldier had great influence upon the public mind, and inspired the people in many of the States to demand public recognition of deserving Negroes. It has been noted already, that in South Carolina, if a Negro, having been captured by the enemy, made good his escape back into the State, he was emancipated; and, if wounded in the line of duty, was rewarded with his freedom. Rhode Island purchased her Negroes for the army, and presented them with fifty dollars bounty and a certificate of freedom at the close of the war. Even Virginia, the mother of slavery, remembered, at the close of the war, the brave Negroes who had fought in her regiments. In October, 1783, the following Act was passed emancipating all slaves who had served in the army with the permission of their masters. It is to be regretted, however, that all slaves who had served in the army were not rewarded with their freedom.

New York enlisted her Negro soldiers under a statutory promise of freedom. They were required to serve three years, or until regularly discharged. Several other States emancipated a few slaves who had served faithfully in the army; and the recital of the noble deeds of black soldiers was listened to with great interest, had an excellent effect upon many white men after the war, and went far towards mollifying public sentiment on the slavery question.

If Massachusetts were ever moved by the valor of her black soldiers to take any action recognizing their services, the record has not been found up to the present time. After commemorating the 5th of March for a long time, as a day on which to inflame the public zeal for the cause of freedom, her Legislature refused to mark the grave of the first martyr of the Revolution, Crispus Attucks!

Slavery flourished during the entire Revolutionary period. It enjoyed the silent acquiescence of the pulpit, the support of the public journals, the sanction of the courts, and the endorsement of the military establishment. In a free land (?), under the flag of the government Negroes fought, bled, sacrificed, and died to establish, slavery held undisputed sway. The colonial government, built by the cruel and voracious avarice of Britain, crumbled under the master-stroke of men who desired political and religious liberty more than jewelled crowns; but the slave institution stood unharmed by the shock of embattled arms. The colonists asked freedom for themselves and children, but forged chains for Negroes and their children. And while a few individual Negro slaves were made a present of themselves at the close of the war, on account of their gallant service, hundreds of thousands of their brethren were still retained in bondage

FOOTNOTES:

See Slavery in Mass., p. 178.
House Journal, pp. 19, 25.
Mass. Archives; Revolutionary Resolves, vol. vii. p. 133.
Hening, vol. ix. p. 226.
Hening, vol. xi pp. 308, 309.

CHAPTER XXXI.: SLAVERY AS A POLITICAL AND LEGAL PROBLEM.: 1775-1800.

British Colonies in North America declare their Independence.—A New Government established.—Slavery the Bane of American Civilization.—The Tory Party accept the Doctrine of Property in Man.—The Doctrine of the Locke Constitution in the South.—The Whig Party the Dominant Political Organization in the Northern States.—Slavery recognized under the New Government.—Anti Slavery Agitation in the States.—Attempted Legislation against Slavery.—Articles of Confederation.—Then Adoption in 1778.—Discussion concerning the Disposal of the Western Territory.—Mr. Jefferson's Recommendation.—Amendment by Mr. Spaight.—Congress in New York in 1787.—Discussion respecting the Government of the Western Territory.—Convention at Philadelphia to frame the Federal Constitution.—Proceedings of the Convention.—The Southern States still advocate Slavery.—Speeches on the Slavery Question by Leading Statesmen.—Constitution adopted by the Convention in 1787.—First Session of Congress under the Federal Constitution held in New York in 1789.—The Introduction of a Tariff-Bill.—An Attempt to amend it by inserting a Clause levying a Tax on Slaves brought by Water.—Extinction of Slavery in Massachusetts.—A Change in the Public Opinion of the Middle and Eastern States on the Subject of Slavery.—Dr. Benjamin Franklin's Address to the Public for promoting the Abolition of Slavery.—Memorial to the United-States Congress.—Congress in 1790.—Bitter Discussion on the Restriction of the Slave-Trade.—Slave-Population.—Vermont and Kentucky admitted into the Union.—A Law providing for the Return of Fugitives from "Labor and Service."—Convention of Friends held in Philadelphia.—An Act against the Foreign Slave-Trade.—Mississippi Territory.—Constitution of Georgia revised.—New York passes a Bill for the Gradual Extinction of Slavery.—Constitution of Kentucky revised.—Slavery as an Institution firmly established.

THE charge that the mother-country forced slavery upon the British colonies in North America held good until the colonies threw off the yoke, declared their independence, and built a new government, on the 4th of July, 1776. After the promulgation of the gospel of human liberty, the United States of America could no longer point to England as the "first man Adam" of the accursed sin of slavery. Henceforth the American government, under the new dispensation of peace and the equality of all men, was responsible for the continuance of slavery, both as a political and legal problem

Slavery did not escheat to the English government upon the expiration of its authority in North America. It became the dreadful inheritance of the new government, and the eyesore of American civilization. Instead of expelling it from the political institutions of the country, it gradually became a factor of great power. Instead of ruling it out of the courts, it was clothed with the ample garments of judicial respectability.

The first article of the immortal Declaration of Independence was a mighty shield of beautifully wrought truths, that the authors intended should protect every human being on the American Continent.

It was to be expected, that, after such a declaration of principles, the United States would have abolished slavery and the slave-trade forever. While the magic words of the Declaration of Independence were not the empty "palaver" of a few ambitious leaders, yet the practices of the local and the national government belied the grand sentiments of that instrument. From the earliest moment of the birth of the United-States government, slavery began to receive political support and encouragement. Though it was the cruel and depraved offspring of the British government, it nevertheless was adopted by the free government of America. Political policy seemed to dictate the methods of a political recognition of the institution. And the fact that the slave-trade was prohibited by Congress at an early day, and by many of the colonies also, did not affect the institution in a local sense.

The Tory party accepted the doctrine of property in man, without hesitation or reservation. Their political fealty to the Crown, their party exclusiveness, and their earnest desire to co-operate with the Royal African Company in the establishment of the slave institution in America, made them, as per necessity, the political guardians of slavery. The institution once planted, property in man having been acquired, it was found to be a difficult task to uproot it. Moreover, the loss of the colonies to the British Crown did not imply death to the Tory party. It doubtless suffered organically; but its individual members did not forfeit their political convictions, nor suffer their interest in the slave-trade to abate. The new States were ambitious to acquire political power. The white population of the South was small when compared with that of the North; but the slave population, added to the former, swelled it to alarming proportions.

The local governments of the South had been organized upon the fundamental principles of the Locke Constitution. The government was lodged with the few, and their rights were built upon landed estates and political titles and favors. Slaves in the Carolinas and Virginias answered to the vassals and villeins of England. This aristocratic element in Tory politics was in harmony, even in a republic, with the later wish of the South to build a great political "government upon Slavery as its chief corner-stone." Added to this was the desire to abrogate the law of indenture of white servants, and thus to the odium of slavery to loan the powerful influence of caste,—ranging the Caucasian against the Ethiopian, the intelligent against the ignorant, the strong against the weak.

New England had better ideas of popular government for and of the people, but her practical position on slavery was no better than any State in the South. The Whig party was the dominant political organization throughout the Northern States; but the universality of slavery made dealers in human flesh members of all parties.

The men who wrote the Declaration of Independence deprecated slavery, as they were pronounced Whigs; but nevertheless many of them owned slaves. They wished the evil exterminated, but confessed themselves ignorant of a plan by which to carry their desire into effect. The good desires of many of the people, born out of the early days of the struggle for independent existence, perished in their very infancy; and, as has been shown, all the States, and the Congress of the United States, recognized slavery as existing under the new political government.

But public sentiment changes in a country where the intellect is unfettered. First, on the eve of the Revolutionary War, Congress and nearly all the States pronounced against slavery; a few years later they all recognized the sacredness of slave property; and still later all sections of the United States seemed to have been agitated by anti-slavery sentiments. In 1780 the Legislature of Pennsylvania prohibited the further introduction of slaves, and gave freedom to the children of all slaves born in the State. Delaware resolved "that no person hereafter imported from Africa ought to be held in slavery under any pretense whatever." In 1784 Connecticut and Rhode Island modified their slave-code, and forbade further importations of slaves. In 1778 Virginia passed a law prohibiting the importation of slaves, and in 1782 repealed the law that confined the power of emancipating to the Legislature, only on account of meritorious conduct. Private emancipations became very numerous, and the sentiment in its favor pronounced. But the restriction was re-enacted in about ten years. The eloquence of Patrick Henry and the logic of Thomas Jefferson went far to enlighten public sentiment; but the political influence of the institution grew so rapidly that in 1785, but two years after the war, Washington wrote LaFayette, "petitions for the abolition of slavery, presented to the Virginia Legislature, could scarcely obtain a hearing." Maryland, New York, and New Jersey prohibited the slave-trade; but the institution held its place among the people until 1830. North Carolina attempted to prohibit in 1777, but-failed; but in 1786 declared the slave-trade "of evil consequences and highly impolitic." South Carolina and Georgia refused to act, and the slave-trade continued along their shores.

After the adoption of the Articles of Confederation in 1778, the Continental Congress found itself charged with the responsibility of deciding the conflicting claims of the various States to the vast territory stretching westward from the Ohio River. The war over, the payment of the public debt thus incurred demanded the consideration of the people and of their representatives. Massachusetts, Connecticut, New York, Virginia, North Carolina, and Georgia laid claim to boundless tracts of lands outside of their State boundaries. But New Hampshire, Rhode Island, New Jersey, Maryland, Delaware, and South Carolina, making no such claims, and lacking the resources to pay their share of the war debt, suggested that the other States should cede all the territory outside of their State lines, to the United States Government, to be used towards liquidating the entire debt. The proposition was accepted by the States named; but not, however, without some modification. Virginia reserved a large territory beyond the Ohio with which to pay the bounties of her soldiers, while Connecticut retained a portion of the Reserve since so famous in the history of Ohio. The duty of framing an ordinance for the government of the Western territory was referred to a select committee by Congress, consisting of Mr. Jefferson of Virginia (chairman), Mr. Chase of Maryland, and Mr. Howell of Rhode Island. The plan reported by the committee contemplated the whole region included within our boundaries west of the old thirteen States, and as far south as our thirty-first degree north latitude. The plan proposed the ultimate division of this territory into seventeen States; eight of which were to be located below the parallel of the Falls of the Ohio (now Louisville), and nine above it. But the most interesting rule reported by Mr. Jefferson was the following, on the 19th of April, 1784:—

Mr. Spaight of North Carolina moved to amend the report by striking out the above clause, which was seconded by Mr. Reed of South Carolina. The question, upon a demand for the yeas and nays, was put: "Shall the words moved to be stricken out stand?" The question was lost, and the words were stricken out. The ordinance was further amended, and finally adopted on the 23d of April

The last Continental Congress was held in the city of New York in 1787. The question of the government of the Western territory came up. A committee was appointed on this subject, with Nathan Dane of Massachusetts as chairman On the 11th of July the committee reported "An Ordinance for the government of the Territory of the United States, Northwest of the Ohio." It embodied many of the features of Mr. Jefferson's bill, concluding with six unalterable articles of perpetual compact, the last being the following: "There shall be neither slavery nor involuntary servitude in the said territory, otherwise than in punishment of crimes, whereof the parties shall be duly convicted." When upon its passage, a stipulation was added for the delivery of fugitives from "labor or service:" and in this shape the entire ordinance passed on the 13th of July, 1787.

Thus it is clear that under the Confederation slavery existed, a part of the political government, as a legal fact. There was no effort made by Congress to abolish it. Mr. Jefferson simply sought to arrest its progress, and confine it to the original thirteen States.

On the 25th of May, 1787, the convention to frame the Federal Constitution met at Philadelphia, although the day appointed was the 14th. George Washington was chosen president, a committee chosen to report rules of proceeding, and a secretary appointed. The sessions were held with closed doors, and all the proceedings were secret. It contained the most eminent men in the United States,—generals of the army, statesmen, lawyers, and men of broad scholarship. The question of congressional apportionment was early before them, and there was great diversity of opinion. But, as there was no census, therefore there could be no just apportionment until an enumeration of the people was taken. Until that was accomplished, the number of delegates was fixed at sixty-five. Massachusetts was the only State in the Union where slavery did not exist. The Northern States desired representation according to the free inhabitants only; while all of the Southern States, where the great mass of slaves was, wanted representation according to the entire population, bond and free. Some of the Northern delegates urged their view with great force and eloquence. Mr. Patterson of New Jersey said he regarded slaves as mere property. They were not represented in the States: why should they be in the general government? They were not allowed to vote: why should they be represented? He regarded it as an encouragement to the slave-trade. Mr. Wilson of Pennsylvania said, "Are they admitted as citizens? then, why not on an equality with citizens? Are they admitted as property? then, why is not other property admitted into the computation?" It was evident that neither extreme view could carry: so the proposition carried to reckon three-fifths of the slaves in estimating taxes, and to make taxation the basis of representation. New Jersey and Delaware voted Nay; Massachusetts and South Carolina were divided; and New York was not represented, her delegates having failed to arrive.

It was apparent during the early stages of the debates, that a constitution had to be made that would be acceptable to the Southern delegates. A clause was inserted relieving the Southern States from duties on exports, and upon the importation of slaves; and that no navigation act should be passed except by a two-thirds vote. By denying Congress the authority of giving preference to American over foreign shipping, it was designed to secure cheap transportation for Southern exports; but, as the shipping was largely owned in the Eastern States, their delegates were zealous in their efforts to prevent any restriction of the power of Congress to enact navigation laws. It has been already shown that all the States, with the exception of North Carolina, South Carolina, and Georgia, had prohibited the importation of slaves. The prohibition of duties on the importation of slaves was demanded by the delegates from South Carolina and Georgia. They assured the Convention that without such a provision they could never give their assent to the constitution. This declaration dragooned some Northern delegates into a support of the restriction, but provoked some very plain remarks concerning slavery. Mr. Pinckney said, that, "If the Southern States were let alone, they would probably of themselves stop importations. He would himself, as a citizen of South Carolina, vote for it."

Mr. Sherman remarked that "the abolition of slavery seemed to be going on in the United States, and that the good sense of the several states would probably by degrees complete it;" and Mr. Ellsworth thought that "slavery, in time, will not be a speck in our country." Mr. Madison said "he thought it wrong to admit in the Constitution the idea of property in men."

Slavery, notwithstanding the high-sounding words just quoted, was recognized in and by three separate clauses of the Constitution The word "slave" was excluded, but the language does not admit of any doubt.

The debate on the above was exciting and interesting, as the subject of slavery was examined in all its bearings. Finally the Constitution was submitted to Gouverneur Morris of Pennsylvania, to receive the finishing touches of his facile pen. On the 8th of August, 1787, during the debate, he delivered the following speech:—

Mr. Rufus King of Massachusetts in the same debate said,—

Mr. Roger Sherman of Connecticut,—

Mr. Luther Martin of Maryland, in the debate, Tuesday, Aug. 21,—

Three days later (Saturday, Aug. 25) the debate on the subject was resumed, and the report of the committee of eleven was taken up. It was in the following words:—

The above specimens of the speeches on the slavery question, during the debate, are sufficient to furnish a fair idea of the personal opinion of the great thinkers of that time on slavery. It is clear that it was the wish of the great majority of the Northern delegates to abolish the institution, in a domestic as well as in a foreign sense; but they were not strong enough to resist the temptation to compromise their profoundest convictions on a question as broad and far-reaching as the Union that they were met to launch anew. Thus by an understanding, or, as Gouverneur Morris called it, "a bargain," between the commercial representatives of the Northern States and the delegates of South Carolina and Georgia, and in spite of the opposition of Maryland and Virginia, the unrestricted power of Congress to enact navigation-laws was conceded to the Northern merchants; and to the Carolina rice-planters, as an equivalent, twenty years' continuance of the African slave-trade. This was the third great "compromise" of the Constitution. The other two were the concession to the smaller States of an equal representation in the Senate; and, to the slaveholders, the counting three-fifths of the slaves in determining the ratio of representation. If this third compromise differed from the other two by involving not merely a political but a moral sacrifice, there was this partial compensation about it, that it was not permanent like the others, but expired, by limitation, at the end of twenty years.

The Constitution was adopted by the Convention, and signed, on the 17th of September, 1787. It was then forwarded to Congress, then in session in New-York City, with the recommendation that that body submit it to the State conventions for ratification; which was accordingly done. Delaware adopted it on the 7th of December, 1787; Pennsylvania, Dec. 12; New Jersey, Dec. 18; Georgia, Jan. 2, 1788; Connecticut, Jan. 9; Massachusetts, Feb. 7; Maryland, April 28; South Carolina, May 23; New Hampshire, June 21 (and, being the ninth ratifying, gave effect to the Constitution); Virginia ratified June 27; New York, July 26. North Carolina gave a conditional ratification on the 7th of August, but Congress did not receive it until January, 1790; nor that of Rhode Island, until June of the same year.

At the conclusion of the deliberations of the convention that framed the Constitution, it was voted that its journal be intrusted to the custody of George Washington. He finally deposited it in the State Department, and it was printed in 1818 by order of Congress.

The first session of Congress, under the new Constitution, was held in the city of New York, in 1789. A quorum was obtained on the 6th of April; and the first measure brought up for consideration was a tariff-bill which Mr. Parker of Virginia sought to amend by inserting a clause levying an impost-tax of ten dollars upon every slave brought by water. "He was sorry the Constitution prevented Congress from prohibiting the importation altogether. It was contrary to revolution principles, and ought not to be permitted." Thus the question of slavery made its appearance early at the first session of the first Congress under the present Constitution. At that time Georgia was the only State in the Union that seemed to retain a pecuniary interest in the importation of slaves. Even South Carolina had passed an Act prohibiting for one year the importation of slaves. In this, as on several occasions before, she was actuated on account of the low prices of produce,—too low to be remunerative. But, notwithstanding this, Mr. Smith, the member from the Charleston district, grew quite captious over the proposition of the gentleman from Virginia. He

Mr. Sherman got the floor, and said he

Mr. Jackson of Georgia

Mr. Parker of Virginia obtained the floor again, and proceeded to reply to the remarks offered upon his amendment by Sherman, Jackson, and Smith. He declared,—

Mr. Ames of Massachusetts

Mr. Madison made an eloquent speech in support of Mr. Parker's amendment. He said,—

Mr. Bland approved the position taken by Mr. Madison, while Mr. Burke of South Carolina charged the gentlemen with having wasted the time of Congress upon a useless proposition. He contended, that, while slaves were not mentioned in the Constitution, they would come under the general five per cent ad valorem duty on all unenumerated articles, which would be equivalent to the proposition of the gentleman from Virginia. Mr. Madison replied by saying, that no collector of customs would presume to apply the terms "goods," "wares," and "merchandise" to persons. Mr. Sherman followed him in the same strain, and denied that persons were anywhere recognised as property in the Constitution. Finally, at the suggestion of Mr. Madison, Mr. Parker consented to withdraw his motion with the understanding that a separate bill should be brought in. A committee was appointed to discharge that duty, but the noble resolve found a quiet grave in the committee-room.

The failure of this first attempt, under the new Constitution, to restrict slavery, did not lame the cause to any great extent. It was rather accelerated. The manner and spirit of the debate on the subject quickened public thought, animated the friends of the Negro, and provoked many people to good works. Slavery had ceased to exist in Massachusetts. Several suits, entered by slaves against their masters for restraining their liberty, had been won. The case of Elizabeth Freeman, better known as "Mum Bet," was regarded as the first-fruits of the Massachusetts Declaration of Rights in the new Constitution of 1780. The Duke de la Rochefoucault Laincort gives the following interesting account of the extinction of slavery in Massachusetts:—

Mr. Nell gives an account of the legal death of slavery in Massachusetts, but unfortunately does not cite any authority. John Quincey Adams, in reply to a question put by John C. Spencer, stated that, "a note had been given for the price of a slave in 1787. This note was sued, and the Court ruled that the maker had received no consideration, as a man could not be sold. From that time forward, slavery died in the Old Bay State." There were several suits instituted by slaves against their reputed masters in 1781-82; but there are strong evidences that slavery died a much slower death in Massachusetts than many are willing to admit. James Sullivan wrote to Dr. Belknap in 1795:—

There are two things in the above that throw considerable uncertainty about the subject as to the precise date of the end of slavery in the Commonwealth. First, the suit referred to was tried in 1783, three years after the adoption of the new Constitution. Second, the good doctor does not say that the decision sealed the fate of slavery, but only that it "was a mortal wound to slavery in Massachusetts."

From 1785-1790, there was a wonderful change in the public opinion of the Middle and Eastern States on the subject of slavery. Most of them had passed laws providing for gradual emancipation. The Friends of New York, New Jersey, and Pennsylvania began to organize a crusade against domestic slavery. In the fall of 1789, while the Congressional debates were still fresh in the minds of the people, the venerable Dr. Benjamin Franklin, as president of the "Pennsylvania Society for Promoting the Abolition of Slavery," etc., issued the following letter:—

And as his last public act, Franklin gave his signature to the subjoined memorial to the United States Congress:—

The session of Congress held in 1790 was stormy. The slavery question came back to haunt the members. On the 12th of February, the memorial from the Pennsylvania society was read. It provoked fresh discussion, and greatly angered many of the Southern members. As soon as its reading was completed, the "Quaker Memorial," that had been read the day previous, was called up; and Mr. Hartley moved its commitment. A long and spirited debate ensued. It was charged that the memorial was "a mischievous attempt, an improper interference, at the best, an act of imprudence;" and that it "would sound an alarm and blow the trumpet of sedition through the Southern States." Mr. Scott of Pennsylvania replied by saying, "I cannot entertain a doubt that the memorial is strictly agreeable to the Constitution. It respects a part of the duty particularly assigned to us by that instrument." Mr. Sherman was in favor of the commitment of the memorial, and gave his reasons in extenso. Mr. Smith of South Carolina said, "Notwithstanding all the calmness with which some gentlemen have viewed the subject, they will find that the mere discussion of it will create alarm. We have been told that, if so, we should have avoided discussion by saying nothing. But it was not for that purpose we were sent here. We look upon this measure as an attack upon property; it is, therefore, our duty to oppose it by every means in our power. When we entered into a political connection with the other States, this property was there. It had been acquired under a former government conformably to the laws and constitution, and every attempt to deprive us of it must be in the nature of an ex post facto law, and, as such, forbidden by our political compact." Following the unwise and undignified example set by the gentlemen who had preceded him on that side of the question, he slurred the Quakers. "His constituents wanted no lessons in religion and morality, and least of all from such teachers."

Madison, Gerry, Boudinot, and Page favored commitment. Upon the question to commit, the yeas and nays being demanded, the reference was made by a vote of forty-three to eleven. Of the latter, six were from Georgia and South Carolina, two from Virginia, two from Maryland, and one from New York. A special committee was announced, to whom the memorial was referred, consisting of one member from each of the following States: New Hampshire, Massachusetts, Connecticut, New York, New Jersey, Pennsylvania, and Virginia. At the end of a month, the committee made the following report to Congress:—

Mr. Tucker took the floor against the report of the committee, and, after a bitter speech upon the unconstitutionality of meddling with the slavery question in any manner, moved a substitute for the whole, in which he pronounced the recommendations of the committee "as unconstitutional, and tending to injure some of the States of the Union." Mr. Jackson seconded the motion in a rather intemperate speech, which was replied to by Mr. Vining. The substitute of Mr. Tucker was declared out of order. Mr. Benson moved to recommit in hopes of getting rid of the subject, but the motion was overwhelmingly voted down. The report was taken up article by article. The three first resolutions (those relating to the authority of Congress over slavery in the States) were adopted; while the second and third were merged into one, stripped of its objectionable features. But on the fourth the debate was carried to a high pitch. This one related to the ten-dollar tax. Mr. Tucker moved to amend by striking out the fourth resolution. Considerable discussion followed; and, upon the question being put, it was carried by one vote. The fifth resolution, affirming the power of Congress to regulate the slave-trade, drew the fire of Jackson, Smith, and Tucker. Mr. Madison offered to modify it somewhat. It was argued by the opponents of this resolution, that Congress, under the plea of regulating the trade, might prohibit it entirely. Mr. Vining of Delaware, somewhat out of patience with the demands of the Southern members, told those gentlemen very plainly that they ought to be satisfied with the changes already made to gratify them; that they should show some respect to the committee; that all the States from Virginia to New Hampshire had passed laws prohibiting the slave-trade; and then delivered an eloquent defence of the Quakers. The resolution, as modified by Mr. Madison, carried.

The sixth resolution, relating to the foreign slave-trade carried on from ports of the United States, received considerable attention. Mr. Scott made an elaborate speech upon it, in which he claimed, that, if it were a question as to the power of Congress to regulate the foreign slave-trade, he had no doubts as to the authority of that body. "I desire," said that gentleman, "that the world should know, I desire that those people in the gallery, about whom so much has been said, should know, that there is at least one member on this floor who believes that Congress have ample powers to do all they have asked respecting the African slave-trade. Nor do I doubt that Congress will, whenever necessity or policy dictates the measure, exercise those powers." Mr. Jackson attempted to reply. He started out with a labored argument showing the divine origin of slavery, quoting Scriptures; showed that the Greeks and Romans had held slaves, etc. He was followed and supported by Smith of South Carolina. Boudinot obtained the floor, and, after defending the Quakers and praising Franklin, declared that there was nothing unreasonable in the memorial; that it simply requested them "to go to the utmost verge of the Constitution," and not beyond it. Further debate was had, when the sixth resolution was adopted.

The seventh resolution, pledging Congress to exert their full powers for the restriction of the slave-trade—and, as some understood it, to discountenance slavery—was struck out. The committee then arose and reported the resolutions to the house. The next day, the 23d March, 1790, after some preliminary business was disposed of, a motion was made to take up the report of the committee. Ames, Madison, and others thought the matter, having occupied so much of the time of the house, should be left where it was; or rather, as Mr. Madison expressed it, simply entered on the Journals as a matter of public record. After some little discussion, this motion prevailed by a vote of twenty-nine to twenty-five. The entry was accordingly made as follows:—

The census of 1790 gave the slave population of the States as follows:—

Slave Population.--Census of 1790.

Vermont was admitted into the Union on the 18th of February, 1791; and the first article of the Bill of Rights declared that "no male person born in this country, or brought from over sea, ought to be bound by law to serve any person as a servant, slave, or apprentice after he arrives at the age of twenty-one years, nor female, in like manner, after she arrives at the age of twenty-one years, unless they are bound by their own consent after they arrive at such age, or are bound by law for the payment of debts, damages, fines, costs, or the like." This provision was contained in the first Constitution of that State, and, therefore, it was the first one to abolish and prohibit slavery in North America.

On the 4th of February, 1791, Kentucky was admitted into the Union by Act of Congress, though it had no Constitution. But the next year a Constitution was framed. By it the Legislature was denied the right to emancipate slaves without the consent of the owner, nor without paying the full price of the slaves before emancipating them; nor could any laws be passed prohibiting emigrants from other states from bringing with them persons deemed slaves by the laws of any other states in the Union, so long as such persons should be continued as slaves in Kentucky. The Legislature had power to prohibit the bringing into the state slaves for the purpose of sale. Masters were required to treat their slaves with humanity, to properly feed and clothe them, and to abstain from inflicting any punishment extending to life and limb. Laws could be passed granting owners the right to emancipate their slaves, but requiring security that the slaves thus emancipated should not become a charge upon the county.

During the session of Congress in 1791, the Pennsylvania Society for the Abolition of Slavery presented another memorial, calling upon Congress to exercise the powers they had been declared to possess by the report of the committee which had been spread upon the Journals of the house. Thus emboldened, other anti-slavery societies, of Rhode Island, Connecticut, New York, Virginia, and a few local societies of Maryland, presented memorials praying for the suppression of slavery in the United States. They were referred to a select committee; and, as they made no report, New Hampshire and Massachusetts, the next year, called the attention of Congress to the subject. On the 24th of November, 1792, a Mr. Warner Mifflin, an anti-slavery Quaker from Delaware, addressed a memorial to Congress on the general subject of slavery, which was read and laid upon the table without debate. On the 26th of November, Mr. Stute of North Carolina offered some sharp remarks upon the presumption of the Quaker, and moved that the petition be returned to the petitioner, and that the clerk be instructed to erase the entry from the Journal. This provoked a heated discussion; but at length the petition was returned to the author, and the motion to erase the record from the Journal was withdrawn by the mover.

In 1793 a law was passed providing for the return of fugitives from justice and from service, "In case of the escape out of any state or territory of any person held to service or labor under the laws thereof, the person to whom such labor was due, his agent, or attorney, might seize the fugitive and carry him before any United States judge, or before any magistrate of the city, town, or county in which the arrest was made; and such judge or magistrate, on proof to his satisfaction, either oral or by affidavit before any other magistrate, that the person seized was really a fugitive, and did owe labor as alleged, was to grant a certificate to that effect to the claimant, this certificate to serve as sufficient warrant for the removal of the fugitive to the state whence he had fled. Any person obstructing in any way such seizure or removal, or harboring or concealing any fugitive after notice, was liable to a penalty of $500, to be recovered by the claimant."

In 1794 an anti-slavery convention was held in Philadelphia, in which nearly all of the abolition societies of the country were represented. A memorial, carefully avoiding constitutional objections, was drawn and addressed to Congress to do whatever they could toward the suppression of the slave-trade. This memorial, with several other petitions, was referred to a special committee. In due time they reported a bill, which passed without much opposition. It was the first act of the government toward repressing the slave-trade, and was as mild as a summer's day. On Wednesday, the 7th of January, 1795, another meeting was held in Philadelphia, the second, to consider anti-slavery measures. The Act of Congress was read.

In 1797 Congress again found themselves confronted by the dark problem of slavery, that would not down at their bidding. The Yearly Meeting of the Quakers of Philadelphia sent a memorial to Congress, complaining that about one hundred and thirty-four Negroes, and others whom they knew not of, having been lawfully emancipated, were afterwards reduced to bondage by an ex post facto law passed by North Carolina, in 1777, for that cruel purpose. After considerable debate, the memorial went to a committee, who subsequently reported that the matter complained of was purely of judicial cognizance, and that Congress had no authority in the premises.

During the same session a bill was introduced creating all that portion of the late British Province of West Florida, within the jurisdiction of the United States, into a government to be called the Mississippi Territory. It was to be conducted in all respects like the territory north-west of the Ohio, with the single exception that slavery should not be prohibited. During the discussion of this section of the bill, Mr. Thatcher of Massachusetts moved to amend by striking out the exception as to slavery, so as to make it conform to the ideas expressed by Mr. Jefferson a few years before in reference to the Western Territory. But, after a warm debate, Mr. Thatcher's motion was lost, having received only twelve votes. An amendment of Mr. Harper of South Carolina, offered a few days later, prohibiting the introduction of slaves into the new Mississippi Territory, from without the limits of the United States, carried without opposition.

Georgia revised her Constitution in 1798, and prohibited the importation of slaves "from Africa or any foreign place." Her slave-code was greatly moderated. Any person maliciously killing or dismembering a slave was to suffer the same punishment as if the act had been committed upon a free white person, except in case of insurrection, or "unless such death should happen by accident, in giving such slave moderate correction." But, like Kentucky, the Georgia constitution forbade the emancipation of slaves without the consent of the individual owner; and encouraged emigrants to bring slaves into the State.

In 1799, after three failures, the Legislature of New York passed a bill for the gradual extinction of slavery. It provided that all persons in slavery at the time of the passage of the bill should remain in bondage for life, but all their children, born after the fourth day of July next following, were to be free, but were required to remain under the direction of the owner of their parents, males until twenty-eight, and females until twenty-five. Exportation of slaves was disallowed; and if the attempt were made, and the parties apprehended, the slaves were to be free instanter. Persons moving into the State were not allowed to bring slaves, except they had owned them for a year previous to coming into the State.

In 1799 Kentucky revised her Constitution to meet the wants of a growing State. An attempt was made to secure a provision providing for gradual emancipation. It was supported by Henry Clay, who, as a young lawyer and promising orator, began on that occasion a brilliant political career that lasted for a half-century. But not even his magic eloquence could secure the passage of the humane amendment, and in regard to the question of slavery the Constitution received no change.

As the shadows gathered about the expiring days of the eighteenth century, it was clear to be seen that slavery, as an institution, had rooted itself into the political and legal life of the American Republic. An estate prolific of evil, fraught with danger to the new government, abhorred and rejected at first, was at length adopted with great political sagacity and deliberateness, and then guarded by the solemn forms of constitutional law and legislative enactments.

FOOTNOTES:

St. Clair Papers, vol. i. p. 120.
The clause "three fifths of all other persons" refers to Negro slaves. The Italics are our own.
The Negro is referred to as person all through the Constitution.
Madison Papers, Elliot, vol. v. pp. 392, 393.
Ibid., vol. v pp. 391, 392.
Madison Papers, Elliot, vol. v. pp. 457-461.
Madison Papers, Elliot, vol. v. pp. 477, 478.
Examine Hildreth and the Secret Debates on the subject of the "compromises."
Travels, etc., vol. ii. p. 166.
M.H.S. Coll., 5th Series, III., p. 403.

FOOTNOTES:

See Dr. Wiseman's Lectures on the connection between Science and Revealed Religion, Am. ed., pp. 95-98

See Nat. Hist. Human Species p. 373.

See British Encyclopædia, vol. ii. pp. 237, 238

Tiedeman, on the Brain of the Negro, in the Phil. Trans., 1838, p. 497

CHAPTER VI.

NEGRO TYPE.

It has often been said that, independently of the woolly hair and the complexion of the Negroes, there are sufficient differences between them and the rest of mankind to mark them as a very peculiar tribe. This is true, and yet the principal differences are perhaps not so constant as many persons imagine. In our West Indian colonies very many Negroes, especially females, are seen, whose figures strike Europeans as remarkably beautiful. This would not be the case if they deviated much from the idea prevalent in Europe, or from the European standard of beauty. Yet the slaves in the colonies, particularly in those of England, were brought from the west coast of intertropical Africa, where the peculiarities of figure, which in our eyes constitute deformity in the Negro, are chiefly prevalent. The black people imported into the French and to some of the Portuguese colonies, from the eastern coast of the African continent, and from Congo, are much better made. The most degraded and savage nations are the ugliest. Among the most improved and the partially civilized, as the Ashantees, and other interior States, the figure and the features of the native people approach much more to the European. The ugliest Negro tribes are confined to the equatorial countries; and on both sides of the equator, as we advance towards the temperate zones, the persons of the inhabitants are most handsome and well formed.

In a later period of this work I shall cite authors who have proved that many races belonging to this department of mankind are noted for the beauty of their features, and their fine stature and proportions. Adanson has made this observation of the Negroes on the Senegal. He thus describes the men. "Leur taille est pour l'ordinaire au-dessus de la mediocre, bien prise et sans défaut. Ils sont forts, robustes, et d'un tempérament propre à la fatigue. Ils ont les yeux noirs et bien fendus, peu de barbe, les traits du visage assez agréables." They are complete Negroes, for it is added that their complexion is of a fine black, that their hair is black, frizzled, cottony, and of extreme fineness. The women are said to be of nearly equal stature with the men, and equally well made. "Leur visage est d'une douceur extrême. Elles ont les yeux noirs, bien fendus, la bouche et les lèvres petites, et les traits du visage bien proportionnés. Il s'en trouve plusieurs d'une beauté parfaite." Mr. Rankin, a highly intelligent traveller, who reports accurately and without prejudice the results of his personal observation, has recently given a similar testimony in regard to some of the numerous tribes of northern Negro-land, who frequent the English colony of Sierra Leone. In the skull of the more improved and civilized nations among the woolly-haired blacks of Africa, there is comparatively slight deviation from the form which may be looked upon as the common type of the human head. We are assured, for example, by M.

Golberry, that the Ioloffs, whose colour is a deep transparent black, and who have woolly hair, are robust and well made, and have regular features. Their countenances, he says, are ingenuous, and inspire confidence: they are honest, hospitable, generous, and faithful. The women are mild, very pretty, well made, and of agreeable manners. On the other side of the equinoctial line, the Congo Negroes, as Pigafetta declares, have not thick lips or ugly features; except in colour they are very like the Portuguese. Kafirs in South Africa frequently resemble Europeans, as many late travellers have declared. It has been the opinion of many that the Kafirs ought to be separated from the Negroes as a distinct branch of the human family. This has been proved to be an error. In the conformation of the skull, which is the leading character, the Kafirs associate themselves with the great majority of woolly African nations.

THE NEGROES.

The Negroes inhabit Africa from the southern margin of the Sahara as far as the territory of the Hottentots and Bushmen, and from the Atlantic to the Indian Ocean, although the extreme east of their domain has been wrested from them by intrusive Hamites and Semites. Most negroes have high and narrow skulls. According to Welcker the average percentage of width begins at 68 and rises to 78. The variations are so great that, among eighteen heads from Equatorial Africa, Barnard Davis found no less than four brachyrephals. In the majority dolichocephalism is combined with a prominence of the upper jaw and an oblique position of the teeth, yet there are whole nations which are purely mesognathous. It is to be regretted that in the opinion of certain mistaken ethnologists, the negro was the ideal of every thing barbarous and beast-like. They endeavoured to deny him any capability of improvement, and even disputed his position as a man. The negro was said to have an oval skull, a flat forehead, snout-like jaws, swollen lips, a broad flat nose, short crimped hair, falsely called wool, long arms, meagre thighs, calfless legs, highly elongated heels, and flat feet. No single tribe, however, possesses all these deformities. The colour of the skin passes through every gradation, from ebony black, as in the Joloffers, to the light tint of the mulattoes, as in the Wakilema, and Barth even describes copper-coloured negroes in Marghi. As to the skull in many tribes, as in the above mentioned Joloffers, the jaws are not prominent, and the lips are not swollen. In some tribes the nose is pointed, straight, or hooked; even "Grecian profiles" are spoken of, and travellers say with surprise that they cannot perceive anything of the so-called negro type among the negroes.

According to Paul Broca, the upper limbs of the negro are comparatively much shorter than the lower, and therefore less ape-like than in Europeans, and, although in the length of the femur the negro may approximate to the proportions of the ape, he differs from them by the shortness of the humerus more than is the case with Europeans. Undoubtedly narrow and more or less high skulls are prevalent among the negroes. But the only persistent character which can be adduced as common to all is greater or less darkness of skin, that is to say, yellow, copper-red, olive, or dark brown, passing into ebony black. The colour is always browner than that of Southern Europe. The hair is generally short, elliptic in section, often split longitudinally, and much crimped. That of the negroes of South Africa, especially of the Kaffirs and Betshuans, is matted into tufts, although not in the same degree as that of the Hottentots. The hair is black, and in old age white, but there are also negroes with red hair, red eye-brows, and eye-lashes, and among the Monbuttoo, on the Uelle, Schweinfurth even discovered negroes with ashy fair hair. Hair on the body and beards exist, though not abundantly; whiskers are rare although not quite unknown.

The negroes form but a single race, for the predominant as well as the constant characters recur in Southern as well as in Central Africa, and it was therefore a mistake to separate the Bantu negroes into a peculiar race. But, according to language, the South Africans can well be separated, as a great family, from the Soudan negroes.

FOOTNOTES:

Prichard's Physical History of Mankind, vol. i. pp. 247-249.
THE RELATION OF PHYSICAL CHARACTER TO CLIMATE.
We shall now find, on comparing these several departments with each other, that marked differences of physical character, and particularly of complexion, distinguished the human races which respectively inhabit them, and that these differences are successive or by gradations.

First, Among the people of level countries within the Mediterranean region, including Spaniards, Italians, Greeks, Moors, and the Mediterranean islanders, black hair with dark eyes is almost universal, scarcely, one person in some hundreds presenting an exception to this remark with this colour of the hair and eyes is conjoined a complexion of brownish white, which the French call the colour of brunettes. We must observe, that throughout all the zones into which we have divided the European region, similar complexions to this of the Mediterranean countries are occasionally seen The qualities, indeed, of climate are not so diverse, but that even the same plants are found sporadically, in the North of Europe as in the Alps and Pyrenees. But if we make a comparison between the prevalent colours of great numbers, we can easily trace a succession of shades or of different hues.

Secondly, In the southernmost of the three zones, to the northward of the Pyreno-Alpine line, namely, in the latitude of France, the prevalent colour of the hair is a chestnut brown, to which the complexion and the colour of the eyes bear a certain relation.

Thirdly, In the northern parts of Germany, England, in Denmark, Finland and a great part of Russia, the xanthous variety, strongly marked, is prevalent The Danes have always been known as a people of florid complexion, blue eyes, and yellow hair The Hollanders were termed by Silius Italicus, "Auricomi Batavi," the golden haired Batavians, and Linnæus has defined the Finns as a tribe distinguished by "capillis flavis prolixis."

Fourthly, In the northern division we find the Norwegians and Swedes to be generally tall, white haired men, with light gray eyes characters so frequent to the northward of the Baltic, that Linnæus has specified them in a definition of the inhabitants of Swedish Gothland. We have then to the northward of Mount Atlas, four well marked varieties of human complexion succeeding each other, and in exact accordance with the gradations of latitude and of climate from south to north. The people are thus far nearly white in the colour of their skin, but in the more southerly of the three regions above defined, with a mixture of brown, or of the complexion of brunettes, or such as we term swarthy or sallow persons.

Fifthly, In the next region, to the southward of Atlas, the native inhabitants, are the "gentes sub fusci coloris" of Leo, and the immigrant Arabs in the same country are, as we have seen by abundant testimonies, of a similar high brown hue, but varying between that and a perfect black.

Sixthly, With the tropic and the latitude of the Senegal, begins the region of predominant and almost universal black, and this continues, if we confine ourselves to the low and plain countries, through all inter tropical Africa.

Seventhly, Beyond this is the country of copper coloured and red people, who, in Kafirland, are the majority, while in inter-tropical Africa there are but few such tribes, and those in countries of mountainous elevation.

Lastly, Towards the Cape are the tawny Hottentots, scarcely darker than the Mongoles, whom they resemble in many other particulars besides colour.

It has long been well known, that as travellers ascend mountains, in whatever region, they find the vegetation at every successive level altering its character, and assuming a more northern aspect, thus indicating that the state of the atmosphere, temperature and physical agencies in general, assimilate as we approach alpine regions, to the peculiarities locally connected with high latitudes. If therefore, complexions and other bodily qualities belonging to races of men depend upon climate and external conditions, we should expect to find them varying in reference to elevation of surface, and if they should be found actually to undergo such variations, this will be a strong argument that these external characters do, in fact, depend upon local conditions. Now, if we inquire respecting the physical characters of the tribes inhabiting high tracts within either of the regions above marked out, we shall find that they coincide with those which prevail in the level or low parts of more northern tracts. The Swiss, in the high mountains above the plains of Lombardy, have sandy or brown hair. What a contrast presents itself to the traveller who descends into the Milanese, where the peasants have black hair and eyes, with strongly-marked Italian and almost Oriental features. In the higher parts of the Biscayan country, instead of the swarthy complexion and black hair of the Castilians, the natives have a fair complexion with light-blue eyes and flaxen or auburn hair. And in Atlantica, while the Berbers of the plains are of brown complexion with black hair, we have seen that the Shuluh mountaineers are fair, and that the inhabitants of the high tracts of Mons Aurasius are completely xanthous, having red or yellow hair and blue eyes, which fancifully, and without the shadow of any proof, they have been conjectured to have derived from the Vandal troops of Genseric.

Even in the inter-tropical region, high elevations of surface, as they produce a cooler climate, seem to occasion the appearance of light complexions. In the high parts of Senegambia, which front the Atlantic, and are cooled by winds from the Western Ocean, where, in fact, the temperature is known to be moderate and even cool at times, the light copper-coloured Frelahs are found surrounded on every side by Negro nations inhabiting lower districts; and nearly in the same parallel, but at the opposite side of Africa, are the high plains of Enarea and Kaffa, where the inhabitants are said to be fairer than the natives of southern Europe. The Galla and the Abyssinians themselves are, in proportion to the elevation of the country inhabited by them, fairer than the natives of low countries; and lest an exception should be taken to a comparison of straight-haired races with woolly Negroes or Shungalla, they bear the same comparison with the Danakil, Hazorta, and the Bishari tribes, resembling them in their hair and features, who inhabit the low tracts between the mountains of Tigre and the shores of the Red Sea, and who are equally or nearly as black as Negroes.

We may find occasion to observe that an equally decided relation exists between local conditions and the existence of other characters of human races in Africa. Those races who have the Negro character in an exaggerated degree, and who may be said to approach to deformity in person—the ugliest blacks with depressed foreheads, flat noses, crooked legs—are in many instances inhabitants of low countries, often of swampy tracts near the sea-coast, where many of them, as the Papels, have scarcely any other means of subsistence than shell fish, and the accidental gifts of the sea. In many places similar Negro tribes occupy thick forests in the hollows beneath high chains of mountains, the summits of which are inhabited by Abyssinian or Ethiopian races. The high table-lands of Africa are chiefly, as far as they are known, the abode or the wandering places of tribes of this character, or of nations who, like the Kafirs, recede very considerably from the Negro type. The Mandingos are, indeed, a Negro race inhabiting a high region; but they have neither the depressed forehead nor the projecting features considered as characteristic of the Negro race.

FOOTNOTES:

Peschel, The Races of Man, pp. 462-464.
CHAPTER VII.
CITIES OF AFRICA.

Carthage. The foundation of this celebrated city is ascribed to Elissa, a Tyrian princess, better known as Dido; it may therefore be fixed at the year of the world 3158; when Joash was king of Judah; 98 years before the building of Rome, and 846 years before Christ. The king of Tyre, father of the famous Jezebel, called in Scripture Ethbaal, was her great grandfather. She married her near relation Acerbas, also called Sicharbas, or Sichæus, an extremely rich prince, Pygmalion, king of Tyre, was her brother. Pygmalion put Sichæus to death in order that he might have an opportunity to seize his immense treasures, but Dido eluded her brother's cruel avarice, by secretly conveying away her deceased husband's possessions. With a large train of followers she left her country, and after wandering some time, landed on the coast of the Mediterranean, in Africa, and located her settlement at the bottom of the gulf, on a peninsula, near the spot where Tunis now stands. Many of the neighboring people, allured by the prospect of gain, repaired thither to sell to those foreigners the necessities of life, and soon became incorporated with them. The people thus gathered from different places soon grew very numerous. And the citizens of Utica, an African city about fifteen miles distant, considering them as their countrymen, as descended from the same common stock, advised them to build a city where they had settled. The other natives of the country, from their natural esteem and respect for strangers, likewise encouraged them to the same object. Thus all things conspiring with Dido's views, she built her city, which was appointed to pay in annual tribute to the Africans for the ground it stood upon, and called it Carthage—a name that in the Phoenician and Hebrew languages, [which have a great affinity,] signifies the "New City." It is said that in digging the foundation, a horse's head was found, which was thought to be a good omen, and a presage of the future warlike genius of that people. Carthage had the same language and national character as its parent state—Tyre. It became at length, particularly at the period of the Punic War, one of the most splendid cities in the world, and had under its dominion 300 cities bordering upon the Mediterranean. From the small beginning we have described, Carthage increased till her population numbered 700,000, and the number of her temples and other public buildings was immense. Her dominion was not long confined to Africa. Her ambitious inhabitants extended their conquest into Europe, by invading Sardinia, seizing a great part of Sicily, and subduing almost all of Spain. Having sent powerful colonies everywhere, they enjoyed the empire of the seas for more than six hundred years and formed a State which was able to dispute pre-eminence with the greatest empire of the world, by their wealth, their commerce, their numerous armies, their formidable fleets, and above all by the courage and ability of their commanders, and she extended her commerce over every part of the known world. A colony of Phoenicians or Ethiopians, known in Scripture as Canaanites, settled in Carthage. The Carthaginians settled in Spain and Portugal. The first inhabitants of Spain were the Celts, a people of Gaul, after them the Phoenicians possessed themselves of the most southern parts of the country, and may well be supposed to have been the first civilizers of this kingdom, and the founders of the most ancient cities. After these, followed the Grecians, then the Carthaginians.

Portugal was anciently called Lusitania, and inhabited by tribes of wandering people, till it became subject to the Carthaginians and Phoenicians, who were dispossessed by the Romans 250 years before Christ. (Rollin.)

The Carthaginians were masters of all the coast which lies on the Mediterranean, and all the country as far as the river Iberus. Their dominions, at the time when Hannibal the Great set out for Italy, all the coast of Africa from the Aræ Phileanorum, by the great Syrtis, to the pillars of Hercules was subject to the Carthaginians, who had maintained three great wars against the Romans. But the Romans finally prevailed by carrying the war into Africa, and the last Punic war terminated with the overthrow of Carthage (Nepos, in Vita Annibalis, liv.)

The celebrated Cyrene was a very powerful city, situated on the Mediterranean, towards the greater Syrtis, in Africa, and had been built by Battus, the Lacedæmonian. (Rollin.)

Cyrene—(Acts xi. 20.) A province and city of Libya. There was anciently a Phoenician colony called Cyrenaica, or "Libya, about Cyrene." (Acts ii. 10.).

Cyrene—A country west of Egypt, and the birthplace of Callimachus the poet, Eratosthenes the historian, and Simon who bore the Saviour's cross. Many Jews from hence were at the Pentecost, and were converted under Peter's sermon (Acts ii.). The region, now under the Turkish power, and has become almost a desert. It is now called Cairoan. Some of the Cyrenians were among the earliest Christians (Acts xi. 20); and one of them, it is supposed, was a preacher at Antioch (Acts xiii. 1). We find also, that among the most violent opposers of Christianity were the Cyrenians, who had a synagogue at Jerusalem, as had those of many other nations. It is said there were four hundred and eighty synagogues in Jerusalem.

Lybia, or Libya (Acts ii. 10), was anciently among the Greeks, a general name for Africa, but properly it embraced only so much of Africa as lay west of Egypt, on the southern coast of the Mediterranean. Profane geographers call it Libya Cyrenaica, because Cyrene was its capitol. It was the country of the Lubims (2 Chron. xii. 3), or Lehabims, of the Old Testament, from which it is supposed to have derived its name.

The ancient city of Cyrene is now called Cyreune, Cairoan, or Cayran and lies in the dominion of Tripoli. This district of the earth has lately occasioned much interest among Italian and French geographers. Great numbers of Jews resided here (Matt. xxvii. 32).

Libya, a part of Africa, bordering on Egypt, famous for its armed chariots and horses (2 Chron. xvi. 8).

Ophir, the son of Joktan, gave name to a country in Africa, famous for gold, which was renowned even in the time of Job (Job xxi. 24, xxviii. 16); and from the time of David to the time of Jehoshaphat the Hebrews traded with it, and Uzziah revived this trade when he made himself master of Elath, a noted port on the Red Sea. In Solomon's time, the Hebrew fleet took up three years in their voyage to Ophir, and brought home gold, apes, peacocks, spices, ivory, ebony and almug-trees (1 Kings ix. 28, x. 11, xxii. 48, 2 Chron. ix. 10).

Tarshish (Isa. xxiii. 1), or Tharsish (1 Kings x. 22). It is supposed that some place of this name existed on the eastern coast of Africa or among the southern ports of Asia, with which the ships of Hiram and Solomon traded in gold and silver, ivory, and apes and peacocks (2 Chron. ix. 21). It is said that once in every three years these ships completed a voyage, and brought home their merchandise. Hence, it is inferred, the place with which they traded must have been distant from Judea.

The vessels given by Hiram to Solomon, and those built by Jehoshaphat, to go to Tarshish, were all launched at Eziongeber, it the northern extremity of the eastern gulf of the Red Sea, now called the Gulf of Ahaba (2 Chron xx. 36). The name of Tarshish was from one of the sons of Javan (Gen. x. 4).

Phut (Gen. x. 6), or Put (Nah. iii. 9), was the third son of Ham, and his descendants, sometimes called Libyans, are supposed to be the Mauritanians, or Moors of modern times. They served the Egyptians and Tyrians as soldiers (Jer. xlvi. 9; Ezek. xxvii. 10, xxx. 5, xxxviii. 5).

Pul. A district in Africa, thought by Bochart to be an island in the Nile, not far from Syene (Isa. lxvi. 19).

Seba (Isa. xliii. 3) A peninsular district of African Ethiopia, deriving its name from the eldest son of Cush (Gen. x. 7), who is supposed to have been the progenitor of the Ethiopians. It is called Seba by the Hebrews.

FOOTNOTES:

Prichard. vol. ii pp. 334-338.

CITIES OF ETHIOPIA

Ethiopian is a name derived from the "land of Ethiopia," the first settled country before the flood. "The second river that went out of Eden, to water the garden, or earth, was Gihon; the same that encompasseth the whole land, or country, of Ethiopia" (Gen. ii. 13). Here Adam and his posterity built their tents and tilled the ground (Gen. iii. 23, 24).

The first city was Enoch, built before the flood in the land of Nod on the east of Eden,—a country now called Arabia. Cain the son of Adam, went out of Eden and dwelt in the land of Nod. We suppose, according to an ancient custom he married his sister and she bare Enoch. And Cain built a city and called the name of the city after the name of his son, Enoch, (Gen. iv. 16, 17). We know there must have been more than Cain and his son Enoch in the land of Nod to build a city but who were they?... (Malcom's Bible Dictionary.)

The first great city described in ancient and sacred history was built by the Cushites, or Ethiopians. They surrounded it with walls which, according to Rollin, were eighty-seven feet in thickness, three hundred and fifty feet in height and four hundred and eighty furlongs in circumference. And even this stupendous work they shortly after eclipsed by another, of which Diodorus says, "Never did any city come up to the greatness and magnificence of this."

It is a fact well attested by history, that the Ethiopians once bore sway, not only in all Africa, but over almost all Asia; and it is said that even two continents, could not afford field enough for the expansion of their energies.

"They found their way into Europe, and built a city on the western coast of Spain, called by them Iberian Ethiopia." "And," says a distinguished writer, "wherever they went, they were rewarded for their wisdom."

The Tower of Babel—Nimrod, the son of Cush, an Ethiopian, attempted to build the Tower of Babel (Gen. x. 8-10 xi. 4-9). One hundred and two years after the flood, in the land of Shinar—an extensive and fertile plain, lying between Mesopotamia on the west and Persia on the east, and watered by the Euphrates,—mankind being all of one language, one color, and one religion,—they agree to erect a tower of prodigious extent and height. Their design was not to secure themselves against a second deluge, or they would have built their tower on a high mountain, but to get themselves a famous character, and to prevent their dispersion by the erection of a monument which should be visible from a great distance. No quarries being found in that alluvial soil, they made bricks for stone, and used slime for mortar. Their haughty and rebellious attempt displeased the Lord; and after they had worked, it is said, twenty-two years, he confounded their language. This effectually stopped the building, procured it the name of Babel, or Confusion, and obliged some of the offspring of Noah to disperse themselves and replenish the world. The tower of Babel was in sight from the great city of Babylon. Nimrod was a hunter and monarch of vast ambition. When he rose to be king of Babylon he re-peopled Babel, which had been desolate since the confusion of tongues, but did not dare to attempt the finishing of the tower. The Scriptures inform us, he became "mighty upon earth;" but the extent of his conquests is not known. (Malcom's Bible Dictionary.)

The private houses, in most of the ancient cities, were simple in external appearance, but exhibited, in the interior, all the splendor and elegance of refined luxury. The floors were of marble; alabaster and gilding were displayed on every side. In every great house there were several fountains, playing in magnificent basins. The smallest house had three pipes,—one for the kitchen, another for the garden, and a third for washing. The same magnificence was displayed in the mosques, churches, and coffee houses. The environs presented, at all seasons of the year, a pleasing verdure, and contained extensive series of gardens and villas.

The Great and Splendid City of Babylon.—This city was founded by Nimrod, about 2,247 years B.C., in the land of Shinar, or Chaldea, and made the capital of his kingdom. It was probably an inconsiderable place, until it was enlarged and embellished by Semiramis; it then became the most magnificent city in the world, surpassing even Nineveh in glory. The circumference of both these cities was the same, but the walls which surrounded Babylon were twice as broad as the walls of Nineveh, and having a hundred brass gates. The city of Babylon stood on the river Euphrates, by which it was divided into two parts, eastern and western; and these were connected by a cedar bridge of wonderful construction, uniting the two divisions. Quays of beautiful marble adorned the banks of the river; and on one bank stood the magnificent Temple of Belus, and on the other the Queen's Palace. These two edifices were connected by a passage under the bed of the river. This city was at least forty-five miles in circumference; and would, of course, include eight cities as large as London and its appendages. It was laid out in six hundred and twenty five squares, formed by the intersection of twenty-five streets at right angles The walls, which were of brick, were three hundred and fifty feet high, and eighty-seven feet broad. A trench surrounded the city, the sides of which were lined with brick and waterproof cement. This city was famous for its hanging gardens, constructed by one of its kings, to please his queen. She was a Persian, and was desirous of seeing meadows on mountains, as in her own country. She prevailed on him to raise artificial gardens, adorned with meadows and trees. For this purpose, vaulted arches were raised from the ground, one above another, to an almost inconceivable height, and of a magnificence and strength sufficient to support the vast weight of the whole garden Babylon was a great commercial city, and traded to all parts of the earth then known, in all kinds of merchandise, and she likewise traded in slaves, and the souls of men. For her sins she has been blotted from existence,—even her location is a matter of supposition. Great was Babylon of old; in merchandise did she trade, and in souls. For her sins she thus became blotted from the sight of men.

THE ETHIOPIAN KINGS OF EGYPT.

1. Menes was the first king of Egypt. We have accounts of but one of his successors—Timans, during the first period, a space of more than two centuries.

2. Shishak was king of Ethiopia, and doubtless of Egypt. After his death

3. Zerah the son of Judah became king of Ethiopia, and made himself master of Egypt and Libya; and intending to add Judea to his dominions made war upon Asa king of Judea. His army

consisted of a million of men, and three hundred chariots of war (2 Chron. xiv. 9).

4. Sabachus, an Ethiopian, king of Ethiopia, being encouraged by an oracle, entered Egypt with a numerous army, and possessed himself of the country. He reigned with great clemency and justice. It is believed, that this Sabachus was the same with Solomon, whose aid was implored by Hosea king of Israel, against Salmanaser king of Assyria.

5. Sethon reigned fourteen years. He is the same with Sabachus, or Savechus the son of Sabacan or Saul the Ethiopian who reigned so long over Egypt.

6. Tharaca, an Ethiopian, joined Sethon, with an Ethiopian army to relieve Jerusalem. After the death of Sethon, who had filled the Egyptian throne fourteen years, Tharaca ascended the throne and reigned eight years over Egypt.

7. Sesach or Shishak was the king of Egypt to whom Jeroboam fled to avoid death at the hands of king Solomon. Jeroboam was entertained till the death of Solomon, when he returned to Judea and was made king of Israel. (2 Chron. xi. and xii.)

This Sesach, in the fifth year of the reign of Rehoboam marched against Jerusalem, because the Jews had transgressed against the Lord. He came with twelve hundred chariots of war, and sixty thousand horses. He had brought numberless multitudes of people, who were all Libyans, Troglodytes, and Ethiopians. He seized upon all the strongest cities of Judah, and advanced as far as Jerusalem. Then the king, and the princes of Israel, having humbled themselves, and implored the protection of the God of Israel, he told them, by his prophet Shemaiah, that, because they humbled themselves, he would not utterly destroy them, as they had deserved but that they should be the servants of Sesach, in order that they might know the difference of his service, and the service of the kingdoms of the country. Sesach retired from Jerusalem, after having plundered the treasures of the house of the Lord, and of the king's house, he carried off every thing with him, and even also the three hundred shields of gold which Salomon had made.

The following are the kings of Egypt mentioned in Scripture by the common appellation of Pharaoh:—

8. Psammetichus.—As this prince owed his preservation to the Ionians and Carians, he settled them in Egypt, from which all foreigners hitherto had been excluded; and, by assigning them sufficient lands and fixed revenues, he made them forget their native country. By his order, Egyptian children were put under their care to learn the Greek tongue; and on this occasion, and by this means, the Egyptians began to have a correspondence with the Greeks, and, from that era, the Egyptian history, which till then had been intermixed with pompous fables, by the artifice of the priests, begins, according to Herodotus, to speak with greater truth and certainty.

As soon as Psammetichus was settled on the throne, he engaged in a war against the king of Assyria, on account of the limits of the two empires. This war was of long continuance. Ever since Syria had been conquered by the Assyrians, Palestine, being the only country that separated the two kingdoms, was the subject of continual discord; as afterwards it was between the Ptolemies and the Seleucidæ. They were perpetually contending for it, and it was alternately won by the stronger. Psammetichus, seeing himself the peaceable possessor of all Egypt, and having restored the ancient form of government, thought it high time for him to look to his frontiers, and to secure them against the Assyrian, his neighbour, whose power increased daily. For this purpose he entered Palestine at the head of an army.

Perhaps we are to refer to the beginning of this war, an incident related by Diodorus; that the Egyptians, provoked to see the Greeks posted on the right wing by the king himself in preference to them, quitted the service, being upwards of two hundred thousand men, and retired into Ethiopia, where they met with an advantageous settlement

Be this as it will, Psammetichus entered Palestine, where his career was stopped by Azotus, one of the principal cities of the country, which gave him so much trouble, that he was forced to besiege it twenty nine years before he could take it. This is the longest siege mentioned in ancient history. Psammetichus died in the 24th year of the reign of Josiah king of Judah; and was succeeded by his son Nechoa or Necho—in Scriptures frequently called Pharaoh Necho.

9. Nechao or Pharaoh-Necho reigned sixteen years king of Egypt, (2 Chron. xxxv. 20,) whose expeditions are often mentioned in profane history

The Babylonians and Medes having destroyed Nineveh, and with it the empire of the Assyrians, were thereby become so formidable, that they drew upon themselves the jealousy of all their neighbours. Nechao, alarmed at the danger, advanced to the Euphrates, at the head of a powerful army, in order to check their progress. Josiah, king of Judah, so famous for his uncommon piety, observing that he took his route through Judea, resolved to oppose his passage. With this view he raised all the forces of his kingdom, and posted himself in the valley of Megiddo (a city on this side of Jordan, belonging to the tribe of Manasseh, and called Magdolus by Herodotus). Nechao informed him by a herald, that his enterprise was not designed against him; that he had other enemies in view, and that he had undertaken this war in the name of God, who was with him; that for this reason he advised Josiah not to concern himself with this war for fear it otherwise should turn to his disadvantage. However, Josiah was not moved by these reasons; he was sensible that the bare march of so powerful an army through Judea would entirely ruin it. And besides, he feared that the victor, after the defeat of the Babylonians, would fall upon him and dispossess him of part of his dominions. He therefore marched to engage Nechao; and was not only overthrown by him, but unfortunately received a wound of which he died at Jerusalem, whither he had ordered himself to be carried.

Nechao, animated by this victory, continued his march and advanced towards the Euphrates. He defeated the Babylonians; took Carchemish, a large city in that country; and securing to himself the possession of it by a strong garrison, returned to his own kingdom after having been absent three months.

Being informed in his march homeward, that Jehoaz had caused himself to be proclaimed king at Jerusalem, without first asking his consent, he commanded him to meet him at Riblah in Syria. The unhappy prince was no sooner arrived there than he was put in chains by Nechao's order, and sent prisoner to Egypt, where he died. From thence, pursuing his march, he came to Jerusalem, where he gave the sceptre to Eliakim (called by him Jehoiakim), another of Josiah's sons, in the room of his brother; and imposed an annual tribute on the land, of a hundred talents of silver, and one talent of gold. This being done, he returned in triumph to Egypt.

Herodotus, mentioning this king's expedition, and the victory gained by him at Magdolus, (as he calls it,) says that he afterwards took the city Cadytis, which he represents as situated in the mountains of Palestine, and equal in extent to Sardis, the capital at that time not only of Lydia, but of all Asia Minor. This description can suit only Jerusalem, which was situated in the manner above described, and was then the only city in those parts that could be compared to Sardis. It appears besides, from Scripture, that Nechao, after his victory, made himself master of this capital of Judea; for he was there in person, when he gave the crown to Jehoiakim. The very name Cadytis, which in Hebrew, signifies the holy, points clearly to the city of Jerusalem, as is proved by the learned dean Prideaux.

10. Psammis.—His reign was but of six years' duration, and history has left us nothing memorable concerning him, except that he made an expedition into Ethiopia.

11. Apries.—In Scripture he is called Pharaoh-Hophra; and, succeeding his father Psammis, reigned twenty-five years.

During the first year of his reign, he was as happy as any of his predecessors. He carried his arms into Cyprus; besieged the city of Sidon by sea and land; took it, and made himself master of all Phoenicia and Palestine.

So rapid a success elated his heart to a prodigious degree, and, as Herodotus informs us, swelled him with so much pride and infatuation, that he boasted it was not in the power of the gods themselves to dethrone him; so great was the idea he had formed to himself of the firm establishment of his own power. It was with a view to these arrogant conceits, that Ezekiel put the vain and impious words following into his mouth: My river is mine own, and I have made it for myself. But the true God proved to him afterwards that he had a master, and that he was a mere man; and he had threatened him long before, by his prophets, with all the calamities he was resolved to bring upon him, in order to punish him for his pride.

12. Amasis.—After the death of Apries, Amasis became peaceable possessor of Egypt, and reigned over it forty years. He was, according to Plato, a native of the city of Sais.

As he was but of mean extraction, he met with no respect, and was contemned by his subjects in the beginning of his reign. He was not insensible of this; but nevertheless thought it his interest to subdue their tempers by an artful carriage, and to win their affection by gentleness and reason. He had a golden cistern, in which himself, and those persons who were admitted to his table, used to wash their feet, he melted it down, and had it cast into a statue, and then exposed the new god to public worship. The people hastened in crowds to pay their adorations to the statue. The king, having assembled the people, informed them of the vile uses to which this statue had once been put, which nevertheless was now the object of their religious prostrations; the application was easy, and had the desired success; the people thenceforward paid the king all the respect that is due to majesty.

He always used to devote the whole morning to public affairs, in order to receive petitions, give audience, pronounce sentences, and hold his councils; the rest of the day was given to pleasure, and as Amasis, in hours of diversion, was extremely gay, and seemed to carry his mirth beyond due bounds, his courtiers took the liberty to represent to him the unsuitableness of such a behaviour; when he answered that it was impossible for the mind to be always serious and intent upon business, as for a bow to continue always bent.

It was this king who obliged the inhabitants of every town to enter their names in a book kept by the magistrates for that purpose, with their profession and manner of living. Solon inserted this custom among his laws.

He built many magnificent temples, especially at Sais the place of his birth. Herodotus admired especially a chapel there, formed of one single stone, and which was twenty-one cubits in front, fourteen in depth, and eight in height; its dimensions within were not quite so large; it had been brought from Elephantina, and two thousand men were employed three years in conveying it along the Nile.

Amasis had a great esteem for the Greeks. He granted them large privileges; and permitted such of them as were desirous of settling in Egypt to live in the city of Naucratis, so famous for its harbour. When the rebuilding of the temple of Delphi, which had been burnt, was debated on, and the expense was computed at three hundred talents, Amasis furnished the Delphians with a very considerable sum towards discharging their quota, which was the fourth part of the whole charge.

He made an alliance with the Cyrenians, and married a wife from among them. He is the only king of Egypt who conquered the island of Cyprus, and made it tributary. Under his reign Pythagorus came into Egypt, being recommended to that monarch by the famous Polycrates, tyrant of Samos, who had contracted a friendship with Amasis, and will be mentioned hereafter. Pythagoras, during his stay in Egypt, was initiated in all the mysteries of the country, and instructed by the priests in whatever was most abstruse and important in their religion. It was here he imbibed his doctrine of the metempsychosis, or transmigration of souls.

In the expedition in which Cyrus conquered so great a part of the world, Egypt doubtless was subdued, like the rest of the provinces, and Xenophon positively declares this in the beginning of his Cyropædia, or institution of that prince. Probably, after that the forty years of desolation, which had been foretold by the prophet, were expired, Egypt beginning gradually to recover itself, Amasis shook off the yoke, and recovered his liberty.

Accordingly we find, that one of the first cares of Cambyses, the son of Cyrus, after he had ascended the throne, was to carry his arms into Egypt. On his arrival there, Amasis was just dead, and succeeded by his son Psammetus.

13. Rameses Miamun, according to Archbishop Usher, was the name of this king, who is called Pharaoh in Scripture. He reigned sixty-six years, and oppressed the Israelites in a most grievous manner. He set over them taskmasters, to afflict them with their burdens, and they built for Pharaoh treasure cities, Pithon and Raamses. And the Egyptians made the children of Israel serve with rigour, and they made their lives bitter with hard bondage, in mortar and in brick, and in all manner of service in the field; all their service wherein they made them serve, was with rigour. This king had two sons, Amenophis and Busiris.

14. Amenophis, the eldest, succeeded him. He was the Pharaoh under whose reign the Israelites departed out of Egypt, and who was drowned in his passage through the Red Sea.

Archbishop Usher says, that Amenophis left two sons, one called Sesothis, or Seaostris, and the other Armais. The Greeks call him Belus, and his two sons, Egyptus and Danaus.

15. Sesostris was not only one of the most powerful kings of Egypt, but one of the greatest conquerors that antiquity boasts of. He was at an advanced age sent by his father against the Arabians, in order that, by fighting with them, he might acquire military knowledge. Here the young prince learned to bear hunger and thirst, and subdued a nation which till then had never been conquered. The youth educated with him, attended him in all his campaigns.

Accustomed by this conquest to martial toils he was next sent by his father to try his fortune westward. He invaded Libya, and subdued the greatest part of that vast continent.

His army consisted of six hundred thousand foot, and twenty thousand horse, besides twenty thousand armed chariots.

He invaded Ethiopia, and obliged the nations of it to furnish him annually with a certain quantity of ebony, ivory, and gold.

He had fitted out a fleet of four hundred sail, and ordering it to sail to the Red Sea, made himself master of the isles and cities lying on the coast of that sea. After having spread desolation through the world for nine years, he returned, laden with the spoils of the vanquished nations. A hundred famous temples, raised as so many monuments of gratitude to the tutelar gods of all the cities, were the first, as well as the most illustrious testimonies of his victories.

16. Pheron succeeded Sesostris in his kingdom, but not in his glory. He probably reigned fifty years.

17. Proteus was son of Memphis, and according to Herodotus, must have succeeded the first—since Proteus lived at the time of the siege of Troy, which, according to Usher, was taken An. Mun. 2820.

18. Rhampsinitus who was richer than any of his predecessors, built a treasury. Till the reign of this king, there had been some shadow at least of justice and moderation in Egypt; but, in the two following reigns, violence and cruelty usurped their place.

19, 20. Cheops and Cephrenus, reigned in all one hundred and six years. Cheops reigned fifty years, and his brother Cephrenus fifty-six years after him. They kept the temples closed during the whole time of their long reign; and forbid the offerings of sacrifice under the severest penalties. They oppressed their subjects.

21. Mycerinus the son of Cheops, reigned but seven years. He opened the temples; restored the sacrifices; and did all in his power to comfort his subjects, and make them forget their past miseries.

22. Asychis one of the kings of Egypt. He valued himself for having surpassed all his predecessors, by building a pyramid of brick, more magnificent, than any hitherto seen.

23. Busiris, built the famous city of Thebes, and made it the seat of his empire. This prince is not to be confounded with Busirus, so infamous for his cruelties.

24. Osymandyas, raised many magnificent edifices, in which were exhibited sculptures and paintings of exquisite beauty.

25. Uchoreus, one of the successors of Osymandyas, built the city of Memphis. This city was

150 furlongs, or more than seven leagues in circumference, and stood at the point of the Delta, in that part where the Nile divides itself into several branches or streams. A city so advantageously situated, and so strongly fortified, became soon the usual residence of the Egyptian kings.

26. Thethmosis or Amosis, having expelled the Shepherd kings, reigned in Lower Egypt.

FOOTNOTES:

Rollin, vol. i. pp. 129-147.
CHAPTER VIII.
AFRICAN LANGUAGES.

In the language of the Kafirs, for example, not only the cases but the numbers and genders of nouns are formed entirely by prefixes, analogous to articles. The prefixes vary according to number, gender and case, while the nouns remain unaltered except by a merely euphonic change of the initial letters. Thus, in Coptic, from sheri, a son, comes the plural neu-sheri, the sons; from sori, accusation, hau-sori, accusations. Analogous to this we have in the Kafir ama marking the plural, as amakosah the plural of kosah, amahashe the plural of ihashe, insana the plural of usana. The Kafir has a great variety of similar prefixes; they are equally numerous in the language of Kongo, in which, as in the Coptic and the Kafir, the genders, numbers, and cases of nouns are almost solely distinguished by similar prefixes.

"The Kafir language is distinguished by one peculiarity which immediately strikes a student whose views of language have been formed upon the examples afforded by the inflected languages of ancient and modern Europe. With the exception of a change of termination in the ablative case of the noun, and five changes of which the verb is susceptible in its principal tenses, the whole business of declension, conjugation, &c., is carried on by prefixes, and by the changes which take place in the initial letters or syllables of words subjected to grammatical government."

Resources are not yet in existence for instituting a general comparison of the languages of Africa. Many years will probably elapse before it will be possible to produce such an analysis of these languages, investigated in their grammatical structure, as it is desirable to possess, or even to compare them by extensive collections of well-arranged vocabularies, after the manner of Klaproth's Asia Polyglotta. Sufficient data however are extant, and I trust that I have adduced evidence to render it extremely probable that a principle of analogy in structure prevails extensively among the native idioms of Africa. They are probably allied, not in the manner or degree in which Semitic or Indo-European idioms resemble each other, but by strong analogies in their general principles of structure, which may be compared to those discoverable between the individual members of two other great classes of languages, by no means connected among themselves by what is called family relation. I allude to the monosyllabic and the polysynthetic languages, the former prevalent in Eastern Asia, the latter throughout the vast regions of the New World. If we have sufficient evidence for constituting such a class of dialects under the title of African languages, we have likewise reason—and it is equal in degree—for associating in this class the language of the ancient Egyptians.

That the written Abyssinian language, which we call Ethiopick, is a dialect of old Chaldean, and sister of Arabick and Hebrew; we know with certainty, not only from the great multitude of identical words, but (which is a far stronger proof) from the similar grammatical arrangement of the several idioms: we know at the same time, that it is written like all the Indian characters, from the left hand to the right, and that the vowels are annexed, as in Devanagari, to the consonants; with which they form a syllabick system extremely clear and convenient, but disposed in a less artificial order than the system of letters now exhibited in the Sanscrit grammars; whence it may justly be inferred, that the order contrived by Panini or his disciples is comparatively modern; and I have no doubt, from a cursory examination of many old inscriptions on pillars and in caves, which have obligingly been sent to me from all parts of India, that the Nagari and Ethiopean letters had at first a similar form. It has long been my opinion, that the Abyssinians of the Arabian stock, having no symbols of their own to represent articulate sounds, borrowed those of the black pagans, whom the Greeks call Troglodytes, from their primeval habitations in natural caverns, or in mountains excavated by their own labour: they were probably the first inhabitants of Africa, where they became in time the builders of magnificent cities, the founders of seminaries for the advancement of science and philosophy, and the inventors (if they were not rather the importers) of symbolical characters. I believe on the whole, that the Ethiops of Meroe were the same people with the first Egyptians, and consequently, as it might easily be shown, with the original Hindus. To the ardent and intrepid Mr. Bruce, whose travels are to my taste, uniformally agreeable and satisfactory, though he thinks very differently from me on the language and genius of the Arabs, we are indebted for more important, and, I believe, more accurate information concerning the nations established near the Nile, from its fountains to its mouths, than all Europe united could before have supplied; but, since he has not been at the pains to compare the seven languages, of which he has exhibited a specimen, and since I have not leisure to make the comparison, I must be satisfied with observing, on his authority, that the dialects of the Gafots and the Gallas, the Agows of both races, and the Falashas, who must originally have used a Chaldean idiom, were never preserved in writing, and the Amharick only in modern times: they must, therefore, have been for ages in fluctuation, and can lead, perhaps, to no certain conclusion as to the origin of the several tribes who anciently spoke them. It is very remarkable, as Mr. Bruce and Mr. Bryan have proved, that the Greeks gave the appellation of Indians both to the southern nations of Africk and to the people, among whom we now live; nor is it less observable, that, according to Ephorus, quoted by Strabo, they called all the southern nations in the world Ethiopians, thus using Indian and Ethiop as convertible terms: but we must leave the gymnosophists of Ethiopia, who seemed to have professed the doctrines of Buddha, and enter the great Indian ocean, of which their Asiatick and African brethren were probably the first navigators.

FOOTNOTES:

Kafir Grammar, p. 3.

Prichard, vol. ii. pp. 216, 217.

SHERBRO MISSION-DISTRICT, WESTERN AFRICA.

Western Africa is one of the most difficult mission-fields in the entire heathen world. The low condition of the people, civilly, socially, and religiously, and the deadly climate to foreigners, make it indeed a hard field to cultivate. I am fully prepared to indorse what Rev. F. Fletcher, in charge of Wesleyan District, Gold Coast, wrote a few months ago in the following language: "The Lord's work in western Africa is as wonderful as it is deadly. In the last forty years more than 120 missionaries have fallen victims to that climate; but to-day the converts to Christianity number at least 30,000, many of whom are true Christians. In this district we have 6,000 church members, and though they are poor, last year they gave over 5,000 dollars for evangelistic and educational work.

"Sherbro Mission now has four stations and chapels and over forty appointments, 112 church members, 164 seekers of religion, 75 acres of clear land, with carpenter, blacksmith, and tailor shops, in and upon which, twenty five boys are taught to labor, and where eleven girls are taught to do all ordinary house work and sewing, with its four day and Sunday schools, 212 in the former and more than that number in the latter, and with an influence for good that now reaches the whole Sherbro tribe, embracing a country at least fifty miles square and containing about 15,000 people. The seed sown is taking deep root there, and the harvest is rapidly ripening, when thousands of souls will be garnered for heaven. Surely we ought to thank God for past success and resolve to do much more for that needy country in the future.

"We now have Revs. Corner, Wilberforce, Evans, and their wives, all excellent missionaries, from America; then Revs. Sawyer, Hero, Pratt, and their wives, Mrs. Lucy Caulker, and other native laborers, all of whom are doing us good service. With these six ordained ministers, and twice that number of teachers and helpers, who are devoting all their time to the mission, the work is going forward gloriously. Still, there should be new stations opened and more laborers sent out immediately."

FOOTNOTES:

Asiatic Researches, vol. iii. pp. 4, 5.
Twenty fifth Annual Report, United Brethren, 1881.

Part II: SLAVERY IN THE COLONIES.

CHAPTER XV.
CONDITION OF SLAVES IN MASSACHUSETTS.

The following memorandum in Judge Sewall's letter book was called forth by Samuel Smith, murderer of his Negro slave at Sandwich. It illustrates the deplorable condition of servants at that time in Massachusetts, and shows Judge Sewall to have been a man of great humanity.

Petition of Slaves in Boston.

On the 23d of June, 1773, the following petition was presented to the General Court of Massachusetts, which was read, and referred to the next session:—

FOOTNOTES:

Slavery in Mass., pp 96, 97.

Neil, pp. 39-41.
CHAPTER XIII.
THE COLONY OF NEW YORK.

1693, August 21st—All Indians, Negroes, and others not "listed in the militia," are ordered to work on the fortification for repairing the same, to be under the command of the captains of the wards they inhabit. And £100 to be raised for the fortifications.

1722, February 20th.—A law passed by the common council of New York, "restraining slaves, negroes, and Indians from gaming with moneys." If found gaming with any sort of money, "copper pennies, copper halfpence, or copper farthings," they shall be publickly whipped at the publick whipping-post of this city, at the discretion of the mayor, recorder, and aldermen, or any one of them, unless the owner pay to the church wardens for the poor, 3s.

1731, November 18th—If more than three negro, mulatto, or Indian slaves assemble on Sunday and play or make noise, (or at any other time at any place from their master's service,) they are to be publickly whipped fifteen lashes at the publick whipping-post.

NEW YORK.

Negro slavery, a favorite measure with England, was rapidly extending its baneful influence in the colonies. The American Register, of 1769, gives the number of negroes brought in slavery from the coast of Africa, between Cape Blanco and the river Congo, by different nations in one year, thus: Great Britain, 53,100; British Americans, 6,300; France, 23,520; Holland, 11,300; Portugal, 1,700; Denmark, 1,200; in all, 104,100, bought by barter for European and Indian manufacturers,—£15 sterling being the average price given for each negro. Thus we see that more than one half of the wretches who were kidnapped, or torn by force from their homes by the agents of European merchants (for such those who supply the market must be considered), were sacrificed to the cupidity of the merchants of Great Britain; the traffic encouraged by the government at the same time that the boast is sounded through the world, that the moment a slave touches the sacred soil, governed by those who encourage the slavemakers, and inhabited by those who revel in the profits derived from murder, he is free. Somerset, the negro, is liberated by the court of king's bench, in 1772, and the world is filled with the fame of English justice and humanity! James Grahame tells us that Somerset's case was not the first in which the judges of Great Britain counteracted in one or two cases the practical inhumanity of the government and the people: he says, that in 1762, his grandfather, Thomas Grahame, judge of the admiralty court of Glasgow, liberated a negro slave imported into Scotland.

It was in vain that the colonists of America protested against the practice of slave dealing. The governors appointed by England were instructed to encourage it, and when the assemblies enacted laws to prohibit the inhuman traffic, they were annulled by the vetoes of the governors. With such encouragement, the reckless and avaricious among the colonists engaged in the trade, and the slaves were purchased when brought to the colonies by those who were blind to the evil, or preferred present ease or profit to all future good. Paley, the moralist, thought the American Revolution was designed by Providence, to put an end to the slave trade, and to show that a nation encouraging it was not fit to be intrusted with the government of extensive colonies. But the planter of the Southern States have discovered, since made free by that revolution, that slavery is no evil; and better moralists than Paley, that the increase of slaves, and their extension over new regions, is the duty of every good democrat. The men who lived in 1773, to whom America owes her liberty, did not think so.

Although resistance to the English policy of increasing the number of negro slaves in America agitated many minds in the colonies, opposition to the system of taxation was the principal source of action; and this opposition now centered in a determination to baffle the designs of Great Britain in respect to the duties on tea. Seventeen millions of pounds of tea were now accumulated in the warehouses of the East-India Company. The government was determined, for reasons I have before given, to assist this mercantile company, as well as the African merchants, at the expense of the colonists of America. The East-India Company were now authorized to export their tea free of all duty. Thus the venders being enabled to offer it cheaper than hitherto to the colonists, it was expected that it would find a welcome market. But the Americans saw the ultimate intent of the whole scheme, and their disgust towards the mother country was proportionably increased.

Printed in Poland
by Amazon Fulfillment
Poland Sp. z o.o., Wrocław